C000264466

RAILWAYS
OF THE
NORTH
PENNINES

RAILWAYS
OF THE
NORTH
PENNINES

THE RISE AND FALL OF THE
RAILWAYS SERVING THE
NORTH PENNINE ORE-FIELD

DR TOM BELL

MARC FITCH FUND

The History Press gratefully acknowledges the support of the Marc Fitch Fund

First published 2015

The History Press
The Mill, Brimscombe Port
Stroud, Gloucestershire, GL5 2QG
www.thehistorypress.co.uk

© Tom Bell, 2015

The right of Tom Bell to be identified as the Author
of this work has been asserted in accordance with the
Copyright, Designs and Patents Act 1988.

All rights reserved. No part of this book may be reprinted
or reproduced or utilised in any form or by any electronic,
mechanical or other means, now known or hereafter invented,
including photocopying and recording, or in any information
storage or retrieval system, without the permission in writing
from the Publishers.

British Library Cataloguing in Publication Data.
A catalogue record for this book is available from the British Library.

ISBN 978 0 7509 6095 3

Typesetting and origination by The History Press
Printed in Malta by Melita Press.

CONTENTS

Foreword by Andrew Scott CBE, Former Director of NRM   6
Preface   7

1. Introduction   11
2. Canal Proposals, Roads and the Early Railways   21
3. The Railway Mania in the North Pennines   43
4. The Main Line of the Proposed Wear Valley Extension Railway of 1845   63
5. The 1845 Proposals for the Allen Valley   76
6. The Alston Branch of the N&CR   85
7. Amalgamation and Financial Restructuring Within the Stockton and Darlington Group of Railways   118
8. Improvements to the Wear and Derwent Junction Railway   131
9. Rookhope, Stanhope and Westgate   152
10. The Hexham and Allendale Railway   165
11. Barnard Castle and the Tees Valley Railway   182
12. The Cumberland and Cleveland Junction Railway   198
13. The Final Attempts to Reach Alston from the Valleys of the Tees and Wear Including the Wear Valley Extension Railway of 1892   215
14. The Long Decline   234
15. The Tourist Railways   244

Appendix A   Relationship of Metric to Imperial Units   250
Appendix B   Railway Companies   251
References   253
Index   280

FOREWORD

N R M

The North Pennine dales are a very special place – one the emptiest places in England, apparently on the road to nowhere, a land of high fells, wide and wild valleys where farming is utterly at the margin.

It is a land where population would have been negligible had it not been for the rocks and minerals for which the area has become well known. Quarries yielded stone – limestone, sandstone and hard whimstone for road works. But igneous activity had also introduced mineral-rich magma, cooling in cracks forced through the rocks and a rich source of important metals and other chemicals. Mining and quarrying became important industries.

As a teenager from the English midlands, I made a pilgrimage with my family to discover where my grandfather had been born, somewhere so different from the modern city where I had been brought up that I have never forgotten that first visit. The place was Harwood in Upper Teesdale, about as wild and remote as one can get in England. My grandparent's family had been farmers and lead miners nearly 2,000ft up in some of the most inhospitable conditions that England has to offer. Life was hard and, by the early twentieth century, it was obvious that the future held little hope, so they emigrated – to Frinton on Sea – but that, as they say, is another story. Tom Bell's fastidious research, published here for the first time, opens the door for me to new facets of my family's history.

For some of the area, the coming of the railway added impetus to quarrying and mining and led to a hundred years of intense economic activity. In the more remote parts, the twin challenges of landscape and economics meant that the railway did not materialise. Transport costs remained high and mining remained a marginal industry. Dr Bell has uncovered the story of the railways that were prepared to confront challenges of the 2,000ft high passes and deep valleys. He paints a picture of what might have been and, in so doing, helps our understanding of the achievements of the miners of the north Pennines and of the limitations that have left this country so lonely today. For those who love this part of the world and the faint traces of its fascinating industria history that remain, he has added a new dimension to the story.

Andrew Scott CBE,
Former Director, National Raillway Museum

PREFACE

The idea for a book outlining the history of the various railway proposals in the North Pennines arose during a study of the nineteenth-century documents relating to the planning, building and later proposals to extend the Alston branch of the Newcastle and Carlisle Railway (N&CR). The majority of people with an interest in railways will have heard of the Alston branch and most of these, as well as many others, will be familiar with its current reincarnation as the narrow-gauge South Tynedale Railway. Similarly, the Wearhead branch is also well known at the time of writing, especially in preservation circles, in its various recent reincarnations as the Weardale Railway. The Middleton-in-Teesdale and Allendale branches, both of which started life as totally independent concerns, are rather less well known, while knowledge of the Stanhope and Tyne, the Wear and Derwent Junction, and Weardale Iron and Coal Company Railways is even more restricted, especially in the case of the latter which was never a public railway and which therefore rarely appears on the various railway maps depicting the pre-grouping era. Those interested in the development of the British railway network will probably have heard of proposals to connect the valleys of the South Tyne and Wear and possibly also the South Tyne and Tees, while the more serious student will be able to name these schemes as the Wear Valley Extension Railway (of 1845) and the Cumberland and Cleveland Junction Railway. What is perhaps less well understood is that these lines were not simply speculative proposals of the Railway Mania, or later, but were genuine proposals, whose supporters were active for over half a century, with the second line coming very close to actually being built.

My interest in railways, and my connection with the North Pennines, extends over all of my almost eighty years. Until I was seven, we lived in the East Allen Valley, a mile north of Allenheads, where I was fortunate to see the last, decaying years of the local lead industry. During that period I was taken, by my father, to Allendale station to collect parcels, although I do not remember ever seeing a train at that rather inconvenient station. In my teens, I cycled over most of the North Pennines, seeing the inclines at Hallbankgate and Stanhope in action, while passenger trains at the railheads of Alston, Middleton-in-Teesdale,

Tow Law and Wearhead were all familiar. I especially remember the station at Alston, with its overall roof, which made it an ideal place to eat one's sandwiches in inclement weather. After twenty years away from the North Pennines, I returned with my family, moving into Alston the weekend the branch closed. This research started three years later, when I produced a small display for the developing South Tynedale Railway Preservation Society. Since that time I have discovered the true extent of the vast efforts made to provide rail connections over the roof of England. I would not claim to have unearthed every piece of relevant information, but certainly there is a much greater quantity than has previously been reported, and if any person reading this history knows of more, I shall be more than happy to hear of it.

Earlier, and incomplete, versions of chapters in this book were written as a series of articles for the *North Eastern Express*, and I am grateful to the then editor, John Richardson, for permission to re-use the material. Although I have received considerable assistance from many individuals in the course of this research, I am solely responsible for the assembly of the information. I have tried to provide as unbiased and complete an account as possible, but the interpretations are my own, and I can blame no one but myself for any errors or omissions. I am aware that others would almost certainly place greater emphasis on different aspects of the story, but I have tried to place the history of the railway plans in the context of contemporary events. For most of the lines I have followed a chronological order, although the final improvements to the Wear and Derwent Junction line occurred after the building of both the Hexham and Allendale and the Tees Valley railways. In addition, I have ventured into the world of 'might-have-been', to see what could have resulted if there had been some relatively minor variations in the decisions taken or the moneys available. From these considerations, I have formed the view that, had the Wear Valley Extension Railway proceeded in 1845, it almost certainly would have obtained its act and been built to become part of one the main lines between London and Glasgow, having a profound effect on the country through which it passed. None of the later planned extensions would have had the same effect, although the future of the railway in Alston might have been different.

I have restricted my account to those standard-gauge railways which were built either as fully authorised public railways, or were private railways operated in a similar manner to a normal public railway, plus those proposed lines for which surveys were carried out, usually with the production of detailed plans. Standard-gauge lines built to serve mines or quarries, but which did not provide a public service for the local population, have been mentioned only briefly in connection with the traffic they contributed, while the story of the various standard- and narrow-gauge systems serving local industries I have left to other authors. For me this has been a labour of love, and I hope that those who read it will find it as fascinating as I found the original research.

The illustrations are a mixture of pictures of the original plans of the railways discussed, contemporary photographs taken by a range of photographers when the railways were open for commercial traffic, or had only recently been closed, and a selection of modern views showing the remains of the railways in the late twentieth or early twenty-first centuries, or where a line that was never built would have passed. The first and last series were taken by the author with the source of the original plans given for each picture. The copyright holder of each of the contemporary pictures is given in the caption and the author is most grateful to the various copyright holders giving permission for the publication of their photographs. Where there is no name attached to a photograph the picture was taken by the author.

The production of this history would have been impossible without the assistance of the staffs of the Record Offices and Archives Services of Cumbria (especially the Carlisle office), Durham, Northumberland, North Riding of Yorkshire, Tyne and Wear; The National Archives; the Literary & Philosophical Society of Newcastle-upon-Tyne, Carlisle City Library, Newcastle City Library, Darlington Public Library, Durham City Library, the Library of the University of Durham; the Darlington Railway Centre and Museum. In particular, I wish to thank the editor and staff of the *Hexham Courant*, who allowed me to spend many Fridays searching through their bound collection of back copies. This is a newspaper which does not feature often in railway literature, yet, from its first publication in 1864, it has proved to be a major source of new information. It seems invidious to single out individuals, but Bob Rennison of the Newcomen Society provided much needed assistance in resolving the convoluted history of the actual building of the Alston branch, and was the inspiration for the paper we jointly wrote on the subject, while Alan Blackburn, Head of Engineering on the South Tynedale Railway, John Crompton of Norpex, Larry Wilson of Allenheads and the Kearton family of Alston have provided information which was otherwise unavailable. I should also like to thank Mike Ryan and Jim Harper, whom I met through the South Tynedale Railway, for reading the manuscript and making constructive comments, particularly by questioning the accuracy of some of the details quoted from the plans. For those who may also wonder, such figures as 1 in 404.06, 2247¼ and 128.78 are taken directly from the original plans! Finally I must thank my long-suffering wife who, for over twenty years, has not only put up with my travels over the North of England, and beyond, in search of information, but who has also read the manuscript and improved the language.

Because of the large number of publications referred to in the text, mostly original and contemporary, they have been placed at the end of the text in order of the date of publication and numbered from 1 (the earliest – 1767) to 839 (the latest – 2014). In the text each reference is shown by a superscript number which is the same as the number in the reference list.

1

INTRODUCTION

While the most northerly counties of England will always be known as the birthplace of the modern railway system, they also have the less enviable distinction of being the only major area of the British Isles whose natural waterways were neither developed to provide safe, non-tidal, inland trading routes, nor connected by a network of navigable canals. There was no shortage of proposals for river improvements and canals but, for a variety of reasons, very little came of these efforts. All that the innumerable surveys and countless meetings managed to achieve was the construction of a small number of completely separate canals, one in the east and three in the west, together with the improvement of navigation over the tidal stretches of the major rivers in the east. Even much of the latter work did not occur until after the establishment of the basic railway network. It was only the northern extension of the Lancaster Canal to Kendal which came close to being connected to the main English inland waterway network and although the Millennium Fund financed a connection known as the Ribble Link it has no bearing on this history, while the short Carlisle Canal, and the even shorter Ulverston Canal, simply connected the towns of their titles to the sea.

At the time when canal networks were being established further south and in Scotland, the coal owners of north-east England were building primitive waggonways to take the output from their collieries to staithes near the river mouths for onward shipping.[738] These early and distinctly rudimentary railways were not only relatively short, but were used solely by the colliery owners for the carriage of their coal to the river staithes and sometimes, in the reverse direction, to transport materials required in their mines. However, on 19 April 1821 the Stockton and Darlington Railway (S&DR) Company was authorised by an Act of Parliament to construct a public railway, which allowed the Company to carry all manner of goods in addition to coal.[31] A second act, granted on 23 May 1823, authorised the railway not only to carry passengers, but also to use steam locomotives.[34] The S&DR is generally recognised as the forerunner of the railway system as we know it today, and the original proposals developed out of one of the early, but unsuccessful, canal schemes. The second of the pioneering public railways in northern England also started life as a waterway scheme, being the only major canal proposal in the northern counties which came anywhere near to fruition. The Newcastle and Carlisle Railway (N&CR) was authorised on 22 May 1829 to connect the river Tyne at Newcastle with the canal basin in Carlisle.[41] The line was opened in sections between 1834 and 1839, by which time the S&DR had started its expansion from the Auckland coalfield into the upper valleys of the North Pennines.

In the last decade of the eighteenth century, the transport of lead ore from the numerous mines in the North Pennines had attracted the attention of the promoters of the unsuccessful Newcastle and Maryport Canal, and this potentially rich traffic continued to entice the railway builders half a century later. Therefore, it is no surprise to find, in 1845, both the N&CR and the Wear Valley Railway (WVR), which was a subsidiary of the S&DR, seeking parliamentary approval for a railway to serve the mines of Allendale and Alston Moor. In the end, it was the Newcastle Company which obtained its Act of Parliament for a line to Alston Moor on 26 August 1846,[249] while three years later a second act was granted, on 13 July 1849, allowing the company to make major alterations to the route.[317] In 1871, nineteen years after the railway finally reached Alston, the Cumberland and Cleveland Junction Railway (C&CJR) Company was promoted to build a line from Alston to the northern terminus of the Tees Valley Railway (TVR) at Middleton-in-Teesdale. Despite further major efforts a decade later, this railway also failed to materialise. Several further attempts to revive the westward extension of the WVR, which would have continued the iron road from the valley of the river Wear through the Pennines to Alston Moor, also failed.

If all the railways surveyed between 1845 and 1871, and for which plans were deposited with the local Justices of the Peace, had actually been built, Alston would have become the focal point of a group of lines serving the entire North Pennine ore-field. Railways would have radiated from Alston in almost every direction as shown on the enclosed maps (Figure 1).

First, a line would have run northwards for 8 miles to Lambley where it would have divided. One branch would have continued down the South Tyne Valley to join the N&CR at Haltwhistle. Another would have turned west and joined the same railway near Brampton, in the valley of the River Irthing, with the Eden Valley and Carlisle close to hand. A second line would have run eastwards, passing through the mining community of Nenthead before tunnelling under Killhope Fell into Weardale, where two branches were to leave before it made an end-on junction with the Wear Valley section of the S&DR. The first branch would have crossed the mountain divide into Allendale where it would later have been joined by the Hexham and Allendale Railway (H&AR), while the second was to connect with the former Stanhope and Tyne section of the S&DR. The third major line would have run southwards over the watershed dividing South Tynedale from Teesdale to connect Alston with the Middleton-in-Teesdale

Railway. Further east, a line was proposed to connect Newcastle with the South Durham and Lancashire Union Railway, making the connected route into a main line from Merseyside to Newcastle.

The promoters of these unsuccessful canal and railway schemes have left behind a mountain of plans, letters, reports and other papers, the very earliest of which show how little was known of the topography of the more remote parts of Great Britain only a little over 200 years ago, and how the pioneering canal and railway engineers sought to overcome their difficulties. Not only do these documents allow one to visualise the railway network that was originally planned but they also shed considerable light on the economics and local politics of the area.

This history is not intended to be a fully comprehensive account of all the railways of the North Pennines, but mainly to demonstrate the network of railways that could have developed to connect Alston Moor with the neighbouring centres of commerce and industry. In order to place the unsuccessful lines in context, it is necessary to describe those that were actually built, together with the relationship between them and the routes which failed to materialise, even some which would have come nowhere near Alston Moor, including those well to the south of the area normally known as the North Pennines, and the line that would have given the London and North Western Railway direct access to Newcastle.[422]

The original railway plans were prepared in great detail, making it relatively easy to follow the proposed routes on modern maps, thereby showing their relationships to the road and river systems. The original plans were prepared by different surveyors using a variety of scales, and the overall map which has been prepared for this work has been drawn from these surveys. The railways shown on this map include all those for which detailed plans have been found, including all those which were actually built. In addition to the routes to be followed, these plans also give details of the expected gradients, the sizes and positions of cuttings and embankments, the heights and lengths of any viaducts and the more important bridges, including road crossings and, in some cases, the proposed sites for stations. No scales are shown on any of the maps reproduced from original plans as the size of each illustration has been determined by a combination of the space available and what is intended to be illustrated. However, on most of the original plans the distance is marked on the surveyed line of each railway in miles and furlongs, usually as a * for miles and a bar + across the line of the route for furlongs.

All the heights, widths and distances on the original plans are given in the Imperial units of inches, feet, yards, chains, furlongs and miles. After careful consideration, it has been decided to give all the figures in the Imperial units used throughout the nineteenth century, but with the metric equivalents following in brackets. The relationship of the Imperial units with each other, and with their

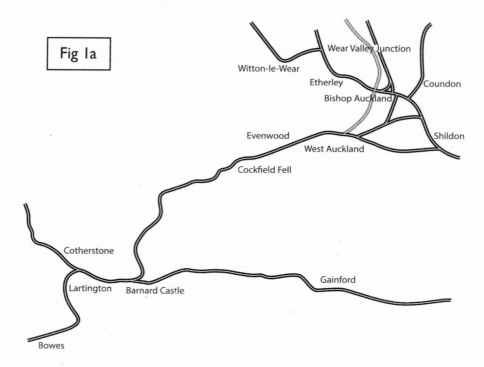

Fig 1a

Six maps showing all the public and major private standard-gauge railways built in the North Pennines, plus those railways for which plans were prepared and submitted to Parliament, but which were either authorised and not built, or were never authorised.

Figure 1a   Railways in the south-east section of the North Pennines.

The scale of these six maps is approximately 1 in 180,000.

Figure 1b   Railways in the north-east section of the North Pennines.

The key to the railways shown on these six maps is as follows:

 represents public railways built, either with initial parliamentary authorisation, or with later parliamentary approval
 railways which were authorised by parliament but not built
 private railways built and operated without any parliamentary authorisation
 railways for which plans were produced, but which were not authorised by parliament
 sections of planned railways following the same route, one of which was authorised by Parliament but not built and the other not authorised

Figure 1c   Railways in the south-central section of the North Pennines.
Figure 1d   Railways in the north-central section of the North Pennines.
Figure 1e   Railways in the south-west section of the North Pennines.
Figure 1f   Railways in the north-west section of the North Pennines.

Note – Where a railway built or proposed that followed the same general route of other, usually earlier, proposals that were not authorised or not built, only major divergences between the routes are shown.

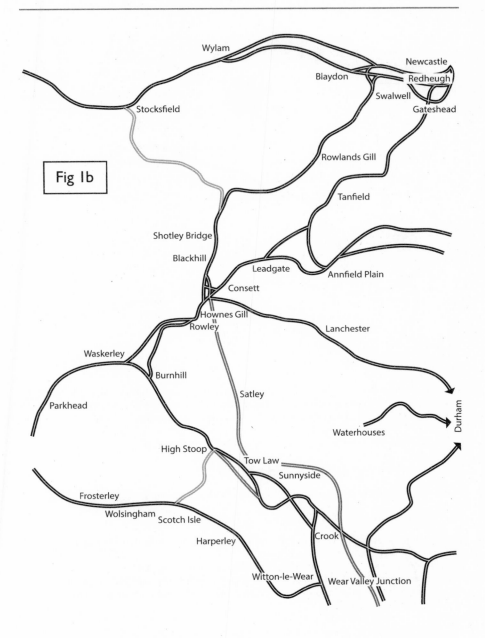

Fig 1b

metric equivalents, is given in Appendix A. In general, place names have been given their current spelling throughout this work.

Most of the documents referred to are to be found in the local record offices and libraries, and fall into a range of different categories. For this work the most important are the plans which were deposited, mainly between 1844 and 1871, with the local Justices of the Peace in compliance with parliamentary procedures.

The majority have been preserved in excellent order and are available for study in the record offices of Cumbria, Durham, Northumberland, North Yorkshire and Tyne and Wear. Plans for the earlier canal schemes are rather fewer in number, but this lack is more than made up for by the wealth of reports prepared by the various engineers commissioned by the different promoters. These can also be found scattered throughout the record offices and libraries in northern England, but the most important are the bound collections in the library of the Literary & Philosophical Society of Newcastle-upon-Tyne and the Central Library of the City of Newcastle-upon-Tyne. The record offices also house collections of personal papers, and those in the Cumbria Record Office in Carlisle and the

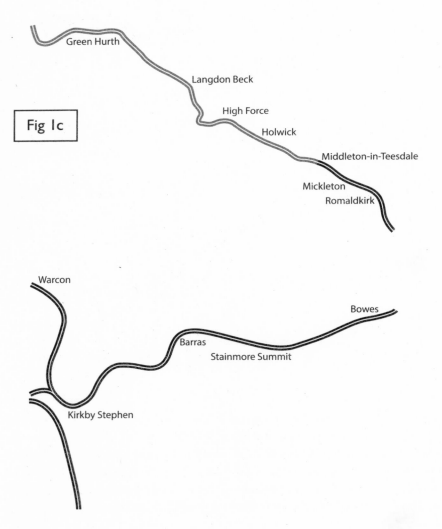

Fig 1c

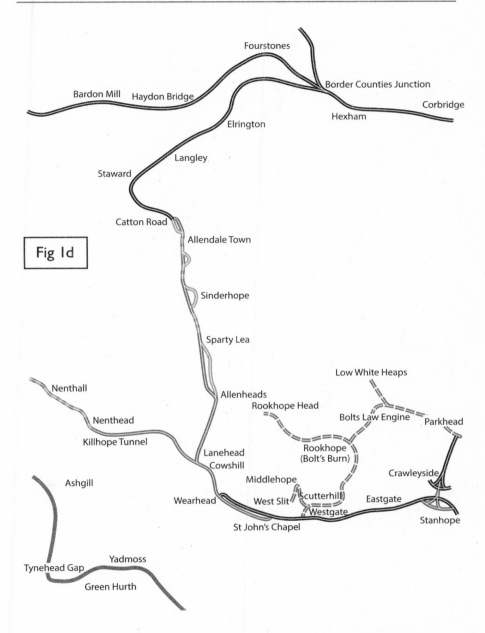

Fig 1d

Fourstones
Border Counties Junction
Bardon Mill Haydon Bridge Corbridge
Hexham
Elrington
Langley
Staward
Catton Road
Allendale Town
Sinderhope
Sparty Lea
Low White Heaps
Nenthall Allenheads
Rookhope Head
Nenthead Bolts Law Engine Parkhead
Killhope Tunnel Rookhope
Lanehead (Bolt's Burn)
Cowshill Crawleyside
Ashgill Middlehope
Wearhead West Slit Scutterhill Eastgate
Westgate
St John's Chapel Stanhope
Yadmoss
Tynehead Gap
Green Hurth

Durham Record Office have provided extensive information. Finally, there is a wealth of information in the pages of the contemporary newspapers, collections of which are to be found in both the libraries and record offices, as well as in the newspaper offices themselves.

As this account is intended to be read by anyone who has an interest in the subject, the authors and titles of the various pamphlets, letters, etc., have not been

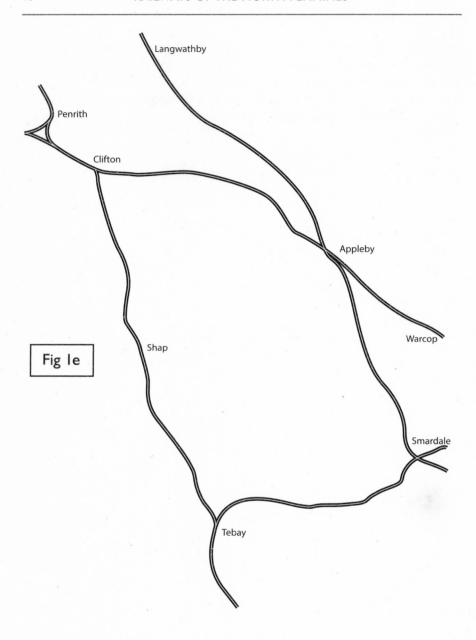

Fig 1e

included in the main body of the text, apart from the names of those who actually carried out the surveys, or who played a major role in the individual projects. Actual quotations from these documents are indicated by quotation marks, while small superscript numbers indicate the references, details of which are given in a separate section at the end of the text. Most of the acts of Parliament referred to have been studied in detail, while the location of the copies quoted are given in the reference list. The modern photographs have been taken to indicate where some of the more interesting features of the unbuilt railways would have occurred, and to attempt to show the scale of the works that would have been required to carry the iron road through the highest parts of the North Pennines, as well as representative views of the remains of the lines actually built. Appendix B gives the names and commonly used abbreviations of all the railways mentioned in this history. For those who wish to trace the courses of the proposed, or abandoned, railways on the ground, this history should be used in conjunction with modern

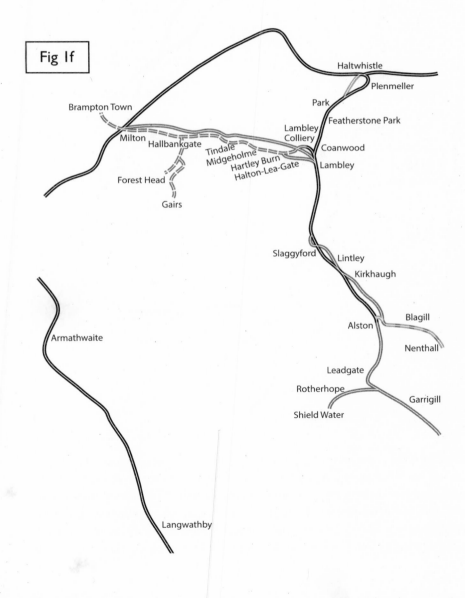

Fig 1f

large-scale Ordnance Survey maps. Although it is possible to follow the routes on the 1:50,000 Landranger Series, the 1:25,000 Explorer and Outdoor Leisure Series provide a much clearer picture of the land through which the lines were planned to pass.

At the time of writing, 2013, the following are the relevant numbers of the 1:25,000 series required to follow each of the proposed railways:

- Newcastle and Carlisle Railway, Nenthead branch of 1845 and Alston branch of 1849 – Explorer OL31 and OL43.
- Newcastle & Carlisle Railway, Allenheads branch proposals – Explorer OL31 and OL43.
- Bishop Auckland and Weardale, and Wear Valley railways – Explorer 305.
- Wear Valley Extension Railway of 1845, main line – Explorer OL31 and OL43.
- Wear Valley Extension Railway of 1845, Allendale branch – Explorer OL31 and OL43.
- Wear and Derwent Junction, and Weardale Iron Company railways – Explorer 305 and 307.
- Hexham and Allendale Railway – Explorer OL43.
- Darlington and Barnard Castle, and South Durham and Lancashire Union railways – Explorer 304.
- Cumberland and Cleveland Junction Railway – Explorer OL31 and OL43.
- Wear Valley Extension Railway of 1892 – Explorer OL31.

2

CANAL PROPOSALS, ROADS AND THE EARLY RAILWAYS

In the second half of the eighteenth century, proposals were put forward for two canals which would have tapped the North Pennines ore-field and, although neither was built, both eventually resulted in the construction of the railways which became the main players in the provision of transport in the area. The first ideas for a canal which would have reached the edge of the North Pennines were discussed in Darlington during October 1767[760] and a firm proposal was made at a meeting held on 9 November 1767.[1,2] At a further meeting, held at the Post House in Darlington on 1 December 1767, a committee was set up to carry the proposal forward.[3] James Brindley was asked to provide a surveyor to investigate a suitable line for a canal to extend the navigation of the river Tees. On 19 September 1768 Robert Whitworth was sent to survey the area towards the inland coalfield and by 24 October 1768 he had completed his survey for a canal just under 27 miles in length,[3] starting at the river Tees in Stockton and rising 328ft (100m) to terminate beside the turnpike road near Winston, a point which was within easy access of the coalfield (p. 22). The cost of constructing the canal and three short branches was estimated at £63,722 by James Brindley and Robert Whitworth, who reported back to the committee on 19 July 1769,[760] but nothing further was done at the time.

The idea of a canal from Winston to Stockton was revived in the 1790s, but this time with two branches, one running northwards to join the proposed Durham Canal and the second running south from Croft Bridge on the river Tees to Boroughbridge on the river Ure. Ralph Dodd painted a bright picture for this canal in a report in 1796.[761] Again nothing came of these proposals, but in 1808 an act was obtained to improve the navigation of the river Tees between Stockton and the sea, including the cutting of a canal through a neck of land near Portrack.[24] The improvements were completed in 1810 and at a dinner to celebrate the opening of the 'New Cut' in Stockton on 18 September 1810 a committee was formed to 'inquire into the practicability and advantage of a railway or canal from Stockton, by Darlington and Winston'.[25,762] Further canal

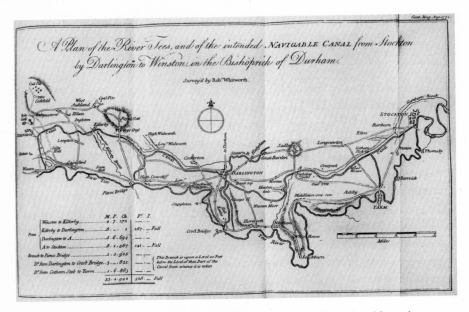

Robert Whitworth's plan for a canal from Stockton to Winston. Reproduced from the *Gentleman's Magazine*, August 1772, by permission of Cumbria County Council, Library Services, Carlisle Group HQ.

proposals were made after the end of the Napoleonic Wars and in 1818 plans were produced and a bill presented to Parliament for a canal running from Stockton to Fighting Cocks with a railway continuing to the coalfield.[27] The bill failed and later in 1818 George Overton was asked to make a survey for a railway. On 13 November 1818, a meeting was held in Darlington Town Hall which decided in favour of a railway,[29,739] and thus the Stockton and Darlington Railway was born.

By the last decade of the eighteenth century, greater quantities of lead were being extracted from the North Pennine ore-field than from any other region in the world, and the town of Alston had become firmly established as the commercial centre of the most important of the mining areas. It was at this time that a group of citizens of Newcastle-upon-Tyne invited Ralph Dodd 'to make superficially a survey' to determine whether it would be practical to build a canal between 'the East and the West Sea'.[5,6]

Although Dodd had just completed a survey for the River Wear Commissioners, and the contemporary North of England press was fulsome with its praise, his experience and abilities as a canal engineer were exceedingly limited.[744] At public meetings held in Newcastle on 1 November and 15 November 1794,[7,8] Dodd indicated that his superficial survey had shown that a canal through Hexham and Carlisle was practical, and he was then asked to make a detailed survey of the route and its probable cost. In addition to the main line, Dodd suggested that several branches would be beneficial, giving as an example 'one that would go nearly to Alston Moor' to accommodate the lead traffic.[7]

At a meeting held in Carlisle on 29 November 1794 to recruit subscribers in Cumberland to the survey for the canal,[9] Dodd's appointment as engineer was confirmed, yet on 27 December the Northumberland Committee decided to request William Chapman, a much more experienced canal engineer, 'to report on the measures to be attended to in the Survey of a line of Navigation, from Newcastle-upon-Tyne to the Irish Channel'.[10] Exactly a week later the Cumberland Committee not only confirmed Chapman's appointment but also the request of the Northumberland Committee that both he and Dodd deliver their reports to a joint meeting of the Northumberland and Cumberland Committees to be held at Hexham on 12 January.[11] Only Chapman delivered his report, and the meeting authorised its publication and asked two other experienced canal engineers, Messrs Jessop and Whitworth, to join with Chapman 'to examine and report their opinion of the best line for a navigation from the River Tyne to the Irish Channel by Hexham and Carlisle…'.[12] In the event, Jessop and Whitworth left Chapman to carry out the actual survey on his own, making their comments later in the light of his detailed report.

Some of the difficulties encountered by the canal and early railway engineers are apparent in the way in which Chapman had to discard any idea of a branch canal to Alston following his first accurate survey of the region. This is in complete contrast to the situation which existed in the second half of the nineteenth century, when the engineer undertaking the survey for the Cumberland and Cleveland Junction Railway was able to use the first edition of the one-inch Ordnance Survey Map when he prepared his plans in 1871.

In his first report of 5 January 1795, Chapman envisaged a broad canal climbing up the South Tyne Valley from Newcastle to Haltwhistle and then following the river Tipalt to a summit on 'the flat ground between the deep Vale of Glenwhelt and the River Irthing'.[13] Chapman expected that it would be possible to build a branch from Haltwhistle into the North Pennines to tap the lead traffic, which he estimated was over 11,000 tons per year. He believed that a small-scale canal could leave the Glenwhelt summit level and follow the west bank of the South Tyne, without requiring any locks, as far as Knaresdale, or possibly even between there and Kirkhaugh. From there he suggested that a high-level canal might be built to run generally eastwards and southwards to penetrate 'the valleys of the lead country'. Chapman proposed that this canal should be on one level, with the rise from the main branch to be the minimum that would allow the canal to reach the lead mines. In his view, the country was not suitable for the construction of a canal on the same scale as the main line, which he believed should be able to take boats carrying 50 tons. It should be noted that the dimensions he suggested are similar to those still to be found on the unmodernized waterways in Yorkshire.[743]

For the lead mine canal Chapman stated that the width and length of the boats for this branch should be half that of those on the main line, so that four small boats could be taken together along the main line where they would be able to pass through the locks roped together. He suggested that the canal to the lead mines should be built by the parties involved in the lead industry and calculated that as it would cost less than half of one (old) penny per ton-mile (about 0.2p) to haul the lead, the circuitous nature of such a canal would not be a disadvantage.

Chapman ended his first report with a postscript in which he stated that he had been informed of a pass between the rivers South Tyne and Eden, to the south of Glenwhelt, but by 10 July 1795 he had made a detailed survey of several routes between the Tyne and Irthing and concluded that the lowest summit lay at Glenwhelt in the valley between the rivers Tipalt and Irthing.[15] This summit level was 55ft (16.8m) above the junction of the rivers South Tyne and Tipalt, whereas the same rise was reached on the South Tyne a little above where it was joined by the Hartley Burn, and therefore he concluded that the plan to make a branch from the summit level towards Alston would not be possible. An undated and unsigned map entitled 'A sketch map of the intended canal between the East and West Seas',[18] with a scale of half an inch to a mile, shows the route of Chapman's canal from the Haymarket in Newcastle running along the valleys of the rivers Tyne, Irthing and Eden, then through Carlisle to reach the sea at Maryport (pp. 25–27).

With the abandonment of the idea for a canal to Alston, Chapman expected that the lead traffic would join the canal at Haydon Bridge, and suggested that a small canal could be built on a high level from the lead country to terminate between Allen Foot and Langley.[15] Following his confirmation that the canal would follow the river Tipalt to the valley of the River Irthing, Chapman proposed the construction of two branches from the western end of the summit level, one in the direction of Penrith and lake Ullswater and the other to within ¼ mile (400m) of Kirkhouse, from which point a railway could communicate with the Tindale Fell collieries (p. 27). Following the delivery of the final reports by both Chapman, for a high-level canal between Newcastle and Haydon Bridge,[15,16] and Dodd, for a low-level canal going only as far as Hexham,[14] there ensued almost two years of wrangling between those who supported Chapman's high-level route on the north side of the Tyne and those who supported Dodd's low-level route (pp. 28–29) on the south side of the river.

During the course of the acrimonious discussions on the relative merits of the two routes, the opinions of several other canal engineers and surveyors were sought. William Jessop supported Chapman's route,[17] while John Sutcliffe thought that a low-level route on the south side of the Tyne was better but suggested a

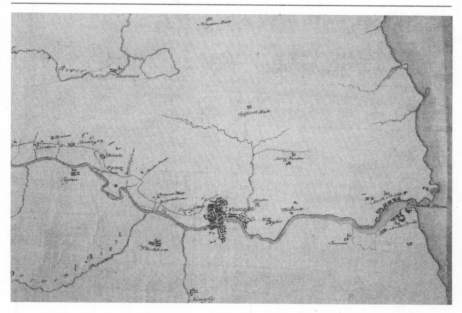

The eastern end of the Newcastle to Maryport canal which was to start near the Haymarket in Newcastle. In the Senhouse Papers, Cumbria Archives Service. Reproduced by permission of Mr J. Scott-Plummer.

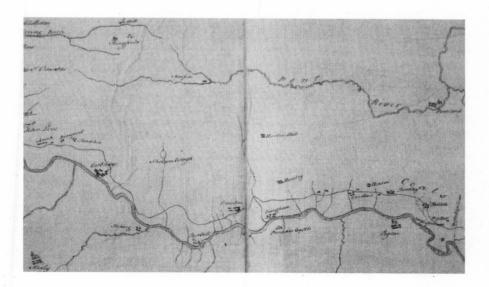

totally different alignment to that proposed by Dodd.[21] In September 1796 plans were deposited for both routes, Chapman for the high-level canal from Newcastle as far as Haydon Bridge,[19] and Bell for the low-level canal as far as Hexham,[20] but the only bill presented to Parliament, in 1797, was for the high-level canal.[23]

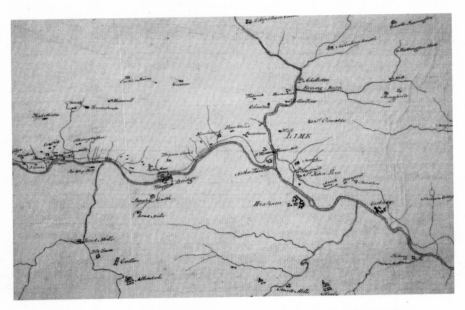

The central part of the Newcastle to Maryport canal with the initial level section from Newcastle ending at Haydon Bridge and then climbing to the summit at Glenwhelt. Note the similarity of this section to the line of the N&CR. In the Senhouse Papers, Cumbria Archives Service. Reproduced by permission of Mr J. Scott-Plummer.

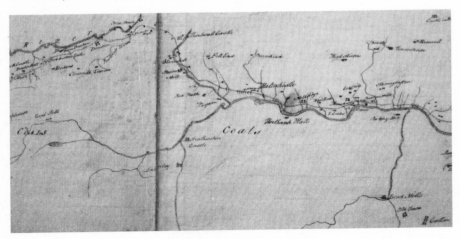

However, the promoters decided to withdraw the bill during a major parliamentary battle, which the contemporary reports suggest they were probably in the process of winning.[22] There were several further attempts to promote a canal westwards from Newcastle, with notice being given in 1810 that a bill was to be introduced in the next parliamentary session,[26] but they all failed due, in part at least, to the economic effects of the Napoleonic Wars.

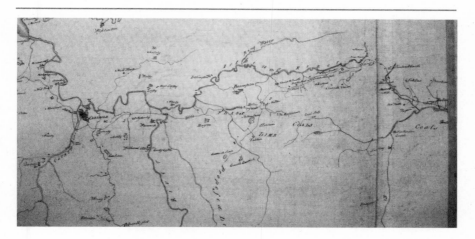

The western and of the Newcastle to Maryport canal showing the heavily locked section south of Brampton and the relatively level section from Carlisle to Maryport. In the Senhouse Papers, Cumbria Archives Service. Reproduced by permission of Mr J. Scott-Plummer.

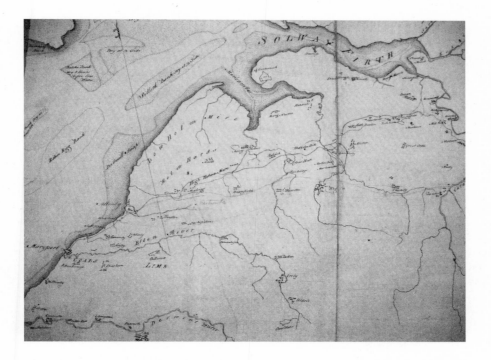

Eventually the Carlisle promoters decided to build a short canal from their city to the sea and asked Chapman to draw up a set of suitable plans, which were deposited with Parliament on 29 September 1818.[26] An act was obtained on 6 April 1819[30] for a canal from Fisher's Cross or Binnacle, the highest point up the Solway Firth that could readily be reached by sea going ships, to a basin in the

City of Carlisle. The Carlisle Canal opened on 12 March 1823[33] and resulted in a final attempt being made to extend the inland navigation to Newcastle. In 1824 Chapman was once again asked to make a survey and then compare the respective advantages of a ship canal or a railway. In his report, Chapman recommended that a railway be built,[36] and thus the Newcastle and Carlisle Railway Company was born. The route Chapman chose for the railway was, in effect, an amalgam of the low-level route to a short distance past Hexham, followed by his high-level route through Haydon Bridge to the basin of the Carlisle Canal.

Less than a year after Chapman suggested that a railway should be built to connect the proposed branch canal to Kirkhouse with the collieries at Tindale Fell,[16] estimates were prepared for a waggonway from the town of Brampton, through Kirkhouse, to the Earl of Carlisle's collieries in the hills to the south. Approved by the Earl, this was the start of the private mineral railway system which is usually known by the name of Lord Carlisle's Railway (LCR),[749] and this primitive wooden waggonway opened from Brampton to the Talkin collieries, near Forest Head, on 15 April 1799.

The original wooden rails of the waggonway were soon replaced by cast iron, while in 1808 it was decided to use wrought, or malleable, iron rails. These proved to be much less liable to break, and were recorded as showing no apparent change after eight years in constant use. This was the first successful use of wrought iron rails on any railway and undoubtedly influenced the contemporary engineers in their decision to abandon the use of cast iron for rails.

Although this first short line was technically in the North Pennines, it was only the later extensions of the completely rebuilt railway that had a direct influence

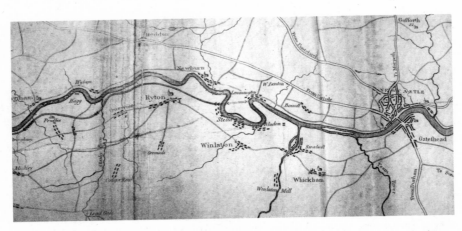

The eastern section of Dodd's 1795 plan of a canal from Newcastle to Hexham, showing his route starting at Stella with a possible line across the bulge of land to Lemington. Reproduced by permission of Local Studies and Family History Centre, Newcastle Libraries and Information Service (NLIS).

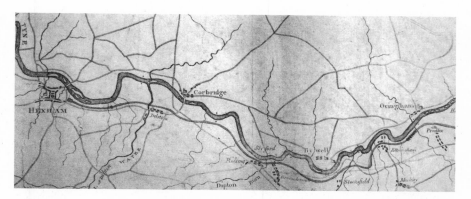

The western section of Dodd's 1795 plan of a canal from Newcastle to Hexham, showing the terminus on the eastern side of Hexham. Reproduced by permission of NLIS.

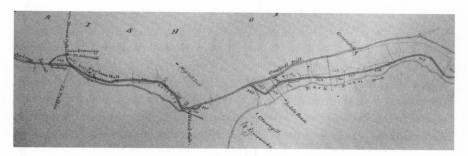

Plan of the proposed turnpike road from Brampton to Alston passing Farlam Hall. The new road (dark) was to follow the original route of Lord Carlisle's Railway to Hallbankgate. Apart from the section beside plot 324, all of the new road appears to have been built. The illustration on p.30 was taken close to the point marked 'tunnel' on the plan. Reproduced by permission of Cumbria Archive Service (CAS).

on the railways reaching into the ore-field at the headwaters of the rivers Allen, Tees, South Tyne and Wear. Much of the information on Lord Carlisle's Railway, also known as the Brampton Railway, is based on the comprehensive history by the late Brian Webb and David Gordon.[748]

As the demand for coal and manufactured goods increased, improvements to the transport system of the United Kingdom became ever more necessary. Throughout the eighteenth century networks of canals and turnpike roads were constructed across the kingdom and, during the last third of the century, several acts of Parliament were passed establishing Turnpike trusts to provide roads in the North Pennines.

The principal areas served by these roads were Alston, West Allendale and the upper Wear Valley, but by the end of the first quarter of the nineteenth century they

Part of the 1799 route of Lord Carlisle's Railway where it runs alongside the A689 between Farlam and Milton, photographed in October 2007. The overgrown cutting is on the right with the A689 road on the left. The building in the background is part of Farlam Hall Hotel. This section of railway ceased to be used when the new line from Hallbankgate to Brampton was opened on 15 July 1836.

were in need of upgrading and extension. In 1823, plans were prepared, under the direction of John Loudon McAdam,[32] for a series of roads centred on Alston which were authorised by an Act of Parliament passed in 1824.[37] This act authorised major improvements to the roads connecting Alston with the outside world, requiring many miles of new construction, in addition to the upgrading of some sections of existing roads, only some of which had been turnpiked previously (pp. 31 and 32). The roads to be improved included the extension to Brampton of the existing turnpike between Burtreeford and Burnstones, improvements to the Hexham to Alston turnpike and its extension to Penrith, and what was essentially a new road from Alston to Barnard Castle. The trustees of the Hexham to Alston turnpike were also authorised to build a road from their existing turnpike at Cupola Bridge in the West Allen Valley, via Haydon Bridge to Fourstones and Bellingham, with a branch from Fourstones to join the Hexham Turnpike close to the point where the modern Hexham bypass leaves the original route. Today, the roads turnpiked by this act form the basis of much of the main road network in the North Pennines and are the A686 in its entirety; the A689 between Cowshill (Burtree Ford) and Brampton; the B6277 in its entirety, plus the unclassified section from Barnard Castle to the south end of Egglestone Abbey Bridge and the B6294 in its entirety. The section from Cupola Bridge to Haydon Bridge forms part of the A686, the road on to Bellingham is now the B6319 and part of the B6320, and the section from Fourstones to the A69 is unclassified.

As soon as the whole line of the turnpike road between Cupola Bridge and Haydon Bridge was completed, the act allowed the Trustees, if they so wished, to

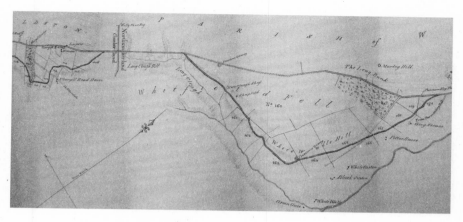

The section of the plans, prepared under the direction of John Loudon McAdam for the improvement of the Alston to Hexham section of the Alston Turnpike Trust, showing the road going over Whitfield Fell with new sections of road replacing the much steeper sections previously used on each side of the summit level. Reproduced by permission of CAS.

abandon their existing road from Cupola Bridge to Summerrods at Hexham. Part of this road is now the B6305 in its entirety, and we shall meet the section that was ultimately abandoned when we consider the building of the Hexham and Allendale Railway. The final length of new road was to run from Newshield Bank, on the Summerrods to Alston turnpike, via Randalholm to Slaggyford, crossing the South Tyne by a new bridge at Kirkhaugh, but this was never completed. The act required that LCR was not to be damaged, and Lord Carlisle was permitted to extend his railway over the turnpike from Alston to Brampton after giving one calendar month's notice of such intention. A later act slightly reduced the scope of the Alston Turnpike Trust,[378] but the section of the former Hexham turnpike from Hexham to Summerrods was transferred to it.

In 1825 plans were prepared by Thomas Bell for a new Turnpike Trust to improve the roads of the Allen valleys.[39] These improvements were authorised by an act of 1826 which required the upgrading of several existing roads, mostly in the East Allen Valley, and involved building some completely new sections.[40] These roads continue in use today as the B6295, B6303 and B6304, plus the unclassified road from Thornley Gate, near Allendale, via Coalcleugh to the A689 near Nenthead. The road connecting Burtree Ford with Gateshead, Crook and Durham was provided by the Lobley Hill Turnpike Trust, originally established in 1793.[4]

In June 1824, at the same time as these road improvements were being planned and authorised, Lord Carlisle sanctioned the construction of a branch from his existing waggonway at Hallbankgate, extending for about 4 miles (6.5km)

Whitfield Fell, looking east along the roads of the Alston Turnpike Trust. The tarmac road in the foreground was authorised by the act of 1778 and retained by the act of 1824. At the end of the straight length the 1778 turnpike continues over the high moors on a gentle curve to the right, while the 1824 road curves more sharply to the right and drops down the hillside on an even gradient.

eastwards to collieries near Midgeholme. The route was first surveyed by Lord Carlisle's colliery agent, James Thompson, and his plans were then approved by George Stephenson. The extension was built to the gauge of 4ft 8in (1.42m), the same as the S&DR, and the construction was of a much higher standard than the original line.[750] The choice of the Stephenson gauge for the new part of LCR also determined the gauge of the N&CR, which was being seriously considered at that time. Because Lord Carlisle's Railway was built without any parliamentary approval there are no deposited plans, but plans deposited for the proposed Wear Valley Extension Railway (WVER), which we will meet in chapter 4, show LCR as the WVER was to run a little to the north of the earlier line. The Midgeholme extension was opened in August 1828, but because of the break of gauge the coal was transhipped at Hallbankgate until the original part of the waggonway was widened over the winter of 1829–30. Even this proved to be only a temporary measure, for early in 1834 it was decided to build a completely new railway from Brampton to Hallbankgate. With these improvements the private railway was expected to carry 'a good amount' of general merchandise and passengers, especially from the Alston area to which further extensions were under consideration.

A connection was also to be made with the N&CR, by then under construction, which Lord Carlisle's new line would cross at Milton station, later called Brampton Junction, and now simply Brampton. A little later in 1834, Lord Carlisle authorised a further extension of his line from Midgeholme to Hartley Burn (Halton Lea Gate). The eastern section of this line, which was outside Lord Carlisle's barony, was to be laid with 1830 rail recovered from the old waggonway between Hallbankgate and Brampton. Although the formation of the eastern extension was ready by November 1835, track-laying did not commence until August of the following year, due to a delay in the completion of the new line to Brampton Town.

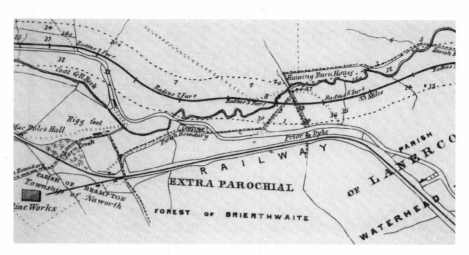

Plan showing LCR running along the valley of the Haining Burn. The Tindale 'battery' or embankment crosses the Tarn Brook. The proposed WVER runs to the north. Reproduced by permission of CAS.

While Thompson was organising the reconstruction of LCR, the N&CR Company had obtained its Act of Parliament on 22 May 1829,[41] with a second act,[42] to raise more money, being granted on 23 June 1832.

In the report in the *Newcastle Courant* of the general meeting of shareholders,[47] held on 25 November 1834, it was stated that considerable quantities of lead were being carried by the line from Hexham and Stocksfield to Blaydon, the effective head of navigation on the river Tyne, using horse-drawn wagons. Tomlinson gives the quantities as 115½ tons from Stocksfield and 491½ tons from Hexham.[767] The *Newcastle Courant* also stated that this part of the line, about 17 miles, was now virtually open and producing revenue for the company. Having decided that horse traction was too slow and inefficient, the directors ordered steam locomotives, although their original act specifically disallowed their use. Nevertheless a service of steam-hauled passenger trains was introduced between Blaydon and Hexham on 9 March 1835,[48] only to be withdrawn on the 28th when an injunction was obtained, by Charles Bacon Grey of Styford, preventing the use of the steam engines.[49] Public opinion was on the side of the railway and services were resumed on 6 May,[50] although it was not until 17 June that the company obtained an Act of Parliament authorising the use of steam locomotives.[53]

Significant amounts of lead were carried on this first 17 miles (27.4km) of railway, but the following year three new sections of line were opened, two of which provided railheads much more convenient for the ore-field.[58] On 28 June 1836, the line was extended 7 miles (11.3km) from Hexham to Haydon Bridge where extensive sidings were provided for the lead traffic coming down the

Looking up the Kirkhouse incline on the 1836 line from Hallbankgate to Brampton. Ken Hoole collection, Head of Steam–Darlington Railway Museum (HoS-DRM).

turnpike roads from Alston Moor and Allendale. At least as significant was the opening, on 19 July, of the 20 miles (32km) from Blenkinsopp, near Greenhead, to the depot at London Road, Carlisle. This connected at Milton with the rebuilt section of LCR from Brampton staithes to Hallbankgate, which had been officially opened just four days previously. The extension of LCR to Hartley Burn from Midgeholme was completed later the same year, providing the northern part of the North Pennines with a second convenient railhead reached by another section of the new turnpike roads.

In the east the Blaydon, Gateshead and Hebburn Railway (BG&HR) had received its act on 22 May 1834[45] to build a railway from the N&CR at Blaydon through Gateshead to Hebburn.[44] A clause empowered the N&CR to construct the line from Blaydon to Gateshead and early in 1835 the N&CR entered into negotiations to take over this section on which work had commenced. The N&CR opened the first part, from Blaydon to the eastern bank of the river Derwent, on 11 June 1836.[58] The BG&HR only constructed the line from the river Derwent to the river Team before being taken over by the N&CR in September 1836, with the final length into Gateshead on the opposite bank of the Tyne to Newcastle opening on 1 March 1837.[63] The remainder of the route to Hebburn was constructed by the Brandling Junction Railway Company,[51,56] and does not concern us. The extension of the western part of the N&CR, from London Road to the terminal basin of the Carlisle Canal, opened on 9 March 1837,[61] while the central section, from Haydon Bridge through Haltwhistle to Blenkinsopp, followed on 18 June 1838, finally connecting the Tyne with the Solway.[65] Rails eventually reached the city of Newcastle-upon-Tyne on 21 May 1839 when the line between Blaydon and the Company's new depot near the Shot Tower in Newcastle was opened for traffic.[71] Although the completed line was of immediate local and regional importance, and most of it remains part of today's railway network, the opening of the central section did nothing to improve the transport situation in the North Pennines, as it was not until 1976 that an adequate road was built to link Haltwhistle with the upper reaches of the South Tyne Valley!

When first completed, the N&CR consisted of 46 miles (74km) of double track and 20 miles (32km) of single track railway,[68] all originally designed to be operated by horses. The directors resolved that, as soon as it was convenient, they would alter some sections of their line to make it more suitable for steam locomotives, as well as doubling it throughout.[79] Because some of the alterations were outside the authorised limits of deviation, yet another act was obtained on 21 June 1841 to allow the company to proceed with the required work, and also to issue a further £225,000 of shares and borrow another £75,000.[85] The work of consolidating and improving the newly opened railway, as well as doubling the 20 miles of single line, occupied the next five years, so that it was not until 1845 that the Newcastle Company felt able to turn its attention to the North Pennines.

It is now necessary to return to the meeting of 1818 where it was decided to apply for an Act of Parliament to build a railway from Stockton, through Darlington to the Auckland coalfield.[29,739] The first act to construct a railway was based on the plans of George Overton, and became law on 19 April 1821.[31] Two months later George Stephenson was asked to make a new survey,[35] and a second act was passed on 23 May 1823,[34] which allowed the company to make several deviations and, more significantly, to use steam locomotives. Before the line was opened a third act was passed, on 17 May 1824,[38] authorising the construction of a branch to Haggerleases Lane (Butterknowle), where roads radiated not only to several local collieries, but beyond to tap the lead mining area around Middleton-in-Teesdale. When the line was eventually opened on 27 September 1825 it consisted of 20 miles (32km) from Stockton to Shildon, on gradients not

The original Haydon Bridge station building photographed in 2004 from the later platform which lies to the north of the original and remains in use today. The goods yard for handling the lead traffic lay behind this building.

exceeding 1 in 104, to be worked by steam locomotives and horses. This was followed by 5 miles (8km) of inclined planes where stationary steam engines hauled the wagons, on gradients of 1 in 30 to 1 in 34, over two ridges to the Phoenix Pit at Etherley in the valley of the river Wear. The next ten years saw the S&DR developing its system in the east, while other companies began to spread through the Durham coalfield, mainly to the north and east, although the Clarence Railway was viewed as a serious competitor.[763]

The first iron road to actually reach the main ore-fields of the North Pennines was the ill-fated Stanhope and Tyne Railway (S&TR), whose history can be found in Tomlinson's account of the North Eastern Railway.[764] The impetus for this extraordinary line came from the formation, in 1831, of a partnership to work coal at Medomsley, north of Consett, and limestone at Stanhope in the Wear Valley. In addition to connecting Stanhope with Medomsley, the partners proposed to continue their railway to staithes on the river Tyne near South Shields. Wishing to keep the extensive nature of their scheme a secret, the partners decided not to apply for an Act of Parliament authorising them to build their railway, which would have given the company established by the Act all the necessary powers to purchase the land they required. Instead the partners had to negotiate 'wayleaves' with the landowners giving them the right to build the railway in exchange for the payment of an annual rent. Using the name Stanhope Railroad Company, the partnership began negotiations on 2 December 1831 for wayleaves across the moors north of Stanhope.

During the first half of 1832 the Stanhope and Tyne Railroad Company was formed, with a capital of £150,000 to take over the 'rights and interests' of the partnership, and held its first meeting in London on 1 June 1832. The establishment of this new company was confirmed by a deed of settlement dated 3 February 1834.[91] Work started at the Stanhope end of the line in July 1832 with Robert Stephenson and Thomas Elliot Harrison as engineers. Although the use of wayleaves saved both the expense of an Act of Parliament and the purchase price of the land, it saddled the company with an annual rent of £5,600 on a main line almost 34 miles (54.5km) long plus 3¾ miles (6.1km) of branch lines. Although the rents for the western portion were relatively inexpensive, being in the region of £40 to £50 per mile, those for the eastern section averaged £280 to £300 per mile.

Work progressed at a reasonable rate and the western 15¼ miles (24.5km) of railway, from Stanhope to Annfield, was opened on 15 May 1834.[46] Unfortunately the day was marred by an accident on the Weatherhill incline when the shackle attaching four wagons, carrying forty to fifty people, broke and the wagons were stopped from continuing down the Crawley incline by being diverted into a siding containing four loaded wagons, killing a man and a 9-year-old boy. The continuation to South Shields was opened on 10 September 1834.[765] Originally, it was not planned that passengers would be carried on the S&TR, which was

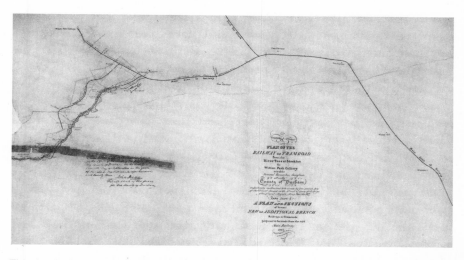

The plan, by Robert Stephenson, of 1823 showing the western end of the Stockton and Darlington Railway with the Haggerleases Branch. Reproduced by permission of Durham County Record Office (DRO).

constructed more on the contemporary principles of a private colliery line than a public railway, with several severely graded sections. In this it was similar to the section of the S&DR west of Shildon, which used inclined planes, worked by stationary steam engines, to carry the iron road into the Auckland coalfield. It is interesting to note that George Stephenson's modernisation of Lord Carlisle's private railway also included a self-acting inclined plane between Hallbankgate and Milton. On the other hand, William Chapman, Josias Jessop and Benjamin Thompson, the engineers of the N&CR, ensured that the maximum gradients on their line could be worked by horses.[704]

Even before the S&TR was completed, or most of the directors of the S&DR had seriously thought of turning their attention to extending their railway westwards, the prospectus for a new railway, called the Tees, Weardale and Tyne Junction Railroad, was published by George H. Wilkinson.[43] According to Wilkinson, the proprietors of the S&TR intended to construct a branch from their main line on Muggleswick Common (Waskerley) to a terminus near Thornley Pit Houses (Tow Law), while the line he proposed was to connect this branch with the termination of the S&DR near Etherley (Fig. 1 col. section). His line was to be 7 miles (11.3km) long and would follow the valley of the Bitchburn Beck down from Thornley Pit Houses, crossing the river Wear about half a mile (0.8km) above the confluence of the Beck with the river. Wilkinson stated that the S&TR branch would be about 5 miles long and almost level, running along the ridge which formed the boundary of the Parishes of Wolsingham and

Lanchester, and his line would have a gradual fall to the river Wear. His final comment was that the current prices of iron, labour, and all that contributed to the formation of railroads were very low. This proposal later resulted in the formation of the Bishop Auckland and Weardale Railway.

As first built, the S&TR used all the contemporary methods of traction, having nine inclined planes operated by stationary steam engines, five self-acting inclined planes, with the intervening level sections being worked by horses in the west and steam locomotive engines in the east. Only the first 11 miles (17.7km), from Stanhope to Carrhouse (Consett), are relevant to this account, and we shall therefore restrict our detailed consideration to this section. Most of the original route, as well as the later deviations, can still be followed on the ground, but a full description of the original route from Stanhope to Consett is in order.[101,765] The line commenced at limekilns near Crawleyside, ½ mile (800m) north of, and 150ft (46m) above, the town of Stanhope, and immediately ascended almost 650ft (200m) in a little under 2 miles (3km). The ascent was accomplished by means of two inclined planes. The first, using gradients of 1 in 8 to 1 in 12, was operated by the Crawley engine, and the second, on the lesser gradients of 1 in 13 to 1 in 21, was worked by the Weatherhill engine. This was the summit of the line which, at 1,445ft (440m) above sea level, was the highest point on a public railway in England.

Initially, horses hauled the wagons over the next 1½ miles (2.4km), which was followed by two inclines, both worked by the Meeting Slacks engine. Nanny Mayor's self-acting incline came next, before another 3 miles (4.8km) of horse operation took the line to the crossing of the 160ft (48m) deep Hownes Gill ravine. It had originally been planned to build a bridge over the ravine, but a pair of inclined planes, operated by a stationary engine at the bottom, was constructed. To keep the wagons horizontal on the steep gradients of 1 in 2½ and 1 in 3, they were carried on special trucks which limited the

Looking west along the original trackbed of the Stanhope and Tyne Railway at 40685471. This photograph was taken on 2 October 2000, over 140 years after this section of the original line was replaced on 4 July 1859 by the line avoiding Nanny Mayor's incline.

capacity of the line to twelve wagons an hour. Beyond Hownes Gill, there was an ascent for 1¼ miles (2km) to the Carr House engine, which also worked the following descent.

The fortunes of the early railway companies can be followed from the tables of share prices and dividends printed in Herepath's Journal, which appeared under various titles (see the references) from 1835. Throughout 1836 no dividend was reported for the S&TR, while the price of the 1,500 shares of £100 nominal value varied from £92 10s (£92.50) during April, to £105 in May and June after which no price at all was quoted.[57] Neither a share price nor a dividend was quoted during 1837, although a reference to the duty paid in respect of passengers carried shows that passenger services were indeed being operated.[64] During August 1839 a dividend of 5 per cent appears for the first time, although the maximum share price remained at £100.[72] Officially, the situation remained the same throughout 1840[76] and 1841[81], but during 1840 the impossible financial position of the Company became apparent.[771]

In order to save the high operating costs of the western section, the 11 miles (17.7km) of line between Stanhope and Carrhouse ceased to be used after 1839, but then the unfortunate owners heard that a combination of the high wayleaves, reduced traffic and unsound financial practices had produced debts and liabilities of upwards of £440,000, which greatly exceeded the value of all the property of the company.[91] At a Special General Meeting, which was started on 29 December 1840[80] and continued on 2 January 1841,[771] the decision was taken to dissolve the old company and this took place on 5 February 1841.[91] Half of the original shareholders raised sufficient new capital to resolve the major part of their financial problems, and on 25 November 1841 applied to Parliament for an act to dissolve the existing company and to 'establish and incorporate a new Company, for the purpose of purchasing the Stanhope & Tyne Railroad',[87] which was to be called the Pontop and South Shields Railway (P&SSR). Among those who lost large sums of money on the failure of the S&TR was Robert Stephenson himself.[83] Clause 94 of the Act[91] empowered the directors to sell the railway, works and branches between Stanhope and Pontop.

Following the proposal for the Tees, Weardale and Tyne Junction Railroad, in 1835 a new group including George Wilkinson proposed, unsuccessfully, to build a line eastwards from Frosterley to connect with the Durham Branch of the Clarence Railway.[52,54] The following year a similar group deposited a modified set of plans,[55] while George Wilkinson reappeared as the Chairman of the Bishop Auckland and Weardale Railway (BA&WR)[75] to propose a similar railway, this time sponsored by the S&DR.[59,60,768] The BA&WR line was designed to take the S&DR from Shildon into the Wear Valley by a tunnel, thus avoiding the existing inclined planes.

The deposited plans (p. 41) show the main line running 16.3 miles (26.2km) from Shildon to Frosterley, with branches to Crook and Bishopley. However, in order to avoid costly parliamentary opposition, it was decided to abandon the section from Witton to Frosterley, including the Bishopley branch. This tactic proved successful, and the BA&WR act received the Royal Assent on 15 July 1837.[62] A second bill, to alter, amend and enlarge some of the powers of the act, was presented to Parliament in 1839.[67] It was read for the first time on 15 March[69] and approved at a special general meeting on 22 April,[70] but nothing further appears of this bill. The scale of the plans for the BA&WR is 4 inches = 1 mile, but no distances, radii of curves, or limits of deviation are given.[59] The section is printed separately and runs left to right from the junction, whereas the plan runs right to left, while the datum line is given as the 'High water line Ordinary Spring Tides at Gauge mark at Stockton'.

The line was to start by a junction with the S&DR main line in Shildon just west of the crossing of the road from Rednorth to Midderidge. A little over 2 furlongs (440m) from the junction the line entered Shildon Tunnel which was 6 furlongs (1.21km) long and passed beneath the Black Boy branch of the S&DR, being preceded and followed by deep cuttings. Through St Andrew Auckland the line ran mainly on an embankment up to 48ft high by which it passed over several highways. The river Gaunless was crossed at a height of 70ft (21.3m), just over 2½ miles from the junction, and then for most of the next 4 miles the line was in cuttings separated by two short sections of embankment, the first of which crossed Etherly Dene at a height of 87ft (26.52m). The line fell at 1 in 250 for most of the first 3 miles and then rose on similarly gentle gradients for the next 4 miles past the point where the plans showed the Crook branch diverging from what should have been the main line to Frosterley. The Crook branch ran for 7 furlongs (2.4km) on an embankment reaching 59ft in height with the river Wear being crossed on a viaduct at 5 miles 5 furlongs 8½ chains (9.22km). The climb to Crook started gently at 1 in 203 1/13 for just over a mile (1.67km), before increasing to 1 in 44 for just over 1¼ miles (2.15km) to the terminus, which was on the south side of the Lobley Hill (Durham section) turnpike, today the A689.

The BA&WR shareholders agreed to a proposal made by the S&DR to build the first section of line, including Shildon Tunnel, as far as South Church (St Andrew Auckland),[66] and a subcommittee was set up to oversee the construction of the Shildon Tunnel, whose members were Thomas Meynell Junior, Henry Stobart, Henry Pease and John Pease.[82,89] On 16 April 1842 this committee asked the BA&WR for permission to build a temporary station near Black Boy Lane, as it appeared that the line through Shildon Tunnel would be ready for use on 16 April 1842.[90] According to Tomlinson[769] Shildon Tunnel was opened on 19 April 1842, although it was not until 5 July 1842 that the BA&WR authorised 'the Shildon Company to provide a temporary coach station at Black Boy Lane for the expected traffic from the north until some further arrangement shall be made'.[92] The line was opened to Bishop Auckland station on 30 January 1843,[94]

The plans showing the Crook Branch of the Bishop Auckland and Weardale Railway, which was built, and the start of the abandoned section to Frosterley. Note the very simple nature of these early plans. Reproduced by permission of DRO.

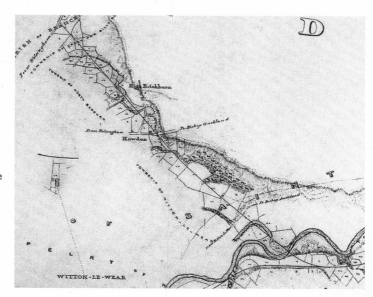

and finally to Crook on 8 November the same year.[96] From the start, the line authorised by the BA&WR Act was leased to and worked by the S&DR.[772]

Returning to the S&TR, the P&SSR Company obtained its act on 13 May 1842, but the new company only took over the eastern part of the former Stanhope and Tyne Railroad.[91] According to a document, which is undated but was probably written in 1847, entitled 'Evidence for the Amalgamation of WVR, BA&WR, WER, W&DR, Shildon Tunnel',[268] the western third, from Carrhouse to Stanhope, was purchased by the Derwent Iron Company 'in pursuance of powers for that purpose contained in an Act of Parliament obtained by the latter Company'. Despite the statement given in evidence to the parliamentary committee, I have been unable to find any Act of Parliament giving the Derwent Iron Company authority to purchase the western section of the former S&TR. The Derwent Iron Company reopened the line, which they called the Wear and Derwent Railway (W&DR), to traffic in 1842.

The following year the Iron Company proposed an extension to Crook to join the West Durham Railway (WDR) and the BA&WR. On 26 May 1843, the directors of the S&DR asked John Harris to report on this proposal and his reply is dated 11 July 1843.[95] Harris stated that until the traffic in limestone, coal and ironstone developed he did not recommend extending the BA&WR. The railway proposed by the Derwent Iron Company would be about 10 miles (16km) long and, although a locomotive line could be built from the top of the proposed Sunniside incline to Meeting Slacks on the S&TR, Harris did not recommend this course of action, but suggested that the BA&WR should be extended to

Frosterley, recommending the plans put forward by Thomas Storey.[93] Harris also believed that the land to the north of Meeting Slacks was too difficult for a railway, but did state that a locomotive line could be made to Wearhead without difficulty. A locomotive line could also connect Alston with the N&CR, but he again believed that the intervening country from Alston to Wearhead was too difficult, and a tunnel under Killhope would be required. He concluded by again stating that the S&DR should wait until traffic had developed before extending the BA&WR.

The Derwent Iron Company then sold the W&DR to Messrs Joseph and Henry Pease, Meynell, Stobart and Hopkins. After selling the W&DR, it was agreed that the line to Crook would be built by the owners of the W&DR, or some of them.[268] Despite the adverse report from Harris, it was recorded, early in 1844, that Emerson Muschamp, Esq. had 'completed the arrangements to construct a railway from the Stanhope line at Meeting Slacks, to join the West Durham Railway and Bishop Auckland & Weardale Railway'.[97] During 1844 arrangements were made by the S&DR to lease not only the new section of line from Crook to Meetings Slacks, called the Weardale Extension Railway (WER), but also the Stanhope to Carrhouse line. The S&DR formally took possession of both lines on 1 January 1845 and named the entire 21 miles (34km) the Wear and Derwent Junction Railway (W&DJR).[772,768] The new line, 10¼ miles (16.5km) long from Crook to Meeting Slacks, was opened in May 1845, either on the 16th according to Tomlinson[772] or the 23rd according to the *Tyne Mercury*,[123] thus bringing to fruition the 1833 proposals of G.H. Wilkinson, who was present at the opening.[123]

At the end of 1844, the first announcement appeared[102] of the proposal for a railway to leave the Crook line 2 miles (3.2km) before the terminus, and proceed up the Wear Valley, into the valley of the river Nent, and then down the South Tyne to join the N&CR at Haltwhistle, despite Harris having stated that a line into the South Tyne Valley would be too difficult to build.[95] Therefore, as 1844 drew to a close, both the S&DR and N&CR were in a position to turn their attention to the promotion of lines which would penetrate into the very heart of the North Pennines, and at last connect the town of Alston with the national railway network.

3

THE RAILWAY MANIA IN THE NORTH PENNINES

The year 1844 was the start of the period known as The Railway Mania, when hundreds of prospective companies were formed, and plans were prepared for the construction of thousands of miles of railway throughout the British Isles. Some of the promoters were genuine in their desire to build lines into areas where they saw a need, while others appear to have formed their companies with the sole object of extracting large sums of money from gullible speculators. Both types of scheme were found in northern England, where several companies were formed to provide direct communication between the south-east and north-west, or south-west and north-east of the region. This chapter briefly examines all of the schemes which would have affected, even if not actually penetrating, the North Pennines. Three acts were passed between 1845 and 1846 for railways into the North Pennines, one in its entirety in 1845, another being only part of the original bill, and the third was an amalgamation of several bills while a fourth, also formed by an amalgamation of related proposals, shared part of its route with the other amalgamated line.

The first proposals for lines to connect the extremities of the region were reported in *Herepath's Journal* of 23 November 1844 under the title of 'New Railway to Carlisle and Newcastle'.[102] Three routes were briefly described, one from Darlington to Newcastle, the second from Northallerton to Richmond and Appleby, joining the N&CR a few miles east of Carlisle while the last was to leave the S&DR 2 miles (3.2km) south of Crook and run through Stanhope to the head of the Wear valley, then down the valleys of the Nent and South Tyne to Haltwhistle on the N&CR. This line was expected to shorten the distance to Glasgow by 28 miles (45km), saving 1½ hours.

It should be remembered that in 1844 no lines were even authorised to connect the railways of central Scotland with the English lines. The Lancaster and Carlisle (L&CR) and North British (NBR) railways had received their acts in June and July 1844, but it was not until 1845 that the Newcastle and Berwick Railway obtained its act, while to the west, the Caledonian and Glasgow, Dumfries and Carlisle railways also brought their bills before Parliament in 1845, with that of the Caledonian being successful. The significance of the Weardale line as part of a through trunk route was clearly considered to be at least as important as its ability to serve the North Pennine ore-fields. Nevertheless, on 7 December 1844, when notice was given to Parliament for a bill for the Wear Valley Railway (WVR), it was for a line only 10 miles (16.1km) long from Wear Valley Junction, on the BA&WR near Witton-le-Wear, to Frosterley, with a branch to tap the limestone deposits at Bishopley. The proposed capital was £82,000 and Robert Stephenson was named as engineer.[104,109]

The plans deposited on 11 November 1844[103] were for a line which was very different from that proposed two years earlier by Thomas Storey[93] and which Harris, the S&DR engineer, appeared to support in his report of 1843,[95] while the engineer was John Dixon. The WVR was to follow the river Wear, starting by a curve of only 15 chains (300m) radius, at the fifth milepost on the BA&WR, on the north side of the highway leading from Witton-Le-Wear to Bishop Auckland.[145] The total length of the main line was 10 miles 5 furlongs 5.1 chains (17.2km), with a ruling gradient of 1 in 144, while the branch to Bishopley Quarries was 1 mile 1 furlong 7.93 chains (1.97km) long, rising all the way at 1 in 43 or 1 in 57.

Although several petitions were received against the WVR bill,[164] it made steady progress through both houses of Parliament. At the committee stage in the House of Commons, the members were informed 'that the object of the line was to open a communication with the rich valley of the Wear, from which were

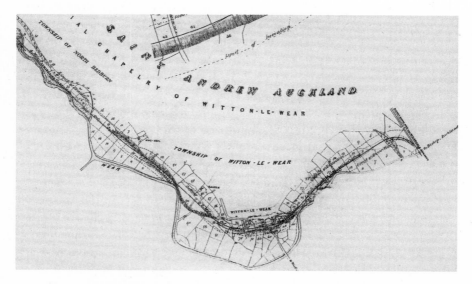

Plans showing the first 4 miles of the WVR from Wear Valley Junction. Note the increase in detail compared with the plans on pp. 37 and 41. Reproduced by permission of DRO.

supplied iron, tin, zinc, copper, lead, stone flagging, slates, spar, and limestone'.[128] It was stated that the proposed railway was essential for the carriage of this traffic, and that by its connection with the Bishop Auckland and Weardale line, it 'would fall in with the Stockton & Darlington Railway'. The committee was informed that the same course had been chosen 20 years earlier as the best line 'by a person who might be called the father of railways, Mr. G. Stephenson'. The proposed line was also expected to result in numerous passengers travelling from Wolsingham, Stanhope, and St Andrew Auckland. The WVR act received the Royal Assent on 31 July[144], being one of the 116 railway bills passed during 1845, a year in which no fewer than 100 railway bills failed.[149] Even before the WVR act became law, the directors had resolved to investigate the best way of extending their line westwards;[134] now, after receiving their Act of Parliament for a line to connect Frosterley with the BA&WR,[145] the directors of the WVR turned their attention seriously to the possibility of extending their line westwards,[150] with the Chairman stating 'They must turn their eyes still further north, and look at this as the great road into Scotland.'[151]

Adverts appeared inviting tenders to be submitted 'on or before Monday, 3rd November 1845' for the construction of the 12 miles (19.3km) of the WVR,[161] while earlier, John Dixon, the WVR engineer, presented the results of his investigation for a westward extension and the meeting authorised a fully comprehensive survey.[153] The directors agreed to take the extension to Milton, adopting, if practicable, the Earl of Carlisle's Railway,[167] and a letter was sent to the Earl of Carlisle to this effect.[168] Unfortunately it appeared that James Thompson had been planning to extend LCR to Alston,[156] and Lord Carlisle was not prepared to sanction the WVER using his railway.[187] However Dixon reported, on 28 October, that he had surveyed a good line independent of LCR and the N&CR appeared to be favourable to a junction at Milton.[184] The directors therefore agreed to adopt Dixon's line with a connecting branch to be built to the eastern end of LCR at Haltonleagate in the hope that Lord Carlisle would not actually oppose the WVER, even if he would not support it,[189] although again according to Webb and Gordon[751] Lord Carlisle supported the branch the N&CR were planning to serve the lead mines around Alston, and to which they claimed his railway was to be connected. It should be remembered that the act authorising the N&CR specifically granted the Earl of Carlisle the right to appoint three of the thirty directors,[141] while even in 1858 one of the reduced number of directors was still recorded as representing Lord Carlisle.[705]

A very detailed set of plans, sections and books of reference were then produced for the proposed extension, which were deposited with the various justices of the peace[198] and the Board of Trade.[203] Plans were also deposited with the justices of the peace for Durham for the Lancashire, Weardale and Hartlepool Union Railway.[204] This 6 mile (9.7km) long railway was to connect the Hartlepool

Junction Railway with the Auckland area, at a cost of £120,000.[206] The advert stated 'by the Weardale, Wear Valley, and projected lines, to join the L&CR, it will form the most direct route from the Baltic, and Northern Europe, to the Western parts of the Kingdom.' The promoters therefore expected that the WVER would form part of a main route to Scotland and, despite the difficult nature of the territory through which it was to pass, it was laid out in such a way that had it been built it would almost certainly have formed part of a through main line connecting Scotland and England.

In reality, both the WVR and the BA&WR were extensions of the S&DR, with which they shared engineers, a secretary and many directors. Therefore, while it was the WVR which deposited the plans for the Wear Valley Extension Railway (WVER) to take the iron road into the valleys of the Tyne and Eden, the driving force was again the S&DR Company, while it was their consulting engineer, John Dixon,[741] who prepared the plans, sections and books of reference which were deposited with the Board of Trade[203] and the Justices of the Peace for the counties of Cumberland, Durham and Northumberland.[198]

The directors of the N&CR had always seen Alston Moor as being within their natural empire, but because of their position at the northern edge of the Pennines they were also involved in the various endeavours to improve communications

Title page of the Wear Valley Extension Railway plans of 1845. The connection between north-east England and Scotland appears to be more important than developing local traffic. Reproduced by permission of CAS.

between Newcastle and Edinburgh, which lay to the north of their line. As already noted, once their line was open the main concerns were to make the route more suitable for operation by steam locomotives, convert the single track sections to double track, and pay off the huge debts that had been incurred in order to complete the construction.[78]

The spring of 1841 saw the first two sections of line doubled,[84] but at the end of that year the Newcastle Company was still not contemplating any other new works.[86] Even as late as the 1845 Annual General Meeting, held on 27 March, no mention was made of any proposed branch lines, the only new construction being discussed was the extension of the main line to a new Central station in Newcastle, alongside an altered Neville Street.[110] This was despite the fact that the Chairman was able to state that the entire line from Newcastle to Carlisle was now double, apart from 73 yards at Farnley Tunnel, where work had been delayed following a partial collapse at the beginning of the year.[105] The financial affairs of the company were also in good order as, following an increase in receipts and a rise in the value of their shares, the directors had been able to pay off the balance of their debt to the Exchequer Bill Loan Commissioners in early February.[108] However, in September 1844 the directors had proceeded by Lord Carlisle's Railway to Hartley Burn and then to Alston and finally to Nenthead,[99] while in October they had examined the location at Allenheads and considered if a branch could be made from Nenthead to Allenheads.[100] It is quite possible these actions were in response to the proposals emanating from the S&DR empire to build a line from Bishop Auckland through Alston to Haltwhistle.

It was not until the beginning of June 1845 that any official proposal appeared for a branch from the N&CR main line, and then it was for an independently promoted line to serve the North Tyne Valley.[124] By the middle of the month, adverts were appearing in the local press[129,131] for the Newcastle and Carlisle and North Tyne Junction Railway. This line was to leave the N&CR near Warden and follow the valley of the North Tyne to Reedsmouth where it would divide with one branch going to Bellingham and a second to Woodburn. The act was to include powers to enable the company to lease the line to the N&CR or to amalgamate with the N&CR.

Nothing further occurred until October when proposals appeared in the *Tyne Mercury*[170] and the *Newcastle Chronicle*[174,182,183] for four further lines to serve parts of the North Tyne Valley. Three were for other independent railways, while the fourth was the announcement of the decision by the N&CR that they intended to construct a branch to Bellingham and Woodburn. Later, the *Tyne Mercury* not only gave information about a fifth proposal to serve the same area[178] but also announced that the Newcastle and Carlisle and North Tyne Junction Railway was to merge with one of the other schemes, the Newcastle-upon-Tyne, Hawick and Edinburgh and Glasgow Junction Railway, to form a single company.[176] This merged scheme, known as the Newcastle-upon-Tyne, Edinburgh and (Direct) Glasgow Junction Railway (NE&DGJR), was also reported in the *Newcastle Chronicle*,[188] and was supported by several influential local business people and landowners, including Ralph William Grey of Chipchase Castle, John Crawford of Warden paper mills, Edward Champion of Hareshaw iron works and John Green of Ridsdale iron works.[192] In the end it was only this merged company and the N&CR which deposited plans for railways in the North Tyne Valley for the 1846 parliamentary session.[204] It was the local support for the NE&DGJR which almost had disastrous consequences for the N&CR bill, which included the branch to Alston Moor, and the extension to Newcastle Central station.

The announcement in the *Tyne Mercury* of 15 October 1845 also reported that the N&CR intended to build a second branch, this time up the valley of the South Tyne.[170] Notice was given to Parliament on 12 November 1845 that the company intended to apply for two separate Acts.[194,202] The first bill was simply for a branch to Allenheads, while the second, called the Newcastle and Carlisle Extension Bill, was more complex. The stated purpose of this bill was:

> ... to alter, amend, and enlarge powers and provisions of Acts relating to the crossing of turnpike roads, on a level and with respect to other turnpike roads, carried over or under the railway; to extend the line from the present terminus at Elswick to Neville Street, near the Town Hall, Newcastle; and to make the following branches, namely, from Haltwhistle to Alston Moor; from Warden to West Woodburn, Corsenside; from Nook to Bellingham; from the main line at West Woodburn, terminating near the Ridsdale iron works, Chesterhope; and to raise a further sum of money.

This decision to include both North and South Tyne branches in the same bill as the extension to Newcastle Central station created considerable difficulties for the N&CR in the months to come. At the beginning of January 1846 it was reported[216] that only those plans, sections and books of reference necessary for the second bill had been deposited at the Private Bill Office,[215] while the Allenheads branch had been abandoned, at least for the time being.

At the same time as the WVR Bill was progressing through Parliament and the WVER was being planned, several railways were proposed which would have reached the southern edges of the North Pennines. Although only the extension of the WVR would have reached the main areas of lead mining from the south, a brief examination of the others will help put into contemporary perspective the Wear Valley Extension Railway (WVER) and the Newcastle and Carlisle Railway's South Tyne branch.

The *Tyne Mercury* of 29 January 1845 reported that 'A new line from Northallerton station on the Great North of England Railway (GNER), through

Title page of the Newcastle and Carlisle Railway plans of 1845 for the extension of the main line to Newcastle Central station and branches along the valleys of the North and South Tyne. Reproduced by permission of the Tyne & Wear Archives Service (TWAS).

Appleby and Richmond, uniting with the Newcastle and Carlisle, is on the anvil.'[106] This information was repeated verbatim in other newspapers, with the editor of the *Carlisle Journal* for 8 February stating 'We presume this must be an error, and suppose it should be to join the Lancaster and Carlisle.'[107] The newspapers carried various references to the survey, but the first concrete proposal, for the York and Carlisle Railway (Y&CR), appeared in *Herepath's Journal* of 12 April 1845 for a line intended 'to connect the Great North of England, Stockton & Darlington, and their associated railways in the east, with the Lancaster & Carlisle, Caledonian, and the lines connected with them in the west'.[111] The following week, *Herepath's Journal*,[113] the *Tyne Mercury*[112] and the *Carlisle Journal*[114] reported that the line was to start 3¼ miles (5.2km) north of Northallerton, taking part of the GNER's proposed branch to Richmond, from which it was to diverge a short distance before the terminus. It was to remain south of the Tees and run up the valley of the river Greta, then follow the route of the Roman road, past Brough, nearly to Kirkby Stephen where the line would divide. One section was to go down the valley of the Eden, through Appleby, to join the Lancaster and Carlisle Railway (L&CR) near Clifton, south of Penrith, while the other was to go by Kirkby Stephen and the vale of Ravenstonedale and join the L&CR near Borrow Bridge (Tebay). A branch was also proposed to run from West Auckland and join the main line at Scargill, between Greta Bridge and Bowes.

On 26 April 1845, the *Carlisle Journal* included the prospectus for the line which was now being called 'The York and Carlisle, and Durham, Westmorland, and Lancashire Junction Railway'.[115] The company had capital of £1,500,000 in 30,000 shares of £50 each and there was a list of forty-one provisional directors, most of whom lived relatively close to the route of the railway and included Joseph Pease of the S&DR. The engineer-in-chief was J.M. Rendel, Esq. FRS. The distance from Northallerton to Clifton was 61 miles (98km), of which 56 miles (90km) would be new construction, while the Orton branch was to be 17 miles (27.4km) long. One third of the capital was to be placed at the disposal of the Lancaster and Carlisle board. A few days later, the *Tyne Mercury* reported that this line had the sanction of the S&DR, the L&CR, and the GNER, and consequently that of Mr Hudson.[116] On 3 May, the *Carlisle Journal* carried an update of the prospectus, which now listed forty-nine provisional directors, although a much smaller Executive Committee had been formed, one of whose members was Henry Pease.[117] At the bottom of the advert it was stated 'No further application can be received for shares in this Company.'

By 24 May the *Carlisle Journal* was reporting 'that some of the shareholders of the York and Carlisle Junction Railway have disposed of their shares at premiums varying from £3.18s (£3.90) to £7'.[121] This is the first real indication of the speculative nature of at least some shareholders of the northern railway schemes proposed during the Railway Mania. The Y&CR line was opposed by the Duke of Cleveland, through whose land it was to pass near Barnard Castle,[158] and it was not until 5 November 1845 that the consent of the duke to allow the survey to be carried out was reported.[190] Two weeks later, the *Tyne Mercury* reported that the directors of the Y&CR had purchased the Haggerleases branch of the S&DR 'from West Auckland to Cockfield Fell, thus securing the influence and assistance of the Stockton & Darlington Railway Co., as well as getting several miles of railway already made over a difficult country'.[195] In common with many of the other railway proposals, *Herepath's Journal* reported, on 6 December 1845,[203] that plans had been deposited with the Board of Trade,[200] in preparation for the 1846 parliamentary session.

The Newcastle, Durham and Lancashire Junction Railway appeared in *Herepath's Journal* of 10 May 1845.[118] The southern part of it could be considered as an alternative to the Auckland branch of the Y&CR. The line was planned to commence on the south side of the Tyne in Gateshead, and run to Durham via the Team valley, Birtley and Chester-le-Street, where it was to join the Sunderland, Durham and Auckland Union Railway,[119] whose bill was before Parliament at that time. That line was to be used for 10 miles (16.1km) before further new construction continued through St Helen's Auckland, Staindrop, Greta Bridge, to join the Y&CR east of Stainmore. The total length of the proposed line was about 32 miles (51.5km) and would reduce the distance between Newcastle and

Liverpool to 147 miles (237km) or 137 miles (220km) providing the Liverpool and Preston Railway was constructed. The line was estimated to cost £500,000 and the engineers were named as Joseph Locke and Thomas Storey.[135]

In early June, the bill for the Sunderland, Durham and Auckland Union Railway was lost by failing to comply with parliamentary standing orders, but it was stated that it would be 'persevered in next session'.[127] Despite this potential setback, the following month the *Tyne Mercury* reported that the Newcastle, Durham, and Lancashire Junction Railway was contemplating a branch from near Staindrop to Richmond'[136] where it was to join the Lancashire and North Yorkshire Railway, whose formation was advertised in the same issue.[137] With a capital of £900,000, this line was to leave the Leeds and Bradford Extension Railway, then under construction, at a point between Colne and Skipton, and proceed by way of Grassington, Kettlewell, Coverdale and Middleham to the Richmond branch of the GNER. John Hawkshaw and Alfred S. Jee were named as the engineers.[137] The combined route was expected to shorten the distance between Lancashire and the north-east of England by more than 50 miles (80.5km),[142] which would be a greater saving of distance than the other projected lines, which were to go via Hawes.

At the beginning of August, a 'constant subscriber' to *Herepath's Journal* made some very uncomplimentary comments about the Newcastle, Durham, and Lancashire Junction Railway.[146] However, the editor of the *Tyne Mercury* had taken a very supportive attitude towards this railway from the start[120] and, later in August, reported an association with another line,[147] which he believed would be advantageous to both. On 15 September 1845, adverts appeared in the *Tyne Mercury* announcing that the Newcastle, Durham and Lancashire Junction Railway was forming a united company with the Manchester, Liverpool and Great North of England Union (which we shall meet later) under the name of the Northumberland and Lancashire Junction Railway (N&LJR) Company.[157] This amalgamation was confirmed in both the *Carlisle Journal*[159] and *Herepath's Journal*[160] of 27 September.

Towards the end of May 1845, the York and Glasgow Union Railway,[128] or the Yorkshire and Glasgow Union Railway (Y&GUR),[125] first appeared in *Herepath's Journal*. Although essentially similar to the Y&CR, it was to take a more southerly route, starting from the GNER near Thirsk, and then running through Bedale, Leyburn and Redmire to Hawes. From there it was to proceed northwards by Mallerstang, Kirkby Stephen and Appleby to Clifton where it would join the L&CR. A branch to join the L&CR south of Orton was also proposed. Once again, a large amount of through traffic was anticipated. A similar advert appeared in the *Carlisle Journal* of 21 June.[132] The capital was to be £1,200,000 and Hamilton H. Fulton, MInstCE, was named as engineer, while the provisional committee numbered forty-nine, most of whom were local to the route. Nothing further appeared in the press until *Herepath's Journal* of 6 December 1845,[203] when it was reported that plans for this line had also been deposited with the Board of Trade.[214]

Yet another company planning to construct a line similar to that of the Y&GUR was advertised in the *Tyne Mercury* of 17 September 1845 as the Leeds and Carlisle or Northern Trunk Railway of England,[154] although it was not reported in *Herepath's Journal* until 4 October.[166] The provisional committee included directors of the Manchester, Liverpool, and Great North of England Union; the North Western; the London & York; and the Newcastle, Durham and Lancashire Junction railways, as well as several other lines in England and Ireland not connecting with the route of the Leeds and Carlisle. The *Carlisle Journal* of 20 September 1845 carried an advert similar to that in the *Tyne Mercury* stating that the capital of the company was £2,000,000.[155] Two weeks later, a second advert appeared in the *Tyne Mercury*,[162] listing an even greater number of members of the provisional committee, although the committee of management was limited to nineteen people. George and John Rennie were named as the engineers for the line which was to start on the Leeds and Thirsk Railway (L&TR), for which an act had been obtained, run up Wharfedale to Otley, Kettlewell and Hawes, from where it would pass through Kirkby Stephen and Appleby, to join the L&CR near Penrith. A branch from Otley to Bradford was also proposed. Once again, a similar advert appeared in the *Carlisle Journal*,[165] in which the provisional committee had reached 168 and the management committee had been increased to twenty. Plans for the Leeds and Carlisle[213] were deposited with the Board of Trade,[203] but common sense now prevailed and, on 20 December 1845, it was announced that the Leeds and Carlisle had amalgamated with the Y&GUR.[211]

The proposals so far considered were primarily intended to provide part of a through route to Glasgow from south of Darlington, but others, which would have had a more direct impact on some of the local traffic, made a brief appearance. The first was the London and Edinburgh Direct Railway, reported in the *Tyne Mercury* of 22 October 1845 where it was estimated that £1,500,000 was required to build the line from Darlington to Hawick, 'which in the event of the London and York Bill receiving the sanction of the legislature will complete a literally straight line between the metropolis of England and that of Scotland'.[177] One week later, there was a preliminary announcement for the East and West Durham, Northumberland and Scottish Junction Railway.[186] This line was to start at Durham City and go via Lanchester, Knitsley, Allensford and Whittonstal to Hexham 'whence it will join one of the proposed lines from the Carlisle railway, by the Vale of the North Tyne, to Hawick, Edinburgh and Glasgow' at an estimated cost of £800,000.

A second series of proposals was for railways that would reduce the distance between Merseyside and Newcastle. The first of these, the Liverpool, Manchester and Newcastle Junction Railway (LM&NJR), appeared in *Herepath's Journal* for 21 June 1845,[133] as a proposal for a line commencing at Preston and running up the valley of the Ribble to Clitheroe. From there it was planned to reach Settle and Hawes 'by the most direct course' and then pass through Askrigg to Richmond where it would join the Richmond branch of the GNER. The total length from Preston to Richmond was estimated to be between 70 and 75 miles (113–121km). This company had a capital of £2,000,000, numbered George Hudson among its supporters and had Robert Stephenson, along with T.E. Harrison, as its engineers.[138,144] The *Tyne Mercury* of 3 September 1845 announced that 'The allotment of shares in this line has just been made, and much dissatisfaction has been expressed in this town by disappointed applicants, many of whom are of the highest respectability. The stock is now at £7.10s and £8 per share premium.'[152] One month later, it was officially announced that George Hudson had joined the provisional Board of Directors, and the share prices rose further.[163] Nevertheless, by the end of the month the price had fallen even further than most other shares in the depression that was afflicting the stock market at that time.[185] However, steady progress was made with the survey, including the addition of a branch to Ripon,[180] and plans were duly deposited with the Board of Trade.[203] Prior to this, on 12 November, it had been agreed to amalgamate the LM&NJR with one of its proposed competitors, the Lancashire and North Yorkshire Railway Company.[196]

The next proposal, following a similar route, appeared in the *Tyne Mercury* of 9 July 1845,[139] and *Herepath's Journal* of 12 July,[140] under the name of the Manchester, Liverpool, and Great North of England Union Railway. With a capital of only £1,000,000, this line was to commence at a point near Settle on the North Western Railway, where the proposed Clitheroe Junction Railway was to join, and then proceed in a north-easterly direction, through Hawes to Muker and Reeth, down the Swale to Richmond, where it would meet the Richmond branch of the GNER. It was also proposed to construct a branch from a point about 12 miles (19km) north of Settle, south-west to the North Western Railway at Ingleton.

A week later, the *Tyne Mercury* reported that the promoters had entered into 'arrangements with the North Western Railway Company, and the Clitheroe Junction Railway Company.[141] Initially, George Watson Buck was named as the engineer on his own, but a fortnight later he was joined by Barnard Dickinson, Jnr.[143]

It was announced, at a meeting held in Richmond on 20 August 1845, that 'plans for a great portion of the line were already prepared'.[148] Nevertheless, on 24 September, adverts appeared in the *Tyne Mercury* announcing the amalgamation with the Newcastle, Durham and Lancashire Junction Company,[157] and details of the Northumberland and Lancashire Junction Railway, which the new line was called, were given in the *Tyne Mercury* of 22 October.[179] The amalgamated line was to be about 70 miles (113km) long, with a capital of £2,000,000, and Joseph Locke was named as engineer. There were eighty-two names on the provisional committee, mostly from northern England, but the committee of management comprised only thirteen people. Plans for the Northumberland and Lancashire Junction Railway and branches were deposited with the local justices of the peace[199] and the Board of Trade.[203]

The advert for a third line designed to connect Lancashire to the GNER, the Lancashire and North Yorkshire Railway, which we have already met, also appeared in the *Tyne Mercury* for 9 July 1845.[137] Three months later, in the *Tyne Mercury* of 1 October 1845, the provisional registration of the Lancaster and Newcastle-upon-Tyne Direct Railway was advertised.[164] This line was to start at Lancaster, follow the Lune valley through Kirkby Lonsdale and Sedbergh to Kirkby Stephen, and then 'take the most practical line to Newcastle', which was expected to run almost parallel to the old coach road, previously the main passenger route from Lancaster to Newcastle. *Herepath's Journal* carried very similar information on 18 October.[172] Later issues of the *Tyne Mercury* in October and November carried the information that the company had a capital of £2,000,000,[175] there were eighty-five members of the provisional committee,[191] and the engineer was Sir John Rennie.[193] However, on 10 December 1845 it was announced that 'the promoters of this line have postponed going to Parliament till the Session of 1847.'[205] Plans were not deposited, and nothing further was heard of this proposal.

The last of the 1845 railway proposals which impinged upon the North Pennines was the Newcastle and Leeds Direct Railway, which first appeared in *Herepath's Journal*,[171] the *Tyne Mercury*[169] and *Carlisle Journal*[173] of 15 or 18 October 1845. At this time it was stated that the line was to commence at a point near Bishop Auckland on the N&LJR, and proceed by Richmond, Bedale, Masham, Ripon and Ripley to Harrogate, where it would join the Leeds and Thirsk Railway. The capital was £800,000, with a provisional committee of forty, of whom about three-quarters were local, and the engineer was named as Thomas Storey. According to the following week's issue of *Herepath's Journal* the line was to start at a junction with the L&TR at Wath, near Ripon, and then pass through Masham, Bedale, Catterick, Richmond, Middleton Tyas, Barton and Manfield to Bishop Auckland, and the junction with the N&LJR.[181] Nothing further appears in any of the papers until *Herepath's Journal* of 13 December 1845,[207] where notice was given of the intention to apply to Parliament to sell or let the undertaking to any other company, although plans had been deposited.[197] Two weeks later, application was made to Parliament for a line along the same route under the name of the Leeds and Thirsk: Auckland Extension.[212]

Plans for a total of 653 railway bills had been deposited by the end of November 1845 for consideration during the 1846 parliamentary session and, with work starting on over 100 railway schemes already authorised in 1845, difficulties were starting to arise in persuading the proprietors of some of these lines to pay the calls on their shares. With genuine capital becoming more difficult to raise, the directors of the WVR Company met on 2 December 1845 and considered:

> … the subject of the prosecution of their line westwards in the approaching Session of Parliament and taking into account the difficult nature of the country and the little time which the Company engineer had for examining the country and for the selection of a line together with other circumstances affecting the railway interests at this time, resolved that the prosecution of the same be postponed till the following Session of Parliament.[201]

The directors met again on 16 December to discuss the proposed extension 'from Frosterley by Alston and Milton to Carlisle'.[210] The meeting, 'having seriously deliberated upon the responsibility incurred by the Board in urging forward extensive works, under the present circumstances attendant on railway enterprise…', resolved:

> … that whilst this Board continues impressed with the importance of the proposed undertaking, and has become increasingly alive to the advantages likely to be secured to the public from its prosecution, it is expedient to postpone for another session any application to Parliament, to sanction the same; thus giving to the engineer full opportunity for further investigation and to other influential bodies who have expressed an anxious desire to co-operate with this Company, the time required for maturing their plans and perfecting their arrangements.[208]

The decision of the directors was confirmed at the half-yearly meeting of the WVR, held on 19 February 1846.[221]

The report of the directors to the half-yearly meeting dated 26 August 1846 states: 'The anticipation of an early extension of the line towards Cumberland postponed at present on account of the large expenditure involved.'[240] This, in effect, was the end of the first WVER, although the intention to construct the line at some later date was confirmed at the half-yearly meeting in September 1846.[244] While the decision not to proceed with the WVER in 1846 effectively ended the possibility of a main line under Killhope, several further attempts were made to construct a similar line, and we shall look at these in Chapter 13.[221] Various explanations have been given for the failure of the WVR to proceed with their line, but it does appear that a combination of the difficult nature of the country, the short time the engineer had for the selection of a suitable line[201] and the huge financial outlay[208] were the main factors inhibiting the directors. We shall see in Chapter 7 that by the end of the decade the financial situation of the entire S&DR group of railways was in turmoil, and it is possible that the first warnings of future problems prompted the directors of the WVR to delay their application to Parliament. On a brighter note, the WVR itself was inspected on Monday 2 August 1847[276] and opened between Wear Valley Junction (p. 44) and Frosterley on Tuesday 3 August.[275]

Before looking in detail at the successful bid by the N&CR to penetrate the North Pennine ore-field from the north, and what differences there might have been if a bill for the WVER had been progressed in the 1846 parliamentary session, we shall briefly review the progress made by the lines which were intended to reach the southern edges of the North Pennines, and whose plans were also deposited during 1845. By the beginning of 1846, only five of the proposals we have reviewed remained to be considered by Parliament.[216] These were: Liverpool, Manchester, and Newcastle-upon-Tyne; Lancashire and North Yorkshire; Northumberland and Lancashire Junction; York and Carlisle; and Yorkshire and Glasgow. *Herepath's Journal* observed that the plans and other information required for 718 railway bills had been deposited in the Private Bill Office, but that this was only about half of the 1,400 bills provisionally registered during 1845.

The details of the proposed amalgamation of the Y&GUR with the Leeds and Carlisle were announced at the beginning of January 1846.[217] The 30 miles (48km) between Clifton and Hawes were common to both these proposals but the route of the Y&GUR had better gradients, while the Leeds and Carlisle had a tunnel 5,482yd (5.01km) long at Mallerstang plus a viaduct over 500yd (460m) long, with twenty arches and a maximum height of 130ft (39.6m), at Appleby.[209] Also, the section of the Leeds and Carlisle between Hawes and the junction with the L&TR would be much more difficult and expensive to construct than the more northerly route of the Y&GUR. The effect of this amalgamation was to place all the resources of both projects behind the line of the Y&GUR.

The bill for the Y&CR was considered by the same committee of the House of Commons as the Y&GUR and, on 7 May 1846,[226] the committee began to examine them together as competing lines. On the following day it was announced that the companies had agreed to amalgamate and 'the Committee resolved to apply to the House for liberty to unite the two lines into one Bill', to which the House consented. The basis for the amalgamation was a decision to construct all of the Y&GUR, together with that part of the Y&CR which was not in direct competition with the former.[227] The committee resumed their consideration of the united railway, which was to be known as the Northern Counties Union Railway (NCUR), and approved the amended bill on 25 May 1846.[230] Towards the end of June, some of the shareholders endeavoured to have the new company wound up,[236] but the bill continued through Parliament and received the Royal Assent on 27 July 1846.[237]

Although the Northumberland and Lancashire Junction Bill was given its second reading by the House of Commons on 30 March 1846,[222] the possibility of petitioning Parliament to dissolve the company was being considered by the shareholders in the latter half of April 1846.[224] On 2 May 1846 *Herepath's Journal* reported that the Northumberland and Lancashire Junction Bill was to be examined by the same committee as the Y&GUR, the Y&CR, and the Liverpool, Manchester and Newcastle-upon-Tyne Junction railways.[225] When this committee met on 5 May, the Northumberland and Lancashire Junction Bill had disappeared, and it was not until 8 June that it reappeared before another committee, whose brief also included the Newcastle and Carlisle (Extension and Branches) Bill.[231] However, at meetings held on 12 and 14 May 1846, the shareholders finally resolved 'that the affairs of this Company be immediately wound up, and that the Directors be required to stop all further expense'.[228] This decision was confirmed by the directors, and the withdrawal of the N&LJR Bill was announced in the House of Commons on 11 June 1846.[231]

At the start of the parliamentary proceedings in 1846 there were individual bills for the Lancashire and North Yorkshire and the Liverpool, Manchester and Newcastle-upon-Tyne Junction railways, but on 7 May 1846, the House of Commons committee agreed to apply to the House to consolidate them under the general name of the Liverpool, Manchester and Newcastle Junction Railway (LM&NJR).[226] The amalgamated company's bill made steady progress, receiving its third reading in the House of Lords on 23 June 1846[235] and the Royal Assent on 26 June 1846.[223]

The route finally authorised by the LM&NJR Act allowed for the construction of the entire Lancashire and North Yorkshire line plus the Hawes branch which was common to both schemes. The authorised lines did not reach the valleys of the Wear or Tees,[239] leaving only the NCUR to be authorised out of all the proposals from the previous year, which would have penetrated the North Pennines from the south. Despite the failure of so many of the 1845 schemes, new proposals for reducing the distance between London and Scotland continued to appear. One of these was for a northwards extension of the London and York, which later became the Great Northern Railway, through Northallerton, Barnard Castle, the Tees Valley, Alston and Haltwhistle to Hawick.[245] It was claimed that this route would reduce the distance between London and Edinburgh from 411 miles (661km) 'by the Hudson line' to 361 miles (581km). Nothing further came of this proposal, which was the first line to be proposed whose route would have taken it over the watershed between the Tees and South Tyne valleys.

Although acts of Parliament were passed in 1846 authorising both the LM&NJR and NCUR, neither line was ever built. By November 1846, notices of three separate applications to Parliament had been made by the LM&NJR.[247] The first was to alter the line and 'to purchase, rent, or use' the Northern Counties Union Railway, the second was to authorise the amalgamation of the two lines and the third was for making certain branches and alterations. These proposals were confirmed at the half-yearly meeting of the LM&NJR Company held early in 1847.[253] The amalgamation bill was later withdrawn by mutual consent, while the bills for the alteration of the main line and making a short branch were passed.[270,271] According to *Herepath*,[278] the first provided that 12 miles (19.3km) of line common to both the LM&NJR and the NCUR in Wensleydale would be made at the joint expense, and for the common use, of both companies. When the plans of the original Y&GUR[214] are compared with those of the deviation of the main line of the NCUR[251] and the Aysgarth alteration of the LM&NJR,[250] it is seen that the actual length of the joint line was a little over 8 miles (16.9km). It should also be noted that the altered LM&NJR was to join the main line of the York and Newcastle Railway (Y&NR) at or near Cowton Station,[270] rather than the Richmond branch as originally authorised.

However, construction work was still not started on the LM&NJR and, in November 1847,[283] notice was given for three completely different bills to be presented to Parliament the following session. The first was for an extension of time, the second was to dissolve the company, while the third was to authorise the sale or lease of the company to the York, Newcastle, and Berwick Railway (YN&BR). Although it was recorded that the directors disclaimed the second and third notices, by the spring of 1848 the possibility of winding up the company was being seriously discussed[290] and, on 8 June 1848,[293] a motion to 'proceed to Parliament for a simple Dissolution Bill' was carried. The bill was passed by the House of Commons, but was thrown out at the committee stage in the House of Lords on 26 July 1848.[294]

Despite this set-back, the following half-yearly meeting of shareholders agreed 'in the present state of monetary affairs, to defer the construction of the works of this railway till a more favourable period, the Directors be and they are hereby required, on the 1st November next, to return to and pay to each Shareholder 13s 4d (66.5 pence) per share of the paid-up capital held by such Shareholder'.[297] The sum to be repaid was altered to 14s (70p), although there was considerable doubt about the legality of this action, which would have the effect of dissolving the company despite the failure of the parliamentary bill, and the directors initially refused to act upon the decision.[298] By the middle of November 1848, 10s (50p) had been repaid to two-thirds of the proprietors, but 'the Directors were unable to fix any date for the payment of the remaining 4s (20p), in consequence of their being liable to construct certain small pieces of railway if called upon by the Lancashire & Yorkshire and Northern Counties Union Companies.'[300] By February 1850, another 1s (5p) had been repaid and support was given to the Railway Abandonment Bill, then under consideration by Parliament.[331] However, six months later it was accepted that it would not be in the interests of the shareholders to place the company within the operation of the Railway Abandonment Act.[334] It was also agreed that a further 2s 4d (11.5p)

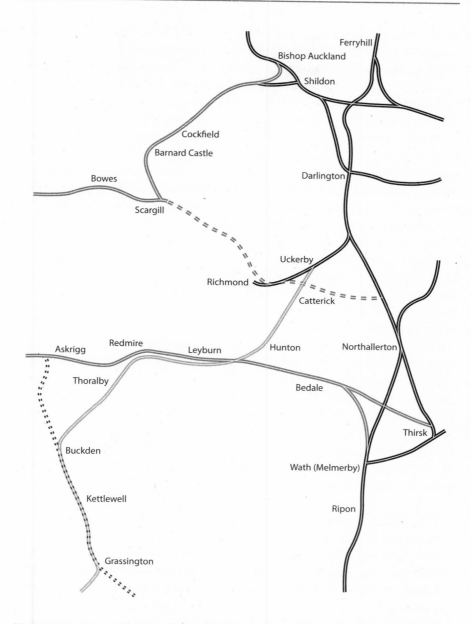

Map showing the railways making up the Northern Counties Union and the Liverpool, Manchester and Newcastle Junction railways – eastern section

represents railways built, under construction or authorised between 1846 and 1850
represents the Northern Counties Union Railway as authorised
represents the section of the York and Carlisle Railway not authorised by the Northern Counties Union Railway Act

would be paid back to the shareholders, which would nearly exhaust the balance of the company's funds, and, although further half-yearly meetings were called by the chairman, George Leeman, who by this time was also chairman of the YN&BR,[347] the LM&NJR Company had effectively ceased to exist.

In contrast to the proprietors of the LM&NJR, those of the NCUR immediately started the proceedings necessary for constructing their line. Unfortunately, one of the requirements in their act was that both authorised lines (from Thirsk, up Wensleydale then down the Eden valley to Clifton; and from Bishop Auckland, through Barnard Castle to Tebay) were to be constructed simultaneously.[237] Notice was given in November 1846 of an application to Parliament for powers to make deviations[251] in the line near Leyburn.[248] At a special meeting of shareholders held on 20 January 1847 it was agreed to add a clause to the deviation bill to repeal the clause requiring simultaneity in the original act, although the members present were unable to decide which of the two lines should be built first![252] The meeting also agreed to negotiate for an amalgamation with the LM&NJR. The images on pp. 59 and 61 show the railways making up the Northern Counties Union and the Liverpool, Manchester and Newcastle Junction railways.

At the half-yearly meeting of the NCUR in February 1847, the chairman reported that their engineer, Mr Fulton, had been instructed to lay out the line between Wath (on the branch to join the L&TR) and Wensleydale, and between Tebay and Kirkby Stephen, as soon as the weather permitted.[256] In addition, the directors deemed 'it advisable to execute the line from Wath to Leyburn (which is of easy construction) without delay, that advantage may be taken of the opening of the L&TR, to secure the traffic from the district of Wensleydale to Leeds and the south'. The report of this meeting appeared in *Herepath's Journal* for 27 February 1847, which also contained the following advert from the NCUR:

> The Directors of this Company are ready to receive tenders for the execution of the earth, brick, and masonry work of this line from Wath to Bedale, called 'The Wath Contract', extending from the Leeds & Thirsk Railway to Bedale, (being about 9 miles [14.5km]); and also from Tebay, on the Lancaster & Carlisle Railway, to Newbiggin, called 'The Tebay Contract' (being about 6½ miles [10.5km]).[254]

Work on the Wath contract was reported as being under way by the beginning of May 1847[263], while the deviation bill received the Royal Assent on 22 July 1847,[273] although with the 'simultaneous clause' of the original act still in place.[272,277]

In November 1847,[283] notice was given of a further bill to amend the original act, and to make several deviations to both the main line and the Auckland to Tebay branch.[285] At the next half-yearly meeting, held on 17 February 1848,[287] it

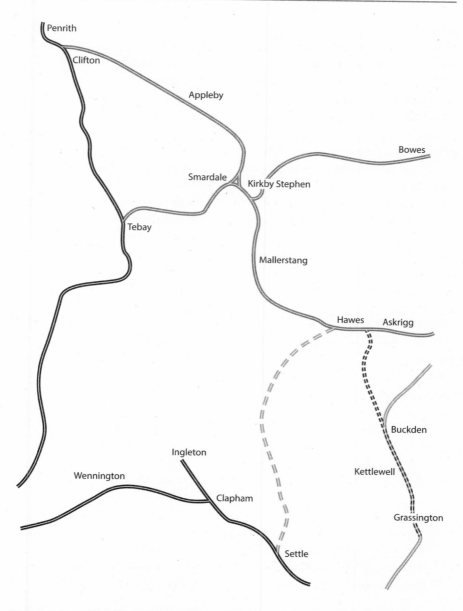

Map showing the railways making up the Northern Counties Union and the Liverpool, Manchester and Newcastle Junction railways – western section

▪ ▪ ▪ ▪ represents the section of the Leeds and Carlisle Railway proposal not replaced by the southern section of the York and Glasgow Union Railway

═════ represents the Liverpool, Manchester & Newcastle Junction Railway as authorised

▬ ▬ ▬ represents the part of the original Liverpool, Manchester and Newcastle-upon-Tyne Junction Railway not authorised

was reported that construction work was confined to the 19 miles (31km) from Wath to Leyburn, which it was hoped to open in the summer of 1849, at the same time as the L&TR was expected to open to Leeds, where it would connect with the Great Northern from Doncaster and Peterborough. The meeting also approved the amendment and deviation bill, which would have reduced the amount of tunnelling required, and again attempted to have the simultaneous clause removed. Yet again Parliament refused to repeal the clause and at the August 1848 meeting the withdrawal of the bill was announced, while a resolution for suspending operations for twelve months was passed unanimously.[296] Three months later, notice was give that an application was to be made to Parliament for the abandonment of the NCUR.[299] At the meeting on 28 February 1849 the shareholders requested that 10s (50p) of the last call be returned, to which the directors agreed, confirming that all work had ceased.[315] Discussions as to the best way of winding up the company at the meeting on 29 August 1850 included the proposal to sell the 'small portion of the line already made'.[335] Despite an offer the following year by the Great Northern Railway to guarantee a certain rate per cent to the Northern Counties Union,[357] nothing further was done.

In 1852 the 2 miles (3.2km) of completed railway were opened as part of the Leeds Northern route from Melmerby to Stockton, having been sold to the L&TR for £6,000.[774] As we shall see later, this was the same year in which the Newcastle and Carlisle Railway Company finally opened the 13 miles (21km) of their truncated Alston branch.[377] These 15 miles (24km) of railway were therefore all that was produced from the multitude of proposals put forward during 1845 and 1846 for railways in the North Pennines.

The northern end of the section of railway built for the joint use of the Northern Counties Union and Leeds and Thirsk railways near Melmerby. The L&TR (later Leeds Northern) line to Northallerton diverges to the right and the incomplete NCUR to Bedale goes straight ahead. Ken Hoole collection, reproduced by permission of HoS-DRM.

4

THE MAIN LINE OF THE PROPOSED WEAR VALLEY EXTENSION RAILWAY OF 1845

In the previous chapter we saw that after receiving their Act of Parliament for a line to connect Frosterley with the BA&WR,[145] the directors of the WVR turned their attention to the possibility of extending their line westwards.[150] In reality it was the S&DR Company that wished to build the extension and it was their consulting engineer, John Dixon,[741] who prepared the plans, sections and books of reference which were deposited with the Board of Trade[203] and the justices of the peace for the counties of Cumberland, Durham and Northumberland (p. 46).[198]

The WVER was to start in Frosterley, at the termination of the WVR, which by then was under construction, and then run west along the Wear Valley, on an alignment generally similar to that of the later Wearhead branch as far as St John's Chapel. From there it was to follow a route south of the turnpike road, today the A689, to the head of the valley of the Killhope Burn where a tunnel would take it under Killhope and into the valley of the river Nent. From Nenthead the route was similar to that of the N&CR branch as far as Alston, where the two diverged, the WVER keeping east of the Tyne to a point just north of Kirkhaugh church, where it crossed the river before joining the general route of the N&CR near Lintley. At Lambley, the WVER turned west and, running north of LCR, joined the main line of the N&CR a short distance east of Milton station.

It was expected that the WVER would form part of a main route to Scotland and, despite the difficult nature of the territory through which it was to pass, every effort was made to produce a line that would not be impossible to operate. Therefore, although three stretches of 1 in 50 to 1 in 55 were required to take the line through the mountains, there were only fourteen changes of gradient in just over 38 miles (61km) of railway. Similarly, although there were nine sections of curvature with a radius of 2 furlongs (400m) totalling 2 miles (3.2km) in all, there were relatively few examples of true reverse curves, with most changes in direction being separated by lengths of straight track. The achievement of this relatively good route through the Pennines was at the expense of some very heavy earthworks, while the company's engineer believed it would be possible to further improve the line.

The plans required by Parliament at that time had not only to show the route of the proposed railway but also the limits of deviation, that is the distance by which the line could be diverted to each side of the surveyed route without requiring a further act to extend the powers of compulsory purchase. The sections showed the gradient of the proposed line and its relationship to the surface of the land through which it was to pass, including the maximum depth of cuttings and height of embankments. Where public roads were to be crossed, any alterations to maintain, or improve, the gradients of the road were shown, while the heights and spans of any bridges were usually given. Although details were rarely provided for simple bridges over rivers, when a viaduct was required, the length and maximum height were shown, and sometimes also the proposed number and size of the arches. In the majority of cases, the radius of each curve was given in chains or furlongs, while the distance from the start was shown in miles and furlongs. Photographs of parts or all of the plans deposited for the lines considered in this book, apart from the Eden Valley Railway, have been included, while variations from the plans while the line was being authorised or built are described in the text. The relationships of imperial to metric units are given in Appendix A.

Because of the origins of the company, the plans showing the route of the WVER start at Frosterley, and we shall follow the same direction in the description of the main line, although this will take us down the valleys of the Nent and South Tyne in the opposite direction to that of the N&CR plans, described in Chapter 6. The datum line, that is the height above which all measurements on the sections are made, is given as 293.73ft (89.53m) below the highest point of Frosterley bridge, while the height recorded for the line at the start of the first section at Frosterley is 270ft (82.3m), which, according to the OS map, is approximately 175m (574ft) above sea level. All distances on the plans and sections are shown from the junction at Frosterley, and all distances in the description are measured from that point. The radii of curves which were to be greater than 1 mile are not shown on the plans. The main line was clearly designed for double track, with all bridges over the railway having a span of 30ft (9.14m) and a height of at least 15ft 6in (4.72m), some being significantly higher. When the line crossed over a turnpike road, the width of the arch was either 25ft or 30ft (7.62m or 9.14m), while the height was 15ft (4.57m) or greater. The bridges over township roads had spans of 20ft or 25ft (6.1m or 7.62m), again with a height of 15ft or more. The line rose all the way from Frosterley to the summit tunnel and then descended, with only two lengths of level and one short section of rising gradient, to join the Newcastle and Carlisle main line a little to the east of Milton station.

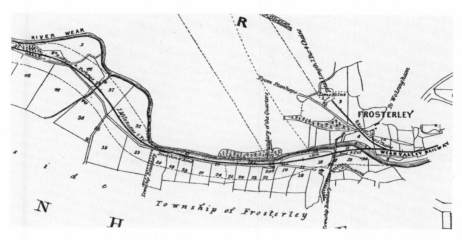

Plan showing the commencement of the WVER at Frosterley, plus the branch to the quarry. *Note*: The solid line shows the projected route of the railway, while the limits of deviation are shown by the dashed lines on either side. Reproduced by permission of Northumberland Collections Service (NCS).

Also included in the plans for the WVER was a branch, 2 furlongs 4 chains (480m) long, starting on the WVR about 6 chains (120m) before the WVER was to commence, rising to lime kilns situated north-west of Frosterley station. The earthworks on the branch were relatively minor, with the Lobley Hill turnpike road (A689) crossing, unaltered, on an arch 12ft (3.7m) high and 20ft (6.1m) wide. During the 1850s a privately owned line, similar to this branch, was built to serve a local limestone quarry,[807] and this line is shown on the 1860 plans for the Frosterley and Stanhope Railway (p. 158).[420]

The main line of the WVER started by an end-on junction with the WVR at the west end of Frosterley station, just to the east of the river Wear, which was immediately crossed. In the lower reaches of the Wear Valley the earthworks were fairly moderate, while the plans show how the line was to run in relation to the river and existing roads. The WVER rose from the start on gradients of 1 in 105 to 1 in 176 for the first 8¼ miles (13.3km) and maintained a position close to the river for most of the way to Daddry Shield (8½ miles or 13.7km).

Moderate earthworks and curvature allowed the line to follow the general direction of the south bank of the river with a branch connecting to the line described as the Derwent Junction Railway, the former S&TR, starting at 2 miles 5 furlongs 2 chains (4.26km). The branch formed a triangular junction with the main line by junctions 1 furlong 3 chains (260m) apart, while the turnpike road to Middleton-in-Teesdale (B6278) was lowered 4ft 6in (1.4m) allowing it to pass under the railway near the eastern junction (p. 66). The river Wear was crossed

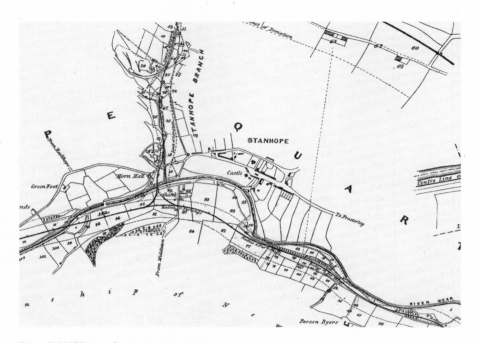

Plan of WVER near Stanhope showing the junctions of the branch to join the Derwent Junction Railway (former Stanhope and Tyne Railway) at the foot of the Crawley incline. This 1845 plan kept the railway on the south side of the river Wear past Stanhope, crossing to the north side a short distance to the west. Reproduced by permission of NCS.

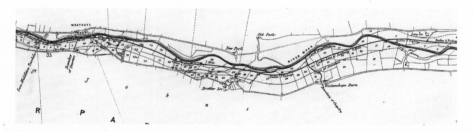

Plan of WVER from the last crossing of the river Wear to Westgate. Reproduced by permission of NCS.

on a bridge of four arches, each 54ft (16.5m) wide and 12ft (3.7m) high just over 3 miles (5.15km) from the start. The line then ran between the turnpike road (A689) and the river until a pair of genuine reverse curves of 60 chains (1.2km) radius took the railway across the river Wear on a bridge with two arches of 50ft (15m) span and 10ft (3m) high.

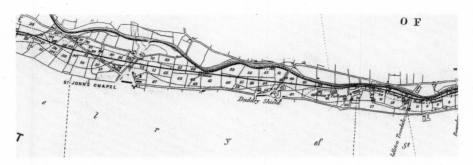

Plan of the WVER through Daddry Shield to St John's Chapel, where it crossed to the south of the turnpike. Reproduced by permission of CAS.

The line maintained a sinuous course, including almost a mile (1.59km) of four reverse curves, which kept the line close to the south bank of the river and carried it past the village of Westgate.

Passing through St John's Chapel the line started to move away from the river with the turnpike road (A689) being lowered 2ft (0.61m) to allow the railway to cross on an arch 16ft (4.9m) high, close to the modern health centre.

From this point the railway remained to the south of the turnpike road all the way to Killhope Tunnel. Although the line avoided most of the high ground to the south, some moderate cuttings and embankments were required to take it through the broken ground past the village of Ireshopeburn. The largest embankment on the line commenced just before Wearhead (shown as Wears Head) and extended for just over 2¾ miles (4.5km), reaching a height of 67ft (20m), with the village being passed on almost half a mile (740m) of right-hand curve of 40 chains (800m). Just 2 chains (40m) from the start of this curve the gradient steepened to 1

St John's Chapel looking west on 9 September 1999 along the A689, the former Lobley Hill Turnpike, which would have been lowered 2ft (0.61m) at this point to allow the WVER to cross on an arch 16ft high.

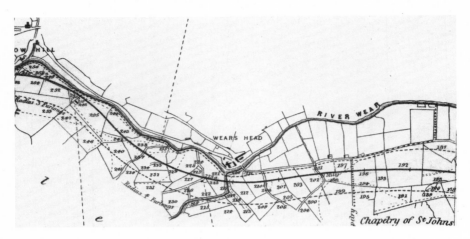

Plan of the WVER passing Wearhead. Reproduced by permission of CAS.

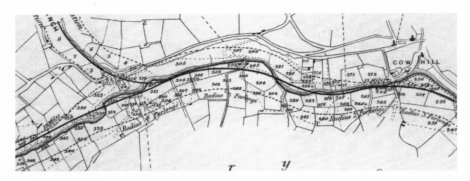

Plan of the WVER from Cowshill, past Lanehead and the divergence of the Allendale branch. Reproduced by permission of CAS.

Plan of the WVER in the upper reaches of the valley of the Killhope Burn to the tunnel under Killhope Fell. Reproduced by permission of CAS.

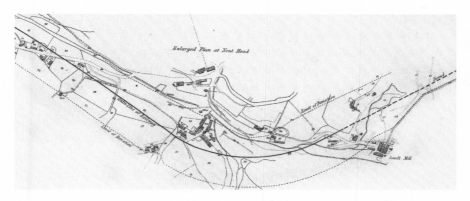

The enlarged plan of Nenthead showing the eastern end of Killhope Tunnel and the line running south of the mining site, then crossing the turnpike road on the level, the only place where this occurred on the WVER. Reproduced by permission of CAS.

in 50, and the line continued to rise at this rate to the entrance to the tunnel under Killhope. The high embankment kept the line well above the level of the river, allowing it to maintain a much less sinuous course than if it had followed the river bed, although the actual route could not be called straight.

The Killhope Burn was crossed four times (see previous page), with the branch to Allendale leaving the main line after the second crossing on an embankment 37ft (11.2m) high, without any break in the 1 in 50 gradient.

The Killhope Burn crossed over the line, on an arch 15 feet 6 inches (4.7m) high with a span of 30ft (9.1m), soon after it entered the summit cutting and almost 1 mile (1.59km) later it entered Killhope Tunnel.

Looking up the Killhope Burn to the entrance to Killhope Tunnel, directly ahead at the point where the river comes in from the right. For the last 100 yards to the tunnel mouth the Killhope Burn was to be diverted to the east (right) to reduce the depth of the cutting required. The road above the river on the right is the A689 which, at Killhope Cross, crosses the hills in the background at a height of 2,056ft (627m) above sea level. The southern portal of Killhope Tunnel was the summit of the WVER at 1,525ft (465m) above sea level.

The summit cutting reached a maximum depth of 70ft (21m) and, just before the entrance to the tunnel, the Killhope Burn was diverted for 5 chains (100m) from the tunnel mouth to reduce the depth of the cutting required, which was 62ft (18.9m) deep at this point. The eastern portal of the tunnel was the summit of the line, 1,525ft (465m) above sea level and 14 miles 6 furlongs 8 chains (23.9km) from Frosterley.

The tunnel itself was 2 miles 2 furlongs 3 chains (3.68km) long, and fell on a gradient of 1 in 142 to emerge into the valley of the river Nent a little to the west of the Nenthead smelt mill, 1,440ft (439m) above sea level. Inside the tunnel, the line left the parish of Stanhope, in the county of Durham, and entered the parish of Alston, in the county of Cumberland. The bore of the tunnel was shown as being 22ft (6.7m) wide, which is considerably narrower than the 30ft (9.1m) span of the over-bridges, and was probably the absolute minimum allowed at the time for double track. Apart from 11 chains (220m) of left-hand curve at the Weardale entrance, the tunnel was straight. A 90° right-hand curve, of 20 chains (400m) radius, started 4 chains (80m) beyond the western portal and carried the railway past the southern edge of Nenthead village. The line emerged just below the building known as Hilltop, and at the exit the descending gradient steepened to 1 in 55, which continued for almost 6¾ miles (10.8km), taking the line to a short distance south of Kirkhaugh church, a little under 2 miles (3.2km) north of Alston.

The line crossed the Nenthead mining area in a cutting which started at a depth of 60ft (18m), but soon became considerably shallower, and then the line continued virtually straight for just over 4 furlongs (825m) crossing the turnpike road (A689) on the level near the north end of Nenthead village. This was the only place where the WVER crossed a turnpike road on the level. Heavy earthworks were required to maintain the relatively straight route and even gradient to Alston.

For most of the distance from Nenthead to Alston, the variations between the WVER and N&CR lines would almost certainly have been accommodated within the 'Limits of Deviation' shown on the plans.

The river Nent was crossed by a single arch, 29ft (8.8m) high and with a span of 50ft (15m), on a short section where the river flows from north to south, rather than the generally east to west course it maintains from Nenthead to Alston. On the approach to Alston, the line then ran along the north side of the valley, keeping north of Gossipgate, before just over 3 furlongs (640m) of right-hand curve of 20 chains (400m) radius took it through 90°, passing between Spency Croft and Low Byer Inn to cross the Hexham turnpike, today's A686, just west of the junction with the South Loaning (p. 231). This was the longest curve with a radius as sharp as 20 chains on the entire WVER. North of the turnpike, the line ran more or less parallel to the main and branch turnpike roads as far as Randalholme, where

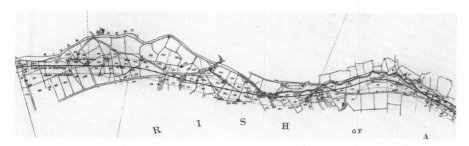

Plan showing the WVER continuing down the valley of the river Nent, passing twice under the Alston turnpike, first near Nentsberry, and then under the junction near Nenthall (A689 and B6284). Reproduced by permission of CAS.

Plan showing the WVER continuing down the River Nent and crossing the Alston turnpike (A686) on an arch 27ft (8.2m) high near Low Byer Inn and then running beside the improved road to the county boundary at Randalholme. Reproduced by permission of CAS.

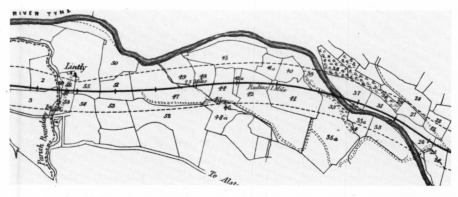

Plan showing the site of the WVER viaduct over the river South Tyne and passing Lintley Farm where the WVER main line and the N&CR branch shared the same alignment. Reproduced by permission of CAS.

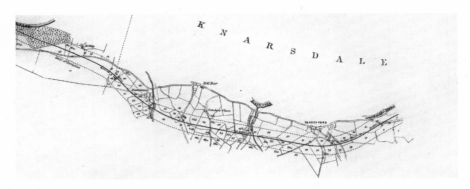

Plan showing the WVER passing Slaggyford village and crossing the Knar and Thinhope burns , then past Burnstones and Softly Farm. Reproduced by permission of CAS.

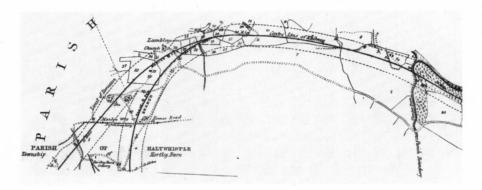

Plan showing the WVER from the Glendue Burn to the division at Lambley. The left-hand section is the main line which continues north of Lord Carlisle's Railway and joins the N&CR main line at Milton. The right-hand section is the branch joining Lord Carlisle's Railway at Hartley Burn. Reproduced by permission of CAS.

it left the county of Cumberland and entered the county of Northumberland in the parish of Kirkhaugh. The branch road is designated a turnpike on the plans, having been authorised by the Alston Turnpike Act of 1824 to cross the South Tyne just past Kirkhaugh church.[37] In common with several other sections of road authorised by the 1824 act, this was never completed, with only the length from the A686 to Randalholme being finished, although it is possible to see the remains of other uncompleted parts between Lintley and the South Tyne. Beyond Kirkhaugh church the line crossed the South Tyne on a viaduct of four arches, each 40ft (12.2m) high and 50ft (15.2m) span which was the largest on the main line of the WVER (p. 71). After Kirkhaugh the descending gradient eased to 1 in 185 and, apart from about 2 miles (3.58km) of ascent at 1 in 194, the generally gentle descent continued until just over 2 miles (3.76km) before the junction with the N&CR.

Once across the river the line ran past Lintley farm, which stands high above, and a few yards north of, the railway (fig. 2 col. section). At this point the WVER was on an almost identical alignment to that of the N&CR, although they diverged a short distance on each side of the farm, with the WVER once more returning to the east side of the N&CR, although staying to the west of the river.

The earthworks from Nenthead were quite extensive and shortly after Lintley the WVER crossed the turnpike with the earthworks substantially reduced beyond Slaggyford where a local road was crossed about 400 yards west of the turnpike (p. 72). Several tributaries of the South Tyne now had to be crossed with a return of moderately heavy earthworks. The WVER ran to the west of the N&CR route for a short distance after Burnstones, returning to the east side after going under the turnpike road. At 1 furlong over 30 miles (48.48km) from Frosterley the WVER divided, with the southern branch, which will be described later, joining Lord Carlisle's Railway.

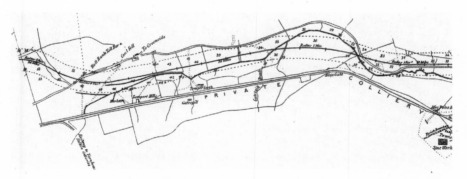

Plan showing the WVER and Lord Carlisle's Railway running along the valley of the Coalfell Beck. The WVER crosses the watershed into the river Eden catchment area shortly after it passes under the turnpike road west of the Hall Bank Toll Bar. Reproduced by permission of CAS.

Plan showing the WVER running north of Lord Carlisle's Railway, past Farlam, to join the N&CR main line just east of Milton station. Reproduced by permission of CAS.

Close to the division the N&CR crossed the route of the WVER before curving sharply to the right to cross the South Tyne. From the junction the main line of the WVER left the South Tyne Valley and turned towards the west, crossing the Black Burn, now the Hartley Burn, and leaving Northumberland County and the parish of Haltwhistle, to re-enter the county of Cumberland, but now in the parish of Lanercost and running along the valley of the Haining Burn (p. 33).

This was where the gradient changed to ascend at 1 in 194 through very broken ground as the line made its way up the valley of the Haining Burn towards the watershed separating the Tyne and Irthing rivers and past the most severe series of reverse curves on the entire route. When the line reached the watershed a massive cutting reaching 59ft (18m) in depth and extending for over 1¼ miles (2.1km) carried it down to Farlam Hall, with the gradient changing to 1 in 52 down, which was maintained all the way to the junction with the N&CR at Milton.

The line of the WVER kept about 150 yards north of, and on easier gradients than, those of the inclined plane approved by George Stephenson, which took Lord Carlisle's Railway down to Kirkhouse, although the 2¼ miles (3.8km) of ascent from the junction at Milton would have remained one of the most severe sections on the WVER main line.

The main line of the WVER was 38 miles 1 furlong 5 chains (61.46km) long and, while it would have included many miles on severe gradients, and several sections of curvature on a radius of 20 chains (400 metres), overall it was laid out in such a way that had it been built it would almost certainly have formed part of a through main line connecting Scotland and England. Although it was stated at the WVR meeting on 16 December 1845 that improvements could be made to the route, the plans produced by the WVER were for a line much superior to that proposed by the N&CR to Nenthead.[210] Webb & Gordon[751] stated that the directors of the WVR failed to obtain the support of Lord Carlisle[187] although the minute of the relevant Board meeting[189] of the WVR held on 4 November 1845 actually states 'A letter received from Lord Morpeth stating that the Earl of Carlisle was not at present prepared to sanction the westward extension of the WVR.' The directors of the WVR then produced plans taking their line well to the north of LCR in the hope that Lord Carlisle would not actually oppose the WVER, even if he would not support it.[189] Although the decision not to proceed with the WVER in 1846[221] effectively ended the possibility of a main line under Killhope, several further attempts were made to construct a similar line, and we shall look at these in detail in Chapter 13. However, we shall also see in Chapter 6 that, if a bill for the WVER had been proceeded with, the N&CR branch to Nenthead would never have obtained its act without major modifications.

BRANCHES FROM THE WVER

In addition to connecting the WVR at Frosterley to the N&CR at Milton, three branches were to be built from the main line. The first would have linked it to the W&DJR at Stanhope, a second to LCR at Halton Lea Gate, while the third would have run to Allendale and will be considered in Chapter 5.

Stanhope Branch

We saw earlier that the branch to the former S&TR at Stanhope started by a triangular junction with the main line. Immediately west of the bridge over the Stanhope to Middleton-in-Teesdale turnpike road (B6278), the eastern side of the triangular junction left the WVER main line to the north on a curve of 10 chains (200m) radius (p. 66). This was the official start of the 6 furlongs (1.2km)-long branch, which connected the WVER to the foot of the Crawley incline of the original S&TR. The western leg of the junction was one furlong (200m) long, on a left-hand curve of only 7½ chains (150m) radius. The branch crossed the river Wear immediately beyond the union of the two arms and for the next 2 furlongs (400m) ran on the west bank of the Stanhope Burn. After crossing the Stanhope Burn it joined the Crawley incline just before it curved west to its terminus beside the lime kilns. In later years this section of the old S&TR became the western arm of the Crawley incline. The Crawley branch of the WVER rose at an inclination of 1 in 7½, which was slightly steeper than the maximum of 1 in 8 on the S&TR section. There is no indication on the plans for a stationary engine specifically designed to operate the WVER incline, and one must assume that the existing, or more probably a new and more powerful, Crawley engine was expected to work the entire incline. As the W&DJR and the WVR were already worked by the S&DR, the use of a single engine for the combined incline would have been quite reasonable.

The Halton Lea Gate Branch

Although from Lambley to Milton the main line of the WVER followed an easier course, to the north of and avoiding LCR, it was one which precluded it from serving most of the local collieries. The branch to join LCR was 1 mile 2 furlongs 8 chains (2.2km) long, and rose at 1 in 563 all the way from the junction to Halton Lea Gate where it joined the colliery railway (p. 72).

5

THE 1845 PROPOSALS FOR THE ALLEN VALLEY

The majority of the railway proposals of the 1840s relating to the most northerly part of the Pennines were designed to connect Alston and the upper South Tyne Valley with the main lines of either or both the N&CR and S&DR, but there was also a perfectly valid reason for wishing to provide similar connections into the neighbouring valleys of the East and West Allen rivers. Although the Allen Valleys did not produce as much lead as Alston Moor, they were home to a sizeable mining industry, while a connection from Alston Moor to the West Allen Valley would have been beneficial to the industry as a whole. This can be seen from the supporting evidence given by the commissioners of the Royal Hospital for Seamen at Greenwich to the parliamentary committee considering the bill for a canal from Newcastle-upon-Tyne to Haydon Bridge in 1797.[22]

A table was produced listing the places where lead from Alston Moor was smelted, which included Langley mill in addition to the mills in the vicinity of Alston itself. Having received the forfeited Derwentwater Estates, the Greenwich Hospital was the owner of a substantial amount of land in the North Pennines, and the commissioners were generally supportive of any measures designed to improve the prospects of their tenants, which included the lead mining industry. It is therefore no surprise to discover that both the N&CR and S&DR included, in their proposals for 1845, branches to serve the mines and smelt mills operating in the East Allen Valley between Allendale town and Allenheads. The Allendale branch of the WVER was an integral part of their proposals, and was included in the sets of plans deposited with the Board of Trade and justices of the peace,[198] as described in Chapter 4. In contrast, the N&CR chose to make their branch to Allenheads the subject of a totally separate application to Parliament.[194] In doing this, the N&CR was following the same practice as the turnpike trusts some twenty years earlier. According to the report in *Herepath's Journal*,[202] the N&CR branch was to start by a junction with their main line at Morralee, close to the confluence of the river Allen with the river South Tyne, and terminate at the north end of Allenheads.

Although due notice was given by the N&CR that they intended to bring their bill for an Allenheads branch before Parliament in 1846, they failed to progress beyond that point. However, at their Annual General Meeting, held on 27 April 1846, it was reported that, in addition to the Alston branch, they were also contemplating making a branch up the river Allen to Allenheads to serve the 'extensive and rich mines'.[223] It was stated that they had been unable to bring the Allenheads bill before Parliament in the current session 'for want of time to complete the necessary surveys and plans'. When a large-scale map of the area is examined, it is no surprise to discover that the N&CR engineer was finding it difficult to survey a satisfactory route, especially when it is remembered that he was also in the middle of producing the plans for the extension to a central station in Newcastle as well as branches to Bellingham and Nenthead. Nevertheless in 1844 the N&CR directors had examined the Allenheads area to determine if a branch could be made from Nenthead to Allenheads.[100]

The main line of the N&CR is approximately 280ft (85m) above sea level at Morralee, while the north end of Allenheads is roughly 1,065ft (325m) higher. This rise is over a distance of approximately 13 miles (21km), requiring an average gradient of around 1 in 65. Between Morralee and Allendale town, where a lead smelting mill was situated, the valley floor rises 410ft (125m) in about 6¼ miles (10km), giving the appearance that the quite acceptable average gradient of 1 in 80 would allow the line to follow the river Allen, which joins the river South Tyne a short distance west of Morralee, all the way to Allendale town. Unfortunately, for over half of this distance, from the junction with the South Tyne to the confluence of the East and West Allen rivers, the river Allen flows through a deep, narrow and steep-sided valley, with many changes of direction, culminating in a magnificent horse-shoe bend about half a mile (1km) downstream from the point of union. It would therefore appear to be virtually impossible to find a satisfactory route along the river valley which could be constructed at a reasonable price.

It would be equally difficult to build a railway directly south from Morralee. To the east of the river Allen the land rises 380ft (115m) in the first half mile (1km) to a gently rising plateau, while a route to the west would have been even more difficult, as the line would have been required to descend almost the same distance to the floor of the West Allen Valley after an ascent of the same magnitude as that to the east of the river Allen. Although the S&DR would probably have accepted an inclined plane to the east of the river Allen, followed by a locomotive-worked line, the N&CR could be called 'a second generation railway' and always expected to work its traffic without recourse to inclined planes, initially using horses, and later steam locomotives. As we shall see in Chapter 10, when a railway into Allendale was eventually authorised in 1865,[466] it commenced near Hexham, and did not reach the Allen Valley until Staward, over 800ft (250m) above sea level, and about 9½ miles (14.5km) from the junction with the N&CR main line.

Even if it had proved possible to construct a line from Morralee to the confluence of the two branches of the river Allen, the remaining 3 miles (5km) along the valley floor to Allendale town would still have been difficult. When the Hexham and Allendale Railway (H&AR) was eventually built, it only reached the East Allen River by a private siding to the Allendale smelt mill. Beyond Allendale town, the East Allen rises approximately 655ft (200m) in the 7 miles (11km) to Allenheads, making the average gradient for that section of the branch 1 in 55. Once again, it was not easy to find a suitable route, but both the WVER, and later the H&AR, succeeded in doing so, even if neither line was constructed.

When the WVR did not proceed with its extension plans, the S&DR was effectively out of the running and it might have been supposed that the N&CR would have had adequate time to prepare suitable plans, for consideration in the next session of Parliament, for a line running into Allendale. However, by the end of 1846 the effects of the Railway Mania were becoming apparent, with the lines already authorised finding it difficult to raise the capital they required. Construction of the Alston branch which, as we shall see in the next chapter, was authorised during the 1846 session,[249] was not started in earnest until after a second act was obtained in 1849 giving permission for major modifications and the abandonment of the steeply graded Nenthead section.[317] The Alston branch proved to be the last part of the N&CR to be built and no further consideration was given to extending into the Allen valley during its remaining years of independent existence.

Despite the failure of the WVER scheme, it is worth looking at the plans of the proposed line for the East Allen Valley in some detail, as it would have been an entirely different type of railway to that authorised from Allendale town to Allenheads by the H&AR Act of 1865.[466] In a letter to Joseph Pease, John Dixon stated that after visiting Allenheads he had considered taking the railway out of the Allen Valley and joining the N&CR towards Haltwhistle, but the land was unsuitable.[156] The plans eventually produced by Dixon for the WVER show a small and varying number of minor additions and alterations, in a different colour of ink, mainly on those sheets covering the Allendale branch.[198] These support the statement made by the directors of the WVR that Dixon had little time examining the country to select a suitable line and could improve the plans, also suggesting that he had completed those for the Allendale branch in rather a hurry.[201] The branch was to be 10 miles 1 furlong 2 chains (16.33km) long, leaving the main line 12 miles 5 furlongs

1 chain (20.34km) from Frosterley, and terminating beside the turnpike road from Haydon Bridge (today the B6295), close to the Allendale smelt mill.

The route of the Allendale branch of the WVER, and its relationship with the unbuilt section of the later H&AR is shown on Figure 1d in Chapter 1. The Allendale Branch is effectively in two sections, the first part being a pair of inclined planes taking the line from the Wear Valley at Lanehead over the hills to Allenheads in the East Allen Valley, while the second was the continuation by a locomotive line from Allenheads to Allendale town.

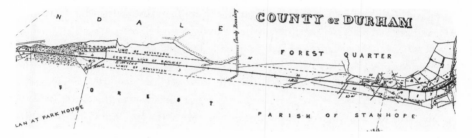

The first section of the WVER Allendale branch from the junction with the main line at Lanehead over two inclined planes to Allenheads. Reproduced by permission of NCS.

Bridge carrying the turnpike road over Heathery Cleugh at Lanehead in September 1997. The photographer is standing where the main line of the WVER would have run on the south side of the river Wear. The Allendale branch would have passed behind the house and through one of the arches of the bridge.

This second section contained some very heavy earthworks which kept it reasonably free from severe curves and frequent variations of the gradient. The S&DR, with its subsidiaries, remained essentially 'a first generation railway' throughout its existence, continuing to use and develop inclined planes, although by 1845 new construction of these was confined to secondary branches. Thus, while a tunnel was to be provided to carry the main line under Killhope to the valley of the river Nent, inclined planes were considered satisfactory for the branch into the valley of the East Allen,[153] although the continuation to Allendale smelt mill was then to be constructed to standards similar to those of the main line. Unlike the triangular junction provided at Stanhope for the branch to the W&DJR, only a single connection, designed for through running towards Frosterley, was to be provided for the Allendale branch at Lanehead.

The junction was on a short length of straight track, but there is no indication on the sections that there was to be any easing of the 1 in 50 gradient on the main line at that point (p. 68). The main line was on an embankment 37ft (11m) high on the south side of the river running along what is now the south bank of an island in the Killhope Burn, while the Allendale branch was to follow what was then the existing south bank of the river, and is now the north bank of the island. The branch first ran along an embankment, of a similar height to that on the main line, before curving to the right and crossing the Killhope Burn on an arch, 50ft (15m) high and 33 feet (10m) wide, at the point where the river turns to the south. The curve took the line through 90° into the valley called Heathery Cleugh (p. 79). At this point the railway was facing directly towards Allenheads to which it ran in a virtually straight line for almost 2¼ miles (3.5km). The branch climbed for just over 1¼ miles (2.1km) from the main line, first at 1 in 53, then at 1 in 17, but mostly at 1 in 10, to a summit level only 1½ furlongs (290m) long, and 1,862ft (570m) above sea level, before descending, mostly at 1 in 12, for almost 1½ miles (2.2km). At the start of the 1 in 17 gradient the line passed beneath the bridge carrying the Alston turnpike (A689) after which it ran below the village of Lanehead. A little beyond the summit level, about 200 yards over the Northumberland county boundary, the railway came to within 100 yards of the turnpike road from Allendale to Burtryford, now the B6295.

Just before the foot of the northern side of the incline, the line curved to the left, again through 90° to pass south-west of the village of Allenheads. The gradient eased first to 1 in 20 and then to 1 in 50, which continued for 2 miles (3.2km). The line kept to the west side of both the road and the headwaters of the river East Allen to a short distance beyond the hamlet which still rejoices in the name of Dirt Pot, despite efforts in the years following the Second World War to change it to Doves Pool!

Beyond Dirt Pot the railway passed along the western edge of the Allenheads smelt mill, keeping west of the river as far as St Peter's church and Allenheads

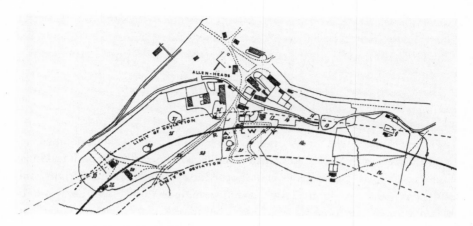

The route of the WVER Allendale branch past Allenheads. The descent at 1 in 12 eased first to 1 in 20 and then to 1 in 50 as the line curved past the south-west edge of the village of Allenheads. The centre of mining activity was on the opposite side of the river. Reproduced by permission of NCS.

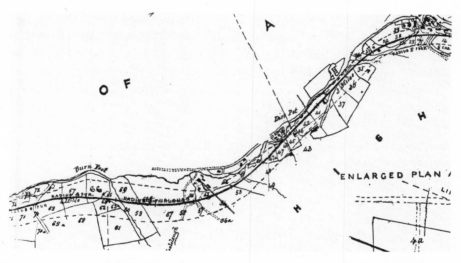

Route of the WVER Allendale Branch past the village of Dirt Pot. Note that the line was to run on the west (right) side of the river East Allen. The Allenheads Smelt Mill was situated between the railway and the river where the railway curves to the east (left). Reproduced by permission of NCS.

corn mill, after which it crossed to the east bank, close to the ford, now a bridge, carrying the road from Spartylea to Swinhope, with the gradient easing to 1 in 67.

Although the earthworks on the inclines were relatively light, once into the Allen Valley they were more extensive and generally became more severe as the line continued down the valley, maintaining a relatively straight course on steep but constant gradients. The river Allen was crossed on an arch 22ft (6.7m) high and 50ft (15.2m) wide at 5 miles 6 chains (8.168km) with the line remaining on the east side of the river.

The line crossed back over the Allen, west of High Sinderhope, on a bridge of two arches each 18ft (5.49m) high and 30ft (9.14m) span at 6 miles 5 furlongs 8 chains (10.823km).

The most extensive earthworks on the branch occurred over the ensuing three-quarters of a mile (1.2km) with an embankment, reaching 64ft (19.5m) in height and almost 3 furlongs (590m) long, taking the line back to the east bank of the river Allen on the largest viaduct anywhere on the WVER. The gradient changed for the last time to 1 in 57 just before this viaduct, which had seven

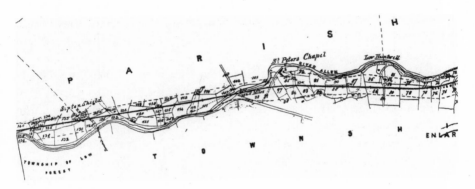

The WVER Allendale branch past Low Huntwell and St Peter's Chapel to Sipton Shield. Reproduced by permission of NCS.

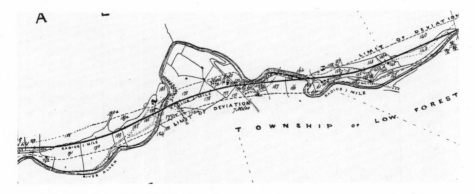

The WVER Allendale branch cutting through the high ground to the west of Sinderhope as it passed Hunt Rods. The line ran in a cutting through the ridge and then crossed the river on the largest viaduct anywhere on the WVER. Reproduced by permission of NCS.

arches each with a span of 60ft (18.3m), three in the centre 56ft (17.1m) high, and two on each side 53ft (16.2m) high. The line crossed the river Allen twice before Allendale town.

Just south of the town the river starts on a series of wide sweeps, first to the west, then back to the east, and finally to the west again, as it changes from the northerly course it has maintained all the way from Dirt Pot, to a more northwesterly direction. The WVER ran below the main part of Allendale town, passing under the turnpike road before crossing over the river yet again. The line stayed on the west bank for just over a furlong (240m) before returning to the east bank for the last time. Immediately after the bridge the line curved to the left to follow the west bank of the river, opposite Allendale smelt mill, before terminating beside the Haydon Bridge turnpike road 100 yards from where Catton Road Station was later built by the H&AR (pp. 177 & 178).

The WVER Directors at their meeting held on 17 September 1845 had authorised Dixon to survey a line with fixed engines or tunnelling to Allendale town via Allenheads, suitable for passenger trains.[153] Throughout its independent existence the S&DR operated regular passenger services over a variety of inclined planes, including the original inclines between Shildon and St Helens Auckland as well as those between Cold Rowley and Crook on the W&DJR.[777] Apart from the existing bridge carrying the Alston turnpike over Heathery Cleugh, all the other over-bridges were to be 30ft (9.1m) wide, adequate for double track. This was a well-planned length of railway and, although the gradients through the East Allen Valley were severe, very extensive earthworks, one long viaduct and several substantial bridges were provided to ensure that it would have been relatively easy to work. In the 7¼ miles (11.76km), from the foot of the inclined plane at Allenheads, to the terminus at Catton Road a total of 4¾ miles (7.6km) of the railway was straight. The lead industry would have been reasonably well served,

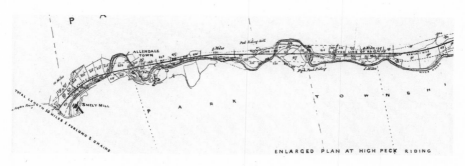

Terminus of the WVER Allendale branch beside the turnpike road from Catton to Allendale Town via Thornley Gate. Reproduced by permission of NCS.

with the route passing close to the smelt mill and mines at Allenheads, while the Allendale smelt mill could have been easily reached by a branch, 2½ furlongs (500m) long, diverging northwards from the main line immediately before it crossed to the east bank of the East Allen for the last time. However, considering the importance of the smelt mill at Langley, it is surprising that the branch was to terminate beside the turnpike near Catton and not extend to Langley.

6

THE ALSTON BRANCH OF THE N&CR

As we saw in Chapter 3, the only bill from the northern part of the North Pennines that was proceeded with in the 1846 parliamentary session was the Newcastle & Carlisle (extension and branches) Bill. Parliament received several petitions against the bill,[218,219] but on Wednesday 17 February 1846 the House of Commons Railway Sub-Committee, No. 5, agreed that it complied with standing orders.[220] At the Annual General Meeting of the N&CR, held on Friday 27 March, the chairman, Matthew Plummer, stated "The Directors have felt themselves called upon, for the protection of the interests of this Company, to apply to Parliament, in the present Session, for powers to make two branches from the main line.'[223] He confirmed that the South Tyne branch would run from Haltwhistle through Alston to Nenthead to serve 'a district abounding in mines of lead and other minerals'. He added that they 'have it also in contemplation to make another branch up the River Allen to Allenheads, in which district are extensive and rich mines'. Taken as a whole, these comments suggest that it had not been the directors' intention to construct any branch lines at that time. It therefore appears that the proposals for the WVER persuaded the N&CR to survey both the South Tyne and the Allen valleys, with the line along the latter being dropped, probably due to failure to find a suitable route as well as rumours, which later proved correct, that the WVR Company might not pursue their extension line in the 1846 parliamentary session.[210] The fact that there were other proposals which could readily encompass the South Tyne Valley, one of which included a line from Northallerton, through Barnard Castle and Alston to Haltwhistle,[245] probably accounts for the retention of this branch. In the case of the North Tyne branch, the Hexham branch of the NE&DGJR was a direct competitor.[231]

At the special meeting of the proprietors of the N&CR, which Parliament required to be held for the purpose of confirming that the shareholders wished the bill to proceed,[229] it was stated that the estimated cost of building the Alston branch was between £200,000 and £210,000, while the expected annual revenue was about £18,000. In contrast, the cost of the North Tyne branch was estimated at between £250,000 and £260,000, with an annual revenue of about £12,600. Doubts were expressed concerning the latter branch, but the meeting agreed to continue with the bill unaltered. Following the consent of the shareholders, the bill entered the committee stage in the House of Commons, where it was considered as part of group 46.[231] This committee met for the first time on 8 June 1846 to consider a total of seven bills. These were: Newcastle and Darlington Junction and Tyne Dock; Newcastle-upon-Tyne, Edinburgh, and Direct Glasgow Junction; Wear Dock Railway; Newcastle and Berwick; Newcastle and Carlisle (extension and branches); Newcastle and Darlington, Durham and Sunderland, and Wearmouth Dock Purchase and Branches; Northumberland and Lancashire Junction.

One week later, the Committee removed the Bellingham branch from the preamble of the N&CR Bill, but passed the preamble for the Alston and Newcastle branches.[232] The preamble for the competing NE&DGJR Bill was found not proved, which meant the end of both proposals for lines up the North Tyne Valley. For those who are not familiar with parliamentary bills, a simple description of the preamble is that it gives the reasons why the act is required. On 22 June 1846 the committee declared the preamble of the truncated N&CR Bill proved, but with the proviso that 'the line from Alston to Nenthead shall not be worked by locomotive engines, without the express sanction of the Board of Trade.'[234] On 7 July 1846[238] the N&CR Bill was passed by the House of Commons and proceeded to the House of Lords where it received a rather difficult passage before receiving the Royal Assent on 26 August 1846.[249] The main opposition to the N&CR Bill was related to the North Tyne branch, but even after this section had been deleted, the opposition continued, and a major effort was made by one MP, Mr John Abel Smith, to discredit financially the N&CR and prevent their bill from passing into law. The probable reason for this is given on page 1169 of *Herepath's Journal* for 12 September 1846, from which the following quotation is taken:

> Mr. Smith represents himself as 'not having the slightest interest one way or the other.' We do not mean to impugn the Hon. member's statement, but we should like to know whether it be true that one of the branches applied for by this Company, to connect the North Tyne iron districts with the main line near Hexham, was intended to pass through part of the estate of Mr. Grey, of Chipchase Castle? – whether Mr. Smith (who married Mr. Grey's mother) attended on behalf of that gentleman to oppose the branch, on the score of injury to the property, in compensation for which he demanded £10,000? – whether the Railway Company refused to entertain any proposition in respect of extra damages, but offered, in case they could not come to an agreement

with Mr. Grey for the value of his property, to give an undertaking that they would, by passing over an adjoining property, avoid it altogether? - whether it be true that, on the continued opposition, the branch was thrown out in Committee, as well as the opposing line on its own demerits, the Committee designating it, (if we remember the exact words) 'a crude, ill-digested scheme, which could neither benefit the Shareholders or the public?' - whether the Chairman and chief supporter of this rejected line, Mr. Charles Atticus Monck, married a daughter of the late Sir Matthew White Ridley, and a brother of Mr. Smith married this lady's sister? We do not say that the former and this second near family connexion, had anything to do with Mr. Smith being chosen as a fit champion to lead a protracted and most vexatious opposition, which could not in the slightest degree benefit the opposing parties; but the opposition certainly had the effect of causing a temporary depression in the price of the Company's stock, and thereby to injure the timid Shareholders, as well as those whom adverse circumstances compelled to sell their shares at a sacrifice - that is the timid and the poor. It would appear to have been the intention to procrastinate the last stages of the Bill for the line to Alston Moor, as to allow the session to close ere it could be passed into a law, and thus to deprive the Company of the power to extend their line into a most central situation in the town of Newcastle, and to unite in a general station, which all the railways north, south, east, and west, will form in one nucleus. Had the opposition succeeded, the effect would have been to deprive the public of a great and manifest convenience, and, again, prevent the formation of a branch to the populous mining district of Alston Moor, and to deprive the inhabitants of the advantage of railway communication - an advantage they know how to appreciate, as was evinced by their demonstrations on the news of the Royal Assent having been given, when the whole district was illuminated, with a general rejoicing; and, to wind up the climax, figures in effigy, intended to represent certain oppositionists, were publicly burned by the people.[243]

In addition to the branch to Alston Moor, the Act also authorised the N&CR to extend its main line into a new Central station in Newcastle, and to raise an extra £240,000 of capital and £80,000 on loan, primarily for the construction of the Alston branch.[243] According to *Herepath's Journal*, the main line was to be 17 miles (37.4km) long, with a branch 3/8 mile (600m) long, and 179 acres of land would be required.[242] The estimated cost of the line was £263,534, with working expenses of 40 per cent. There were to be no tunnels, while the maximum gradient on the main line was stated to be 1 in 100, rising to 1 in 33½ on the branch. Four turnpike and five other public roads were to be crossed on the level. Finally, Mr. N. Woods was named as engineer.

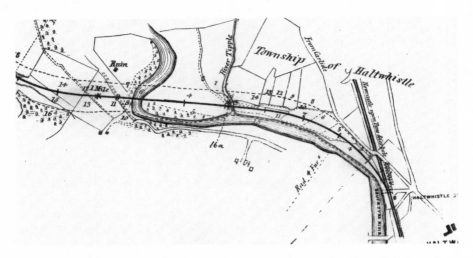

First 1¼ miles of the 1845 N&CR plans for the Haltwhistle to Nenthead branch showing the junction with the main line at the west end of Haltwhistle station and the branch crossing the rivers Tipple (Tipalt) and South Tyne. Reproduced by permission of CAS.

Even a cursory examination of the plans deposited with the justices of the peace shows that this information is somewhat inaccurate.[215] There is no indication anywhere of any branch, the gradient of 1 in 33½ occurs between Alston and Nenthead and other sections steeper than 1 in 100 are to be found between Haltwhistle and Alston, while the name of the 'acting' engineer is John Bourne. The scale of the plans and sections is 4 inches = 1 mile, with the distances from Haltwhistle marked off in furlongs. The radius of each curve is given when it is of 8 furlongs (1 mile or 1.6km) or less. For the sections, the datum line is stated as being '50 feet below the level of the first step on entering the office door of the Haltwhistle station upon the Newcastle and Carlisle Railway'. From the 1 in 25,000 OS map, the height of Haltwhistle Station is approximately 360 feet, so the datum line is approximately 310 feet (94.5 metres) above sea level. The line was to leave the N&CR main line at the west, or Carlisle, end of Haltwhistle station and cross both the rivers Tipalt and South Tyne before joining the alignment of the branch, as built, near Broomhouse. We shall now look in detail at the Haltwhistle to Nenthead branch that was actually authorised on 26 August 1846.

The plans, sections and books of reference were deposited with the justices of the peace in the counties of Cumberland and Northumberland, and the city and county of Newcastle-upon-Tyne.[215] All sets remain available for study, although those at the record offices in Carlisle and Woodhorn are very fragile with extensive use, while the set at Newcastle is in excellent condition. In the book of reference, all roads not described as occupation roads are stated as being

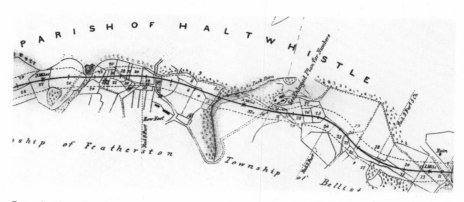

From 1 mile to 3 miles 1 furlong of the 1845 plans of the Haltwhistle to Nenthead branch of the N&CR showing the embankment over the Park Burn. Most of this section of line was retained in the 1849 Act. Reproduced by permission of TWAS.

either turnpikes, or the property of the Surveyor of Highways of the local parish or township, and in this description the latter have been grouped together as 'public roads'. All bridges carrying roads over the railway were 28ft (8.5m) wide and at least 15ft (4.6m) high.

From the junction at Haltwhistle, the branch curved to the left on a radius of 40 chains (800m) and rose, first at 1 in 2138 and then at 1 in 49½ for 1½ miles (2.3km), to a point just over ½ mile (935m) beyond the Haltwhistle to Park Village road, crossing the rivers Tipalt and South Tyne on viaducts 122 yards (112m) and 176 yards (161m) long and 52ft (15.8m) and 85ft (25.9m) high respectively. At the end of the 1 in 49½ ascent the gradient eased to 1 in 130 and the branch continued to rise on easier gradients, apart from about ¾ mile (1.1km) descent to the crossing of the South Tyne at Lambley, and half a mile (0.75km) of level, all the way to Alston.

The line passed under the road to Park Village in a deep cutting and, after passing Park village it crossed the Park Burn on an embankment 68ft (20.7m) high with a large culvert to carry the water (p. 90), while ¼ mile (0.54km) further on, the public road from Rowfoot to Featherstone was raised and crossed on the level.

The Herdley Burn was crossed on an embankment shortly before Lambley viaduct, 268 yards (245m) long and 100ft (30.5m) high, took the line to the west bank of the South Tyne. Immediately south of the viaduct a curve only 7 chains (140m) long but of 10 chains (200m) radius took the line through nearly 90° (p. 90).

After the sharp curve the N&CR became virtually straight for just less than 1 mile (1.6km), while the WVER would have entered the valley of the South

Embankment with culvert carrying the N&CR Alston branch over the Park Burn. The section of just over 1 mile (2km), which included this embankment, was built using the 1845 plans and was possibly the only place where work actually commenced in 1847.

1845 plan of the N&CR Nenthead branch showing the crossing of the river South Tyne at Lambley. Reproduced by permission of TWAS.

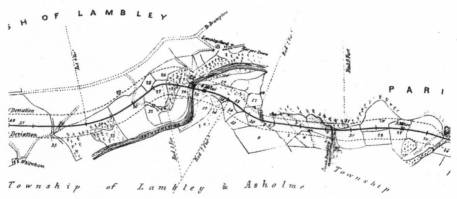

Tyne to the west of the N&CR at Lambley, and then crossed to run between the N&CR and the river.

Unlike the WVER the N&CR branch crossed the roads of the Alston Turnpike Trust several times on the level, with the first crossing being shortly before the burn at Burnt Stones (the Thinhope Burn) was crossed.

The Knar Burn was to be crossed on another high embankment, but we now come to those parts of the plans and sections which would not have passed any thorough examination, such as would have been required if the directors of the WVR had proceeded with their bill for the WVER.

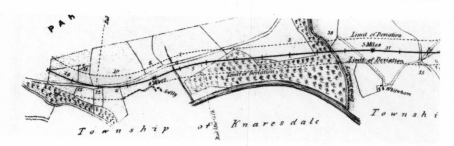

The 1845 plan of the N&CR Nenthead branch between Whitwham and the level crossing of the turnpike road south of Softly. Reproduced by permission of TWAS.

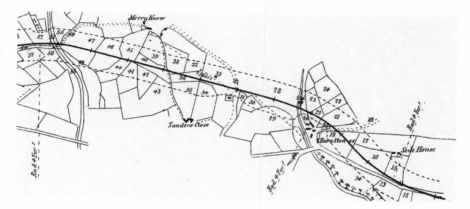

The 1845 plan of the N&CR Nenthead branch from the level crossing north of Burnstones to the Knar Burn. Reproduced by permission of TWAS.

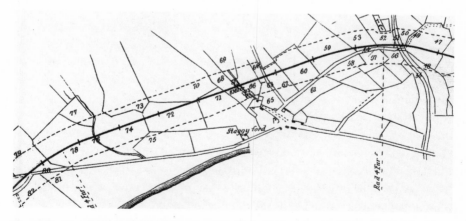

The 1845 plan of the N&CR Nenthead branch between the Knar Burn and the crossing of the turnpike north of Slaggyford showing part of the length where there were several discrepancies between the plan, which is reasonably accurate, and the section, which is not. Reproduced by permission of TWAS.

For 3 furlongs (600m) south of 7 miles 7 furlongs (12.7km) there are several discrepancies between the plans and the sections in the 1845 N&CR documents. First, the road that exists at the south end of Slaggyford station is shown correctly on the plan, and is described in the book of reference as 'a road or highway', the property of the parish of Knaresdale. There is nothing shown on the section at this point, but a road is shown crossing the railway, without any alteration to its level, at 8 miles 1 furlong 1 chain (13.1km) from Haltwhistle.

Second, on the plan a second road is shown, described in the book of reference as 'road to the common', crossing the line 1 chain (20m) before the 8 miles (12.85km) mark. Once again, there is nothing on the section at this point, although a track, and a stream, are crossed today, by a two-arched bridge, about 140m south of the public road, which again coincides reasonably well with the plan, but not the section.

Third, on the length immediately after the second road crossing, between 8 miles 1 furlong and 8 miles 2 furlongs (13.08km and 13.28km), a stream was crossed at a height of 23ft (7m) on the section. There is nothing on the plan at this point, although a stream is shown at 8 miles 3 furlongs 6 chains (13.6km), which could be the Thompson's Well shown on today's OS map.

It is interesting to note that on both the WVER and N&CR plans from 1845 the road leading to the site of the present Slaggyford station was devoid of buildings.

Close to Lintley Farm the line passed under the turnpike road, then over the Thornhope Burn on an embankment 43ft (13.1m) high, while immediately north of the Burn, the WVER converged on the N&CR and for about 2½ furlongs (500m) they both followed the same alignment, passing below Lintley Farm (fig. 2 col. section). South of the Thornhope Burn the lines intersected what was described in the N&CR book of reference as 'Turnpike Road. Not Completed,' owned by the Alston Turnpike Trust. This was the new road from Alston to Slaggyford, authorised by the Alston Turnpike Trust Act of 1824[37] but never actually built, that we met in Chapter 2.

For almost two miles (3.11km) from just beyond the Slaggyford road-crossing the line was to rise at 1 in 107, before easing to 1 in 379¼ for almost a mile (1.39km), over which length it went under two streams and over the Gilderdale Burn on an embankment 42ft (12.8m) in height, to enter the parish of Alston in what was then the county of Cumberland.

Approximately 5 chains (100m) after Gilderdale Burn the gradient steepened to 1 in 82, taking the line to a point just south of the Haydon Bridge section of the Alston turnpike, today's A686. The turnpike (A686) was crossed, on the level, close to its junction with the much steeper earlier road, today known as North Loaning, about 5 chains (100m) east of Lowbyer Manor Hotel (p. 231) and this was the southern

The 1845 plan of the N&CR Nenthead branch between the bridge over the turnpike road south of Slaggyford and Gilderdale Burn. Note the double dashed line, labelled 4a, 7a & 11, is the unbuilt section of the Alston turnpike. Reproduced by permission of TWAS.

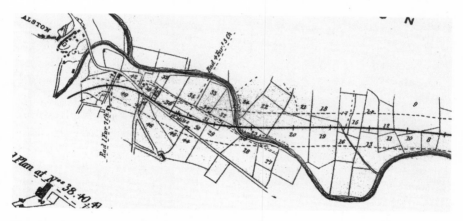

The plan of the 1845 N&CR Nenthead branch at the crossing of the Hexham to Alston turnpike (A686) on the outskirts of Alston. Reproduced by permission of TWAS.

limit authorised for operation by locomotives, with the gradient steepening to 1 in 39.

The WVER converged on the N&CR just south of the road crossing and the two alignments cannot then be distinguished on a modern map to a point immediately before Gossipgate, although they crossed the turnpike at different levels. The WVER then maintained a much straighter alignment, but with significantly heavier earthworks, although the N&CR crossed the river Nent, on a single arch 40ft (12.2m) wide and 37ft (11.3m) high.

The gradient eased to 1 in 54 one furlong (200m) before the river Nent was crossed, while the public road running through Blagill which connected the two sections of the Alston turnpike was lowered and crossed on the level 1 furlong (200m) south of the river Nent (p. 94 and fig. 3 col. section).

The plan of the 1845 N&CR branch from Alston to just east of the crossing of Nent.
Reproduced by permission of CAS.

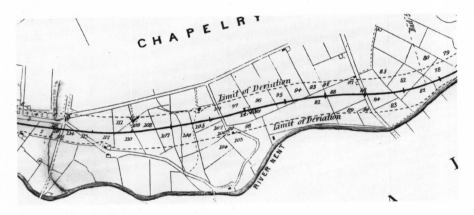

Plan of the 1845 N&CR Nenthead branch from the Blagill road to the Hudgill crossroads.
Reproduced by permission of CAS.

The B6294, was crossed on the level, as was the occupation road to Lovelady
Shield, near the end of the 1 in 54, with the gradient easing to 1 in 147. The
Cowshill turnpike (A689) was crossed over to the west of Nenthall (p. 95), on an
arch 20ft (6.1m) wide and 15ft (4.6m) high.

The two lines ran together for 2½ furlongs (500m) from a point opposite
Nentsberry, until just before both lines passed beneath the Cowshill turnpike,
with the gradient steepening to 1 in 33½ for almost a mile (1.6km). The
ascending gradient changed for the last time, to 1 in 68½ and then the turnpike
was crossed, on the level, for the last time. The line terminated just beyond the
road to Garrigill beside the Dowgang stream and the occupation road of the
Dougang Mining Company. The branch was exactly 17 miles (27.36km) long
and was stated to rise 1,048ft 5in (320m) from the junction, making the terminus
approximately 1,410ft (430m) above sea level.

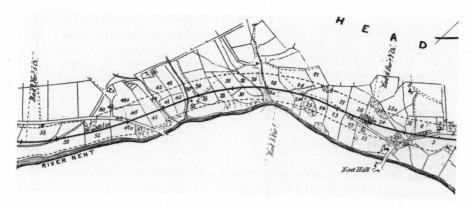

Plan of the 1845 N&CR Nenthead branch from Nenthall to the outskirts of Nenthead. Reproduced by permission of CAS.

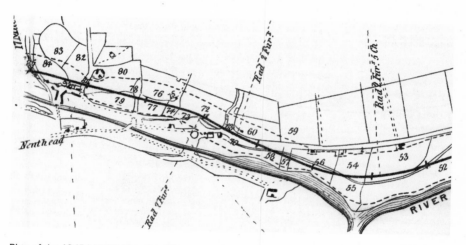

Plan of the 1845 N&CR Nenthead branch through Nenthead to the terminus. Reproduced by permission of CAS.

This was the railway authorised by the N&CR Act of 1846. Although the 28ft (8.5m) width of the over-bridges indicated that it was designed for double track, the severity of the gradients and some of the curves make it clear that this line could never realistically have been seen as part of a major through route. Furthermore, there were seventeen changes of gradient, with a maximum of 1 in 33½ in the 17 miles of the N&CR branch, whereas there were only fourteen changes, producing nothing steeper than 1 in 50, in the entire 38 miles of the WVER.

We have seen that the attempts financially to discredit the N&CR failed, but an examination of the plans and sections suggests that this would have been a more productive approach. The discrepancies between the plans and the sections in the region of Slaggyford must not have been discovered by the parliamentary committee for if they had it is unlikely that the bill would then have been allowed to continue with the Nenthead branch included. Certainly, there is every reason to believe that if the directors of the WVR had continued with their bill for the WVER, the two lines would have been considered by the same parliamentary committee, probably as competing lines in the same group as the NE&DGJR. This committee would then have had to decide if either or both preambles had been proved. The parliamentary committee which did examine the N&CR plans, even in isolation, placed severe restrictions on the use of steam locomotives over the section from Alston to Nenthead. The much more accurate plans and sections of the WVER, for what was obviously a vastly superior line, would almost certainly have received parliamentary approval. It is also clear that if John Abel Smith had attacked the N&CR on the quality of its plans and documentation, rather than on its financial probity, he would probably have been more successful.

From the manner in which parliamentary committees treated other competing lines in that session of Parliament, it is improbable that the N&CR branch would have been allowed to proceed unaltered in the presence of the WVER. There is every possibility that the parliamentary committee would have suggested one of three alternatives to be considered by the N&CR and WVR. The first, and I believe least likely alternative, is that a full amalgamation of the N&CR and WVR/WVER would have been proposed. The second, and in my opinion most probable outcome, is that only the line of the WVER would have been authorised between Lambley (possibly Burnstones) and Nenthead, to be constructed at the joint expense, and for the joint use, of both railways. The third possibility, which would have depended partly on the success of the general opposition to the N&CR, and partly on the reaction of the members of the committee to the flaws in the N&CR plans, is that the South Tyne branch would have been removed from the preamble of the N&CR bill at the same time as the North Tyne branch was removed, allowing the WVER to proceed unopposed.

It seems highly improbable that any parliamentary committee would have been prepared to allow the N&CR application, which, when viewed today, is based on what appears to have been a hastily and ill-prepared set of plans for a definitely inferior line, to take precedence over the much superior WVER line. However, no one can ever be certain of the outcome of a *might have been* situation, especially with the Earl of Carlisle backing the N&CR. Even if the WVER had been authorised, there is no certainty that it would ever have been built, in view of the general financial collapse which followed the Railway Mania and the looming financial problems of the entire S&DR group of railways. Nevertheless, with the financial backing of the wealthy directors of the S&DR it seems highly likely that at least the main line, from Frosterley to Brampton, would have been completed, making the railway map of northern England very different today.

When the Act authorising the N&CR to construct their branch to Nenthead was passed at the end of August 1846,[249] the Railway Mania was at its height and no action was taken by the directors of the N&CR until after the next Annual General Meeting, held on 25 March 1847. Here the chairman stated that 'A careful examination of the country through which the line of the Alston branch passes, has suggested various alterations and improvements, all of which may be carried into effect without further authority from Parliament.'[259] There would, however, be a delay in commencing work on the branch, although it was hoped to complete it rapidly. The chairman also stated that the directors considered the Alston branch to be very important, with the mines in the district greatly increasing the general traffic of the railway.

The decision by the parliamentary committee to restrict the use of steam locomotives between Alston and Nenthead was undoubtedly one of the reasons why the route was looked at again by the company's engineers. The N&CR placed advertisements in the local newspapers and *Herepath's Journal* towards the end of March 1847 requesting tenders for the formation of portions of the line for which the plans and specifications would be ready on 12 April 1847,[257,258] and in April for rails, chairs and sleepers for 'a portion of their Alston branch'.[261,262] One of the alterations to the branch was to be a deviation near its commencement at Haltwhistle,[264] and assuming that the 1847 proposal was the same as that adopted in the plans produced in 1848 this, at least, would have required a second Act of Parliament. On 10 May the directors accepted the tender from Cowan, Marshall and Ridley for 'the earthworks from Haltwhistle to within a distance to be determined on this side of Shafthill', and that from Edward Reed for Haltwhistle bridge.[265] The *Newcastle Chronicle* reported in June that not only had contracts been signed for Haltwhistle viaduct and a portion of the earthworks, but that work had commenced.[266] However, very little appears to have been undertaken at this time. Nevertheless, on 26 July it was announced that the £240,000 authorised to be raised as capital would be offered in the form of 2,400 shares of £100 each, payable in seven instalments during 1847 and 1848.[274] These shares became known as Alston Branch shares.

The words spoken by Matthew Plummer in March 1847, that improvements might be made to the route, again suggest that the original survey, and the resulting plans, were drawn up in 1845 primarily in response to the proposals for the WVER, in order that a viable parliamentary bill could be presented for the 1846 session. In November 1847 it was reported that the N&CR had given notice that they intended to apply for a further act to alter the branch line from 'Haltwhistle to Knaresdall'.[283] Webb and Gordon[752] quote correspondence from John Ramshay, on behalf of Lord Carlisle, which states that this alteration would keep the line on the east bank of the South Tyne, making it very difficult to provide the promised connection with LCR. Nothing further was heard of this proposed bill, possibly because of Lord Carlisle's opposition to the route of the deviation. An undated and very fragile map shows what appears to be the plan for this first proposal.[284] From Shafthill Farm the proposed new line was to pass above Low Ash Holm before crossing the South Tyne on a viaduct 84ft (25.6m) high and about 300 yards long, some distance beyond Waughold Holme, almost a mile (1.6km) south of where Lambley Junction was eventually built. This route would have reduced the height of the viaduct over the South Tyne by 16ft (4.9m) and the maximum gradient of the climb from the viaduct from 1 in 60 to 1 in 90. It would also have eliminated the curve of 10 chains (200m) radius which occurred immediately south of Lambley viaduct on both the 1845 and 1848 plans.

At the Annual General Meeting held on 28 March 1848 it was reported that 'During the prevalence of the high prices of labour and materials, it was not deemed expedient to press forward the works on the Alston branch.'[289] It was stated, 'That portion of the works which will require most time has been let, and is in course of execution', while several deviations, making great improvements in the line, had been agreed; but they would require a further Act of Parliament. Once the new act had been obtained, it was expected to complete the line within the time originally contemplated. Further time was to be allowed for payment of the calls on the Alston Branch shares, and it was proposed that the call payable

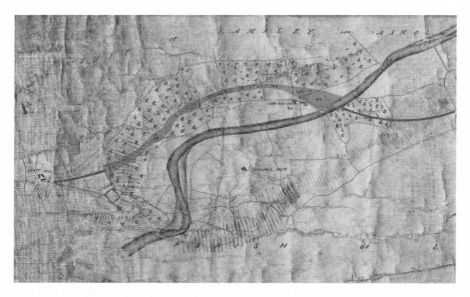

Undated map, probably 1847, showing the first proposed modification of the Alston branch at Lambley. The new route, mostly north of the river, was to leave the authorised route just north of Shafthill Farm and not cross the South Tyne until a short distance south of Waughold Holme. Reproduced by permission of J. M. Clark & Partners.

on 21 April be postponed till 21 June 1848. On 13 April 1848, *Herepath's Journal* reported that the Alston Branch shares were selling in Newcastle at a premium of £3,[291] while 'A Correspondent' provided him with the following information which was published in the issue of 20 May 1848: 'The (N&CR) shares have fluctuated a good deal … this is caused by parties selling their old £100 shares to buy the Alston £40 paid, which are £9 premium".[292]

The story now becomes rather more complicated as both the Newcastle and Carlisle and the Maryport and Carlisle railways had been leased, officially by the York, Newcastle, and Berwick Railway (YN&BR), but in reality by George Hudson himself,[301] although this proved to be only a temporary situation. Eventually, a modified route along the South Tyne Valley was agreed, which included a connection to the LCR, and *Herepath's Journal* was able to report on 25 November 1848 that the N&CR had applied to Parliament for a bill 'To make deviations in the Alston branch, and also in the branch line from the Alston branch, and to make a branch therefrom; also to extend time for the completion of the works.'[302] Plans, sections and books of reference were deposited with the various justices of the peace[303] and at the Private Bill Office.[304]

The bill started its passage through Parliament in February 1849, being given a first reading[307] on the 5th and a second[311] on the 13th. Also before Parliament at this time was a bill to allow the YN&BR to lease, or amalgamate with, the N&CR.[311] Concern was expressed in February 1849 over the £150,000 it was said to cost to relay the Newcastle and Carlisle line with heavier rail, which had to be carried out immediately.[308] Despite the progress of the amalgamation bill, *Herepath's Journal* reported at the beginning of March that it was expected that the agreement to lease the N&CR would soon be cancelled.[310] A special meeting of the Newcastle and Carlisle Railway Company, held on 27 March 1849, sanctioned the Alston Branch Bill, but requested that the clauses relating to amalgamation be removed from the leasing bill.[312] The Alston Branch Bill continued to make steady progress through Parliament, being given its third reading in the House of Commons on 30 April 1849,[313] and concluding its passage through the House of Lords on 3 July 1849,[316] with the Royal Assent being granted on 13 July 1849.[317] Shortly after this the railway commissioners reported against the amalgamation scheme,[319] and that bill was lost at the end of July.[320]

We shall now look at the alterations authorised to be made to the 1846 Nenthead branch by the 1849 Act.[317] The plans of the deviations are in four sections.[303] Two sections of the original route in Northumberland, and the bulk of the line in Cumberland, were to be replaced by new alignments. Between Haltwhistle and Alston a total of 7 miles (11.26km) was to be replaced by 7¾ miles (12.47km) of new line, while the final 4¾ miles (7.64km) from Alston to Nenthead were to be abandoned. In addition, a branch of 1½ miles (2.41km) was authorised to connect the Alston branch with LCR at Halton Lea Gate. These plans and sections were drawn to the much larger scale of 1 inch = 5 chains. Although the plans of the three deviations show both the 1846 or parliamentary route, as it is called in the text of the 1849 act, and the 1848 proposals, the limits of deviation are only given for the 1848 line. At the end of the plan for deviation 1, at both the start and finish of the plan for deviation 2, and at the start of the plan for deviation 3, it is stated: 'Junction with Parliamentary line at the authorised level.' Unfortunately, the parliamentary line is neither shown beyond the ends of each deviation, nor is the distance by it from Haltwhistle given, so the exact points at which each section of deviation commenced or terminated on the 1845 plans have to be worked out from the information on the 1848 plans.

We will now look at each of the deviations from the parliamentary route, including the 'branch of the branch', and follow this with an account of the construction of the branch from contemporary reports. Finally the entire route authorised by the 1849 Act will be compared with what was actually built. This last point is particularly important in several places, particularly between Lambley and Gilderdale, where there were significant deviations from the plans as originally authorised by the two acts.

The First Deviation covered the initial section of the branch where most of the 1 in 49½ gradient was reduced to 1 in 70 or 80. This was achieved by moving the junction from the west to the east end of Haltwhistle station, giving a connection facing Carlisle instead of Newcastle and increasing the distance by ½ mile (800m). The price for this change was the introduction of some severe curvature; the earthworks were reduced, but still remained extensive. The viaduct over South Tyne was 145 yards (133m) long with four arches 30ft (9.1m) high and 42ft

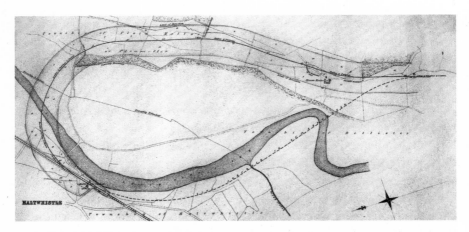

Plan showing the first deviation of the Alston branch with the junction moved from the west to the east end of Haltwhistle station. The broken line shows the 1846 or parliamentary route. Reproduced by permission of CAS.

Looking through the northern arch, and the intermediate arches of the viaduct at Haltwhistle, to the blank wall at the southern end. This is the southern arch which was rebuilt in 1853 after being destroyed by flood damage shortly after Lambley viaduct was finally completed, allowing the branch to be opened throughout. The N&CR was authorised to build the viaduct to carry both road and rail traffic, and the central spaces in the arches may have been originally intended for a roadway.

(12.8m) wide, and two arches 25ft (7.6m) high and 25ft wide, at a maximum height above the river of 48ft (14.6m).

An embankment, 53ft (16.2m) high, carried the line across the flood plain, while the curvature took it through 180°. This first deviation was 1 mile 6 furlongs 3 chains (2.9km) long, and replaced a distance of 1 mile 2 furlongs 1 chain (2km) of the parliamentary route, and although the gradients remained severe, they were easier than on the original route. The deviation also allowed the line to serve the then relatively new Plenmeller Colliery (p. 102) and eliminated the viaduct over the river Tipalt.

The 1845 plan (p. 89) was then followed for 1 mile 1 furlong 8½ chains (2km) before the second deviation commenced, 2½ chains (50m) south of the road from Featherstone Castle, and 2 miles 3 furlongs 9½ chains (4km) from Haltwhistle by the parliamentary route, but 3 miles 1½ chains (4.9km) when the first deviation is taken into account. It is possible that this section of the alignment authorised in 1846 was retained because enough work had actually been carried out over it

Plenmeller Colliery and halt. Ken Hoole collection, reproduced by permission of the HoS-DRM.

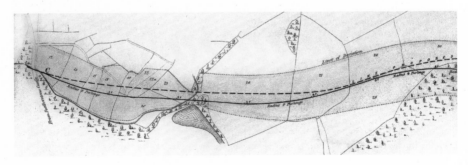

The start of the second deviation of the 1848 plans, showing the rather crude junction between the 1845 and 1848 alignments south of Featherstone station and the altered crossing of the South Tyne. Reproduced by permission of CAS.

to make it financially more acceptable to use the original route than to alter it, although there does not appear to be any documentary evidence in support of this theory.

There are discrepancies between what is shown on the 1845 and 1848 plans, and as we saw earlier that the survey for the original Nenthead branch was inaccurate in places, it is reasonable to assume that the 1848 plans are more likely to be correct.

The new plans took the line over the South Tyne on a section of level at a different angle and in a slightly different place to the 1845 plans, with the

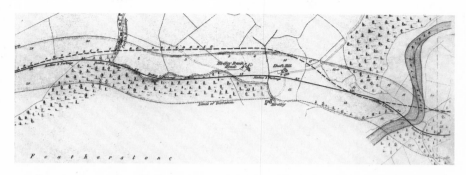

The second deviation of the 1848 plans, showing the approach to the altered crossing of the South Tyne. Reproduced by permission of CAS.

Lambley viaduct over the river South Tyne, showing the curve of 10 chains radius, after the branch to Lambley Colliery had closed. The viaduct was restored by the North Pennines Heritage Trust and is now owned by the South Tynedale Railway Preservation Society. This viaduct is the only length of the branch built for single track. Reproduced by permission of NCS.

gradients altered to eliminate the drop towards the viaduct, although the Herdley Burn was still crossed on an embankment 53ft (16.2m) high (p. 104).

The plans showed that Lambley viaduct was to have 24 arches of 20ft (6.1m) span, with a maximum height above the river South Tyne of 100ft (30m).

Immediately across the South Tyne, almost 2 furlongs (380m) of left-hand curve, of only 1 furlong (200m) radius, took the new line through more than 90°. Not only was Lambley station to be built on this severe curve but the branch to LCR was to diverge from the main line on the curve, just north of the passenger platform. It should be remembered that a left-hand curve of only 1 furlong radius was also to be found on the parliamentary line, but it started about 100 yards south of the river crossing and was significantly shorter.

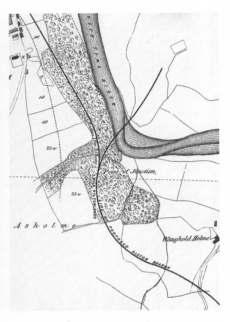

Embankment carrying the N&CR branch over the Herdley Burn on the north side of Lambley viaduct, north of Coanwood station. This section was built by Cowan, Marshall & Ridley using the plans of Peter Tate, who designed embankments with culverts over the side streams.

Section of 1848 plan with the viaduct over the South Tyne at Lambley and the junction of the branch to Lord Carlisle's Railway. Lambley station was situated on the bend immediately south of the junction. Reproduced by permission of CAS.

From Lambley to Burnstones the curvature on the new route was more severe than on the line it replaced. The new route remained east of the parliamentary line all the way to the end of the deviation, with the distance separating the two lines varying from 50 yards (45m) to almost one furlong (200m).

From Lambley to Softly, there are some discrepancies between the different N&CR surveys, but the alignment proposed in 1848 was very similar to that of the WVER.[198] The WVER route converged with the N&CR close to where the parliamentary route crossed the deviation, and diverged before Softly, remaining on the west of the deviation until just before the old and new alignments united.

The Glendue Burn was to be crossed on an embankment 91ft (28m) high and 150 yards nearer to the river than the parliamentary line.

The new alignment took the line much closer to Softly Farm than the 1846 plans.

There are few details given on the plans for the site of what is today Burnstones viaduct. No enlarged cross-sections of the road or river crossings

View looking north from Lambley station. The route is set to the right, for the main line over Lambley viaduct. The line to the left is the branch to Lambley Colliery, where it originally connected with Lord Carlisle's Railway. The locomotive is waiting to take coal wagons from the colliery to the N&CR main line at Haltwhistle. Ken Hoole collection, reproduced by permission of the HoS-DRM.

The 1848 line past Waughold Holm and Low Ash Holm. Compare this with the 1847 map which had the branch on the east side of the river at this point. Reproduced by permission of CAS.

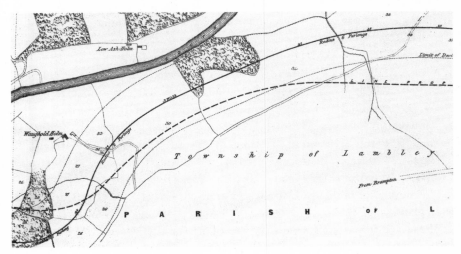

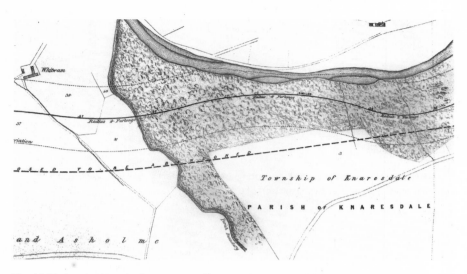

The 1848 plan showing the line crossing Glendue Burn, with 1845 alignment, in places, outside the 1848 limits of deviation. Reproduced by permission of CAS.

Viaduct over the Glendue Burn. The section at this point indicates that the crossing was designed as an embankment with a culvert at the bottom for the waters of the stream to flow through, similar to the Herdley Burn shown on page 104. This was the first of six viaducts built in place of embankments over tributary streams.

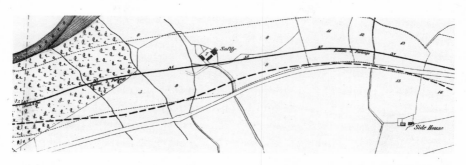

The 1848 plans showing the second deviation past Softly avoiding the level crossing of the turnpike road. Reproduced by permission of CAS.

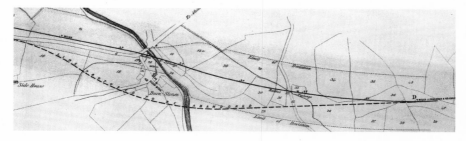

The 1848 plans showing the end of the second deviation past Burnstones with the 1845 alignment much further south. Reproduced by permission of CAS.

are given, while printed on the section is 'Turnpike road one arch 35ft span 16ft high, level unaltered'.

The deviation was 4 miles 5 furlongs 8½ chains (7.6km) long, and replaced a section which was approximately 7½ chains (150m) shorter. The loss of height on the parliamentary line, caused by the drop to the centre of Lambley viaduct was avoided, while the deviation reduced the maximum gradients north of the viaduct from 1 in 79 to 1 in 100, and from 1 in 60 to 1 in 128.78 to the south. However, the curvature on the deviation was more severe and, while the heights of all but one of the major embankments were reduced, in general the earthworks were more extensive, although there was a better relationship between the volume to be extracted from the cuttings and the quantities of fill required for the embankments. The parliamentary line was then followed from Merry Knowe for the next 4 miles 9½ chains (6.6km), which included the length containing several discrepancies between the plans and sections of 1845.

The third, and final, deviation commenced 11 miles (17.7km) from Haltwhistle by the parliamentary line, at a point north-east of Howgillrigg, 1½ furlongs (300m) after the line entered the county of Cumberland. In reality, this deviation was a completely new section of railway, because although the parliamentary line was crossed shortly before the final viaduct over the South Tyne, the remaining part of the route authorised in 1846 was to be abandoned.

Just north of the South Tyne, the new route intersected the parliamentary line and crossed the river 50 yards upstream of, and at a different angle to, the original plans. This last viaduct over the South Tyne was to be built of three arches, each of 30ft (9.1m) span and 29ft 6in (9m) above the water and it was half a mile from the terminus, which was close to the bridge carrying the Alston to Hexham turnpike, today's A686, over the river Nent at Alston Town Foot. The length of this final section of the main branch was 1 mile 2 furlongs 9¼ chains (2.2km). The new terminus was some distance south-west of the probable site for the

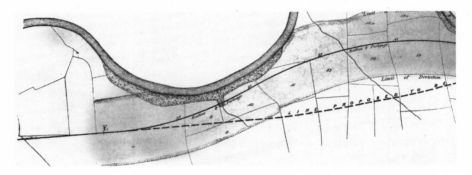

Start of the final deviation of 1848. Most of the authorised route in Cumberland was abandoned or replaced. The first part of the new route kept closer to the river South Tyne to avoid the bulk of the severe earthworks which would otherwise have been required. Reproduced by permission of CAS.

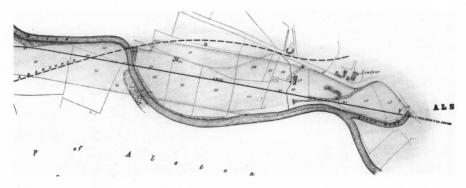

The end of the final deviation of 1848. The new terminus was beside the river Nent in Alston and the route is shown running straight from a little north of the viaduct over the river South Tyne, although most of the line built south of the viaduct is a series of reverse curves. Reproduced by permission of CAS.

through passenger station on the parliamentary line, it was also several feet lower and more convenient for the town of Alston.

Not only was the heavily graded section to Nenthead abandoned by the 1849 Act, the situation of the new terminus virtually precluded the construction, at a later date, of any direct extension of the line up the valleys of either the rivers Nent or South Tyne. The new line rose 497ft 4in (152m) from Haltwhistle and, according to the plans, the total length of the branch from Haltwhistle to Alston was 13 miles 1 furlong 8¾ chains (21.3km), of which 7 miles 7 furlongs and ¾ chain (12.7km) was new route, authorised by the Act of 1849, while only 5 miles 2 furlongs 8 chains (8.6km) remained from the route authorised by the Act of 1846. On balance, the new line would be easier to operate, with the gradients generally less severe, while the difficult section to Nenthead was abandoned. The heaviest of the earthworks were also reduced although the curvature was definitely more severe.

In addition to the alterations to the main branch, the 1849 Act also authorised a 'branch of the branch' from Lambley to the terminus of LCR at Halton Lea Gate. This branch diverged from the main branch, in a northerly direction, 100 yards from the west bank of the South Tyne, at a point 4 miles 5 furlongs ½ chain (7.6km) from Haltwhistle.

The branch was designed with a minimum of earthworks and with some very severe curvature. The branch was level at the start, then rose, first at 1 in 80 before easing to 1 in 165.

The line became level just before it crossed the section of LCR serving Thompson's Hartleyburn Colliery to the north of the branch railway. The two lines then ran side-by-side to the terminus of the branch, while the gradient changed to 1 in 82½ up for the final 3 furlongs (600m). The branch was 1 mile 4 furlongs 5 chains (2.5km) long, while the terminus was on land belonging to

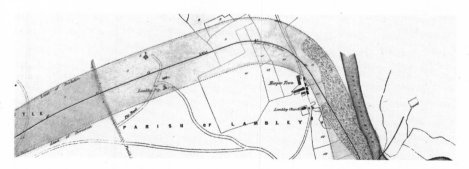

Plan of the branch from Lambley Junction to Halton Lea Gate as it passed Lambley Pit. The section from Halton Lea Gate to Lambley Colliery was built as part of Lord Carlisle's Railway, but was out of use by the early 1900s. Reproduced by permission of CAS.

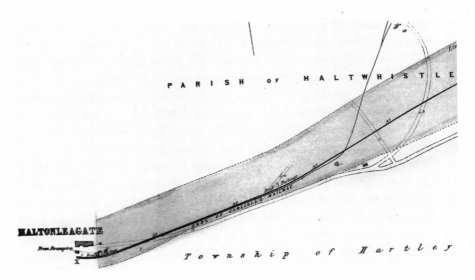

Terminus of the branch from Halton Lea Gate to Lambley Junction. As far as Lambley Pit the line was built as part of Lord Carlisle's Railway. Reproduced by permission of CAS.

LCR, alongside the buildings provided by Thompson at Halton Lea Gate to serve Hartleyburn township.

In addition to authorising the deviations to the Alston branch, the N&CR Act of 13 July 1849 granted a range of powers to the company, imposing certain new restrictions, but relaxing others.[317] The company was allowed three years to purchase the land required, during which time they had also to complete the railway and all the associated works. Compensation was to be made to all persons with whom contracts had already been entered into, or if notice had been given by the company for purchasing any lands on the sections of line to be abandoned. Clause 8 of the act authorised the company, if they so wished, to construct the bridge over the river South Tyne at Haltwhistle in such a manner as to include a public roadway, while clause 9 specified the tolls which could be charged for the use of this road by horse-drawn vehicles, foot passengers and animals. The requirement, included in the original act, forbidding the company to open any part of the branch before the entire section from Haltwhistle to Alston had been completed was repealed.

Although their railway was being worked by Mr Allport, the manager of the YN&BR, on behalf of George Hudson the N&CR Directors were responsible for maintaining the line and building the Alston branch.[323] On 1 September 1849 the N&CR advertised for large quantities of permanent way materials,[322] while on 25 October the shareholders of the YN&BR Company were told that they should not contemplate leasing the N&CR due to the large outlay required to relay the main line and complete the Alston branch.[323] At a meeting of the N&CR shareholders, held on 7 November 1849, the offer from Hudson to give up the lease of their railway from 31 December 1849 was accepted.[324]

Meanwhile work on the branch was progressing, with the staking out completed by 1 November 1849,[411] with the meeting being told that between £60,000 and £70,000 had been already spent on it. Thus, on 1 January 1850, the working of the railway reverted to the company's own board of directors,[329] who then proceeded to inject a much greater degree of vigour into the construction of the Alston branch. Also at the half yearly meeting of the N&CR, started on 28 March 1850, the chairman, Matthew Plummer, was able to report that 'Very serious attention has been paid by the Directors to the formation of the Alston branch; the works are progressing, and negotiations are and have been going on with the proprietors of the land required, many have been arranged with to the satisfaction of the Directors, and without the necessity of any appeal to a jury.'[329] He also announced that a bill had been introduced to raise more money, which the Directors estimated would be required to complete the Central station in Newcastle, and the Alston branch, on which £56,320 17s 7d (£56,320.88) had already been spent. This Newcastle and Carlisle Amendment Bill had already started its passage through Parliament and received its first reading in the House of Commons on 5 February 1850.[328]

The adjourned half-yearly meeting was continued on 1 May 1850 when it was announced that 'The contract for the unfinished portion of the Alston branch is let to Rush and Lawton at £60,000.'[332] The Newcastle and Carlisle Amendment Bill made steady progress through Parliament and the act received the Royal Assent on 29 July 1850.[333] The main purpose of this act was to permit the N&CR to raise a further sum of £150,000. In addition, there was also clause XIII which allowed the Vicar of Alston to sell and convey to the railway company land belonging to the vicarage required by the company for the purposes of the Newcastle-upon-Tyne and Carlisle (Alston branch) Railway Act 1849, in consideration of a perpetual annual rent-charge.

At the Annual General Meeting of the N&CR held on 28 March 1851 it was announced: 'The line from Haltwhistle to near Lambley, about four miles, is now finished and is already used for the carriage of minerals and goods. It will be opened for passengers as soon as it shall have been surveyed and approved by the officer of the railway commissioners.'[348] It was also stated that another £115,230 16s 11d (£115,230.85) would be required to complete the Alston branch, that the viaduct across the South Tyne at Lambley was the only major work remaining, and that the remainder of the line to Alston would be completed before the end of the year. On 7 May 1851 the adjourned AGM agreed to create 1,500 shares of £100 each, with a preferential dividend of 4 per cent, to raise the money required to complete the branch.[349]

The end of the line at Alston; a typical train arriving from Haltwhistle after nationalisation. Gresley J39 0-6-0 locomotives were regularly used on the branch in the 1950s. The building on the right exists but the overall roof, the engine shed and other buildings have gone and the area on the left is now a car park. Photographed by the late Arthur Chambers.

At the beginning of June, Matthew Plummer, who was in his 80th year, resigned as chairman of the N&CR after eighteen years in office[351] and, on Wednesday 18 June 1851, James Losh, Esq., whose father had been the first chairman of the company, was unanimously elected chairman.[352] A report to a committee meeting held on 9 July stated that the inspecting officer had gone over the line on the 8th,[353] and the following week it was announced that, the licence having been obtained, the Alston branch would be opened on Saturday 2 August.[354] On 31 July 1851 the directors circulated an advertisement in the local press asking for sealed tenders for the erection of stations, coal depots, etc. on the Alston branch, to be received by 18 August.[355]

A long article appeared in the *Newcastle Journal* for 13 September 1851 describing an inspection of the works by the directors.[356] According to the paper, work on the branch had commenced in June 1849. The party travelled the 4¼ miles (6.8km) to Shafthill, which had been open for some time, by special train and first inspected Lambley viaduct on which construction had only recently commenced, as the company had been awaiting the arrival of the tracks to bring in the necessary materials. Although only some of the piers had been completed, a pathway had been constructed for passengers along the scaffolding. Unlike the other viaducts which had been constructed for double track, Lambley Viaduct was stated to be only 13ft wide and would carry only a single track. From Lambley to Alston the party travelled in ballast wagons with planks for seats, drawn by two horses. Apart from Gilderdale, the other viaducts on the branch had been completed, although the position for a station to serve the Slaggyford and Burnstones area had not been decided. The report noted that the works on the line were necessarily heavy, with a total of forty bridges required.

Two further adverts from the N&CR appeared in the local press in October 1851. The first, at the beginning of the month stated: 'On weekdays an omnibus leaves Alston at 5.50 a.m., arriving at Haltwhistle at 7.9 a.m. The omnibus returns from Shafthill on the arrival of the 1.30 p.m. train from Newcastle and the 2.45 p.m. from Carlisle, arriving at Alston about 5.30 p.m.'[358] The second, at the end of the month, gave the times of trains from Newcastle to Carlisle, but there was no mention of the Alston branch.[359] According to Tomlinson,[773] the branch was opened to Shafthill (Coanwood) for goods in March, and for passengers on 19 July 1851, although the company's minute books state that the line was to be opened on Saturday 2 August.[354] According to the contemporary diary of Joseph

Looking north at Alston station around 1900. The station building and passenger platform is on the left and the goods shed is on the right. An NER Fletcher 0-4-4 BPT is arriving with a train from Haltwhistle. A horse-drawn vehicle is waiting to take passengers to Nenthead. Reproduced by permission of Robin Walton.

Pearson, an Alston resident, a railway-operated road coach started running three times a week from Alston to Harper town (Lambley) on 8 August 1851.[411]

The 9 miles (14.5km) of line from Lambley Colliery to Alston was opened for goods on 5 January 1852, the ¾ mile (1.2km) from Halton Lea Gate to Lambley Colliery having been opened as the final eastward extension of LCR in 1849.[750a] Pearson's diary[411] and the Carlisle[362] and Newcastle[361] papers give accounts of the opening for goods traffic which would not have been inappropriate as a ceremony for the commencement of passenger services, and included the distribution of coal to the poor.

The information provided by various adverts in the local press indicate that passenger trains started using the section from Alston to Lambley some time before Lambley viaduct was completed. On 30 January 1852 an advertisement appeared similar to that in October stating that on weekdays an omnibus left Alston at 6.35 a.m., arriving at Haltwhistle at 8.13 a.m.[363] The omnibus returned from Shafthill on the arrival of the 1.20 p.m. train from Newcastle and the 2.40 p.m. train from Carlisle, arriving at Alston about 5.30 p.m.

At the Annual General Meeting, held in March 1852, it was stated that in 1851 £61,880 had been spent on the Alston branch, and it was expected to complete it for another £50,023 12s 6d (£50,023.62½).[364] It was also announced that the branch was open at both ends and Lambley viaduct was expected to be completed in the autumn, allowing the whole line to be opened. The chairman

Slaggyford station and signal box looking north from the road crossing. Ken Hoole collection, reproduced by permission of HoS-DRM.

promised that trains would run on Sundays to Alston, just as on the main line. Another advertisement, on 23 April 1852, gave the times of the trains between Newcastle and Carlisle, but did not mention the Alston branch.[365] Two weeks later a new timetable for the Alston branch was published stating that on weekdays an omnibus left Alston at 6.15 a.m., arriving at Shafthill in time for the train leaving at 7.15 a.m. and arriving at Haltwhistle at 8.13 a.m.[366] The omnibus returned from Shafthill on the arrival of the 1.20 p.m. train from Newcastle and the 2.40 p.m. train from Carlisle, arriving at Alston about 5.30 p.m. At this time it was clear that passenger trains were running between Shafthill and Haltwhistle, but not between Alston and Lambley.

The following week it was announced that an agreement had been made with the British Electric Telegraph Company to establish a telegraph line between Newcastle and Carlisle and along the Alston branch.[367] According to Pearson's diary, on 14 May 1852, the 'Government Inspector' visited the line from Lambley to Alston, which was then opened for passenger traffic on Friday 21 May 1852.[411] On 18 June 1852 an advertisement for excursions to Carlisle races on 29 June to 1 July showed that trains were indeed now running from Aston itself, as it was stated that 'return tickets will be issued on the Alston Branch by the 7.20 a.m. train each day, available for return by the 5.15 p.m. train on either Tuesday, Wednesday or Thursday.'[369] The *Newcastle Chronicle* of 23 July 1852 advertised a cheap excursion train on Monday 26 July, leaving Newcastle for Alston at 6.45 a.m. returning from Alston at 5 p.m. and arriving in Newcastle about 8.15 p.m.[370] The return fares were 5s first, 4s second and 3s third.

Another timetable, also published in the *Newcastle Chronicle*, indicated that trains were running regularly, from Haltwhistle at 8.50 a.m. and 6.20 p.m., and from Alston at 7.20 a.m. and 5 p.m.[371] A further excursion was advertised from Newcastle to Alston for Saturday 28 August,[372] while the morning train for Alston was re-timed to leave at 8.55 a.m.[373] From the beginning of January 1853, the timetable was altered again, with trains from Haltwhistle at 8.42 a.m. and 6.20 p.m. and from Alston at 6.50 a.m. and 4.30 p.m.[375] By this time trains were running right through, the Alston branch having been opened throughout on 17 November 1852.[377]

An article written in 1912 stated that the viaduct was not opened until 1854, and that passengers were required to alight at Coanwood and make their own way to join the train at Lambley.[790] However, the statement made to the AGM on 17 March 1853 says quite specifically that 'The Alston branch was opened throughout on 17 November 1852, parts of it having been previously used,[377] while at the previous AGM it had been stated that the Alston branch was opened at both ends and Lambley viaduct was expected to be completed in the autumn,[364] allowing the whole line to be opened. We have seen that in September 1851 there was a footpath over the scaffolding on Lambley viaduct, while from 21 May 1852 until the viaduct was completed, trains were running from Alston to Lambley, and from Shafthill (Coanwood) to Haltwhistle. Therefore, although the article was correct in suggesting that passenger trains did operate in two sections for a period before the viaduct was completed, the date of 17 November 1852 for the opening of the viaduct is also correct. It would appear that not only was LCR used to take the freight traffic to and from Alston during most of 1852, but it was also used to take a locomotive and carriages to Alston. According to Pearson's diary the locomotive was *Carlisle*,[411] a six-wheeled engine built by Thompson Brothers and delivered to the N&CR in June 1837.[706]

The line as actually built differs from the line as represented on the plans, particularly in regard to the section from Lambley to Gilderdale, with the number of viaducts constructed greatly exceeding the number in the plans. A short distance from the junction with the main line the South Tyne is crossed on a viaduct that became known as Alston Arches. According to the section, this viaduct was to have six arches with a maximum span of 42ft (12.8m). Although it does have six arches, the maximum span is 53ft (16.2m). Unlike most of the larger tributary valleys south of Lambley, embankments were used to cross the Park and Herdley burns, with culverts to carry the water. According to the sections, Lambley viaduct was supposed to be 190 yards (174m) long and have twenty-four arches, each with a span of 20ft (6.1m), whereas it is actually 290 yards (265m) long and has eighteen arches.[792] There are nine arches, each 58ft (17.7m) wide, taking the line across the river itself, plus seven arches, each 20ft (6.1m) wide, three to the north and four to the south of the massive thrust blocks on each side of the main river spans, in which were incorporated 12ft (3.7m) wide arches. Unlike the remainder of the branch, all of which was built for double track, Lambley viaduct is only 12ft wide.

In the next 7 miles (11.3km), six viaducts were built over tributaries of the South Tyne, none of which were indicated on the sections produced either in 1845 or in 1848. The reason for the differences in the way the northern and southern sections of the branch were built is probably due to different engineers being involved with the details of each part. We have seen that the plans and specifications from Haltwhistle to Shafthill were produced in 1847, presumably under the direction of Peter Tate, the N&CR's engineer, and the contracts for this section were let on 10 May 1847. By the time the second act was passed, in 1849, the N&CR was committed to relaying the main line with heavier rail and as he was fully engaged in this activity, Tate was unable to undertake the management of the building of the Alston branch.[325] Two weeks later Mr J. T. Harrison, who had been employed in making the 1848 survey, was appointed as engineer in charge of the Alston branch.[326] The plans and specifications from Shafthill to Alston, including Lambley viaduct were therefore produced by Harrison and the three separate contracts were let to Rush & Lawton. The details of the contracts include all the viaducts as built, although Whitley viaduct is described as a three-arch bridge.[340]

However, more changes were to come as, at the end of 1850, Harrison requested to leave his employment and was replaced by the resident engineer for the recently completed Royal Border bridge at Berwick, Mr George Barclay Bruce.[337] Finally, in November 1851, Mr Bruce obtained an appointment in India and Mr Charlton was appointed engineer to complete the Alston branch.[360] From all these changes in supervising engineer it is not surprising that the Alston branch shows so many different styles.

After Lambley, the Glendue Burn came first, with a viaduct of five arches replacing the embankment shown on the 1848 section. This was followed by the unusual Burnstones viaduct over both the turnpike road and the Thinhope Burn. Only the first arch over the turnpike is shown on the 1848 section. This arch is skewed in one direction, while the remaining arches over the valley of the burn are skewed in the opposite direction. In fact, the intermediate arch is a V, blind at the eastern side of the structure. The Knar Burn, stated to be a rivulet in the 1845 book of reference, and the Thornhope Burn at Lintley are each crossed with viaducts of four arches which replace the embankments shown on the 1845 section, and from Lintley the line rises at up to 1 in 56 for almost a mile. Shortly after the gradient eases, the small, but deep Whitley viaduct of three arches takes the line over the Lort Burn, whereas the 1845 section shows the burn going over the railway. One of the few long straight sections on the branch takes the line to the high three-arch Gilderdale viaduct, again replacing an embankment shown on the 1845 plans. The final viaduct over the South Tyne was in the sections, and has three arches as shown.

In addition to the six extra viaducts, the gradients south of Slaggyford bear no relationship to those on the 1845 plans, while the branch follows a relatively sinuous course from the South Tyne to the terminus, although the 1848 plans show it running straight over the last 5½ furlongs (1.1km). Finally, several of the roads to the larger farms, which are shown crossing the line on the level, were provided with bridges. In their report to the Annual General Meeting held on Thursday 17 March 1853,[376] the directors stated that the Alston branch had cost £205,027 to build, which was within the £200,000 to £210,000 estimate made to the shareholders in 1846[229] and £58,500 less than the figure of £263,534 given to Parliament[242] for the original Nenthead branch, although that line would have been about 4 miles longer. The line which was eventually built served the town of Alston well, providing all-year-round transport from 5 January 1852 until 1 May 1976. We shall look at the later fortunes of this branch in Chapter 14.

7

AMALGAMATION AND FINANCIAL RESTRUCTURING WITHIN THE STOCKTON AND DARLINGTON GROUP OF RAILWAYS

We saw in Chapter 3 that, although the WVR deposited plans for the WVER with the required authorities in 1845,[203] the project was not pursued into the 1846 parliamentary session, at least partly due to the cost of the project.[208] At the end of August 1846 it was announced that due to the increase in the value of labour and materials, the WVR was likely to exceed the original estimate, and the authorised loan of £27,300 was to be raised by the issue of new shares.[241] Next, at the general meeting of the BA&WR it was stated that 'the unforeseen expenses which were incurred in the formation of the line, and the amount of capital requisite for perfecting those arrangements which a rapidly extending traffic have already called for'[246], required the company to broaden the basis of its capital. It was therefore resolved to amalgamate with the neighbouring lines. Similar resolutions were carried at a meeting held subsequently of the S&DR Company. On 5 December 1846, *Herepath's Journal*[248] announced that a bill was to be introduced in Parliament to allow the Bishop Auckland and Weardale, Weardale Extension, Wear and Derwent, and Shildon Tunnel railway companies to amalgamate with the WVR, which was to be allowed 'to raise a further sum of money'. Special meetings of the WVR and BA&WR companies approved the bill,[260] which was unopposed[267] and received the Royal Assent on 22 July 1847.[269]

The act incorporating the BA&WR had authorised that company to build the entire line from the junction with the S&DR at Shildon to Crook,[62] including Shildon Tunnel but, as we saw in Chapter 3, the tunnel section was constructed by the Shildon subcommittee of the S&DR. According to Jeans,[740] there was a

Southern entrance to Shildon Tunnel after the line through it had been singled. Ken Hoole collection, reproduced by permission of HoS-DRM.

separate 'Shildon Tunnel Company', composed of the proprietors of the Stockton and Middlesbrough Railway, another organisation which did not actually exist. In fact, the first clause of the WVR Act of 1847 states that the Weardale Extension, Wear and Derwent, and Shildon Tunnel railway companies were owned by a group of proprietors of the S&DR.[269] Joseph Pease, Thomas Meynell, Henry Stobart, John Castell Hopkins and Henry Pease were stated as being the owners of the W&DR, which was that part of the former S&TR from Stanhope to Carrhouse (Consett) originally purchased by the Derwent Iron Company, who then sold it on. Joseph Pease, Thomas Meynell and John Castell Hopkins were owners of the WER, which was the line built for the Derwent Iron Company to connect their W&DR, from Meeting Slacks (Waskerley) at the head of Nanny Mayor's incline in the township of Muggleswick, to the BA&WR by a junction at Crook; while Joseph Pease, Thomas Meynell and Henry Stobart were the owners of the Shildon Tunnel Railway.

While the Act authorising the purchase of the connected lines was being obtained, construction of the WVR progressed steadily, with the secretary, Mr MacNay, able to announce that he expected the line to be opened before the next half-yearly meeting.[255] The act incorporating the company had authorised capital of £82,000 and borrowing of up to £27,300,[145] although this had been raised as shares. At the date of the meeting £89,403 4s 2d (£89,403.21) had been received and £80,403 1s 2d (£80,403.06) spent. The line was inspected and approved on Monday 2 August 1847 by Captain Coddrington, allowing the directors to open it the following day. The party headed by the chairman, Thomas Meynell, left Darlington at noon and travelled first along the S&DR to Shildon, then along the BA&WR to Witton Junction, before proceeding along the WVR to Wolsingham and Frosterley, where they arrived at about 1.45 p.m. They returned to Wolsingham at 2.30 p.m., where dinner was provided by the Black Bull Inn with about sixty gentlemen sitting down.[275] In addition to the engineer, John Dixon, and the secretary, Thomas MacNay, several directors of the S&DR attended.

After the formal business at the half-yearly meeting of the WVR on 31 August 1847, the meeting was declared special and resolutions were passed authorising the purchase of the Shildon Tunnel, Bishop Auckland & Weardale, and the Wear and Derwent Junction railway companies.[279] The capital required for these purchases was £674,650 and was to be raised by the issue of 26,986 shares of £25 each, although up to £168,668 of this could be raised by mortgage rather than shares once three-quarters of the £674,672 capital authorised had been subscribed and half paid up.[269] Each of the proprietors was to take two new

Looking towards Tow Law station on the route avoiding the Sunniside incline, which curves to the right, with the original route of the Weardale Extension Railway to the head of Sunniside incline going more or less straight ahead, taken on 7 April 1956. Ken Hoole collection, reproduced by permission of the HoS-DRM.

shares for every original share, with the calls spread over a period of five years, at the discretion of the directors. Arrangements had also been agreed to lease the railways thus amalgamated to the Stockton and Darlington Railway Company, for a term of twenty-one years, at a dividend of 6 per cent per annum.

The previous day, at a special meeting of the BA&WR, the shareholders had resolved to sell their line to the WVR.[280] A series of railway meetings was held on the same day in Darlington, at which the Middlesbrough and Redcar (M&RR) and the amalgamated WVR agreed to lease their lines to the S&DR with effect from 1 October 1847, while the S&DR agreed to take the leases.[281] The S&DR was to pay an annual rental of £47,037, less income tax, to the WVR which was equivalent to 6 per cent on the old and new share capital of the WVR, provided the S&DR spent a sum not exceeding £60,000 improving the leased lines during the next seven years. The first call of £5 on the new shares was made on 1 October.[282] In practice, this huge sum which the WVR was required to raise absorbed all the spare capital available in the region, curtailing further extensions up the Wear Valley during the remaining independent life of the S&DR to the tiny F&SR. A further call of £1 5s (£1.25) was made, due on 1 February,[286] and at the half-yearly meeting, held on 25 February 1848,[288] the directors reported that the whole of the arrangements of the amalgamation act were now satisfactorily completed.

In the railway share lists published in *Herepath's Journal*,[305] the WVR first appears at the beginning of April 1848, where there were stated to be 2,186 shares of £50 each with £42 15s (£42.75) paid up and 2,880 shares of £25 with £25 paid up, both with a guaranteed dividend of 6 per cent. The face value of the £50 shares was £109,300, being the sum of the share and loan capital authorised by the original WVR Act. The £72,000 value of the £25 shares was the capital authorised by the BA&WR Act. No price was shown for the £50 shares, but the £25 shares were quoted at £27 10s (£27.50) to £27. It was not until 10 June that the share list stated that there were 24,106 shares of £25 with £6 5s (£6.25) paid up, of which the London price was £8 5s (£8.25). These new £25 shares represented £602,650 of the £674,672 capital authorised by the act of 1847. On 17 June the £25 shares had £7 15s (£7.75) paid up, with a dividend of 6 per cent guaranteed.

On 26 August another call of £2 5s (£2.25) was made on the £25 shares,[295] to be paid by two instalments, £1 5s (£1.25) on 1 September and £1 on 1 November 1848, making £10 per share paid. The price of these shares rose to £10 2s 6d (£10.22), while the paid-up £25 shares reached £27 17s 6d (£27.87). On 16 September the £50 shares were fully paid up. The prices continued to rise, with the £50 shares being worth £55, the new £25 shares reaching £12 10s to £12 12s 6d (£12.50 to £12.62), and the paid-up £25 shares no less than £28 5s to £28 10s (£28.25 to £28.50) by the end of December 1848.

During 1849 two further calls were made on the new £25 shares. The first, of £2 10s (£2.50) was to be paid by Monday 26 February,[306] while the second, also of £2 10s (£2.50) was due on 10 July.[314] At the half-yearly general meeting in February, it was announced that the cost of completing the WVR itself would be about £160,000. While this exceeded the authorised capital, the average cost of this section of the S&DR group was about £13,500 per mile, which was considered satisfactory in comparison with other lines.[309]

At around this time the difficult and uncertain financial position of the S&DR itself became apparent and the company applied to Parliament for an act to dissolve the original company, incorporate a new company, and legalise its financial situation. The original company had been authorised to raise £252,000 of share capital by their four previous acts; £100,000 had been raised by 1,000 shares of £100 each, £100,000 by 2,000 shares of £50 each, while £52,000 had been borrowed, which remained unpaid. The old company also had outstanding debts of about £340,000 for engines, carriages, wagons, etc., as well as £160,000 for the construction of Middlesbrough dock. A deviation of the main line of the S&DR was also authorised by the act at an estimated cost of £25,000.[318] The new S&DR Company was therefore authorised to raise additional capital of £525,000 to pay off the debts and build the new line.

The WVR shares continued to rise in value, reaching £61 for the £50 shares in February and March, £30 10s (£30.50) for the fully paid up £25 shares, and £15 12s 6d (£15.62) for the £25 shares with £10 paid up. The value fluctuated around these levels for some months, and then fell to £55 5s (£55.25) for the £50 shares, and £25 7s 6d (£25.37) for the fully paid-up £25 shares.[327] At the second WVR half-yearly meeting for 1849 it was agreed to borrow £90,000 of the £168,668 allowed, to reduce the amount of future calls on the new £25 shares.[321] Further calls of £3 15s (£3.75) were made on these shares during 1850, but due to the emerging financial crisis of the S&DR the prices of the paid-up shares fell during the second half of the year, reaching £42 for the £50 shares and £18 15s (£18.75) for the £25 shares.[341]

It was at the half-yearly meeting of the S&DR, on 27 February 1850, that the first real indications that all was not well were announced.[330] It was stated the railways within the group amounted to '33¼ miles of double way, 58 miles of single way, and 49¼ miles of sidings, standing places, and sheds, a total of 140½ miles'. Nearly 40 miles belonged to the S&DR, and had cost about £14,200 per mile, while 50 miles of the lines under lease cost about £14,400 per mile. The engines, coal wagons (upwards of 6,000) and carriages averaged £2,300 per mile. The accounts showed that the traffic on the leased lines was insufficient to pay the rents without some recourse to the guarantee fund. A summary of the capital account of the S&DR at 31 December 1849 was included in the report in *Herepath's Journal* and is given in Table 1, although some of the figures presented do not add up.

TABLE 1   Summary of the capital account of the Stockton and Darlington Railway at 31 December 1849

Payments	£	s	d
Amount expended in expenses, and in the formation of railway and works	556,966	7	4
Rolling stock viz. - Locomotive engines, coaches, and wagons	209,396	13	2
Dock and shipping staithes	172,471	16	10
Expended on Wear Valley line for lime works, buildings	35,381	8	4
Balance	55,582	0	6
TOTAL (?)	1,025,748	6	2
Receipts			
8,000 shares at £25 each	200,000		
Premiums received on the Old Company's shares	127,837		
Company's bonds	587,175	1	0
Bonds and notes in respect of Middlesboro' Dock	159,928	10	2
Wagon bonds	4,484	7	10
Bonds and Directors' notes for Wear and Derwent lines, payable February 18th 1855	40,000		
Notes, reserved dividends, &c.	45,236	12	8
TOTAL	1,164,661	11	8
Deduct amounts due from Wear Valley Co. and others	138,913	5	6
TOTAL	1,025,748	6	2

Although the balance on the working of the lines for the half year was £15,273, it was not sufficient to pay the 6 per cent guaranteed interest to the Wear Valley and Redcar companies. At the end of November 1850, it was reported that for the year ending 30 June 1850, the net profit of £28,500 from all three lines was only just over half the rents of £48,732.[338] In order to bring some order to the situation it was proposed to amalgamate the WVR and Middlesbrough and Redcar Railway (M&RR) with the S&DR, and notice for a bill to that effect was given for the ensuing session of Parliament.[336] One of the terms of this bill stated: 'until the united profits shall be able to pay 6%, 90% of the said profits shall be applied towards that object, and the remaining 10% be divided among the Stockton and Darlington Shareholders.' Also, in an attempt to reduce the bonded debt, powers were sought to create 4 per cent preference shares, to take dividends immediately after the payment of the working expenses, and before all other claims. A letter from a Mr Yeats to *Herepath's Journal* pointed out that the mortgage debt of the S&DR was £720,000 and that:

It is of the highest importance, therefore, for the Wear Valley proprietors to satisfy themselves that this enormous amount of loan capital has been raised under proper legislative powers or sanctioned by some subsequent act of Parliament. If such powers have not been granted, or the assumption of them has not been confirmed, the interest on this excess of mortgage capital cannot be legally chargeable against the revenues of the Company to the detriment of the rents payable to the Wear Valley, and Middlesbrough and Redcar Companies.[339]

Although the financial position of the S&DR had improved by the time of the meeting held in January 1851,[343] the overall profit of the group, after paying the interest charges, was still insufficient to pay the 6 per cent rental on the leased lines. It was stated that the proposed amalgamation bill contained provisions for the conversion of the £693,313 of loans into share capital, although the act of 1849 had already authorised the conversion of a large part of this.[318]

At that time the WVR accounts showed that the total receipts amounted to £850,861, including £749,087 from shares, £60,145 as loans, and £41,450 W&DR (due to them). The expenditure was £820,524, including £155,739 for the line from Witton Junction to Frosterley, £238,335 for the line from Shildon Junction to Crook, £223,450 for Shildon tunnel, and £203,000 for the North Branch or Wear and Derwent Junction Railway (W&DJR), leaving a balance of £80,107. Another letter from Mr Yeats to *Herepath's Journal* advised the proprietors of the WVR to look carefully at the position of sharing their secretary and solicitors with the S&DR.[342]

At an extraordinary meeting of the WVR, held in Darlington on Friday 31 January 1851 to consider the amalgamation bill, a motion to adjourn to London, proposed by Mr Yeats, was carried.[344] At the adjourned meeting it was agreed to delete the amalgamation clauses from the bill, to create 4 per cent preference shares to capitalise the S&DR debt, and to alter the terms of the leases so that when the leased lines received 4 per cent, the S&DR would receive one tenth of the sum paid for the leased lines to pay a dividend on the non-preference shares, ensuring that the S&DR Company would have some interest in increasing the net revenue.[345] The whole of the net earnings of the three lines was to be divided in that proportion until the dividend on the leased lines amounted to 6 per cent, and on the S&DR to 4 per cent; the surplus, if any, was to be appropriated to paying the arrears of dividend on the leased lines.

Once agreement had been reached on the new leases, the value of the shares rose again, reaching close to their nominal value by the end of February 1851.[346] The bill, now called the Stockton and Darlington (Arrangements) Bill, made steady progress through Parliament and received the Royal Assent on 19 May

1851.[350] This act allowed the shares created by the act of 1849 to carry a guaranteed dividend of not more than 4 per cent, while a further £98,000 could be created with a 4 per cent dividend. However, the original £52,000 mortgage was to take priority over the preferential dividend, although the company could raise preference shares to pay off this debt. The act also allowed the WVR to borrow a further £40,000, with the S&DR responsible for paying the interest, while the M&RR was authorised to raise a further £18,000 in shares. Yet another act was obtained in 1852, which listed the S&DR share capital as £650,000 in 4 per cent preference shares and £200,000 in ordinary shares, and authorised the creation of a further £200,000 in £25 shares.[368] A total of £130,000 had been paid by the ordinary shareholders on a voluntary basis, the premiums of £127,837 received on the old company's shares as shown in Table 1. The holders of the original 8,000 shares were entitled to new shares in proportion to their original holding, with each share deemed to have £16 5s (£16.25) paid up.

Two years later, on 3 July 1854,[383] the S&DR obtained another act allowing it to raise a further £200,000 in £25 shares, and stating that the existing share capital of the company, prior to creating the extra £200,000, was £650,000 in preference shares of £25, with £400,000 designated class A and £250,000 designated class B; plus £400,000 in ordinary shares of £25. The Act stated that the net revenue of the company was to be used to pay, in order:

1) payment of 4 per cent preferential dividend on £650,000;
2) payment of rents (£47,037 to WVR and £3,960 to M&RR) and interest on the debts of the WVR and M&RR;
3) payment of dividend up to 4 per cent on ordinary shares;
4) payment of further 1 per cent dividend above 4 per cent on £400,000 class A and on ordinary shares.
5) payment of dividend on ordinary share capital.

On the day before the 1854 Act received the Royal Assent, an act authorising the first section of another group of lines which eventually became part of the S&DR also received the Royal Assent.[382] This was the Darlington and Barnard Castle Railway (D&BCR), which included Joseph and Henry Pease and Thomas MacNay among its subscribers, with the S&DR being authorised to work the line. Returning to the S&DR itself, only 2,000 of the 10,000 class B preference shares had been issued and, in 1855, a further act was obtained allowing the company to obtain a surrender and cancellation of the 2,000 shares issued, replacing them with class A preference shares.[386] The act also permitted the company to cancel the 8,000 unissued shares, and to create and issue £200,000 worth of new ordinary £25 shares in their place. These shares were to be offered to the original shareholders.

There now followed a period during which the final series of lines belonging to the S&DR group were authorised. The D&BCR was opened on 28 July 1856,[390] while the following year the act authorising the South Durham and Lancashire Union Railway (SD&LUR) received the Royal Assent.[399] This line was very similar to the Auckland to Tebay section of the unsuccessful Northern Counties Union, and again the list of subscribers included Henry Pease, although this time only in the company of Thomas MacNay. Once again the act included clauses allowing it to be worked by the S&DR, which was also permitted to subscribe and hold shares in the new company. The last of this series of lines, the Eden Valley Railway (EVR), obtained its act in May 1858,[405] once again having Henry Pease among the list of subscribers and with the S&DR allowed to work the traffic, although the SD&LUR and the L&CR were also authorised to work, lease or purchase it.

TABLE 2   Summary of the capital and borrowing powers of the Stockton and Darlington Railway and its subsidiaries prior to amalgamation

Railway	Capital £	Borrowing £	Comments
Bishop Auckland and Weardale	32,000	24,000	Paid by WVR out of money raised by 1847 act
Wear Valley 1845 Act	82,000	27,300	£27,300 issued as shares
Wear Valley 1847 Act	674,672	168,668	
Total capital of Wear Valley	783,950	40,000	
Total capital of M&RR	66,000	22,000	
Total capital of M&GR	96,000		
Total capital of D&BCR	82,000	33,300	£34,700 extra borrowed
Capital of S&DR			
Preference A shares	450,000		
Ordinary shares	1,000,000		
Borrowed debt		572,592	
Total capital of new S&DR	2,477,950		
Total borrowed debt		667,592	
Extra D&BCR borrowed		34,700	

TABLE 3   Organisation of the capital of the enlarged Stockton & Darlington Railway according to the amalgamation act of 1858

Type of share	Total value £	Original source
Class A preferential	450,000	ex S&DR shares
Class B preferential	849,950	ex WVR & M&RR shares
	62,000	conversion of WVR and M&RR debt
Class C preferential	178,000	ex M&GR and D&BCR shares
	68,000	conversion of M&GR and D&BCR debt
Other preferential		if required by further acts
Ordinary shares	1,000,000	ex S&DR ordinary shares

Just over two months later Parliament finally allowed the S&DR to amalgamate with the WVR.[408] The preamble of the act included a detailed account of the amalgamation forming the enlarged WVR Company, and gave a comprehensive list of the capital and borrowing powers permitted by the acts for the railways authorised to be amalgamated into the S&DR. These included the M&RR, Middlesbrough and Guisbrough Railway (M&GR) and the D&BCR in addition to the WVR. The list is summarised in Table 2, while the capital of the newly enlarged company was authorised in the form shown in Table 3, with the net revenue divided as shown in Table 4.

TABLE 4   Division of the net revenue of the Stockton and Darlington Railway according to the amalgamation Act of 1858

Order of payment	Type of shares
First	5% dividend on Class A
Second	6% dividend on Class B + interest on WVR and M&RR debts
Third	Interest on D&BCR debt, then 6% dividend on Class C
Fourth	dividend on any other preferential shares
Fifth	dividend on ordinary shares

It was another two years before the S&DR found it necessary to go back to Parliament for the authority to raise more capital.[418] A further £250,000 was to be raised as ordinary share capital, with another £83,000 authorised to be borrowed. The following year, 1861, yet another act was obtained to raise a further £220,000 in ordinary shares, with up to an extra £67,000 authorised to be borrowed.[429] The money was to be used for works authorised by previous acts. Table 5 gives details of the S&DR capital as it stood on 1 December 1860, before the further £220,000 was added. Just three weeks before this S&DR Act received the Royal Assent, another act was passed authorising the construction of the 2¼ mile-long F&SR.[425] Yet again Henry Pease headed the list of subscribers, with the S&DR authorised to work the line.

TABLE 5   Summary of the capital and borrowing powers of the Stockton and Darlington Railway on 1 December 1860

Type of capital	£	s	d
PREFERENTIAL CAPITAL			
Class A preferential	450,000	0	0
Class B preferential	850,000	0	0
Class C preferential	200,000	0	0
TOTAL (Which is fully paid up)	1,500,000	0	0
ORDINARY CAPITAL			
Under the amalgamation act of 1858	1,000,000	0	0
Under the North Riding Lines Act of 1858	45,000	0	0
Under the Durham lines, etc. Act of 1858	335,000	0	0
Under the act of 1860	333,000	0	0
TOTAL	1,713,000	0	0
Which is paid up to the amount of	1,034,418	4	10
Leaving unpaid	678,581	15	2
The DEBENTURE debts were			
Wear Valley	15,849	0	0
Redcar	11,630	0	0
Barnard Castle	26,748	0	0
Stockton and Darlington	518,119	0	0
TOTAL	572,346	0	0

The year 1862 was a busy one in Parliament for the S&DR group, with new lines and deviations authorised for the EVR, F&SR and S&DR, as well as the amalgamation of the SD&LUR, EVR and F&SR with the S&DR.[442] The preamble for this bill stated that the total share capital of the S&DR was £3,433,000, while the borrowing power was £639,346, and gave the details of the share capital and borrowing powers of the three companies to be incorporated in the S&DR which are shown in Table 6. The act authorised the S&DR to create £535,000 in £25 shares called class D preferential capital to pay off the SD&LUR and EVR capital, while the shareholders of the F&SR were to be repaid. The debenture debts of the three companies were to be added to the existing debenture debt of S&DR. The class D shares for the SD&LUR were to receive a preferential dividend of 4½ per cent for eighteen months, then 5 per cent for two years and 5½ per cent thereafter, while the EVR was to receive 4 per cent for the first three years after opening, then 5 per cent for two years and 5½ per cent thereafter.

TABLE 6   Capital and borrowing powers of the South Durham and Lancashire Union, the Eden Valley and the Frosterley and Stanhope railways

Railway	Capital in £	Total allowed to be borrowed in £
SD&LUR	400,000	133,000
EVR	135,000	45,000
F&SR	15,000	4,300

The following year saw the end of the S&DR Company as a separate entity, with the passing of an act authorising the amalgamation of the S&DR Company with the NER Company.[446] The preamble stated that the total authorised capital of the NER was £22,290,057 10s (£22,290,057.50) and the total sum authorised to be borrowed was £7,429,900, while the total authorised capital of the S&DR was £4,052,000 and the total authorised to be borrowed was £759,946. The capital of the S&DR was to be added to the NER capital and known as the Darlington capital stock, while the debenture debt of the S&DR was added to that of NER, so that the NER was now authorised to borrow up to £8,189,346. The number of directors of the NER was increased from eighteen to twenty-one, with the extra three being called the Darlington directors.

Although this was effectively the end of the S&DR, its influence continued to be felt for another decade as the act set up a Darlington Committee to manage the former S&DR lines until 31 December 1873. This committee was composed of two directors appointed by the board of the NER, the three Darlington directors and seven other shareholders elected by the Darlington section. An ordinary meeting of the Darlington section, at which one of the Darlington directors was to be re-elected each year in rotation, was to be held in January or February until 1874. From receiving the Royal Assent for their original act on 19 April 1821, authorising a main line almost 27 miles (43km) long, to its amalgamation with the NER in 1863, the Stockton and Darlington Railway had extended to 200 miles (322km), and was one of the most profitable railway companies in the land. Finally, Table 7 gives details of how the joint net revenue of the enlarged NER was to be divided among the different sections making up the railway.

TABLE 7   Division of the net revenue the of North Eastern Railway according to the amalgamation act of 1863

Section	Proportion (%)
Berwick	44.10
York	25.41
Leeds	7.72
Malton	0.29
Carlisle	8.58
Darlington	13.90

8

IMPROVEMENTS TO THE WEAR AND DERWENT JUNCTION RAILWAY

We saw in previous chapters (2 and 7) how the western section of the S&TR, from Stanhope to Carrhouse, was closed by the original company in 1839 and then purchased by the Derwent Iron Company in 1842.[770] The Iron Company reopened the line for the carriage of limestone from the quarries above Stanhope, in the Wear Valley, to their rapidly developing iron works at Consett,[721] overlooking the Derwent Valley, calling it the Wear and Derwent Railway (W&DR), which they then sold on to a group of S&DR directors. Three years later, on 23 May 1845,[123] the Weardale Extension Railway (WER) was opened, connecting the W&DR to the BA&WR at Crook. This allowed the S&DR to work traffic between Bishop Auckland and Consett, although passenger services initially only operated as far as Cold Rowley on the west side of Hownes Gill. Both the S&TR and WER were built without any parliamentary approval, using wayleaves to obtain a right of passage and thereby avoiding the cost of purchasing the land for their trackbed.

The WER was built on behalf of the Derwent Iron Company by a group of proprietors of the S&DR,[269] although acting as private individuals using borrowed money. The line ran from the BA&WR at Crook to Waskerley Park Junction, a little over a mile from the Meeting Slacks engine.[101] A railway community later developed at the junction called Waskerley. The W&DR had been purchased from the Iron Company by a larger number of S&DR proprietors,[269,772] again using borrowed money, and the entire section was then worked as part of the S&DR. According to Tomlinson and the *Tyne Mercury*, the combined railway was then called the Wear and Derwent Junction Railway (W&DJR).[123,772] This name does not appear in any of the subsequent S&DR plans or acts of Parliament relating to the line, although it does occur in other plans and papers long after the line had become part of the NER. An extended rationalisation and improvement programme started in 1847 when the WER and W&DR were absorbed, along with the BA&WR and the privately constructed section known as the Shildon Tunnel Railway, into an enlarged WVR.[269] As we saw in the previous chapter, the money which had been borrowed by the existing owners of the WER, W&DR and Shildon Tunnel Railway was repaid out of the greatly enlarged capital authorised for the expanded WVR.

In their original forms, the W&DR and WER were difficult and expensive railways to operate. Tomlinson[777] includes an excellent description of the W&DJR in the middle 1850s, when two composite carriages were sufficient for the passenger traffic between Crook and Cold Rowley. Leaving Crook, trains were first raised by a stationary engine up the 1¾ miles (2.8km) of the Sunniside incline. Locomotives then hauled the trains to Waskerley Park Junction, at a maximum speed of 15mph (24kph) over the single line. Next, the vehicles were let down the ¾ mile (1.2km) of Nanny Mayer's incline where another locomotive hauled them to Cold Rowley. Only a little earlier, the method of operating the inclines at Hownes Gill had been altered to eliminate the original special trucks, with sets of three wagons now being attached directly to the ropes which lowered and raised them. Although this had increased the capacity of the incline to between 550 and 650 wagons per day,[778] it still placed a severe restriction on the amount of traffic that could be carried to the expanding Consett iron works, and was unsuitable for passenger trains. Although the Hownes Gill inclines presented the greatest problem to the S&DR, the Sunniside and Nanny Mayer's inclines also placed severe restrictions on the traffic that could be carried to Consett.

From the lime quarries at Stanhope to Waskerley the S&TR had built four inclines, worked by three stationary engines.[766] The Crawley engine operated the ½ mile (800m) of the first incline up from Stanhope, which had gradients between 1 in 8 and 1 in 12; while the Weatherhill engine was used to haul the wagons up the next incline, which was 1 mile (1.6km) long and had gradients between 1 in 13 and 1 in 21. Horses then took the wagons for the next 1½ miles (2.4km) to Park Head wheel. Here they were attached to a tail-rope from the Meeting Slacks engine which lowered them down the 1 in 80 to the engine house, where a second rope lowered them to Waskerley on gradients of 1 in 35 to 1 in 47.

At the end of May 1844 Jenkinson examined the Stanhope Railway and lime works in relation to the extension of the BA&WR, and reported that the railway and inclines were in a poor state of repair.[98] Later in 1844 William Bouch reported on the engineering features and mode of working from Crawley Incline to Hownes Gill.[101] From the start of 1844 the wagons were worked from the top of Weatherhill incline to Meeting Slacks by the Weatherhill and Meeting Slacks engines. Bouch reported that this method taxed the Weatherhill engine, as the power of the engines was insufficient to work both inclines and the 3 miles 352 yards (5.15km) between the Weatherhill and Meeting Slacks engines, beyond which the line descended at maximum gradients of 1 in 31 and 1 in 33. The Weatherhill engine took about the same time to get twelve wagons up from the

Crawley engine as sending twelve wagons to Meeting Slacks, and Bouch stated that the most efficient remedy would be to convert the line into a locomotive line. To convert the entire line from the junction to Weatherhill engine into a locomotive line it would be desirable to have a uniform gradient of 1 in 92 for the 4¼ miles (6.84km) from the junction to Weatherhill. The land was suitable for this conversion and would not require a very great deviation from the existing line. If ¼ mile (400m) of level was provided before the Weatherhill engine the gradient would be 1 in 85. Before the WVR absorbed the W&DJR, this deviation was

Looking towards Weatherhill bank top from Crawley bank top. Ken Hoole collection, reproduced by permission of HoS-DRM.

Train on the deviation avoiding Parkhead wheel approaching Blanchland station, in the distance. Ken Hoole collection, reproduced by permission of HoS-DRM.

built, like the original line, without any parliamentary powers.[724] It ran at a lower level avoiding the Parkhead wheel-house, thus allowing the line to be worked by locomotives from the junction with the WER to the Weatherhill engine (p. 133).

The act enabling the WVR to raise sufficient share capital for the purchase of the BA&WR, W&DR, WER and the Shildon Tunnel Company was the first step in providing parliamentary authority for the W&DJR,[269] while the enlarged WVR was leased to the S&DR from 1 October 1847.[281] The next steps in the regularisation of the position of the W&DJR came when the S&DR began to put its own financial and legal position in order.

In addition to enlarging the capital of the S&DR and detailing the method of payment of dividends, the act of 3 July 1854 authorised the S&DR to purchase, or take on lease, the lands on which the W&DR and WER had been built using wayleaves.[383]

This act also authorised the S&DR to build a line, known as the tunnel branch,[380] part of which we shall meet later, to connect the Haggerleases branch with the west end of Shildon tunnel, thus removing the requirement for trains to and from the branch to use the Brusselton inclines. Traffic to the iron works at Consett was steadily increasing, with ore coming from both

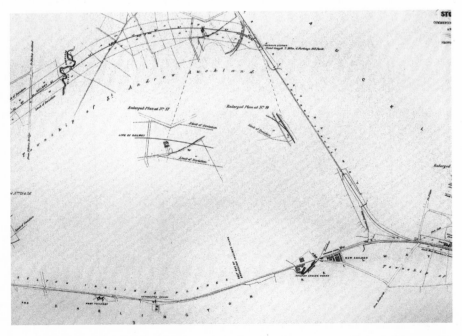

Plan showing Shildon tunnel and the start of the Tunnel branch at the north end of the tunnel. The line over the Brusselton inclines is at the bottom of the picture. Reproduced by permission of DRO.

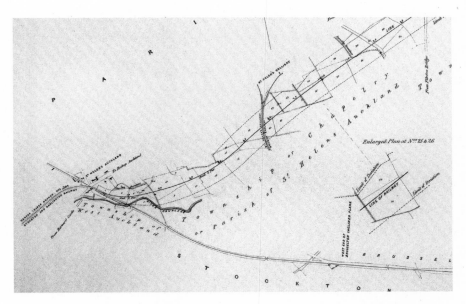

Plan showing the junction of the Tunnel branch with the original line of the S&DR close to the point where the Haggerleases branch left the line to Witton Park Colliery. Reproduced by permission of DRO.

Cleveland and Cumbria. There were, at that time, three routes to Consett: the Pontop and South Shields section of the former S&TR, the Tanfield branch of the Brandling Junction Railway, and the W&DJR, on all of which traffic was operated over rope-worked inclined planes. With the M&GR as part of their group, the S&DR had an initial advantage in the carriage of the Cleveland ore, as it could travel the entire distance over their rails. In addition, by the 1850s, locomotive development was sufficiently advanced for heavy traffic to be satisfactorily worked over gradients as steep as 1 in 35 without requiring the use of stationary engines.

This still left Sunniside incline on the WER with gradients as steep as 1 in 13,[780] Nanny Mayer's incline with a gradient of 1 in 14,[766] as well as Hownes Gill on the W&DR as major obstacles to the effective transport of the Cleveland ore. In November 1854, the S&DR engineers, John Dixon and William Cudworth, deposited plans showing the land required to build a viaduct over Hownes Gill (p. 136), and for a line to bypass Nanny Mayer's incline (pp. 137–138), as well as a new, but very steep, route from Tow Law to Wolsingham.[385] On 16 July 1855, the S&DR obtained another act authorising, amongst other items, these improvements to the W&DJR, although the lines are referred to in the act as those parts of the WVR which were formerly the W&DR and WER.[386]

Plan of 1854 showing the arrangement at Hownes Gill on the former Stanhope and Tyne Railway where a viaduct was to be built to avoid the inclined planes. Reproduced by permission of DRO.

Hownes Gill viaduct looking towards Tow Law. Ken Hoole collection, reproduced by permission of HoS-DRM.

Work proceeded reasonably rapidly, with Hownes Gill viaduct being completed on 1 July 1858 according to Tomlinson,[779] but on 25 June 1858 according to the *Newcastle Courant*.[406] The quite detailed report in the *Newcastle Courant* describes what appears to have been the testing of the viaduct by various combinations of locomotives and wagons, before stating that the viaduct was 700ft (213m) long, 175ft (53m) high with twelve arches of 50ft (15m) span each. It was built for a single line and took fifteen months to erect at a cost of £14,000. The deviation line was not opened until a year later, on 4 July 1859,[412] by which time the S&DR

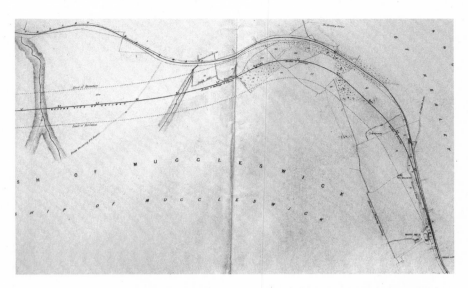

Plan of the eastern end of the line from White Hall to Burnhill station, showing the original, upper, Stanhope and Tyne route. Reproduced by permission of DRO.

had absorbed the WVR. The line bypassing Nanny Mayer's incline was not going to be easy to work, although the steepest incline fell in the direction in which the ore trains would be travelling, while the reversal at Waskerley for trains to Consett was eliminated. The plans show the deviation starting at a junction on the WER (p. 138), about 1 mile (1.6km) before Waskerley, and falling for 2 miles 7 furlongs 3 chains (4.69km) to join the W&DR close to Whitehall Farm, about ¼ mile (400m) before the W&DR passed under the Corbridge turnpike (today the A68), where a new Rowley station was built.

The gradients varied from 1 in 224½ to almost ¾ mile (1.17km) at 1 in 35, and another mile (1.55km) at 1 in 44 or 1 in 44½, with the line falling through 293ft (89m) in the process. According to the plans two public roads were to be crossed on the level, one close to Whitehall, which is shown as a bridge under the railway on the OS map of 1947, and the other mid-way along the deviation (p. 138), which is shown on the OS map as an unmetalled road crossing over the line on a bridge. This section of line was built as double track, with a station, called Burnhill, being built just east of the junction with the line from Waskerley. No work appears to have been done on the 3 miles (4.8km) of line from near Tow Law to Wolsingham, which would have been at least as difficult to work as the Sunniside incline down to Crook, and the S&DR obtained authority to abandon this branch in their act of 1858.[407]

The act of 1855 also authorised the S&DR to build a branch from the former WER at Crook to collieries near High Waterhouses, as well as acquiring the

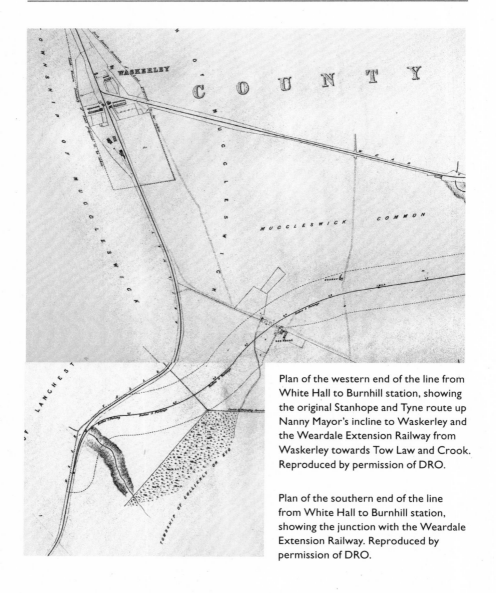

Plan of the western end of the line from White Hall to Burnhill station, showing the original Stanhope and Tyne route up Nanny Mayor's incline to Waskerley and the Weardale Extension Railway from Waskerley towards Tow Law and Crook. Reproduced by permission of DRO.

Plan of the southern end of the line from White Hall to Burnhill station, showing the junction with the Weardale Extension Railway. Reproduced by permission of DRO.

private railway connecting the foot of Sunniside Incline with the West Durham Railway at Roddymoor Colliery.[386] Apart from the Tow law to Wolsingham section, all the provisions of this act appear to have been carried out reasonably rapidly.

While work on Hownes Gill viaduct and the Nanny Mayer's deviation was being carried out, two railways were authorised to improve the carriage of Cumbrian haematite ores to Consett. The first would have more or less eliminated the S&DR as it would have allowed ore trains to reach the iron works from the N&CR main line without travelling over any inclined planes, while the second was to divert much of the Cumbrian ore traffic to the W&DJR. Plans for the Stockton & Darlington & Newcastle & Carlisle Union Railway (S&D&N&CUR) were prepared in 1855,[387] and an act authorising the construction of what was to be a single line, but capable of being widened later to double track if required, was obtained the following year.[391]

The line was to be 10 miles 3 furlongs 4½ chains (16.79km) long to a junction with the W&DR section of the S&DR and have a branch 1 mile 3 furlongs 2 chains (2.25km) long to the Derwent Iron Company's internal railway. It had an authorised capital of £100,000, much of which was subscribed by persons connected with the Derwent Iron Company.[778] Although the line was expected to carry large quantities of ore, it was very sinuous and heavily graded. The line started on the N&CR at Stocksfield by a junction giving through running from Carlisle, and then followed up the Stocksfield Burn. The line rose at 1 in 44 to the watershed between the rivers Tyne and Derwent, and then fell at 1 in 56 to cross the Derwent, before rising to Consett on gradients as steep as 1 in 44. The line joined the S&DR 21 chains (420m) east of Hownes Gill, and was laid out for through running towards Stanhope and Crook. Just before the junction, a branch of almost 1½ miles (2.23km) climbed to join the iron company's private railway, nearly 800ft (245m) above Stocksfield.

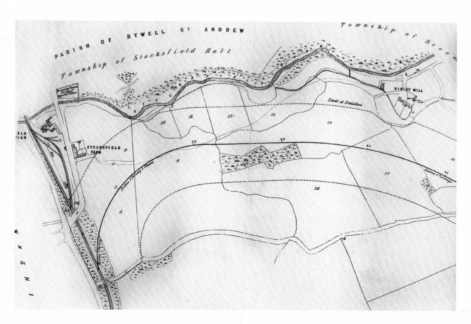

Plan showing the start of the Stockton and Darlington and Newcastle and Carlisle Union Railway at Stocksfield. Reproduced by permission of DRO.

William Bouch wrote a report on the authorised route, dated 31 October 1856, in which he states that there were to be stations, with passing places, at Blackhill and Shotley Bridge.[395] He goes on to say that the viaduct over the river Derwent was to carry double track, be on a descending gradient of 1 in 132 and a curve of 1 furlong (200m) radius, possibly eased to 12 chains (240m), while there was to be another passing place at the summit up from the viaduct. Bouch ends by making the point that the line would be difficult and potentially dangerous to work. In the same file there is a letter from David Dale to Henry Pease stating that it might be better to take a line from Bolts Law (on the Weardale Iron and Coal Company Railway [WI&CCR]), to which the S&DR engines were stated to run, over to Alston to join the N&CR branch.[396]

Work started at the Consett end of the line, but on 26 November 1857 the Northumberland and Durham District Bank, to whom the Derwent Iron Company owed nearly a million pounds, ceased trading.[404,775] Despite the statement by the directors, at a special general meeting of the shareholders to consider the voluntary w1375*12inding-up of the bank, that there was an arrangement with the Consett Iron Works Company, construction ceased, and the powers for the line expired before it could be restarted. It is worth noting that in their final report in December 1859, the official liquidators required the reformed, and refinanced, Derwent Iron Company (Limited) to pay £425,000.[417]

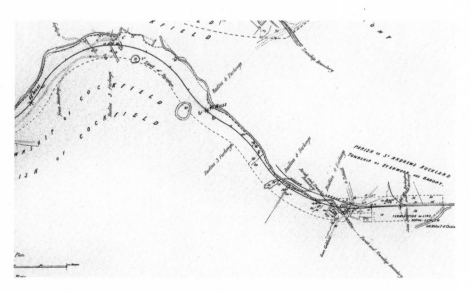

Plan showing the eastern end of the South Durham and Lancashire Union Railway where it joined the Haggerleases branch of the Stockton and Darlington Railway as authorised by the original act of 1857. Reproduced by permission of DRO.

The same year in which the line from Stocksfield to Consett received its authorisation, plans were deposited for the South Durham and Lancashire Union Railway (SD&LUR).[398] Once again, directors of the S&DR were named as shareholders, while the act, which received Royal Assent on 13 July 1857,[399] contained clauses allowing the S&DR to subscribe to and hold shares in the new railway, as well as authorising the S&DR to work the line. This route was to connect with the L&CR and provide a more direct route for Cumbrian ore to reach the iron works on the Tees and at Consett, although the W&DJR would require further improvements to make it suitable for the expected increase in traffic. Later in 1857 plans were deposited for the EVR, again with S&DR directors as subscribers.[401] This was effectively a branch of the SD&LUR, starting at Kirkby Stephen and connecting at Penrith with the L&CR and the Cockermouth, Keswick and Penrith Railway. The latter connection was also expected to provide large amounts of ore traffic for the Tees and Consett Iron industries. The act for the EVR received Royal Assent on 2 May 1858, and included clauses allowing the S&DR and L&CR to work the traffic.[405] The Haggerleases branch of the S&DR formed the eastern section of the SD&LUR, so that iron ore from Cumbria to Consett would have to pass through Bishop Auckland to reach the line to Consett.

Plans were therefore deposited in 1857 for a short line to allow traffic from the tunnel branch to travel west along the former BA&WR without having to reverse direction.[402] Also included were plans for a line just less than 6 miles (9.46km) long which, although sinuous and steep, was suitable for locomotives and avoided

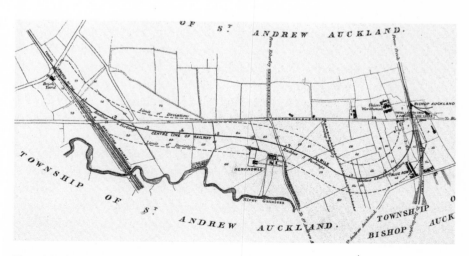

Plan of the line connecting the Tunnel branch to the east end of Bishop Auckland station. Reproduced by permission of DRO.

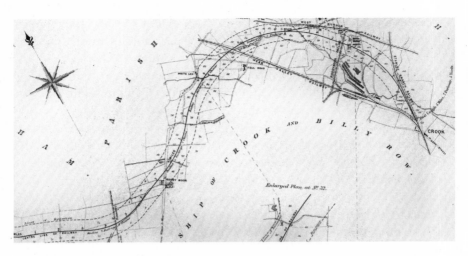

Eastern section of the 1857 line to avoid the Sunniside incline, which joined the B&WR close to the start of the WER incline. Reproduced by permission of DRO.

the rope-worked Sunniside incline. The short line at Bishop Auckland was not contentious and was authorised by the S&DR Act of 1858.[407]

On the other hand the line to avoid Sunniside incline was withdrawn from the bill, following objections from Charles Attwood of the Weardale Iron Company. According to Tomlinson[780] Attwood claimed that the avoiding line would pass over ground on which he was contemplating erecting several blast furnaces. The S&DR plans[402] show the new line leaving the former WER at High Stoop and then running a little to the south of the Corbridge turnpike before making a sweeping S-bend down the hill to Crook. Although there were about 3¼ miles (5.22km) on gradients of 1 in 50 or 1 in 48, and almost ¾ mile (1.1km) of curvature with radii of 15 to 16 chains (300m to 320m), this line would actually have been easier to operate than the Waskerley deviation. Plans in Durham Record Office showing the W&DJR in relation to the blast furnaces at Tow Law, one dated 1908[682] and the other undated[683], but possibly earlier, certainly suggest that the line proposed in 1857 would have passed through the land on which the blast furnaces were later built.

While these improvements to the W&DJR were in progress, plans for the nominally independent Newcastle-upon-Tyne and Derwent Valley Railway (N&DVR) were deposited on 30 November 1859.[415,416] This was for a line, 13 miles 2 furlongs 3.8 chains (21.4km) long, starting on the W&DJR at the north end of Hownes Gill viaduct (p. 144) and running down the Derwent Valley to join the N&CR between Scotswood and Blaydon, with junctions facing towards both Newcastle and Carlisle. According to Tomlinson[781] the idea originated with some directors of the SD&LUR and would have formed an important link in a

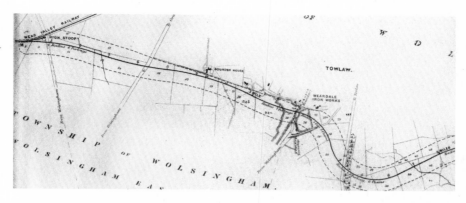

Western section of the 1857 line to avoid the Sunniside incline, leaving the WER at High Stoop and passing close to the existing Weardale ironworks. Reproduced by permission of DRO.

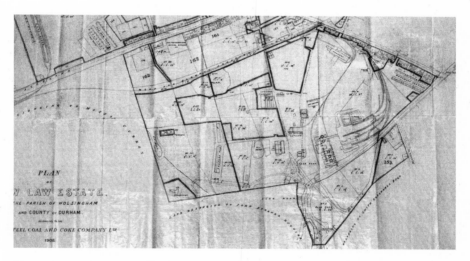

Plan of the blast furnaces at Tow Law in 1908. Note the railway is called the Wear and Derwent Junction Railway long after it had become the North Eastern Railway. Reproduced by permission of the DRO.

through line between Edinburgh and Liverpool, as well as giving the S&DR a route into Newcastle-upon-Tyne independent of the NER, a point emphasised by a report in the *Durham County Advertiser*.[416] The line was to maintain an even descent of 1 in 70 for just over 8½ miles (13.7km) from the start, which would have required some rather extensive earthworks.

In addition to three bridges over the river Derwent a viaduct 135 yards (123m) long and 100ft (30.5m) high was required to take the line over the Pont Burn,

6 miles 7 furlongs (10.86km) from the W&DJR. Spurred on by these independent proposals, the NER also surveyed the route between Scotswood and Conside, as Consett was then called, and deposited their plans in November 1859.[414]

The general route of the NER branch was similar to that of the N&DVR, but it was not designed to be a main line and so would have been cheaper to build. It was to start at the south end of the N&CR Scotswood Bridge and then run for just over 12½ miles (20.34km) to a junction with the authorised, but at that time incomplete, line of the Lanchester Valley Branch of the NER. A junction with the

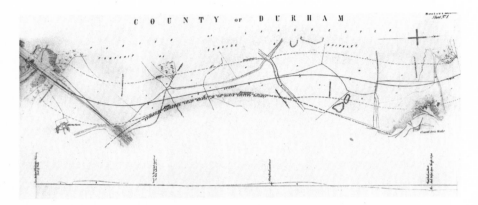

Plan showing the start of the Newcastle-upon-Tyne and Derwent Valley Railway near Hownes Gill. Reproduced by permission of DRO.

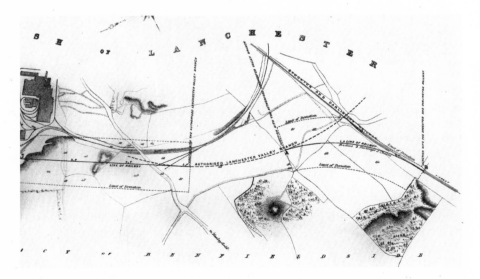

Hownes Gill Junction on the plans of the NER branch from Blaydon to Conside (Consett). Reproduced by permission of DRO.

N&CR for through running to Carlisle was to be provided 2 furlongs 9½ chains (590m) from the start and three viaducts were planned to carry the line over the river Derwent.

After following a short section of the Lanchester Valley branch near Consett, a connection, 2 furlongs 6 chains (520m) long, was to be made with the W&DJR just north of Hownes Gill viaduct. This was a poorer line, with worse gradients, than the N&DVR, and both bills were rejected by Parliament.

The following year the NER presented the same route for parliamentary approval, but the N&DVR group submitted a very different set of plans for a

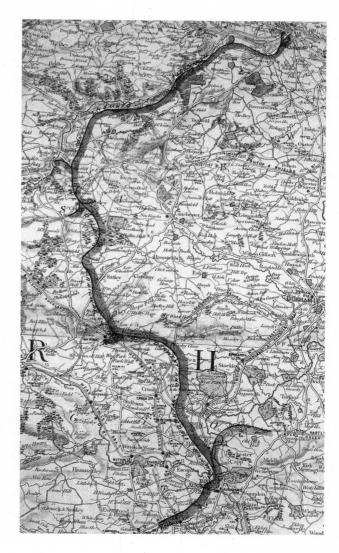

Route of the Newcastle, Derwent and Weardale Railway and its branches, shown in grey on a map made up of the joined sheets 53 and 58 of the series published by G. F. Crutchley, London. Reproduced by permission of DRO.

bill for a line that was very much longer.[422] The hand of the London and North Western Railway (L&NWR) was clearly to be seen in this proposal, with the *Newcastle Courant* reporting that a spokesman for the committee promoting the railway stated that the L&NWR was to be given 'the most unlimited right to use their railway'.[419] It was also proposed to give the NBR running powers over the line. The dependence on the S&DR, which had caused problems the previous year, was to be avoided by doubling the length of the line and constructing it to a junction with the SD&LUR just beyond Bishop Auckland (p. 148).

The *Durham County Advertiser* left the reader in no doubt that this was to be a main through route by entitling its report: 'Proposed new railway from the Northeast Ports by the Derwent and Weardale to Liverpool.'[421] The deposited plans of the Newcastle, Derwent and Weardale Railway (ND&WR) show a line starting from a station in Gateshead, between Church Walk and Hillgate, about 1 furlong (200m) east of the High Level Bridge, and proceeding independently of all other railways, including the W&DJR section of the S&DR, to join the SD&LUR on the former Haggerleases branch of the S&DR, a total distance of approximately 37 miles (59.5km).[422] The decision to apply for powers for a line which would completely avoid the W&DJR confirms Tomlinson's statement[781] that the S&DR, as a whole, was less inclined to support the L&NWR at the expense of the NER, than were the SD&LUR directors. From Gateshead the ND&WR was to throw off branches, one to the NER (Brandling Junction section) close to the locomotive works and the other, 5 furlongs 2.5 chains (1.06km) long, to the N&CR and hence Central station, leaving the main line

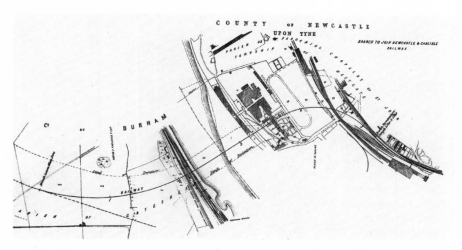

Plans of the branch of the Newcastle, Derwent and Weardale Railway to the N&CR at Newcastle. Reproduced by permission of DRO.

at the 1 mile (1.61km) point and crossing the river Tyne on a viaduct 400 yards (366m) long and 105 feet (32m) high.

The main line of the ND&WR then ran some way from the south bank of the Tyne, crossing over the Team, passing Dunston and Swalwell where another branch joined the N&CR, designed for through running from Hexham to Weardale. The line turned up the valley of the river Derwent, throwing off a branch to Winlaton mill, and crossing the Pont Burn on a viaduct 105 yards (96m) long. A branch from the main line joined the Lanchester Valley line of the NER and then crossed the W&DJR section of the S&DR immediately south of its own viaduct over Hownes Gill, which was to be 112ft (34m) high and 168 yards (154m) long.

A branch to Tow Law iron works left at 24 miles 7 chains (38.8km) and then it passed within 3½ chains (70m) of the Bishop Auckland and Durham branch of the NER, where a branch from Byers Green joined.

The river Wear was crossed on a viaduct 211yds (192.93m) long and 98ft (29.87m) high at 34 miles 1 furlong (54.92km), while ½ mile (0.93km) further on a branch, just over 2 furlongs (0.42km) long, went off to join the S&DR west of Bishop Auckland station (p. 148). Just over 1 furlong (270m) later the S&DR (the former BA&WR) was crossed over with an end-on junction being made with the SD&LUR just past the start of the Haggerleases branch (p. 148), at 38 miles 6 chains (61.28km).

An advert from the ND&WR in the *Newcastle Courant* in late December announced: 'the NER having commenced soliciting names to a petition to

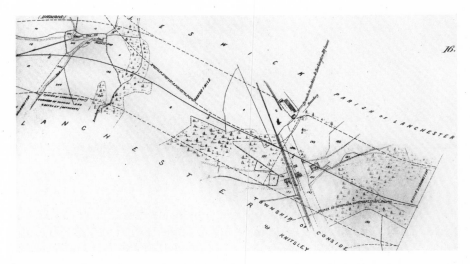

Plan of ND&WR showing the crossing of the S&DR (W&DJR) line near Hownes Gill.
Reproduced by permission of DRO.

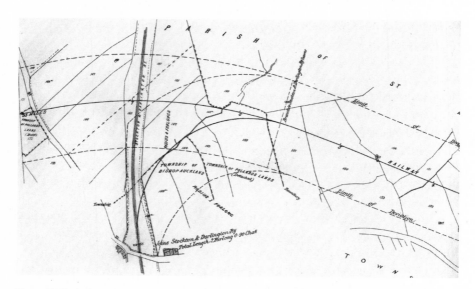

Plan of ND&WR showing the crossing of, and branch to, the S&DR (BA&WR) to the west of Bishop Auckland station. Reproduced by permission of DRO.

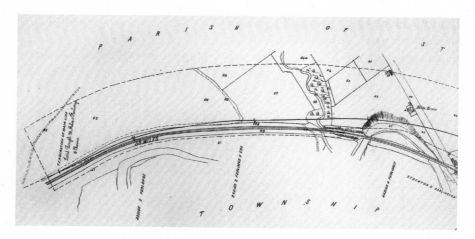

Plans of the Newcastle, Derwent and Weardale Railway showing the junction with SD&LUR. Reproduced by permission of TWAS.

Parliament in favour of their Bill forming a branch railway from Conside to Blaydon. This advert is for a petition on behalf of the above line, otherwise the traffic to Newcastle will be entirely in the control of the NER.'[423] Another advert in the *Newcastle Courant* in January 1861 stated that the capital of the company was to be £450,000 in shares of £20 each,[424] while the involvement of the

L&NWR and the NBR was made clear when two members of the committee were directors of the L&NWR and two were from the NBR. Despite this, most of those signing the application were from the north-east, including Charles Attwood, in this case stated to be of Tow Law iron works, and Charles Cookson of Derwent Cote iron works. Despite all the efforts, both bills were once again thrown out by Parliament, with the ND&WR only being rejected by the committee of the House of Lords after it had spent fifty hours hearing the case.[430]

Proposals for the final improvements to the W&DJR were made by the S&DR in 1861, when a new set of plans was deposited for a line to avoid the Sunniside incline.[435] This time the deviation was to start close to the passenger station in Tow Law, east of the site of the proposed iron works, and this bill passed through Parliament without any problems, receiving Royal Assent on 3 June 1862.[439] The following month the NER finally obtained their act for their Blaydon to Consett line,[444] while in 1863 the S&DR and NER amalgamated.[446]

The second Sunniside deviation route was a little over 4¼ miles (7.29km) long and, apart from 13 chains (260m) of level at the top, fell all the way to Crook (see below and p. 150) at 1 in 50¼. The line curved continuously throughout its length, with no less than six changes in direction on the descent, although the sharpest curves had radii never less than 30 chains (600m). Much of the line was built through moderately broken ground, but close to the top there was a cutting reaching a depth of 65ft (19.8m). Although the overall length of this line was considerably less than that of the 1857 plans, it was a better line for locomotives to work.

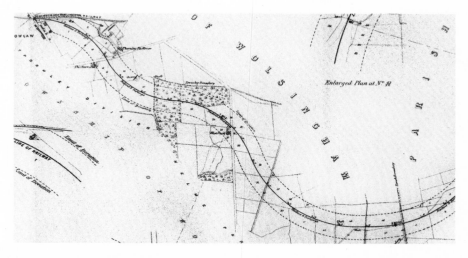

Western section of the plans for the railway from Tow Law to Crook, showing the new point of departure avoiding Tow law iron works. Reproduced by permission of DRO.

The Sunniside deviation was opened for goods traffic on 10 April 1867,[726] but problems with two Board of Trade inspectors delayed the opening for passengers. The saga started on 12 June 1867 when the secretary, Thomas MacNay, wrote to the Board of Trade giving them ten days notification that the line from Crook to Tow Law was ready for inspection.[491] A second letter was sent on 12 July 1867 postponing the opening of the line,[492] but a letter dated the same day from Col. Hutchinson stated that he would inspect the line on Friday 19 July.[493] A second letter from Col. Hutchinson, dated 17 July, confirmed that 9 a.m. on Friday (19 July) would suit him very well to start from Crook station.[494]

Col. Hutchinson was accompanied by Thomas MacNay and the engineer who explained the difficulty of having two platforms at Crook, while the plans for the new station at Tow Law obviated the necessity for a double line past the old platform at Tow Law. Col. Hutchinson agreed that there was not much work required, and said the new platform at Tow Law should be started at once.[495] However, he wrote later the same day stating that Col. Rich, who originally required two platforms at Crook and Tow Law, was unwilling to change his view as he thought he had originally required too little for the safety of the passenger traffic rather than too much.[496] Nevertheless on 24 July the Traffic Committee agreed that a single platform and booking office for temporary use should be provided at Tow Law at once.[497]

The next development occurred in October when the engineer reported he had met with Col. Rich and some requirements had been waived, but others had

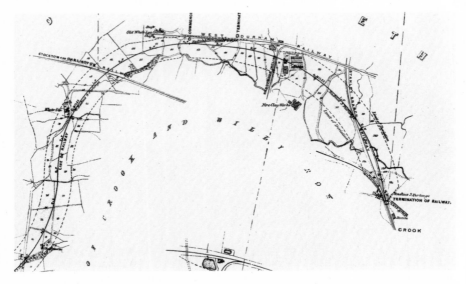

Eastern section of the plans for the railway from Tow Law to Crook, showing the new line leaving the BA&WR at the foot of Sunniside incline. Reproduced by permission of DRO.

not.[500] The next letter was from Thomas MacNay to Col. Hutchinson stating: 'that in order to build a double line past the site of the old passenger station, that platform had to be removed and passenger trains must now use the new line and station to allow the work to progress.'[501] MacNay also pointed out that the new line was vastly superior to the old line. On 31 January 1868, Thomas MacNay wrote to Col. Hutchinson stating that 'Captain Tyler was passing through Tow Law on the same train as the manager of the line. He was shown the arrangements planned for accommodating the passenger traffic upon the new line.'[504] MacNay hoped this letter might assist in the Board of Trade coming to its conclusion. The final document in this file is a notice stating that the Crook and Tow Law Deviation Railway will be officially opened for passenger trains on 2 March 1868.[508]

A timetable published in the *Auckland Chronicle* in January 1868 shows two trains in each direction between Bishop Auckland and Carr House, with the ascent from Crook to Tow Law via the Sunniside incline taking twenty-five or thirty minutes, and the descent twenty-five minutes.[503] After the deviation line was opened, passenger trains took only twelve minutes in each direction.[758] The W&DJR continued to provide an essential link in the carriage of ore to Consett until just before the start of the Second World War, but if the London and North Western Railway had succeeded in its efforts to reach Newcastle in 1860, the W&DJR could have become part of a main through route from Merseyside to Newcastle. Finally, the North Eastern's Blaydon to Consett branch opened on 2 December 1868.[518]

Train at Tow Law station. Ken Hoole collection, reproduced by permission of HoS-DRM.

9

ROOKHOPE, STANHOPE AND WESTGATE

In Chapter 3 we examined the financial reasons why the S&DR group failed to pursue the idea of building a railway through the North Pennines in the middle of the nineteenth century. Nevertheless, the decision by the directors of the WVR not to proceed with the WVER did not mean the end of railway construction in the upper Wear Valley, although for almost half a century it took a very different course from that in the neighbouring valleys. In this chapter we shall start by considering the development of the WI&CCR, which was centred on Rookhope; then look at the F&SR which, despite its short length, required two acts of Parliament before it settled upon a suitable terminus, and finally see how the private WI&CCR became an important part of the general freight transport network of the upper Wear Valley.

During the course of researching this book, reference to the involvement of Charles Attwood in the promotion of railways in the North Pennines has occurred several times, but definitive evidence for his involvement in building the railways in the Rookhope area has been very difficult to discover. The records of Stanton, Croft and Company, the firm of Newcastle Solicitors who handled the affairs of the Weardale Steel, Coal and Coke Company, have relatively little concerning the railways built to and from Rookhope, while Tomlinson[759] does not mention them at all. We do know that after failing in his attempt to represent Newcastle as a Radical Member of Parliament at the 1832 general election, Charles Attwood concentrated his energies on the iron trade, becoming the general manager of the Weardale Iron and Coal Company.[676]

Despite the silence of Tomlinson on railways in the Rookhope area, there are several volumes which include information on the railways in the Wear Valley area of County Durham,[727, 731, 747, 798] all of which refer to the lines built by what they, and all the contemporary local press, call the Weardale Iron Company, while two articles in *Backtrack*[786, 789] also give considerable information on the lines of this company. All these sources agree that the line from a junction with the former S&TR at Parkhead, in the hills above Stanhope, to the Rookhope Valley was started in 1846, although there is disagreement on when the Weardale Iron and Coal Company itself was formed; 1845 as stated by Whittle[731] and Mountford[798], or 1846 according to Rounthwaite[727] and Earnshaw[786]. Like the original S&TR and WER, the lines of the Weardale Iron and Coal Company were built without any parliamentary authority and therefore there are no deposited plans to study.

In 1835 Charles Attwood moved from Whickham to Wolsingham and obtained a lease of the ironstone in the manor of Stanhope and Wolsingham,[676] although it has not been possible to find the date of this lease. With finance from the Baring family,[727,786] Charles Attwood founded and became manager of the Weardale Iron and Coal Company which, under his direction, erected iron works at Tow Law, Tudhoe and Stanhope. An indenture was made on 23 September 1882 between Thomas George, Earl of Northbrook, Francis Henry Baring and Thomas Charles Baring transferring the property, etc. of the Weardale Iron and Coal Company Ltd to the Weardale, Steel, Coal and Coke Company Ltd, which comprised Francis Henry Baring and Victor William Bates van de Weyer.[580] In the first part of the second schedule it is stated that Charles Attwood leased the farm called Lanehead in the valley of the Stanhope Burn in the parish of Stanhope on 25 November 1844, while on 10 May 1845 Matthew Foster Johnson assigned to Charles Attwood the mineral rights in various parts of the parishes of Stanhope and Wolsingham.

A second collection of documents, dated 16 June 1845, includes the lease of a lead mine, various mills and land at Lanehead to Charles Attwood.[130] From these documents it is reasonable to assume that the Weardale Iron and Coal Company was formed in 1845. According to Whittle[731] and Rounthwaite[727] the S&DR considered building a line to Rookhope from the refurbished western section of the S&TR. On the other hand, Mountford[798] and Berry[789] state that Charles Attwood asked the S&DR to build the line, but they declined as they were already too heavily committed[789] or the nature of the country was unfavourable[798]. In the end it was the Weardale Iron and Coal Company itself which built the 5½ miles (8.8km) of railway from a junction on the moors originally called Parkhead, but later Blanchland (see fig. 4 col. section).

The line built by the Weardale Iron and Coal Company originally terminated at Bolt's Burn in the Rookhope Valley, which was the local centre of the mining and quarrying activities for limestone, iron and lead. This first section of the WI&CCR, or the Weatherhill and Rookhope Railway as it was called on the OS maps, was certainly started in 1846 and probably opened in 1847 or 1848.

The junction at Parkhead was laid out for through running from Rookhope to Waskerley with the new line curving through more than 90° to head north-west before crossing over the Stanhope to Edmondbyers turnpike, today the B6278. Then the line, climbing steadily, ran below and more or less parallel to the Blanchland road until the road turned to the north, leaving the railway to continue climbing westwards to a summit near Bolts Law. There were few earthworks on this first section until a deep cutting at Redgate Head took the line through a shoulder of Bolts Law to a point overlooking the valley of the Rookhope Burn. At this point the line was 1,670ft (536m) above sea level and about 600ft (180m) above the village of Bolt's Burn in the Rookhope Valley. To reach the village, the railway required an inclined plane around 2,000 yards (1.83km) long, with the gradient mostly about 1 in 12, but nearer 1 in 6 at the top and also near the foot of the incline where it crossed over Bolts Burn on a wooden trestle viaduct before passing under the main road in the village. Buildings to house a stationary engine for operating the incline, and two locomotives, for use on the section from Parkhead were constructed at Bolts Law.

Apart from loops and sidings at Bolts Law, and a passing loop in the middle of the incline, the entire line from Parkhead to Rookhope was single track. According to Rounthwaite[727] it is believed that once Rookhope had been reached work stopped for several years, probably for financial reasons, even though the main ironstone workings had not been reached. Eventually the Weardale Iron and Coal Company extended their railway from Rookhope round the hills onto a ledge above upper Weardale where it was able to serve the many productive lead and ironstone mines of the area. According to Rounthwaite[727], this Rookhope and Middlehope Railway, as it was called on the OS maps, reached the West Slit mines by 1855, and the 6 inches to the mile OS map, drawn from the 1857–58 survey,[403] shows the line terminating a short distance after turning north into the valley of the Middlehope Burn. From the village of Rookhope, or Bolts Burn as it is called on the 1857 map, the line ran close to the 1,100 feet (335 metres) contour, above and almost parallel to the Rookhope Burn, before crossing the Smails Burn where there was a short loop.

The line then turned south-west and ascended the double track of Bishop's Seat incline, where an engine house is shown at the top, built in 1852 according to Berry.[789] Reaching almost 1,300 feet (395 metres) at the top of the incline, the line followed a very sinuous ledge round the hillside, into and out of Sunderland Cleugh, where an embankment was required to keep the line more or less level, before turning almost due west, high above the Wear, between the villages of Eastgate and Westgate. The line then followed a relatively straight and level westward course, close to the 1,250ft (380m) contour, to Scutterhill depot about 300ft (90m) above Westgate village, on the west side of the road which climbs up from the bottom of the valley (fig. 5 col. section).

No sidings are shown at Scutterhill on the 1858 edition of the OS map, while the depot carries the legend 'Coal and Ironstone'. This depot became the place where massive quantities of ironstone and limestone were tipped from horse-drawn carts into railway wagons which were then taken to Rookhope and hauled up Bolts Law incline to be handed over to the S&DR section of the NER at

View of Rookhope showing the incline to Bolts Law in operation. Ken Hoole collection, reproduced by permission of HoS-DRM.

Parkhead, although it is stated that S&DR engines ran to Bolts Law in 1856.[396] From Scutterhill the WI&CCR line turned north into the Middlehope Gorge where it terminated at the Slit Pasture ironstone mine.

The 1858 map shows three tracks at the foot of the incline from Bolts Law and there appears to be a triangular layout in Bolts Burn village, although at this time the line is shown continuing north for only a few yards up the Rookhope Burn to the West Level lead mine. I have found nothing to indicate when the line was extended beyond Slit Pasture mine, although the section beyond was certainly in use with steam haulage by 1868.[515] The 6 inches to the mile OS map drawn from the 1895 survey shows several changes to the WI&CCR system.[649] At the foot of the incline at Bolt's Burn, as it was then spelt, only one track is shown, with a single connection facing towards Westgate, although a new, and unnamed, line continues up the valley of the Rookhope Burn. Beyond Bolt's Burn the Rookhope Burn continues in a north–westerly direction, with the headwaters being only about 1 mile (1.6km) from Allenheads. Both lead ore and ironstone are to be found in this valley, while the massive Rookhope lead smelter, now usually known as Lintzgarth smelt mill, lay just over a mile upstream from the village. The WI&CCR was extended up the valley of the Rookhope Burn, past Rookhope smelt mill to terminate at Fraser's Hush, probably around 1860 to 1864 according to Berry,[789] or 1865 to 1866 according to Rounthwaite,[727] and it was fully operational by 1869.[789] The 1895 OS map[649] shows it going only as far as Grove Rake Mine, although even today, evidence can be seen on the ground suggesting that it did extend further up the valley towards the quarries at Fraser's Hush and North Grain, while the report of an accident in the *Hexham Courant* indicates that the line was in use from Rookhope Head in 1875,[558] while Berry[789] records that 30,000 tons of ironstone were produced from this area in 1872.

On the Rookhope and Middlehope line, the 1895 OS map no longer shows a loop at Smailsburn, nor an engine house at the top of Bishop's Seat incline. According to Rounthwaite,[727] Bishop's Seat incline was self-acting, and this certainly appears to have been the case from some time before the survey was made for the 1895 OS map, but the presence of an engine house on the earlier survey indicates that a winding engine was installed when the line was constructed. As the bulk of the traffic would go east from Scutterhill depot, it was probably soon discovered that a winding engine was not required and that the incline could be made self-acting. According to Berry,[789] a number of old S&DR tenders were employed on this incline, being used full to haul supplies for the west up the incline and then taken back empty by descending loaded wagons. Beyond Scutterhill the line is shown continuing up the east side of the Middlehope Gorge to cross a wooden bridge[515] over the burn. Immediately beyond the bridge the line reverses direction before climbing south along the west side of the burn to terminate near Middlehope Shield at Slit Vein. The map accompanying Berry's article does not show this reversal, rather a simple curve.[789] Slit Vein was the most westerly point reached by the WI&CCR and, according to Rounthwaite,[727] the distance from Parkhead to the West Slit mines was 11 miles 1 furlong 5 chains (13.98km).

Scutterhill depot is again shown on the west side of the road climbing up from the valley, but now there is a siding in addition to the main line. Almost ½ mile (800m) east of the depot, Scutterhill incline is shown dropping down the hillside to terminate on the north-east side of Westgate church. On the map Westgate depot has three tracks and is called a coal and ironstone depot. A building, called Scutterhill Engine, is shown in the V between the tracks of the incline and those to Middlehope Burn, with the incline designed for direct running to and from Rookhope. In the early 1860s huge quantities of mineral ores from the upper end of the Wear Valley were being taken to the village of Westgate in horse-drawn carts which then had to be laboriously hauled up the 1 in 5 gradient of the narrow road to Scutterhill depot. The Scutterhill inclined plane thus gave the WI&CCR a much more convenient terminus close to the turnpike road (A689). According to Berry,[727] this line was opened between 1869 and 1872, although the winding engine was not completed until 1870 or 1871.

Also shown on the OS map based on the 1895 survey is an 'old railway' which left the WI&CCR a little over half-way from Parkhead Junction to Bolt's Burn and dropped northwards to a mine at Ramshaw, near Blanchland, in the valley of the river Derwent. An unsigned and undated copy of a lease states that the Rev.

David Capper, of Huntley Rectory, Gloucestershire, will lease to Richard Cordner, of Crawley House, Stanhope, for twenty-one years from 13 May 1862, a railway from a junction on the Weatherhill and Rookhope Railway 3 miles (4.8km) from Parkhead station on the S&TR to Low White Heaps (see fig. 6 col. section).[438]

The Rev. Capper owned land near Hunstanworth in the valley of the river Derwent which included several mines in the Ramshaw area, while Cordner had built the railway and engine houses at a cost of £3,500 provided by Capper. The annual rent for the railway was to be £280, while William Shaw, an engineer at Tow Law iron works, part of the Weardale Iron and Coal Company, would stand as surety for Richard Cordner in his operation of the railway. The lease required Richard Cordner to provide all rolling stock, equipment and labour and to carry all passengers and goods 'as shall require it' from Low White Heaps to Parkhead or other intermediate stations in a good and efficient manner, although he was not required to carry ironstone without permission of the owner of the Weatherhill and Rookhope Railway, again the Weardale Iron and Coal Company. Cordner agreed to run, weather permitting, a goods train twice a week to Parkhead and back, and also provide a passenger train to Parkhead and back on such days as the Darlington and/or Bishop Auckland markets were held, stated as once per week.

Until reading the records of Stanton, Croft and Company, I used the name Weardale Iron Company Railways for the lines built by Attwood's company, but a document, dated 2 August 1884,[584] includes a map (p. 158) showing the Iron Company's Railway almost at its fullest extent. This includes the Weatherhill and Rookhope Railway, the Middlehope and Rookhope line all the way to the West side of Middlehope Burn, including the Westgate incline, plus the route past Rookhope Smelter, although only going as far as Grove Rake mine. On the map the entire railway system is called the Weardale Iron and Coal Company Railway (WI&CCR) and I have therefore used this name throughout. The names Weatherhill and Rookhope Railway and Rookhope and Middlehope Railway were used by the Ordnance Survey on all their maps, including the New Popular Edition One-Inch maps published in 1947, after the lines had all been closed and lifted, although it must be admitted that the last full revision of this map had been made in 1920 before the system closed.

While the Weardale Iron and Coal Company was building its railways in the hills and valleys to the north of the Wear Valley, efforts continued towards extending the railway along the valley floor. Plans were deposited for the F&SR on 27 November 1860, produced by William Bryson their engineer (pp. 158–159).[420]

This line was 2 miles 1 furlong (3.42km) long and started by an end-on junction with the WVR at Frosterley, crossing the Bishopley road on the level and then crossing the Wear at 6 furlongs 4 chains (1.29km) from Frosterley. Once over the river, the F&SR followed a route similar to the WVER and terminated

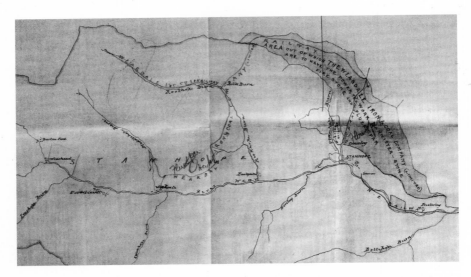

Map in records of Stanton, Croft and Company, with documents dated between May and August 1884, showing the railway built by the Weardale Iron and Coal Company. Reproduced by permission of DRO.

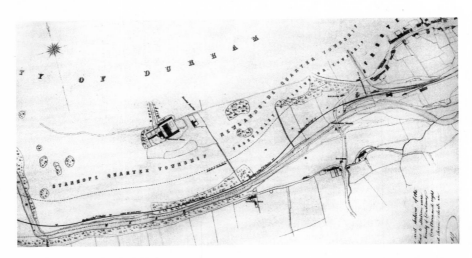

Plan showing the start of the Frosterley and Stanhope Railway at Frosterley with the branch to the limestone quarry. Reproduced by permission of DRO.

on the south bank of the river Wear at West Ferryfield, below Newlandside and opposite Stanhope. A road, with a bridge over the river, was to be built to connect the station with the town of Stanhope. Yet again the Pease family was involved and, on 28 June 1861, the F&SR Act[425] was passed with Henry Pease as the first chairman.[428]

Plan showing the Frosterley and Stanhope Railway crossing the river Wear. Reproduced by permission of DRO.

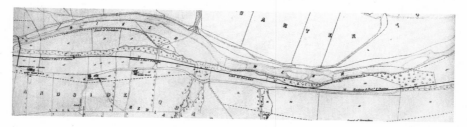

Plan showing the end of the Frosterley and Stanhope Railway with the start of the road over the Wear to Stanhope. Reproduced by permission of DRO.

The authorised capital of the new company was £10,000, in 500 shares of £20 each, with the S&DR allowed to subscribe up to £2,500. The greatest call was to be £2 per share, with at least two months between calls and £10 to be the maximum amount called in one year.

The Company was also allowed to borrow up to £3,300, while the land was to be purchased in two years with the railway being completed in three years. Although the plans show the Bishopley road at Frosterley and the public highway from Parson Byers, near Stanhope, crossing the line on the level, the act required both roads to be carried over the railway on bridges. The S&DR was also authorised to enter into an agreement to work the line.

The first general meeting of the F&SR was held on 27 July 1861,[428] and the directors soon had second thoughts about the position of the terminus for Stanhope, with Bryson drawing up a second set of plans which were deposited on 27 November 1861.[434] The line was now to be taken across the river Wear into Stanhope, terminating 2.2 chains (44m) from the turnpike road (A689) through the town (p. 160). The deviation was 4 furlongs 1.2 chains (0.83km) long, and started 1 mile 5 furlongs 0.5 chain (2.63km) from Frosterley on the

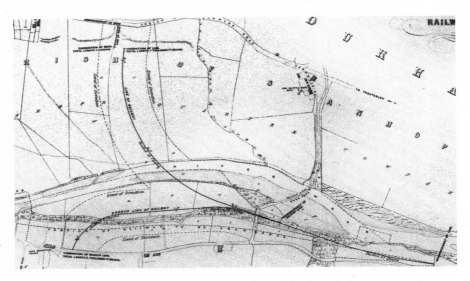

The 1861 plan showing the deviation of the Frosterley and Stanhope Railway to cross the Wear into Stanhope. Reproduced by permission of DRO.

original line. The quarries at Newlandside were to be served by a branch leaving the main line at a point 1 furlong 5.5 chains (310m) from the junction with the originally authorised route. A special general meeting was held on 25 April 1862 to approve the bill for the deviation as well as one which included the absorption of the F&SR by the S&DR.[436] At the meeting the engineer stated that the line to Newlandside was completed and almost ready for opening.[437]

Both bills successfully passed through Parliament,[441,442] with the deviation act authorising the F&SR to abandon part of the original main line and station approach road, while allowing it to build the main line to a new terminus close to the Lobley Hill turnpike. The Newlandside branch was opened for mineral traffic on 12 April 1862,[784] before the deviation act was passed, although the entire branch was within the limits of deviation of the main line authorised by the original act. The line to the revised station in Stanhope was opened for passengers on Wednesday 22 October 1862.[445] The Wear Valley and Frosterley and Stanhope railways form a continuous route up the Wear Valley from the Bishop Auckland and Weardale Railway, and we shall now look in detail at this line, which still exists, from Wear Valley Junction to Stanhope.

The plans of the WVR, and both sets for the F&SR, are on the same sheets as their respective sections,[103,420,434] allowing the line, as authorised, to be described relatively easily. The plans state that the WVR was to start 90 yards (82.3m) south of milepost 5 (8.05km) measured from the Bishop Auckland terminus of the BA&WR (p. 44), and near (3 chains [60m] north of) the bridge over the road

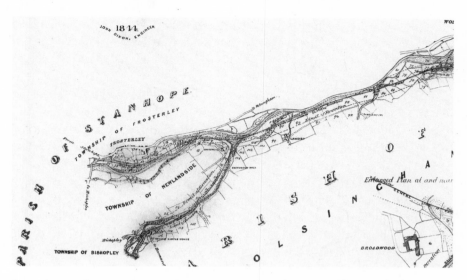

Plans of the Wear Valley Railway showing the western termini, at Frosterley and the freight-only line to Bishopley. Reproduced by permission of DRO.

from Witton-le-Wear to Bishop Auckland, which is 7 miles 2 furlongs 2 chains (11.71km) from the junction with the original S&DR at Shildon. The new railway started on a left-hand curve, of 15 chains (300m) radius, on a rising gradient of 1 in 264. The earthworks on the line from Wear Valley Junction to Frosterley were, in general, relatively minor, with the turnpike from West Auckland to Elishaw (today the A68) to be raised 6ft (1.8m) and crossed on the level, at a point 1 mile 3 furlongs 4½ chains (2.30km) from the junction, but the act required it to be crossed on an overbridge (see fig. 7 col. section).[145] There were two short level sections and almost a mile (1.53km) descending at 1 in 254, but otherwise the line ascended on gradients not exceeding 1 in 144 all the way to Frosterley. At a point just over 4 miles from the start (6.63km), the river Wear was to be diverted to the south of the railway for 8 chains (160m) thus avoiding two bridges over the river in close succession although the river was crossed twice in the last 4 miles (6.63km) to Frosterley.

The mineral branch to Bishopley curved away to the south at 9 miles 4 furlongs 7 chains (15.43km), while the WVR main line terminated beside the road to Bishopley, 10 miles 5 furlongs 5.1 chains (17.20km) from the junction with the BA&WR. The first F&SR plans[420] show the new line commencing by an end-on junction with the WVR, while the second set of plans[434] shows the deviation of the main line diverging from the route of the original line. The second F&SR Act[441] stated that the start of the deviation was to be in a field, originally owned by William Nicholas Darnel, which is 1 mile 5 furlongs ½ chain (2.63km) from ·

Frosterley, and the termination 2.2 chains (44 metres) from the turnpike road (A689) in Stanhope (p. 160). This terminus was 2 miles 1 furlong 1.7 chains (3.45km) from the end of the WVR, or 12 miles 6 furlongs 6.8 chains (20.66km) from the junction with the BA&WR.

Apart from the last ½ chain (10m), the entire length of the originally authorised line was a series of six continuous reverse curves with radii varying from 20 to 57 chains (400m to 1.15km), rising all the way on gradients varying from 1 in 82 to 1 in 325. Most of the earthworks were negligible, with the river Wear being crossed 6 furlongs 4 chains (1.29km) from the start, at a height of 17ft (5.2m). The deviation authorised by the act of 1862 initially ran a little south of the originally authorised line,[434,441] while the Wear was crossed 1 mile 7 furlongs 8½ chains (3.19km) from Frosterley with the line rising to the terminus on a gradient of 1 in 303. The branch was 2 furlongs 1.2 chains (425m) long and terminated beside the road from West Ferryfield House.

While the extension of the railway from Frosterley improved the transport facilities for the output from the various mines and quarries in the valley of the river Wear as far west as Stanhope, especially those on the south side of the river, those to the north and west continued to rely on the WI&CCR and the inclines of the W&DJR section of the S&DR. During the second half of the

Stanhope old station, opened on 22 October 1862 for passenger traffic and closed on 21 October 1895 when the line was extended to Wearhead, leaving the terminal station on a short spur for goods traffic, with the new passenger station on the through line seen in the lower left corner of the picture. Ken Hoole collection, reproduced by permission of HoS-DRM.

nineteenth century the Weardale Iron and Coal Company moved large quantities of ironstone and limestone, much won from its own quarries and mines, over its railway system, all of which had then to be taken up Bolts Law incline. According to reports in the *Hexham Courant* of accidents at Rookhope and on Bolts Law incline,[447,558] the WI&CCR was operated in a similar manner to a public freight line, with lead ore being carried for the Weardale Lead Company from various mines to Rookhope smelter, smelted lead taken up the incline, and provisions including flour and oatmeal brought down into Rookhope. Rounthwaite[727] reports that wool was taken up the incline while coal was brought down into the valley, as might be assumed from the information given on the OS maps for the depots at Westgate,[403,649] while Berry[789] also records that food, drink, animal feed, ironmongery and general household goods were carried.

Although passenger trains did not operate over most of the WI&CCR, Rounthwaite[727] and Berry[789] record that a passenger service was provided between Park Head and Bolts Law for Ramshaw miners, while we have seen that Cordner provided a weekly passenger train from Low White Heaps to Parkhead during the period between 1862 and about 1883.[438] At the western end of the WI&CCR system, huge quantities of ironstone as well as limestone and lead ore were loaded onto wagons at the various depots. By the beginning of January 1877 the Weardale Iron and Coal Company was employing a traction engine, 'carrying' 10 tons, to move ironstone from Cows Hill to Westgate.[561] By the very nature of the contemporary working methods for inclined planes, accidents kept occurring, sometimes with loss of life, as happened at Bolts Law in July 1873 when a young man became entangled between the wire rope and the winding drum.[556] Other accidents were reported on the locomotive-worked sections of line, sometimes due to the foolishness of the workers involved,[553,594] and sometimes caused by mechanical failures.[558] It is interesting to note that the locomotive involved in a major accident at Bolts Burn, where several wagons were destroyed, although in this instance fortunately without loss of life, was called Charles Attwood.[558]

In addition to the usual problems of working the inclined planes, winter snow caused major difficulties on the lines of both the WI&CCR and the S&DR, with the inclines and adjoining locomotive-worked mineral railways being frequently blocked,[559,590,598] often for long periods of time.[591,643] Nevertheless, despite the problems with snow, and the inherent limitations of the inclined planes on both the WI&CCR and W&DJR sections of the S&DR, for over thirty years the large quantities of ironstone, limestone, lead and other minerals produced by the quarries and mines of the upper section of the Wear Valley were successfully taken away by these two railway systems. However, by 1880 the lead industry was in serious decline, mainly due to competition from foreign ores, while even the boom in ironstone had ended. It was in the light of these changes in the prospects of the extractive industries that the high costs of hauling large tonnages over

Site of the WI&CCR depot at Rookhope (Bolts Burn) showing the foot of the incline from Bolt's Law. Ken Hoole collection, reproduced by permission of HoS-DRM.

the inclines between Westgate, or Stanhope, and the main rail network began to make the difference between success and failure, not just of individual mines and quarries but also of the entire industry in the area. In Chapter 13 we shall look at the final efforts that were made to connect Alston to Teesdale and Weardale, and record the last extensions of the railway system in the North Pennines.

10

THE HEXHAM AND ALLENDALE RAILWAY

We saw that the proposals for the WVER seem to have been the reason why the N&CR decided to survey both the South Tyne and the Allen valleys in 1844–45,[210] but only the N&CR's branch from Haltwhistle to Alston was authorised, opening on 17 November 1852.[377] The N&CR built no further branches although the independent Border Counties Railway (BCR) was authorised,[384] with the first length, from Hexham to Chollerford, being opened on 5 April 1858.[714] On 17 July 1862, following several unsuccessful attempts, Parliament finally allowed the Newcastle and Carlisle and the North Eastern railway companies to unite,[783] thus ending any real prospect of a main line company extending into the area south and west of Hexham. Nevertheless, lead mining prospered in the Allen valleys, despite the relatively poor transport facilities, with the nearest railheads being at Alston, Haydon Bridge or Rookhope. The population of Allendale parish continued to rise, reaching 6,400, the highest level ever recorded, in 1861,[571] with productive smelters owned by the Beaumont Lead Company operating at Allenheads and Allendale and a third, owned by the Greenwich Hospital Trust, at Langley. Despite the quantities of lead being produced, it was apparent that, if there was going to be a railway in the Allen valleys, it would have to be built by local initiative.

The next genuine proposal to build a railway into the East Allen Valley was made at the dinner following the annual show of the Allendale, Hexhamshire, and Whitfield Agricultural Society held on Monday 22 August 1864 in Allendale Town,[449] where Wentworth Blackett Beaumont offered to subscribe £20,000, being one-third of the estimate of the capital required to build the line. In addition to being the local MP, and controlling most of the lead industry in the valleys of the rivers Allen and Upper Wear through his Beaumont Lead Company, W.B. Beaumont now became the main driving force behind the construction of a railway into Allendale. On Wednesday 31 August 1864 he chaired a meeting in Allendale town to consider the proposal for a railway running to Hexham.[450] Charles Grey, the receiver of the Greenwich Hospital Estates, endorsed the proposals, and stated that the commissioners of the Greenwich Hospital were in favour of the scheme and would contribute £10,000, providing Parliament agreed. It was proposed to start the railway at Allendale town, and run by Langley to Hexham, passing through part of the Greenwich Hospital Estates. Mr Dinning, of Langley smelt mill, offered to subscribe £2,000, and a committee was set up to see the local landowners. Three weeks later an extensive report appeared in the *Hexham Courant*, the recently established local newspaper, of a second meeting held on 23 September 1864, also in Allendale town and again chaired by W.B. Beaumont, to hear the report of the committee.[551]

The paper's editorial section outlined the advantages a railway line would bring to the district, and was followed by a short description of the route surveyed by Mr Bewick, the engineer of the Beaumont Lead Mines. The railway would leave the N&CR main line west of Hexham and:

> … pass by Westwood and Coastley, past Greenshaw Plain, and on the north of Glendue, then by a gradual curve to Ellfoot House and Elrington, which it passes south side, and from thence, in a nearly direct line, by Langley Lead Works, to near Staward, where it turns southward up the valley of the East Allen River, continues nearly parallel with that river to Catton, and proceeds thence to Allendale Town.

None of the landowners objected, and preliminary enquiries had received a favourable response from the NER. No great works would be required to build the line, which was to be 13 miles (21km) long, rising for the first 6¾ miles (10.9km) at 1 in 58. It was thought probable that the line would be extended to

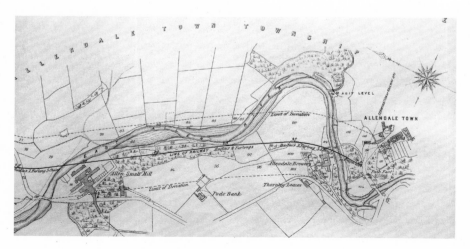

Plan showing the Allendale terminus of Hexham and Allendale Railway No. 1. Reproduced by permission of NCS.

the lead mines at Allenheads, and Bewick was named as engineer. A single line was to be built, but with enough land bought and bridges built that could be adapted for a double line later. Shares were to be £10 each and £29,360 of the required £60,000 had been subscribed, although this did include the £20,000 from W.B. Beaumont. A committee of thirteen was appointed to take the plans forward.

The next meeting was held in Hexham,[453] where it was announced that a total of £37,040 had been subscribed, with local committees established to raise more capital. A notice announcing the intended formation of the company was published on 10 November 1864,[454] in which it was stated that powers to construct two railways, one from Hexham to Allendale town, and a second from Allendale town to Allenheads, would be sought. The plans, sections and books of reference were deposited with the authorities on 29 November.[455,459]

The H&AR Bill was one of 349 railway bills presented during the 1865 parliamentary session.[457] Unopposed, it was considered second by the House of Commons committee.[460] The bill passed parliamentary standing orders on 18 January 1865[461] and the committee stage of the House of Commons the following month.[462] A general meeting of the shareholders was held on Wednesday 29 March where Mr Bewick, who was now secretary and treasurer as well as engineer, and Mr Beaumont as chairman outlined the progress made so far.[464] Mr Bewick stated that with the encouragement they had received for the line from Hexham to Allendale, the directors had decided to apply for powers to extend it to Allenheads. Subscriptions had been received for £42,850 worth of shares, of which £2,500 was on the understanding that the railway would be continued to Allenheads. The chairman then stressed that the Allenheads section would only be built if the shareholders approved. The NER Company had promised to subscribe £10,000 in exchange for the appointment of one director, providing their shareholders agreed, while the commissioners of the Greenwich Hospital were to be treated in the same way. Some dissent was expressed concerning the Allenheads extension, but it was agreed to adopt the bill as it stood.

Only one local problem had to be resolved, caused by the proposed site for the station to serve Staward being on the turnpike road, today's A686 (p. 168). It was agreed that the company would build a bridge over the railway and a new road to connect the station with the road to Catton.[463] The bill remained unopposed, receiving its third reading in the House of Commons on Wednesday 10 May 1865[465] and Royal Assent on Monday 19 June.[466] Before considering the building of the railway, we shall look at the details of the rather complex H&AR Act.[466]

The act allowed the Greenwich Hospital and NER to make substantial contributions. The capital of the Company was to be £120,000 in shares of £10 each, made up of £75,000 in respect of Railway No. 1, and £45,000 in respect of Railway No. 2. The two railways authorised by the act formed a continuous

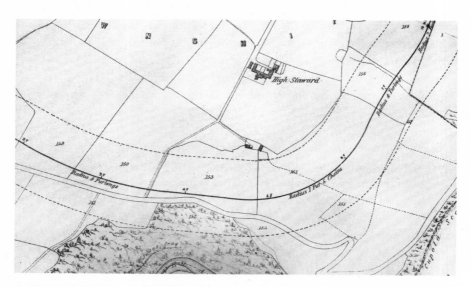

Plan of railway past Staward. The level site for the station was just past the 9 mile 4 furlong point, close to the 1823 section of the Alston turnpike, whereas High Staward was served by the old section. Reproduced by permission of NCS.

route from Hexham to Allenheads. The line abounded in severe curves and steep gradients, but with mainly relatively light earthworks. Of the 12 miles 7 furlongs ½ chain (20.73km) of railway No. 1 to Allendale town, less than one-third was straight, made up of twenty sections totalling 3 miles 6 furlongs 2½ chains (6.1km). The rest of the line was on curves with radii as severe as 15 chains (300m). Several of the straight sections were less than a furlong (200m) long, while the longest, past Catton, was just over ½ mile (900m). The line rose almost continuously for the first 9½ miles (15.35km) to a summit level a little over a furlong (200m) in length. It then fell for almost 2¾ miles (4.25km) before rising again over the last ½ mile (815m) to the terminus in Allendale town, with the ruling gradient being 1 in 50 in both directions.

Railway No. 1 was to start by a junction, laid out for direct running towards Hexham, just over 1 furlong (210m) west of the point at which the BCR joined the N&CR (p. 181). Only one major river, the East Allen, was to be crossed, although there were three large streams whose valleys required quite massive embankments. The company was allowed to borrow up to £40,000 when the whole £120,000 had been subscribed and one half paid up 'or', as the clause also stated, the company could borrow up to £25,000 when £75,000 in respect of Railway No. 1 had been subscribed and one half paid up, and £15,000 in respect of Railway No. 2 when £45,000 was subscribed and half paid up. At least £2 per share had to be paid before any money could be borrowed.

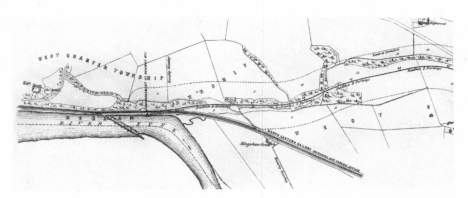

The authorised junction with N&CR, just 1 furlong (200m) west of the Border Counties line. Reproduced by permission of NCS.

Plan showing the route of the H&AR going under the Fourstones to the Hexham section of the Alston turnpike, then over Coastley Burn and finally under the Hexham turnpike, now the A69. Reproduced by permission of NCS.

Not only did clauses 24 to 31 authorise the NER to subscribe £10,000, they also detailed how it could be raised and stated that the representatives of the NER were not allowed to vote in the election of directors, but could vote on other issues up to the value of the shares. Five years were allowed to complete the line. Individual earthworks tended to be less than 1 furlong (200m) long, and were rarely more than 20ft (6.1m) high or deep. The line started with a pair of reverse curves, each 7 chains (140m) long, first to the left on a radius of 30 chains (600m) and then to the right on a radius of 40 chains (800m). Just under a furlong (190m) of straight followed before there was another pair of reverse curves on radii of 20 and 40 chains (400m or 800m). This pattern was repeated all along the route although sometimes there was only a single curve after each section of straight line, and sometimes as many as five reverse curves one after the other. Curves of 20 chains (400m) radius abounded, but at least their use usually avoided the requirement for heavy earthworks.

The climbing started straight from the junction, with almost a mile (1.4km) of 1 in 53½ followed by just under 2¾ miles (4.2km) of 1 in 50.

The Coastley Burn was crossed on an embankment 68ft (20.7m) high and almost a furlong (190m) long with a road from Lowgate to West Boat going under the embankment (p. 169 and below). The Hexham turnpike, today's A69, crossed over the line just under 1½ miles (2.4km) from the junction (p. 169), but no details were given of the size of the arch to take this, or any other, road over the railway.

Coastley embankment showing the bridge carrying the H&AR over the former public road from Lowgate to West Boat in June 2004, more than half a century after the line closed. This road is now only used as a path.

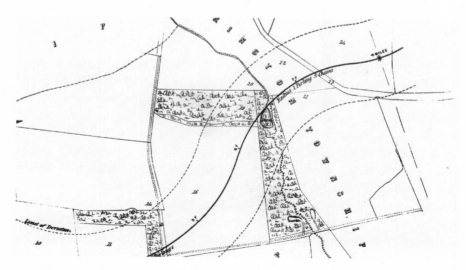

Plan showing the route of the H&AR on the approach to Elrington. The former Hexham turnpike (23 on plan) is shown crossing the line. Reproduced by permission of NCS.

The most severe series of five consecutive reverse curves on Railway No. 1 took the line under the former Hexham turnpike and brought it close to Elrington.

Elrington station was to be built on a furlong (200m) where the rising gradient was only 1 in 330 on an embankment 26ft (7.9m) high and almost ½ mile long (680m), under which a public road was to pass.

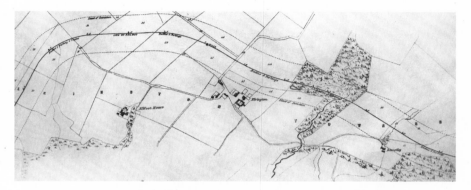

Plan showing the route of the H&AR going past Elrington. The road crossing the line of the railway and passing to the east of the houses was diverted to pass to the west as shown below. Reproduced by permission of NCS.

View of the former Elrington station from the bridge over the H&AR in June 2004. The plans showed this minor road going under the railway, but when it was built the road was taken over the railway. Elrington was one of the two intermediate stations to have a single platform.

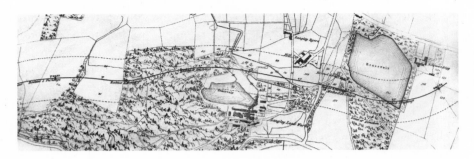

Plan showing the route of the H&AR going past Langley. Reproduced by permission of NCS.

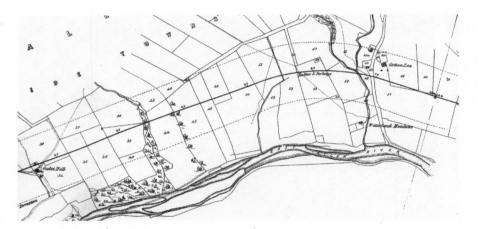

Plan showing the half mile of straight line on the H&AR on the descent to Catton. Reproduced by permission of NCS.

The gradient steepened again to 1 in 55 for the next 1¼ miles (2km) and then a series of four consecutive curves took the line to 1½ furlongs (290m) of straight past Langley Mills where the Greenwich Hospital's lead smelting plant lay between 100 and 250 yards to the north.

Just over 3 furlongs (0.65km) past Langley station the Allendale turnpike, today the B6295, passed under the line and then the first summit was reached as the line cut off the corner of Nilstone Rigg reservoir, part of the water supply for the lead works. After falling at 1 in 50 for 3 furlongs (550m) the line started to climb again, crossing the Alston turnpike, today the B6305, just south of Carts Bog Inn before reaching the summit of Railway No. 1 just over 9½ miles (15.35km) from Border Counties Junction (p. 168). The descent started from Staward station site, initially at 1 in 50, but then on varying gradients until the river East Allen was finally reached.

The railway followed the general line of the river East Allen past Catton with the descent continuing to the centre of the bridge over the river Allen after which the line rose all the way to the terminus 12 miles 7 furlongs 0.56 chains (20.73km) from Border Counties Junction.

Railway No. 2 was simply a continuation of Railway No. 1, and started with a tunnel, 4 chains (80m) long under the Allendale turnpike, today's B6295, on the same left-hand curve of 15 chains (300m) radius by which Railway No. 1 ended, (see below and p. 166). However, the two lines were very different in design. Railway No. 1 was clearly intended for all types of traffic, whereas it is difficult to envisage a passenger service being successfully operated at reasonable

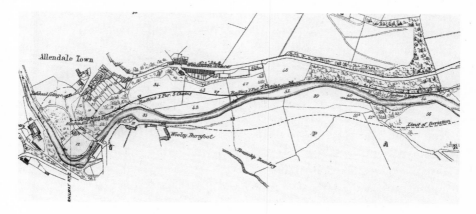

Plan showing the start of Railway No. 2 at Allendale. Reproduced by permission of NCS.

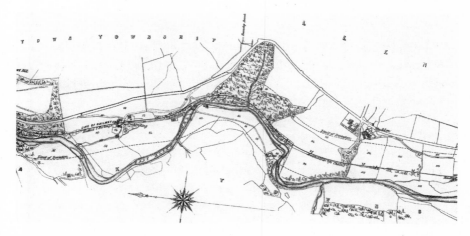

Plan showing the route of H&AR No. 2 past the 1 mile post from Allendale town. Reproduced by permission of NCS.

speeds south of Allendale town. Railway No. 2 was 7 miles (11.3km) long, with just seven sections of straight totalling only 1½ miles (2.4km), of which the final 4½ furlongs (900m) to the terminus accounted for over a third. There were nine consecutive reverse curves in the first 1 mile 3 furlongs, most with radii between 10 and 20 chains (200m and 400m) (p. 173). Apart from two lengths of level line totalling just over ¼ mile (440m), Railway No. 2 rose all the way from Allendale to Allenheads on eleven changes of gradient varying from 1 in 50 to 1 in 100, with over half (6km) of the distance at 1 in 50.

Apart from 3 furlongs (600m) to the west as it avoided the wide eastern sweep of the river at Sinderhope, the H&AR remained to the east of the river Allen all the way to Allenheads. The earthworks were heavier than might have been expected, considering the gradients and curvature. The largest earthwork of all was an embankment 59ft (18m) high and almost ½ mile (780m) long where the line passed above Peasmeadows House and crossed the Byerhope Burn.

One final point of interest was that all the public roads were either to be crossed by bridges, or closed and stopped up.

On 13 September 1865 the *Hexham Courant* reported that the contract for constructing Railway No. 1, from Hexham to Allendale, had been let to Mr W. Ritson of Redcar, and work was expected to commence immediately.[469] Three weeks later, the *Hexham Courant* stated that Mr. Ritson had 'begun with vigour to execute the works'.[472] On the same day, both it and the *Newcastle Daily Chronicle* announced that preliminary surveys were being made for a railway from Stanhope to join the H&AR at Allenheads.[471,472] This would have been similar to the proposed Allendale Branch of the WVER and, like its predecessor, it too came to nothing. By the middle of November 1865, the Company felt ready to

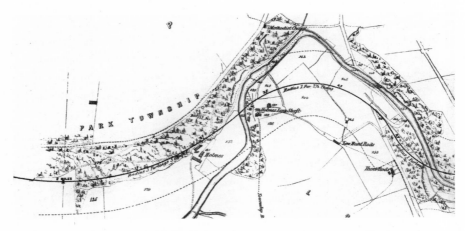

Plan showing the route of H&AR No. 2 past Holmes where the river East Allen is crossed twice west of Sinderhope. Reproduced by permission of NCS.

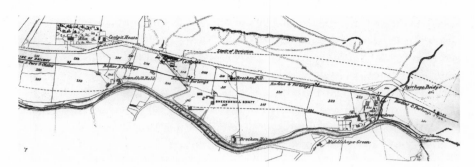

Plan showing the route of H&AR No. 2 running west of the turnpike road past Peasmeadows House, where the author lived as a child, and Byerhope Burn. Reproduced by permission of NCS.

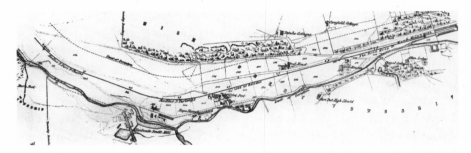

Plan of terminus of H&A Railway No. 2 at Allenheads. The H&AR ran to the east of the river East Allen most of the way from Allendale town, whereas the WVER Allendale branch ran on the west of the river as far as Sparty Lea. Reproduced by permission of NCS.

place advertisements in the local papers asking for tenders for rails, fish–plates, nuts, bolts, spikes and sleepers,[474] while at the second half-yearly general meeting, held on Tuesday 3 April 1866,[480] satisfactory progress on the construction of the line was again reported, despite the frost, snow and rain which had occurred.

Unfortunately there were found to be ambiguities in some sections of the act authorising the line and, in order to clarify these, a second bill was brought before Parliament in the following session. Although it was the NER which gave notice of a bill to allow that company to double its holding in H&AR shares, and to enable the Greenwich Hospital Estates to invest in the line, the bill was actually presented to Parliament by the H&AR Company.[479]

The H&AR Bill was unopposed,[481] and passed rapidly through the various parliamentary stages, receiving the Royal Assent on 11 June 1866.[482] The H&AR Act of 1866 stated that the line was to pass for 7 miles (11.3km) through the Greenwich Hospital Estate and specifically authorised the Greenwich Hospital to subscribe £10,000 to the company, and the NER company to subscribe a further

£10,000, making £20,000 in all. There were also fears that under the original act the company could only exercise its powers of compulsory purchase when the entire capital of £120,000 had been subscribed, and the 1866 act stated that only the £75,000 for Railway No. 1 was required to be subscribed before the land required for railway No. 1 could be obtained by compulsory purchase. This was the last time the H&AR Company found it necessary to approach Parliament.

Because the works were so dependent upon the weather, the directors were unable to give an accurate forecast for the opening of the first part of the line to Langley. However, they hoped it might be open for goods traffic in 'the autumn or early winter of this year [1866]'. It was recorded that the total expenditure to date was £10,105 5s 3d (£10,105.26). Prior to the third half-yearly meeting on 30 August 1866,[484] the directors inspected the line from the junction to Nilstone Ridge, near Langley, and found that although there had been considerable progress, the weather and state of the labour market had delayed progress by two or three months. Most of the earthworks on the first 8 miles (12.9km) were complete, and 4½ miles (7.2km) of permanent way had been laid. Bewick expected the line would be ready for opening as far as Langley by the end of the year, while the chairman expected that Railway No. 1 would be completed during the following year, and hoped that Railway No. 2 would also be finished. The Greenwich Hospital had not only taken 1,000 shares but had already paid the company £6,000 in calls. An item in the report that the junction with the N&CR had not yet been definitely arranged was soon to present serious problems. After three optimistic reports, the fourth meeting, held on 2 February 1867 presented a rather gloomier picture.[487] Bad weather had affected both the progress and stability of the works, and had increased the costs.

The main problem was Coastley Dene (p. 170), where the large embankment had continued to slip since the previous August. It had also proved difficult to reach an agreement with the NER over the site of the permanent junction (p. 169), although a temporary connection had been allowed. Fortunately, the local landowner, Mr Leadbitter, allowed the company to have the required area of land, even though it lay outside the limits of deviation allowed by the act. A site for the station for Allendale Town had been found beside the turnpike road between Catton and the river, just over ½ mile (1km) from Allendale Town. This point was 12¼ miles (19.7km) from the junction, was convenient for traffic to both East and West Allendale and coincidently was on the opposite side of the turnpike to the proposed terminus of the WVER Allendale branch (p. 84).

The cost of the last ½ mile (1km) of Railway No. 1 was estimated at between £6,000 and £8,000, and was not expected to generate any additional traffic. Bewick saw no justification for building this section until the line was to be extended up the valley and, at that time, there was no prospect of building Railway No. 2, as the additional capital necessary could not be raised. To that date

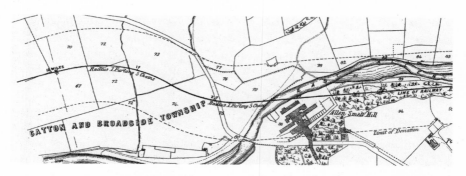

Plan showing the H&AR near Catton. The site chosen for the *temporary* terminus of Catton Road was beside the Allendale turnpike in the field marked 73, at the edge of the limits of deviation. Reproduced by permission of NCS.

the company had received £49,319 10s 3d (£49,319.51) of which £3,546 7s (£3,546.35) remained on hand, while the call for the last £2 on each share of £10 had been made that day. It was confirmed that H&AR trains would use the NER's Hexham station, and Mr Hunter, the director appointed by the NER, hoped that Hexham station would have been improved by that time. Almost a year later than expected, the line from Hexham to Langley was opened for goods traffic on Monday 19 August 1867,[498] and found to be in excellent condition, with the Coastley Dene embankment now firm and solid. Trains were to run regularly from Hexham about 10 a.m. each morning for the conveyance of goods, minerals, stock and parcels; returning from Langley about 12 p.m. The fifth half-yearly general meeting was held on the following Saturday, 24 August 1867,[499] where the pleasure at the opening of the Hexham to Langley section was tempered by the news of the financial difficulties in which the company now found itself. The NER was working the traffic, so that the H&AR had not needed to purchase any rolling stock for itself. The temporary junction with the NER had been brought into use during May 1867 for works traffic, and the works for the new road at Staward were progressing well (p. 178), although it was expected to be at least three months before the line could be opened to the temporary terminus at Catton Road.

However, up to 30 June 1867 the Company had received £66,648 5s 5d (£66,648.27), while expenditure amounted to £60,229 12s 11d (£60,229.65). There were 334 shares on which no payment had been made and the company could not exercise their borrowing powers unless at least £2 deposit was paid on each of these shares. The cost of making the line ready for passenger traffic, including the permanent junction at Hexham, would be £3,000 to £4,000.

As it had not been possible to start constructing the continuation of the line to Allendale Town, or start the formation of Railway No. 2, the chairman would

The steep southern approach to the bridge carrying the road to Catton from the Alston turnpike over the H&AR at Staward. This road was built by the H&AR to accommodate the local population and was another example of the negotiating powers of Wentworth Blackett Beaumont, the driving force behind the line.

Catton Road (Allendale) station when the passenger service was running. Ken Hoole collection, reproduced by permission of HoS-DRM.

have to build a branch into the Allen smelt mill. The line was finally opened through to Allendale, or Catton Road as the temporary terminus was originally called, for goods, minerals, livestock and parcels, on 13 January 1868, following an inspection the week before.[502,504] Large numbers of people turned out to welcome the first train at Catton Road. It was reported at the sixth half-yearly meeting[506] that there were now 12¼ miles (19.7km) of railway open for freight traffic. Stations were provided at Elrington, Langley, Staward and Catton Road, each with a small shed where goods could be kept, while arrangements were being made to erect a large shed for storing wagons at Catton Road. It should be noted that from 12 miles 1 furlong (19.5km) the eastern limit of deviation on the deposited plans ran alongside the turnpike road, on land owned by W.B. Beaumont, and this is where the so-called 'temporary terminus' was built. The completion of the line in two years from the start of work, and two and half years from obtaining the act, was considered to be very satisfactory.

The Chairman had spent between £1,200 and £1,300 on building the branch from Catton Road Station to the Allen smelt mill, while the Greenwich Hospital had also constructed a branch line from their Langley Mills to the railway at a cost of £1,000. It was estimated that the cost of completing the junction with the N&CR would be £2,600; another £1,400 would be needed for passenger stations etc., while it would cost a further £9,000 to £10,000 to complete the line to Allendale town. The problem of the permanent junction with the main line occupied the remainder of 1868. The new site was about ¼ mile (400m) nearer Hexham than the junction shown on the plans, and it was originally expected that the railway would be open for passengers by 1 July 1868.

By the end of March 1868 the signs of serious problems for the H&AR were beginning to appear when the *Hexham Courant* reported on the reduced price of lead, resulting in less traffic than expected on the railway.[509] Then, in July, despite an earlier announcement, the H&AR advertised for tenders to build the permanent junction with the NER and to erect stations.[516] At the next general meeting it was announced that the remaining 334 shares had not all been sold until May 1868,[517] when the directors gave instructions for the immediate formation of the permanent junction, the erection of stations and all other works necessary to make the line fit for passenger traffic. Mr Ritson, the contractor, had not only failed to proceed with the works but instead had made substantial claims against the company. This had lead to the loss of the best part of the season. The shareholders agreed to make an application for an extension of time to complete their lines, although it was stressed that this did not mean that Railway No. 2 would definitely be built.

At last, on Tuesday 2 February 1869,[519] the government inspector, Colonel Yolland inspected the line, accompanied by Mr Bewick and other H&AR and NER officials. Col. Yolland recommended the formation of a siding at Langley, and some minor changes in the signals, before he would pass the line for passenger traffic. He also expressed himself thoroughly disgusted with Hexham railway station, much to the delight of the town's inhabitants. Col. Yolland made a second inspection on Thursday 25 February 1869,[520] and passed the line for passenger traffic, which was to start on Monday 1 March. Immediate arrangements were made with the NER, and an advert appeared in the *Hexham Courant* of the following Saturday, announcing the date of the official opening, and that a service of two passenger trains would run each way daily, except Sundays, with an extra train on Tuesday, Hexham market day.[521] At the eighth half-yearly meeting it was reported that a turntable had been erected at Catton Road, as the company was not allowed to operate engines tender first.[522] The signals necessary for the passenger service had been erected, and those at the junction had proved expensive, as the Board of Trade had required the H&AR to provide safety locking apparatus not only for their own line but also for the BCR, which joined the main line at the same place. Arrangements had been made for the NER to supply the motive power and rolling stock necessary for working all the traffic on the line.

The Board of Trade had extended the time for the construction of Railway No. 2 for two years. Despite the fact that Catton Road was stated to be a temporary station, it remained the terminus of the public railway until it closed, the only southward extension being W.B. Beaumont's private branch into the Allen smelt mills. It should be noted, however, that the NER changed the name of Catton Road to Allendale in 1898.[657] Twenty-two years after the line was absorbed into the North Eastern Railway, an extension to the Leadgate in Allendale town was surveyed,[658] but that appears to have been the final attempt to complete Railway No. 1, although rumours that the line was to be extended continued to appear in the local papers.[667]

The H&AR was a fairly typical example of a line built largely with local initiative, to serve a relatively sparsely populated rural area in which there was a single extractive industry, in this case lead. Not only did the H&AR fail to reach its intended destination but, within a decade of opening, the lead mining industry was failing and the population emigrating. Although it is true that lack of available finance caused the railway to terminate about half a mile short of Allendale town, the line was actually built well within the share and loan capital it was authorised to raise. In fact, dividends were paid on three occasions, while the original shareholders saw around 60 per cent of their investment returned when the line was sold to the NER in 1876. In other words, this railway was not the unmitigated financial disaster that was displayed by several of its contemporaries, and for which, locally, it has always had an unjustified reputation. The trains run during the independent existence of the company carried over 240,000 passengers without any accident either to passengers or servants of the company. As the chairman said in his address to the final meeting of shareholders, 'That said much for the careful management on the part of the officials and servants of the Company.'

As has proved to be the case quite frequently in the North Pennines, the H&AR was not built exactly as shown on the deposited plans. At Elrington, the road shown on the plans as being lowered to go under the railway was taken 6 chains (120 yards) further west and raised to go over the line. The embankment

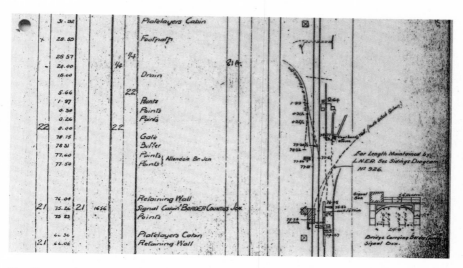

The diagram above is part of the LNER engineers' track diagrams showing the track plan at Border Counties Junction, with 2¼ chains (50 yards) separating the Allendale branch points from the Border Counties points. This was the true picture of the junction, not the situation as shown by the OS map (see fig. 8 col. section). Reproduced by permission of A. Cudlipp.

on which the railway was built past Elrington ended at the road bridge, 7 chains (140 yards) further east than stated on the plans, with the cutting which followed starting under the road bridge. Near Langley two bridges were built, one over the line to the east and one under it to the west of the station, providing access to the lead smelter owned by the Greenwich Hospital Trust. The flu from Langley smelt works also crossed the line on an over bridge, to the east of the road bridge.

These bridges were always shown on the OS maps, and exist to this day, but one anomaly remained right up until the line was lifted in the early years of British Rail, although it was obliterated by the building of the Hexham bypass on the A69. It even appeared on the seventh edition of the 1-inch OS map, published in 1956 after the line had been closed completely, and showing that the tracks had already been lifted beyond Elfoot House. The deposited plans (p. 169) show the junction with the N&CR some way west of the junction with the BCR. This is what was authorised and how the junction was always shown on the OS maps. When the NER refused to accept this junction, the private agreement negotiated by Wentworth Blackett Beaumont with Mr Leadbitter allowed the junction to be moved to within a few yards of the junction with the BCR. However, this was never shown on any OS map, or on any maps, such as Bartholomew's Half Inch series, that were based on the OS maps (see fig. 8 col. section).

11

BARNARD CASTLE AND THE TEES VALLEY RAILWAY

In earlier chapters we examined the efforts made during 1845 and 1846 by both the S&DR and the N&CR to connect the lead-mining district of the North Pennines with the outside world. The plans produced at that time by these companies involved the valleys of the rivers Allen, Tyne and Wear, but completely ignored the Tees, although significant quantities of lead were being extracted from the upper reaches of this valley. Although the town of Barnard Castle lies some distance from the ore-field, it occupies a key position for the provision of transport into the upper regions of the Tees Valley, as well as providing an approach to Stainmore which offers one of the lower crossings of the Pennine chain. Rather like the towns of Allendale, Alston and Hexham, most of Barnard Castle has been built on a site well above the river Tees on which it stands but, unlike these northern towns where most of the plans kept the railway close to the level of the river, all the plans for railways, including those which were built, show lines which terminated in, or passed through, the higher parts of Barnard Castle.

The first suggestions that a railway might be built connecting Barnard Castle to the developing rail network appeared in November 1839.[73] Two weeks later *Herepath* reported that a well-attended meeting had been held in Barnard Castle on Thursday 7 November 1839, when a provisional committee was formed to arrange for a survey to be made for a railway to connect Barnard Castle with the S&DR.[74] Despite this early promise, in February 1840 *Herepath* announced that 'The railway projected from Barnard Castle to join the Stockton & Darlington is to be given up in consequence of the strenuous opposition of the Duke of Cleveland, through a portion of whose estates it would pass.'[77]

The next series of proposals to bring a railway to Barnard Castle appeared in 1845 and, as we saw in Chapter 3, resulted in the authorisation of the NCUR, which was an amalgam of three separate schemes.[230] The railway authorised to be built by this act included a line from Bishop Auckland, through Barnard Castle, to join the NCUR main line from Thirsk to Penrith near Kirkby Stephen,[227] plus a branch from Kirkby Stephen to Tebay. The plans for the NCUR were derived from those of the Y&GUR and the Y&CR.[200]

As we saw in Chapter 3 the NCUR management ceased trying to build their line when Parliament refused to repeal the clause requiring both sections of the railway to be built simultaneously.[296] Another scheme which failed even to submit plans for a bill was the proposal, in 1846, for a line from Northallerton, through Barnard Castle, Alston and Haltwhistle to Hawick, which would have served as an extension of the London and York, giving that line a direct route to Edinburgh.[245] When it became obvious that none of the lines of the NCUR would ever be built, plans were produced by members of the S&DR Company for a line which revived the idea of connecting Barnard Castle with the S&DR at Darlington.[374] The first attempt failed in the 1853 session of Parliament, but new plans were submitted for the following year (p. 184).[379] Opponents of the S&DR promoted, as an alternative, the Barnard Castle and Bishop Auckland Junction Railway (BC&BAJR) starting by a junction with the authorised, but at that time not yet built, Bishop Auckland branch of the YN&BR, and terminating at Barnard Castle. A junction with the WVR at Bishop Auckland was also included in the plans and an attempt was made to obtain an act in the 1854 parliamentary session.[381]

However, after a fierce battle, the BC&BAJR failed, whereas the scheme supported by the S&DR succeeded,[776] with the D&BCR Act receiving the Royal Assent on 2 July 1854.[382] The D&BCR was opened on Tuesday 8 July 1856[390] with the arrival at Barnard Castle of a train carrying the directors and their friends,[389] and this was followed by the departure, at 11 a.m., of a crowded excursion train for Darlington and Redcar.[390] In fact the first train had arrived

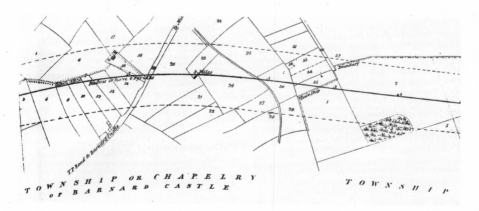

The route of the NCUR, former Y&CR, past Barnard Castle, crossing the Middleton-in-Teesdale turnpike road in a similar place to the SD&LUR (p. 187). Reproduced by permission of DRO.

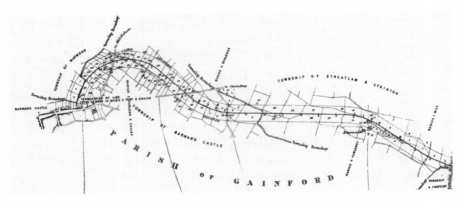

The western end of the plans of the D&BCR showing the Barnard Castle terminus.
Reproduced by permission of DRO.

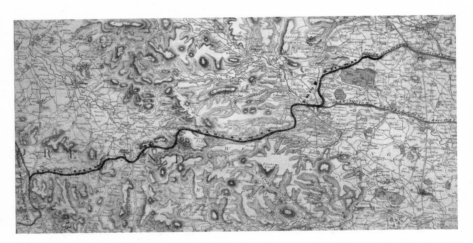

Copy of sheet 48 of G. F. Cruchley's map showing the route, marked in grey, of the South
Durham and Lancashire Union Railway, as originally authorised. Reproduced by permission
of DRO.

from Darlington on Tuesday 24 June with a number of directors and friends,
while the first parcel was forwarded from Barnard Castle the same day from
the office of the *Teesdale Mercury*.[388] Initially there were three trains each way
between Darlington and Barnard Castle,[390] but this was increased to four from
1 August.[392,393]

At the half-yearly meeting of shareholders[394] it was stated that from the
opening a coach had commenced running from Barnard Castle to Brough to
connect with the Penrith mail, and that the works to equip the line to deal with
merchandise, coal or mineral traffic were being pushed ahead. In November

1856, following the opening to Barnard Castle,[397] the prospectus was issued for a line to run from the Hagger Leases branch of the S&DR near Bishop Auckland, through Barnard Castle to Tebay on the L&CR, following a route similar to that proposed in the NCUR Bill of 1847.[285] The new railway was promoted by directors of the D&BCR, S&DR and L&CR, with plans being deposited for the South Durham and Lancashire Union Railway (SD&LUR) the same month,[398] while the act received the Royal Assent on 13 July 1857.[399] The first meeting of the shareholders of the SD&LUR took place on 5 August 1857,[431] with the first sod being cut on 25 August, at Kirkby Stephen, by the Duke of Cleveland.[400] However, rather like the South Tyne branch of the N&CR ten years earlier, the promoters had second thoughts about part of their route and, in November 1858, deposited a revised set of plans for the section from Bishop Auckland to Barnard Castle.[410]

Parliament granted the SD&LUR a second act authorising these changes on 1 August 1859.[413] The original route had joined the Hagger Leases branch of the S&DR close to Lands Colliery (p. 140), whereas the new line was to join the same branch closer to Bishop Auckland, about 2¼ miles (3.6km) further east (p. 186). However the distance from Barnard Castle to the junction was only increased from 9 miles 9.6 chains (14.68km) to 10 miles 5 furlongs 3.6 chains (17.17km). The reason for the apparent discrepancy was that the new route ran further south than the original, was a little straighter and had a rather lower summit level. Even

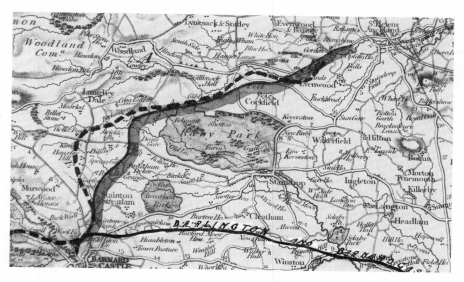

Copy of sheet 48 of G F. Cruchley's map showing the revised route, the shaded line, of the SD&LUR, between Barnard Castle and the Hagger Leases branch of the S&DR. Reproduced by permission of DRO.

the steepest gradient was slightly less, although the new line did have almost 5 miles (7.65km) of 1 in 71 descending towards Bishop Auckland, whereas the longest gradient on the original line was 2½ miles (4.04km) climbing from Barnard Castle at 1 in 70.

In the same year that plans for the direct line from the Hagger Leases branch to Bishop Auckland were prepared, plans for the Eden Valley Railway (EVR) were also deposited.[401] Although it is slightly outside the scope of this monograph, the Eden Valley line virtually completed the northern section of the NCUR while, by connecting the L&CR at Clifton, just south of Penrith, with the SD&LUR near Kirkby Stephen, it provided another route between the West Cumberland ore-fields and the iron works and coalfields of County Durham. The act for the Eden Valley Railway was passed on 2 May 1858,[405] with the first sod being cut on 4 August 1858 at Appleby by Lord Brougham.[409]

The SD&LUR was opened for goods traffic between Tebay and Barnard Castle on 1 July 1861, with hundreds of tons of coke, ironstone, etc. immediately being conveyed along this first section.[427] The line was opened for passenger traffic just five weeks later, on 7 August.[431] The construction of the SD&LUR left the original Barnard Castle station of the D&BCR at the end of the short branch, with the new station for through trains being built just west of the junction.

Initially two of the trains from Darlington continued through to Tebay,[432] only drawing up at the new station, although those terminating at Barnard Castle continued to use the old station,[433] whereas all trains started from the new station. Work continued satisfactorily on the Barnard Castle to West Auckland section[426] while the EVR was opened for all traffic in June

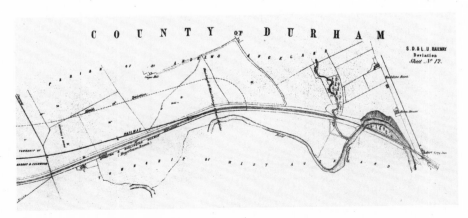

Plan showing the new junction, closer to Bishop Auckland, of the SD&LUR with the Hagger Leases branch of the S&DR, as authorised by the Act of 1859. Reproduced by permission of DRO.

1862,[440] although a second act had been passed on 7 July 1862 to improve the carriage of mineral traffic to and from the Cockermouth, Keswick and Penrith Railway.[443]

The final section of the SD&LUR from Barnard Castle to the junction with the Hagger Leases branch of the S&DR, near St Helen's Auckland, was opened on 1 August 1863. According to the *Teesdale Mercury* of 29 July a second inspection had been required before 'the government official' was satisfied with the line.[447] Just over two weeks earlier the act allowing the amalgamation

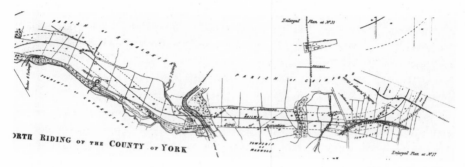

SD&LUR plans showing the crossing of the river Tees and the junctions with D&BCR to the north of Barnard Castle. The line crosses the Middleton-in-Teesdale turnpike in a place similar to the NCUR, which was the site of the new through station. Reproduced by permission of DRO.

Through station at Barnard Castle, built for the South Durham and Lancashire Union Railway, looking east. Ken Hoole collection, reproduced by permission of HoS-DRM.

of the S&DR with the NER had received the Royal Assent[446] and so it was the NER which inaugurated services over the new line. A full account of the South Durham and Lancashire Union Railway is to be found in the book *The Stainmore Railway* by K. Hoole,[737] and of the Eden Valley Railway in the book of that name by Robert Weston.[791] I have found no reference to a separate opening of the section of line from the tunnel branch to Bishop Auckland, and it is therefore probable that the entire line from Barnard Castle to Bishop Auckland was opened on 1 August 1863. The total distance from the junction at Barnard Castle to the east end of Bishop Auckland station was 14 miles 5 furlongs 5 chains (23.64km) and the initial passenger service on the SD&LUR was two trains each way from Darlington to Tebay with coaches for Penrith, one train each way from Darlington to Penrith, two trains each way from Darlington to Barnard Castle only and two trains each way from Barnard Castle to Bishop Auckland,[448] although the latter service was increased to four trains each way before the end of 1864.[458]

Although the line from Bishop Auckland to Barnard Castle became, in effect, part of the main line from West Cumberland and the Furness region to Consett, the 14 miles 5 furlongs 5 chains from Barnard Castle to Bishop Auckland was made up of lines authorised by four different acts of Parliament. The first 1 mile 3 furlongs 9.18 chains (2.4km) was the section from the east end of Bishop Auckland station to the tunnel branch (p. 141), authorised by the S&DR Act of 1858.[407] This line rose all the way from Bishop Auckland at 1 in 2247¼ and, although the radius of curvature was never less than 40 chains (800m), it followed a fairly sinuous route, although the earthworks were not severe. The next 1 mile 2 furlongs 1 chain (2.03km) was the western section of the tunnel branch (p. 135), authorised by the S&DR Act of 1854,[383] taking the line to St Helen Auckland where it crossed the line of the original Stockton and Darlington Railway at West Auckland station. Again the earthworks were relatively light on this section while the only severe curve was 15 chains (300m) to the right on a radius of 20 chains (400m) at the point where the tunnel branch joined the original line of the S&DR.

The next part of the route used 1 mile 2 furlongs 1 chain (2.03km) of the Hagger Leases branch (p. 37) authorised by the S&DR Act of 1824.[38] The plans[380] for the tunnel branch state that the new line commenced at the junction with the Hagger Leases branch but it does look as if a few yards of the original S&DR were used between the junctions. I have therefore added 18 yards (0.82 chains or 16.5 metres) to the distance at St Helen Auckland. These plans,[35] signed by Robert Stephenson, showing the Hagger Leases branch and the entire S&DR, are among the earliest of railway plans and show no radii for the curves, no limits of deviation, and have a very crude method of indicating earthworks and gradients.

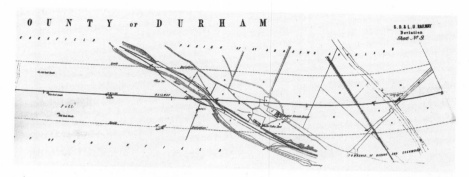

Plans of the deviation of the Barnard Castle to Auckland section of the SD&LUR, showing the new crossing of the river Gaunless near Butterknowle House. Reproduced by permission of DRO.

The plans of the deviation of the Bishop Auckland section of the SD&LUR show the new line joining the Hagger Leases branch 2 furlongs (400m) west of the second crossing of the river Gaunless, or a further 9 chains (180m) west of the Earl Grey Inn, at the crossing of the Darlington to Corbridge turnpike (p. 186).[410] From the S&DR plans, the distance from the main line to the second crossing of the river Gaunless is 1 chain over 1 mile (1.63km), making the total distance of the Hagger Leases branch which the new route followed 1 mile 2 furlongs 1 chain (2.03km), all rising at 1 in 150. According to the distance table in *The Stainmore Railway* by K. Hoole,[737] 1 mile 2 furlongs 6 chains (2.13km) of the Hagger Leases branch was used.

The river Gaunless was crossed on 7 furlongs (1.4km) of straight a little over 3¾ miles (6.07km) from Bishop Auckland.

There were some quite heavy earthworks on this section of the SD&LUR, with several embankments over intermediate streams and rivers, although in no case was the method of crossing indicated. The first was over the Gordon Beck at a height of 42ft (12.8m), followed by the river Gaunless which was to be crossed at a height of 91ft (27.7m) and the Langley Beck at a height of 74ft (22.5m), with viaducts being built over the last two watercourses. On the early plans dimensions were not given for the bridges taking the railway over public roads, but for the last three sets the height of the bridges over public roads varied from 15ft to 35ft (4.6m to 10.7m), while the width varied from 16ft to 25ft (4.9m to 7.6m). No dimensions were given for bridges over the railway on any of the plans. A large amount of industry, mainly coal mining and coke production, developed along this section of railway, and a private branch 5 miles (8km) long was built from the SD&LUR just east of Lands viaduct to serve the Woodlands group of collieries.[811] Initially the NER worked this branch, but the local company took over in 1885

Train of empties crossing Lands viaduct where the SD&LUR crossed the river Gaunless and the Haggerleases branch of the S&DR. Ken Hoole collection, reproduced by permission of HoS-DRM.

Viaduct carrying the SD&LUR over the river Tees near Barnard Castle. Ken Hoole collection, reproduced by permission of HoS-DRM.

using normal locomotive operating practices. However from the 1890s the loaded wagons were run by gravity down to the junction with the NER, while the locomotive was used only to haul the empties back up the gradient.

The stage was now set for the extension of the railway system to Middleton-in-Teesdale, the headquarters of the Tees Valley lead-mining region. Following a meeting held in the Rose and Crown Inn, Middleton-in-Teesdale on

8 October 1864 to promote the building of a railway from the S&DR east of Lartington on the south side of the river Tees to Middleton,[452] plans for the TVR.[456] were deposited on 29 November 1864 and the act authorising the line received the Royal Assent on 19 June 1865.[467] Although the chairman was the Rev. Thomas Witham of Lartington Hall, three of the other directors were Henry Pease, Henry Fell Pease and Thomas MacNay, while the NER subscribed half of the £50,000 authorised capital.[729] On Monday 12 September 1865 the Duke of Cleveland cut the first sod, and the local press reported that the line would be 7 miles (11.3km) long, starting from a junction with the South Durham and Lancashire Union Railway a short distance west of the viaduct over the Tees (p. 190) and about 1½ miles (2.4km) from Barnard Castle (p. 187).[469] According to the report, it was 'to run along the valley of the Tees by way of Lartington, Cotherstone, Romaldkirk, Egglestone, and Mickleton, terminating for the present at Middleton-in-Teesdale, a stretch of the most beautiful territory; but at some future day the line might be extended as far as Alston.'

The new line did not go through Lartington, which was served by a station on the SD&LUR a short distance beyond the start of the TVR, while Egglestone lies on the Durham side of the river, and was served by the station for Romalkirk (p. 193). It was also stated that previous efforts had been made to build this railway, but nothing had happened. The authorised capital of £50,000 was divided into 1,000 shares of £50 each. Although the Tees Valley Railway connected Middleton-in-Teesdale with Barnard Castle, both of which are, and were, in the county of Durham, the route lay entirely within what was then the North Riding of the county of Yorkshire.

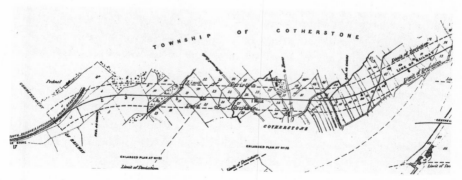

The start of the Tees Valley Railway by a junction with the SD&LUR about 1 mile (1.6km) beyond the Tees viaduct and passing the village of Cotherstone just over a mile further west. Cotherstone station lay on the 1 in 200 gradient just before the road running from the village. Reproduced by permission of NYCRO.

Tees Valley Junction, taken on 17 June 1959, with the SD&LUR on the left and the line to Middleton-in-Teesdale diverging to the right. Ken Hoole collection, reproduced by permission of HoS-DRM.

In June the doubling of about one mile (1.6km) of the SD&LUR line from the junction with the Tees Valley Railway to Barnard Castle was authorised to commence immediately.[468] The contract for building the line was let to Messrs Bolton & Co. of Newcastle, who expected to have it completed in eighteen months, while the S&DR, by that time the NER, had agreed to work it. The line was to start from the SD&LUR, approximately 4 furlongs (800m) west of the viaduct over the river Tees and 1½ miles (2.4km) from the junction of the SD&LUR and the D&BCR at Barnard Castle, at a point 367 yards (336m) west of the mile-post marked 17.[456]

Except where river valleys were to be crossed, the earthworks were moderate to light, with embankments only exceeding 27ft (8.2m) on three occasions, while the cuttings were never more than 29ft (8.8m) deep. The line crossed over the public road to Barnard Castle just before Cotherstone station, the only intermediate station for which a level section of track was not provided. This road was supposed to have been replaced on a new alignment by the Alston Turnpike Trust Act of 1824,[37] but whereas most of the new sections of road from Alston to Middleton-in-Teesdale were built, those between Middleton and Barnard Castle were not.

It is interesting to note that at the majority of road crossings the railway was to pass over the roads on arches 16ft (4.9m) high, with the width varying from 20ft to 35ft (6.1m to 10.7m), while the plans showed three level crossings, but no bridges carrying roads over the railway. The river Balder was crossed on a viaduct

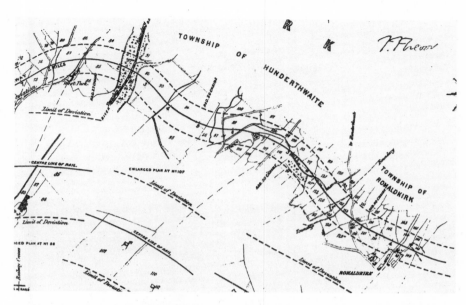

The Tees Valley Railway between Cotherstone and Romaldkirk. Balder viaduct was between the 2 miles 2 and 3 furlong marks. The 18½ chains of level for Romaldkirk station lay just past the road crossing after the 3 miles 4 furlong point. Reproduced by permission of NYCRO.

The Tees Valley Railway between Romaldkirk and Mickleton. Reproduced by permission of NYCRO.

91ft (27.7m) high and 103 yards (94m) long at 3 miles 6 furlongs 8½ chains (6.05km) from Barnard Castle.

The level section for Romaldkirk station commenced 5 miles 5½ chains (8km) from Barnard Castle. The summit of the line was 812ft (247.5m) above sea level and Mickleton station was situated on the summit level just over 6 miles 5 furlongs (10.52km) from Barnard Castle. The river Lune was crossed on a viaduct a little over 60ft (18.4m) high and 118 yards (108m) long (p. 194) at 7 miles 4 furlongs 8 chains (12.08km) from Barnard Castle.

The TVR was to terminate some way above the west bank of the river Tees, beside the Step Ends Toll Bar on the Brough to Middleton-in-Teesdale turnpike

The end of the Tees Valley Railway. Mickleton station was built near the 5 mile 3 furlong point, 2 furlongs past the summit of the line. The valley of the river Lune was crossed between the 6 mile and 6 mile 1 furlong marks. Reproduced by permisson of NYCRO.

The Lune viaduct with the former Alston turnpike from Middleton (B6277) running to the left (east), on 3 October 2002. The former section of the B6277 (now unclassified) leaves at the signpost and passes under the viaduct.

road, today the B6276/B6277. The line was to be 1 chain over 7 miles (11.29km) long from the junction with the SD&LUR and the company was permitted to enter into working, maintenance and traffic arrangements with the NER which, as we have seen, was allowed to subscribe capital to what was essentially a branch from the SD&LUR.

Following the cutting of the first sod, progress was reasonably rapid, with the shareholders being told at the half-yearly meeting in February 1866 that not only had the contract for building the line been signed but that the working plans had been prepared and the contractors had started work.[478] At this time the local press carried regular notices advertising the Teesdale Mail Omnibus which ran to and from Middleton-in-Teesdale and connected with trains, either at Lartington station on the SD&LUR, or at Barnard Castle station itself.[476] It was reported at the next half-yearly meeting in August 1866 that work was continuing to progress well,[483] and this was repeated in November 1866 in a report in the *Teesdale Mercury*.[485] This report also stated that should the weather continue favourable it would shortly be possible for a locomotive to get as far as Cotherstone. Most of the permanent way had been laid and the foundations for the Balder and Lune viaducts were in place, while all the minor bridges and culverts had been completed. By December 1866 the TVR was facing problems similar to those of the H&AR further north, with the *Teesdale Mercury* reporting that 'the works are proceeding as well as the weather will permit.'[486]

It was also announced that the contract for the stations at Cotherstone and Mickleton had been let to a Mr D.P. Appleby of Barnard Castle, while six weeks later the building of Middleton station was awarded to a Mr B. Hepworth, also of Barnard Castle.[488] The report at the next half-yearly meeting at the end of February 1867 remained reasonably optimistic, stating that only about one quarter of the works remained to be executed and that it was hoped to open in August.[489] There was another favourable report in the *Teesdale Mercury* at the end of April 1867 where the contractors were congratulated in 'pressing forward so well in view of the unfavourable weather of the previous year', and stating that

View over Middleton-in-Teesdale station from above the line to the quarries. Ken Hoole collection, reproduced by permission of HoS-DRM.

'with favourable weather, there will be no difficulty on completing the works in the time contemplated.'[490]

Nevertheless, the line did not open in 1867. The report of the half-yearly meeting at the end of February 1868 stated that the works were so far advanced that a train was able to cover the whole line and the opening for passengers was expected in two months, and for goods traffic almost immediately.[507] Col. C.L. Hutchison inspected the line on 1 May 1868 and reported that the junction with the SD&LUR had been moved about one mile closer to Barnard Castle, presumably to avoid the necessity of having a staff station at the intended junction.[510] The line used was originally a mineral line of the Barnard Castle branch. Various relatively minor defects had been found and had to be repaired before permission would be granted to open the line.

Finally, on 8 May 1868, it was announced that the directors of the TVR would make their final inspection on Tuesday 12 May before the opening of the line on Wednesday 13 May 1868.[511] Col. Hutchinson, the government inspector, duly made his final inspection on Tuesday 12 May[512] and the opening of the line the following day was celebrated by a dinner and other festivities. In the TVR Book of Reports, Letters, etc there is a letter from Col. Hutchison dated 16 May 1868,[513] stating that the line had been re-inspected and passed, followed by a letter from the Board of Trade of 18 May 1868 stating that 'the line was now allowed to be open.'[514] Although the plans show no bridges carrying roads over the TVR, according to the 1947 edition of the OS 1-inch map, three were included when

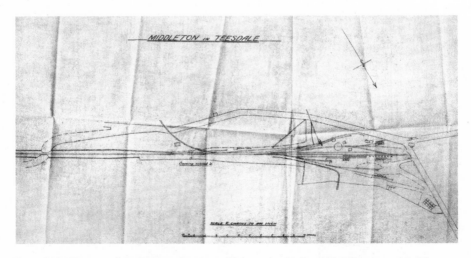

Plan of Middleton station showing the mineral line to the Ord and Maddison quarries. The line to the quarries left at the east end of the station. Reproduced by permission of Lord Strathmore and DRO.

the line was built. The first was one of the roads to Hunderthwaite, which should have been lowered 21ft (6.4m). The other two were roads to Mickleton, where the actual earthworks appear to be rather different from the low embankments shown on the plans, with the line running at ground level for the first road and in a cutting for the second.

Initially the passenger service on the TVR was three trains each way per day,[523] but this was later increased to six each way,[578] which was the number being operated in the 1951 British Rail timetable. Unlike the H&AR, whose expected freight traffic failed to materialise due to the depression in the British lead industry, while the line itself failed to generate any significant new traffic, a considerable amount of new traffic rapidly developed on the TVR, especially whinstone from a new siding provided at Middleton at the request of Messrs Ord and Maddison.[523a] Just three years after the line was opened the *Teesdale Mercury* reported that the ironstone works of Messrs Pease, at Park End, 1½ miles (2.41km) further up the valley, were sending large quantities of iron ore by rail from Middleton-in-Teesdale.[526] Less than a year later an editorial in the same paper stated that the TVR was carrying about 1,000 tons of limestone daily.[551] In fact the bulk of the stone despatched from Middleton-in-Teesdale station was whinstone for road making and most came from Middleton quarry owned by Ord and Maddison. This quarry was situated to the south-east of the station to which it was connected by a private branch.[569,806]

However, not everything continued to go well for the company, with the *Hexham Courant* reporting the suspension of the telegraph service in 1875 when the Post Office authorities in London refused to pay the extra 3*d* (1.25 pence) per message being demanded by the railway company.[557] The new mineral traffic generated by the opening of the line more than compensated for the loss of the lead traffic, when the failure of the British lead industry to compete with foreign markets finally hit Teesdale in 1878.[565] However, according to an editorial in the *Teesdale Mercury*, 'urgent requirements of the Board of Trade as to general traffic regulations' forced many of the shareholders to agree to the absorption of the TVR by the NER.[622] This was accomplished by the NER Act of 19 June 1882,[557] which left the NER company in absolute control of all the public lines in the North Pennines.

THE CUMBERLAND AND CLEVELAND JUNCTION RAILWAY

Three years after the opening of the TVR the local press reported that a survey had started for the planned extension of the railway from Middleton-in-Teesdale to Alston.[527,529] In reporting the survey the *Carlisle Patriot* stated that the district was rich in ores, while the line would be 'an important link towards shortening the distance into Scotland'.[528] On 17 November 1871 the *Carlisle Journal* carried a notice of application to Parliament for the Cumberland and Cleveland Junction Railway (C&CJR), stating that printed copies of the proposed bill would be deposited on or before 21 December 1871.[530] The *Carlisle Journal* carried this notice in two more issues, while on 22 November the *Teesdale Mercury* announced that the survey was complete and confirmed that a prospectus of the new line would shortly be issued.[531] On 24 November the *Auckland Times and Herald* also reported that the survey had been completed, adding that the railway would pass through a rich metalliferous country, which was generally thought to contain a large amount of iron ore of good quality, and would reach a height of 1,750ft (530m) nearly 500ft (150m) higher than the railway across Stainmore, which was understood to be the highest in England.[532] On 1 December the *Carlisle Patriot*[535] reported that the C&CJR Bill had been deposited with the Private Bill Office.

Also at the beginning of December the *Hexham Courant* reported the completion of the survey, saying that the line was to be 22 miles (35km) long and 'will open out, not only a wild and very romantic district, but one rich in mineral wealth'.[536] On 22 December the *Auckland Times and Herald* reported that plans and sections had been deposited with the justices of the peace for Cumberland, Durham and the North Riding of Yorkshire by Messrs Dickinson, Solicitors, Alston.[537] Also included in this report, as well as one in the *Teesdale Mercury* for 27 December,[539] were comprehensive descriptions of the proposed railway, stating that it would start by a junction with the Alston branch a little north of the station, about 350 yards (320m) south of the Tyne viaduct. It was to run east of the Raise, cross the Alston to Penrith turnpike (A686) near the junction with the road to Leadgate and Rodderup Fell, then pass by the town of Garrigill, over Yadmoss and pass close to the villages of Greenhead, Harwood,

Langdon for Caldron Snout, Forrest and Frith, High Force, Bowlees and Holwick to Middleton station. The line was to pass through 'a district abounding with minerals, which are undisturbed on account of the present want of facilities for a ready transport'.

In the early 1870s, several lead mines were to be found at the headwaters of the South Tyne and Tees, and one with considerable potential, Green Hurth, was expected to benefit greatly from this railway as, at that time, the ore was carried by road carts to the trains at Alston.[554,566] On 26 December 1871 the *Carlisle Journal* reported that the Directors of the C&CJR were Lord William Montagu Hay, Jonathan Neild, Wm. Thos. Scarth, Robert Thompson and C. Wilson, that the proposed capital was £250,000 in 25,000 shares of £10 each, while powers were being sought to borrow £83,000.[538] The time for construction of the line was to be five years.

In addition to depositing the plans with the various authorities, the local landowners had been circulated with the schedules of land required to be purchased for building the railway.[540] Everything now appeared to be progressing smoothly, despite the fact that this was the only unopposed railway proposal to appear for a line in the Pennine area of County Durham which did not have any member of the Pease family on the committee. On the other hand, Lord William Hay was chairman of the Anglo–Mediterranean Telegraph Company,[730] while W.T. Scarth and Robert Thompson were directors of the TVR.[729] In a letter to Mr C.R. Wilkinson, the secretary of the NER Company, Richardson, Gutch & Co. stated:

> … the following Bills affect the N.E.Co's interests, as here mentioned, and will either have to be watched or opposed as the Board may direct:– The Cumberland & Cleveland Junction Railway. This line is proposed to commence by a junction with the N.E.Co's Alston Branch and to terminate by a junction with the Tees Valley Railway. Its Bill also contains a power for the N.E.Co. to work and maintain it and assuming the junction to be unobjectionable, we see no reason for opposing this Bill. The consent of the N.E. shareholders is requested if it proceeds.[542]

It is interesting to note that this letter is the only reference I have discovered in the National Archives, and no reference is made to the Cumberland and Cleveland Junction Railway in the TVR Minute Books.

Despite the apparent favour with which the NER Company's agents viewed this line, it was never built. Tomlinson[785] states that nothing came of the proposal for the C&CJR due to the failure of the promoters to raise sufficient capital, but this is clearly incorrect. Reports in the *Carlisle Journal* of 6 February 1872[543] and the *Teesdale Mercury* of 7 February 1872[544] state that the bill for the C&CJR

By the time plans for the Cumberland and Cleveland Junction Railway were being prepared, the first edition of the 1-Inch Ordnance Survey maps were available. The route of the railway was shown on a map made up from two Ordnance Survey sheets. Reproduced by permission of CAS.

came before Examiner Robinson in the House of Commons, who was satisfied that standing orders had been complied with. The bill had therefore passed the standing orders of the House of Commons, meaning that subscriptions had been obtained for the bulk of the shares, making Tomlinson's statement quite incorrect. Next, a letter dated 9 March 1872 from Tilleard & Co. to J.D. Holmes, the clerk of the C&CJR, states:

> The Committee of the House of Lords on this Bill is appointed to meet on Tuesday next 12th inst at 11 o'clock precisely in one of the Committee Rooms at the House of Lords. The only opposition to the Bill is that of Mr. & Mrs. Horrocks of Buses Hill who allege that the No. 2 Railway (to the Shield Water lead mines) will be injurious to their property – we are endeavouring to arrange with their agents, but if we fail it will be necessary for witnesses to attend the Committee to support the Bill.[545]

Two days later a telegram was sent to Mr Holmes saying that his presence was no longer required,[546] indicating that the Horrocks' had withdrawn their opposition. This was confirmed by the report in the *Carlisle Journal* of 16 April that the C&CJR bill had come before Lord Redesdale's committee on unopposed bills in the House of Lords.[548] The report continued: 'the clauses having been gone through the Committee passed the Bill and ordered it to be reported in the House.' Reports in the *Carlisle Patriot* of 17 May[549] and the *Newcastle Weekly Chronicle* of 18 May 1872[550] stated that on Monday 13 May 1872 the bill had again come before Examiner Robinson in the House of Commons Committee on Standing Orders, which had been adjourned due to the omission of a signature required to complete compliance. The signature had been obtained and the examiner advanced the bill a stage.

On Friday 17 June the C&CJR bill came before the Committee on Ways and Means, again as an unopposed measure.[552,553] Certain explanations were given by the promoters, then the clauses were gone through, after which the committee passed the bill. Finally, on Wednesday 22 June 1872 the bill received its third reading in the House of Commons, and the *Carlisle Patriot* stated on 28 June 1872 that 'the extension of the Tees Valley Railway to Alston will commence in or about the month of August.'[553] However, the bill is not recorded as having passed into law, therefore the C&CJR was never authorised.[555] Proposals for a similar line appeared twenty years later, in 1892, at which time a report in the *Teesdale Mercury* quoted a letter from Mr Macnay stating that in 1871 he had prepared plans for a line from Middleton to Alston and that the bill went through Parliament almost to the point of receiving the Royal Assent when it was withdrawn by the promoters who were apparently dissatisfied with some mineral royalties near Alston.[624] This appears to be correct as the bill clearly passed the House of Lords in April 1872 and the House of Commons in June 1872, but never received the Royal Assent, so the line could not even be started, despite the announcement in the local press.

The plans deposited with the justices of the peace for the counties of Cumberland, Durham and the North Riding of Yorkshire on 30 November 1871 show a railway with formidable gradients and much severe curvature, which would have crossed the watershed between the rivers Tees and Tyne at the highest point reached by any standard-gauge line in the British Isles.[534] One item setting these 1871 plans apart from those we have examined previously is that the surveyors were able to show the route of their line on the first edition of the one-inch-to-the-mile OS maps of the area. Bound into the accompanying book of reference is a copy of the notice of application to Parliament, in which three railways are described.

Railway No. 1 was the main line from Alston to Middleton-in-Teesdale. Railway No. 2 was a branch to the lead mines in the valley of the Black Burn and

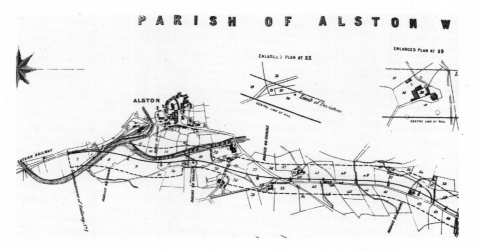

First part of the plans for the Cumberland and Cleveland Junction Railway showing the start of the line 1¼ furlongs (500m) north of Alston terminus. The line passed under the Brampton and Penrith sections of the Alston turnpike roads with the site for a passenger halt between. Reproduced by permission of CAS.

was designed to allow through running towards Middleton. Railway No. 3 was a short link from the branch to the main line, forming a triangular junction, and allowing trains to run directly to Alston. However, when the plans were prepared for submission, Railway No. 3 had been abandoned, perhaps to satisfy earlier objections by Mr and Mrs Horrocks.

The junction with the Alston branch was designed for through running towards Haltwhistle and would have been situated close to the present Water Authority Crossing, where the road to the Northumbria Water sewage works crosses the modern narrow-gauge South Tynedale Railway (STR). The C&CJR crossed the South Tyne just over a furlong (250m) from the junction and immediately commenced the climb to the summit, initially at 1 in 60. A level section in the triangle of land between the Brampton and Penrith turnpike roads was probably intended to provide a passenger halt for Alston so that trains would not have been required to reverse into the original N&CR terminus. Most of the road crossings were by bridges, while the climbing was almost continuous all the way to the summit. There were to be several major viaducts on the line with the first being over the Blackburn at 2 miles 4 furlongs ½ chain (4.03km), which was to be 96ft (29m) high and 600ft (183m) long, on a rising gradient of 1 in 50 and a 20 chain (400m) radius curve. The line then stayed on the west side of the South Tyne until it reached the watershed with the river Tees.

Half a mile (840m) after the Black Burn the branch serving the mines in the valley of the Black Burn (Railway No. 2) trailed in (p. 213), and

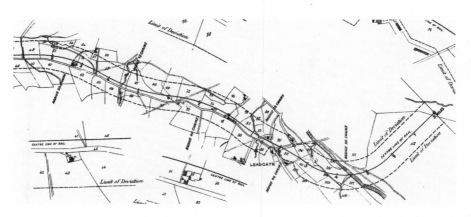

Plan of the C&CJR near Leadgate showing where the Black Burn was to be crossed on a viaduct 96ft high, 600ft long and on a curve of 20 chains radius, with the line riding on a gradient of 1 in 50. Reproduced by permission of CAS.

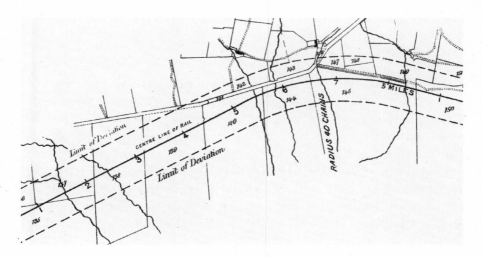

Plan of the C&CJR showing the site for Garrigill station close to where the road turns away from the railway, which is on a curve of 40 chains radius, to drop down into Garrigill. Reproduced by permission of CAS.

1¼ miles (1.92km) later there was a level section for Garrigill station. For most of its length the C&CJR crossed difficult country resulting in a sinuous line with some severe earthworks, although not as bad as might have been expected.

Another 1¼ miles (1.92km) took the line to the next major viaduct over Crossgill which was to be 528ft (161m) long, and 146ft (44.5m) high, again on a rising gradient of 1 in 50, but with a curvature of only 25 chains (500m) radius.

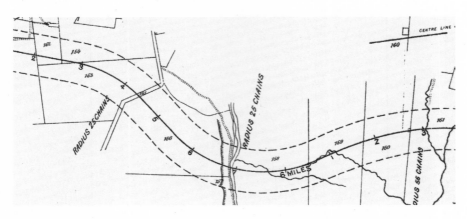

Plan of the C&CJR showing, in the centre, the curving viaduct over Crossgill, which was to be 528ft long and 146ft high. The Pennine Way lies to the left. Reproduced by permission of CAS.

Looking over the South Tyne Valley to Crossgill. The C&CJR was to run from the right, above the top field wall, pass under the road a little above where it turns right, and over the valley on a viaduct built on a curve of 25 chains radius, 528ft long and 146ft high, climbing at 1 in 50.

Crossgill viaduct would have been the largest structure on the line and one of the most impressive viaducts in the North Pennines.

Beyond Crossgill the earthworks were generally less severe.

Several minor occupation roads and footpaths were crossed all along the route, although few signs of any of these roads and paths are to be found anywhere on the hillside today. The 1 in 50 extended for a total of 7 miles 5 furlongs 7 chains (12.4km), but the climbing continued even after the railway reached the

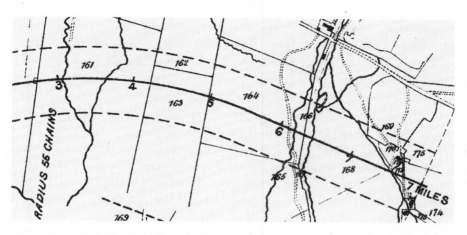

Route of the C&CJR passing West Ashgill, high above the river South Tyne. Apart from the road to Tynehead, most of the paths in this area have disappeared from the map. Reproduced by permission of CAS.

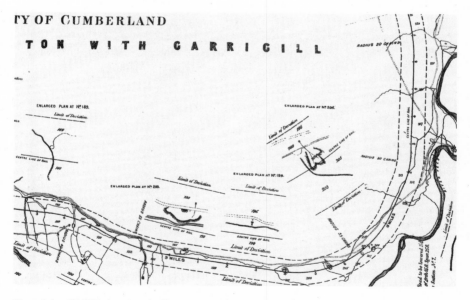

Plan of the C&CJR showing the line crossing the watershed between the river South Tyne, which runs from the lower left, ending just before the line curves towards the top of the picture, and the river Tees, which runs on the right, from the bottom. The 1 in 50 ended 1 furlong after the end of the straight at the bottom of the picture. Reproduced by permission of CAS.

watershed dividing the rivers South Tyne and Tees, although on the much easier gradient of 1 in 355. The reason for this was the decision to descend the valley of a tributary of the river Tees and thus avoid what would have been an extremely difficult passage down the main valley past Caldron Snout. However, to reach the Harwood Beck the line had to follow a series of left-hand curves taking the line through 180° before changing direction again through 90° to follow the valley of yet another tributary of the Tees, the Crook Burn.

As the line crossed the Crook Burn, it left the parish of Alston with Garrigill in the county of Cumberland, and entered the parish of Middleton-in-Teesdale in the county of Durham. The line continued to climb until the summit of the railway was reached at a height of 1,878ft (572m) above sea level. The summit level was just under 2 furlongs (390m) long and in a cutting which reached a depth of 43ft (13.1m) at the point where the descent into Teesdale began. According to the sections, the C&CJR would have had to climb 1,007ft 4in (310m) in 11 miles 7 furlongs 3½ chains (19.2km) from the junction with the Alston branch, giving an average gradient of 1 in 62.3. A very sinuous route took the line down into the valley of the Harwood Beck, on an unbroken gradient of 1 in 50.

Although the Ashgill Beck is quite small, it flows in a deep and narrow valley which was to be crossed on a viaduct 300ft (91m) long and 62ft (19m) high, again on a gradient of 1 in 50 and curving with a radius of 25 chains (500m).

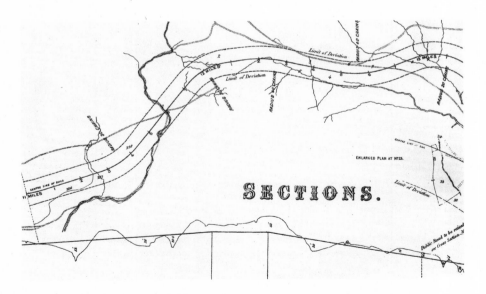

Plan of the C&CJR showing the line climbing up the valley of the Crook Burn and then dropping into the valley of the Harwood Beck. At the bottom of the picture is the section showing the very short summit level. Reproduced by permission of CAS.

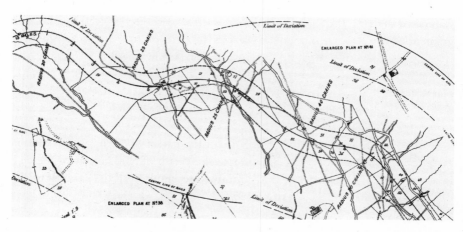

Plan of the C&CJR showing the line descending the valley of the Harwood Beck. The viaduct over Ashgill Beck is close to the 14-mile mark. This curving viaduct was to be 300ft long, 62ft high on the 1 in 50 descent. The railway kept below the former turnpike road (B6277). Reproduced by permission of CAS.

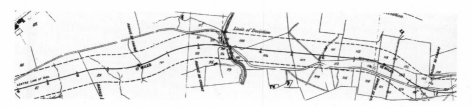

Plan of the C&CJR showing the railway crossing the turnpike road (B6277) and the Langdon Beck on a viaduct near the Langdon Beck Hotel. Reproduced by permission of CAS.

As in the South Tyne Valley several roads are shown crossing the line on the plans but only that to Harwood, apart from the B6277 in the upper Tees valley, has a tarmac surface today.

The line crossed over both the turnpike road and the Langdon Beck on a viaduct 399ft (122m) long which was to be 64ft 9in (20m) above the road and no less than 83ft 4in (25m) above the river.

Less than a mile (1.44km) after crossing over the turnpike, the line went under it on its way to the crossing of the river Tees, only a short distance downstream of the point where the combined Langdon and Harwood becks join the main river (p. 208–209).

The bridge over the Tees was on a curve of only 15 chains (300m), where the 1 in 50 descent, which had continued unbroken for 7 miles 1 furlong 2½ chains (11.5km), ended.

Looking along the turnpike road (B6277) towards Alston. Langdon Beck Hotel lies below the trees from which the C&CJR would have emerged to cross the valley on a viaduct 399ft long, 64ft 9in above the road and 83ft 4in above the river.

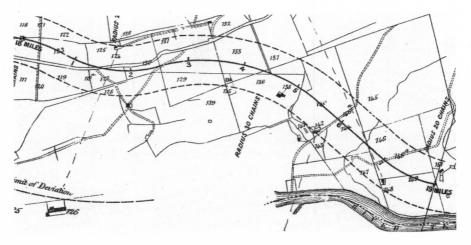

Plan showing the C&CJR going under the turnpike and approaching the north bank of the river Tees. Reproduced by permission of CAS.

Although today both sides of the Tees are in County Durham, in 1871 the river was the county boundary and the railway would have entered the parish of Romaldkirk in 'The North Riding of the County of York' as it crossed the river. A level section carried the line past Holwick Head House and it seems probable that this level section was to be used to provide a passenger station for visitors to High Force Waterfall and Holwick Lodge, as well as for the hamlet of Holwick which was about a mile away in the direction of Middleton-in-Teesdale.

A gradient of 1 in 52 took the line past Holwick hamlet (p. 210).

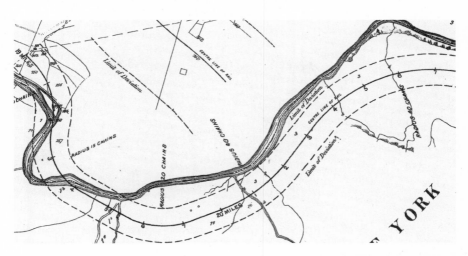

Plan of C&CJR showing the river Tees crossing above High Force on a 15-chain radius curve and then becoming level after 7 miles (11.5km) of 1 in 50 descent. Reproduced by permission of CAS.

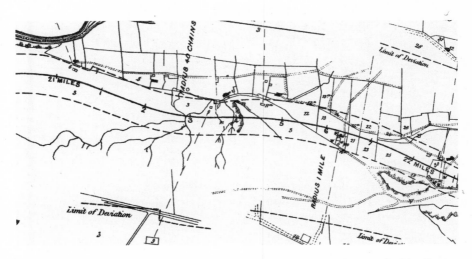

Plan showing the C&CJR approaching Holwick village, passing the level site, at the 21-mile point, for a station for High Force or Holwick. Reproduced by permission of CAS.

Over the final 3 miles (4.8km) from Holwick the majority of the earthworks were relatively light, while a southward sweep of the Tees brought the river and railway close together for about 1½ furlongs (300m) (p. 210).

Road and rail then ran virtually side-by-side to the terminus of the TVR, which lay on the south side of the turnpike road (p. 211). In the schedule[541] sent by the clerk of the railway to the trustees of the Brough and Middleton-in-Teesdale

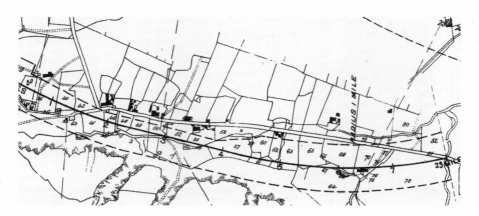

Plan showing the C&CJR passing Holwick village with a cutting through the ridge represented by plots 40, 41 and 42 on the plan. The line then runs in the valley to the south of the village. Reproduced by permission of CAS.

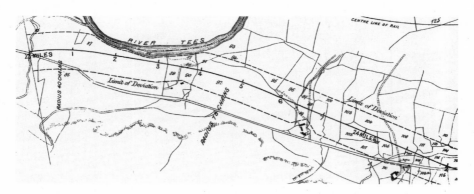

The C&CJR running to the north of the road between Holwick and Middleton-in-Teesdale, from the bridge over the road to Holwick at 23 miles to the level crossing at 24 miles 2 furlongs. Reproduced by permission of CAS.

Bridge and Egglestone Bridge turnpike road, who maintained this road at that time, a level crossing had been envisaged, to which the trustees objected. However, when the final plans were drawn up, the road was to be lowered 12ft 4in (3.8m) for the railway to cross on an arch 16ft (4.9m) high and 35ft (11m) wide. It should be noted that this road was originally part of the Alston turnpike trust authorised in 1824, and today is part of the southernmost section of the B6277.

Middleton-in-Teesdale station was 92ft 3in below the level of the junction with the Alston branch, giving an overall drop from the summit of 1,099ft 7in (335m). A total of 7 miles 5 furlongs 6½ chains (12.4km) of the 13 miles 5½ chains (21km) from the summit was on the ruling gradient of 1 in 50, giving

Plan showing the termination of the C&CJR at Middleton-in-Teesdale station. The plans show the turnpike lowered and the line crossing on a bridge. Reproduced by permission of CAS.

The closed Middleton-in-Teesdale station in use as the offices etc. of a caravan site on 3 October 2002. The tables are on the single platform and the projected Cumberland and Cleveland Junction Railway would have started by an end-on junction with the Tees Valley Railway at the platform end.

an average gradient of 1 in 63.5, which is slightly less than that of the ascent. According to the plans the line was to be 25 miles 1 furlong 8.3 chains (40.6km) long. Although there was a level section immediately before the junction with the TVR, it seems probable that trains from the C&CJR would have used the existing TVR station at Middleton-in-Teesdale, especially as the NER would have been authorised to work the new line.

Although the C&CJR failed to come to fruition, rails did eventually run for about 1¼ miles (2km) beyond the terminus of the TVR. Towards the end of the nineteenth century, Ord and Maddison extended their line serving Middleton quarry for about 1½ miles (2.4km) to a new quarry at Park End. Soon after it was decided to concentrate their work at Crossthwaite quarry, ¼ mile (0.4km) nearer to Middleton, where the stone was of much better quality.[806] This line was built on an alignment much higher up the hillside than the proposed C&CJR, with the connection (p. 196) curving away to the south-east, in a semi-circle from the TVR, 17 chains (340m) from the buffer stops at Middleton,[569] and could never have been seen as part of a route through to the South Tyne, although we shall see in Chapter 13 that, before the end of the nineteenth century, further attempts were made to build a line to Alston similar to the C&CJR.

We shall now look briefly at Railway No. 2, which was to serve the mines beside the Black Burn and leave the parish of Alston with Garrigill to enter the parish of Melmerby when it crossed the Shield Water. It is almost certainly this short mineral branch that gave rise to the local Alston tradition that a railway had been planned to run from Alston to the village of Melmerby, which lies in the Eden Valley, on the other side of the Pennines. In the Notice of Application to Parliament, there is a very detailed description of the point where the branch was to leave the main line, and it was stated that the branch would terminate 'at the entrance to a lead mine, situated on the west side of a stream called Shield Water'. There were equally detailed descriptions in the Notice of Application of the points at which Railway No. 3 was to leave the main line and join Railway No. 2, but there is no sign of this line on any of the plans or sections.

The branch was to start by a junction for direct running towards Middleton, on the 1 in 50 incline at the south end of the straight section which started immediately after the viaduct over the Black Burn. The branch first fell at 1 in 50, reducing the height of the crossing of Rotherhope Cleugh to 44ft (13.4m), and then rose at 1 in 60 before becoming level for the final 2 miles (3.16km). The branch was mainly of curves taking it above Rotherhope mine which, although it existed at the time, was not shown on the plans, and below the Rotherhope Fell mining complex.

The final 27 chains (540m) of the branch ran on the west side of the Shield Water which, at that time, separated the parish of Melmerby from the parish of Alston with Garrigill and terminated in the mining ground owned by the Reverend Henry Houghton, Lord of the Manor, giving a total length of the branch of 2 miles 3 furlongs 4 chains (5.51km).

Neither Parliament nor the NER Company appears to have seen any major obstacles standing in the way of constructing this railway. It would have been rather expensive to build and even more expensive to operate, presenting serious problems for the operating department of the NER. While the ruling gradient of 1 in 50 is not as severe as those to be found on other lines in the North Pennines, the distances involved would have made it one of the most difficult railways in England to operate. The severe curvature would also have presented problems, especially the curve of 15 chains (300m) radius at the crossing of the Tees, which would have made it impossible to approach the main part of the northbound

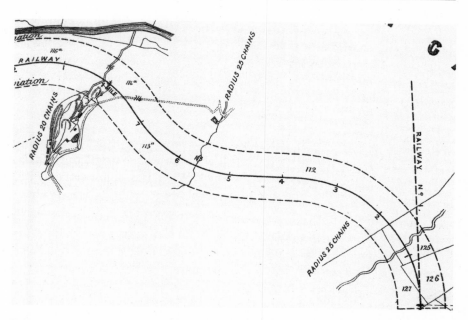

Plan showing the Blackburn branch of the C&CJR. The branch starts from the main line at the end of the straight from the Blackburn viaduct and runs past Rotherhope Fell mine. Reproduced by permission of CAS.

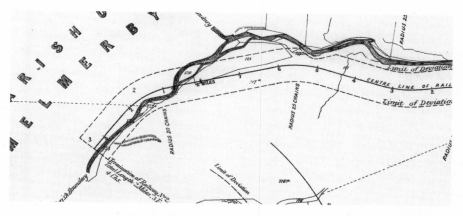

Plan showing the termination of the Blackburn branch of the C&CJR. The branch ends on the west side of the Shield Water in the parish of Melmerby. Reproduced by permission of CAS.

climb at anything but a low speed. Not only would the ascending gradients have taxed the motive power, but the equally long and steep descents would have caused considerable wear and tear to any braking system, not forgetting the possible hazard of vehicles running away on unfitted freights. Apart from the branch to the mines in the valleys of the Black Burn and Shield Water, the potential for intermediate traffic would have been restricted to the output of the quarries between Middleton and High Force, the lead mines of the headwaters of the rivers Tees and South Tyne, and the possible ironstone traffic from Yadmoss. Despite the comments in the *Carlisle Patriot*,[528] it is difficult to see how the C&CJR could ever have been seriously considered as part of a main through route for either passengers or freight.

Local passenger traffic would have been light, as the line traverses what is one of the most sparsely populated parts of the North Pennines and only five level sections are shown on the plans. Ideally stations should be built on level track, while it is usually considered inadvisable for passenger trains to be stopped on gradients of 1 in 50. The first level section was almost certainly for a passenger halt for Alston while, in the 16 miles 2 furlongs 3 chains (26.21km) between Garrigill, where a straight and level section in a shallow cutting would have made a very adequate site for a station with full facilities, and the much poorer level site close to High Force, the only other level sections were at the summit, and on the severe curves above High Force. It is true that a station could easily have been built on the 1 in 355 gradient near the headwaters of the Tees, but even in 1871 there would have been little requirement for a passenger halt at this point, although it could have served as a central freight yard to collect the output from the mines and potential quarries in the upper reaches of the Tees and South Tyne valleys.

The summit level (p. 206) was convenient for both the successful Green Hurth mine and the untapped reserves of ironstone on Yadmoss, but being on a curve of 20 chains (400m) radius, and in a deep cutting, it would not have made an ideal site for any type of station. Another serious problem which would have faced the operating department was the difficulty of keeping the line open during the winter, in particular the summit cutting which inevitably would have rapidly become filled with drifting snow in all but the mildest of winters. It is difficult to see how the C&CJR could ever have been a paying proposition unless the ironstone deposits at Yadmoss had proved highly productive and capable of being used to make steel. Had it been built, it is probable that it would have succumbed to a combination of the economic depression and road competition in the 1920s or 1930s. On the other hand, if by some miracle the railway had assisted production to continue into the second half of the twentieth century from the Rotherhope and Green Hurth lead mines and the Yadmoss ironstone quarries, coupled with stone traffic from the High Force quarries, it could have survived into the era of preservation, when there is little doubt that a society would have been formed to take it over, with every chance of success, given that it would have been by far the highest standard-gauge railway anywhere in the British Isles. On the other hand, perhaps the promoters were correct in withdrawing the bill from Parliament just as it was about to pass into law.

13

THE FINAL ATTEMPTS TO REACH ALSTON FROM THE VALLEYS OF THE TEES AND WEAR INCLUDING THE WEAR VALLEY EXTENSION RAILWAY OF 1892

The authorisation of the H&AR in 1865[466] stimulated the first of a succession of proposals to build a line west and north from Stanhope, at least three of which planned to go over, rather than under, Killhope. We saw in the last chapter how an attempt, in 1872, to extend the Middleton-in-Teesdale Railway over the mountains to Alston almost succeeded. In this chapter we shall look at all the other proposals that were put forward in the last third of the nineteenth century to connect Alston with the valleys to the south and east. The only result of all these efforts was the extension of the railway along the floor of the Wear Valley from Stanhope to Wearhead, finally bringing to fruition the recommendations put forward by John Harris half a century earlier.[95] The second Wear Valley Extension Railway (WVER92) proved to be the last major extension of the railway system in the North Pennines and was only partially successful in its attempt to arrest the decline of the mining industries in Upper Weardale. Even if the alternative St John's Chapel Railway (SJCR) had succeeded, and that railway had then been extended under, or even over, Killhope to Nenthead and Alston, it is doubtful if the eventual demise of the all lines in the North Pennines would have been prevented, or even significantly postponed, although this will be discussed in the next chapter.

Almost as soon as the Act authorising the H&AR[466] was passed, the *Hexham Courant* reported that preliminary surveys were being made, at the beginning of October 1865, with the intention of presenting a bill to Parliament for a railway running up the Wear Valley from Stanhope to Cowshill, then over the mountains to Allenheads, where it would join the H&AR.[472] At the first general meeting of the H&AR Company, held on 21 October 1865, the chairman, W.B. Beaumont, concluded that the proposal for a line from Stanhope to Allenheads justified their decision to obtain powers to extend their line to Allenheads.[473] However, nothing further was heard of this line from Weardale, which would have been very similar to the Allendale branch of the WVER.

The next proposal was put forward in 1870, when the engineers Messrs Wilkinson and Smith, of Duke Street, Westminster, presented plans for a railway from Stanhope to Alston, first at a meeting in Stanhope on Friday 8 April 1870, then the following day at St John's Chapel.[524] Meetings were held in Alston town hall on Saturday 23 April, and at Mr Dent's school, in Garrigill, on Monday 25 April. The editor of the *Hexham Courant*, Mr J. Catherill, attended the Alston meeting and has left us a very detailed account of the proceedings.[525]

At the Alston meeting Mr C.G. Grey, of Dilston Hall, took the chair, acting in his private capacity, and not as the representative of the lords of the Admiralty who, as the trustees of the Greenwich Hospital, were the largest local landowners. He confirmed his support for the proposed railway, stating that if the local population approved, 'the Lords of the Admiralty would not be lacking in their duty to the district'. Among other advantages, he believed that building the railway would increase the production of ironstone. Mr Wilkinson said that the line would be 500ft (150m) higher than any other line in the kingdom, and while it would present considerable difficulties, it would be a comparatively cheap line to build. The total length would be 25 miles (40km) and the estimate of the cost was £95,000. The plans had been prepared from the Government Survey (presumably the Ordnance Survey) while Mr Wilkinson also stated that the NER had nothing to do with the line, that there were no promoters of the railway and the work had been done because of Mr Attwood's interest. The worst gradient was 1 in 40, but this could easily be operated with suitable locomotives. In another account the estimated cost was given as £97,000 while a tunnel under Killhope was expected to cost £90,000.[797]

The line was to start from the Alston Branch, about 200 yards on the Haltwhistle side of the station, and would cross the road (A686) near the Brewery Bridge, passing Cowgap to reach Whitesyke mines, then by Seldom Seen, near Ashgill, and on towards Nenthead, round Killhopehead, and down by Burtryford to Stanhope. The gradient at the Alston end would be 1 in 40, but at Stanhope it would be comparatively level, being about 1 in 145. Wilkinson said an easier line could be made with a tunnel, costing £100,000, through Killhope, but this would not pay. There were to be 9,700 shares of £10 each, and provisional committees were set up in Stanhope, St John's Chapel and Alston. Although there was general support for a connection with Weardale, the bulk of the public support in Alston was for the C&CJR, described in the previous chapter, and nothing further was heard of this project to take a railway over rather than under Killhope. Nevertheless, the desire for a line from Weardale to Tynedale was never far from people's minds and, when the press announced the successful testing of Killhope ironstone at the end of 1871,[547] the report ended by stating that it was hoped the railway from Weardale would soon be built.

By the end of the 1870s, the availability of cheap foreign lead, with imports reaching no less than 74,351 tons in 1874,[587] had caused a major decline in the lead-mining industry, especially in the north of England,[563] although Green Hurth mine continued to be very successful. In 1879 the *Hexham Courant* published an article on the problems of the lead industry whose first three sentences read: 'The condition and prospects of the North of England Lead Mining have attracted much attention of late. Seldom, if ever, has the industry been in such a depressed state. Prices are low, the demand small, working more costly, and the outlook anything but encouraging.'[567] The mining of ironstone in the North Pennines was also going through one of its periods of decline, with the Weardale Iron and Coal Company's workings in Upper Weardale being suspended in March 1878,[562] and their Tow Law iron works reduced to only one furnace in blast by October 1878.[564]

Agitation for the construction of a railway from Alston to Middleton-in-Teesdale started again in 1881,[570] with the *Hexham Courant* giving a slightly inaccurate account of the previous attempts to build such a line.[572] According to the author of the article, transport of the local ironstone via Alston station was too expensive, and the proposed line would allow it to be extracted. Among the people who were rumoured to support the line were the Duke of Devonshire, the Duke of Cleveland, Colonel Byng, Mr Bowes, and Mr C.G. Grey on behalf of the lords of the Admiralty. The article ended by stating that the connection from Alston to Middleton would form the shortest route between Edinburgh and London. At the half-yearly meeting of shareholders of the NER held in August 1881, the chairman said that the NER was not prepared to build the line, but if other parties were prepared to construct such a line and come forward with proposals, the directors would carefully consider them.[574] Later in 1881, the NER applied to Parliament for a bill to allow them to absorb the TVR, and the *Hexham Courant* assumed that this would only be a 'stepping stone to the extension of the North Eastern system to Alston'.[575] After the purchase of the TVR in 1882,[577] a letter to the editor of the *Hexham Courant* suggested that the prospects for building the line from Alston to Middleton, or the Cumberland Junction Railway as the writer called it, were more promising than ever before,[576] but yet again nothing further developed.

The mining of ironstone in Weardale boomed again in the early 1880s, with no less than seventy-two carts being employed to carry hundreds of tons daily to the depot at Westgate.[579] Although there was also a short-lived improvement in the demand for lead in 1881,[573] the decline in lead mining continued and the mines leased by W.B. Beaumont in Weardale closed at the beginning of June

1883 when the Beaumont Lead Company ceased operations in Weardale.[582] A new organisation, the Weardale Lead Company, took over some of the mines, and started operating them on a smaller scale in July 1883.[583]

Just over a year later a meeting was held in St John's Chapel to consider a railway scheme for Weardale.[585] A committee was set up to progress the proposed extension of the railway up Weardale, with some people wanting the line to go through to Alston. A meeting of this committee decided that it was too late to go to Parliament the following session, although both the Bishop of Durham and the Weardale Lead Company supported the plan.[586] A report in the *Hexham Courant* in February 1885 stated that the projected Weardale Railway, which a Mr Hopkins was expected to survey in the spring, would help both the lead and iron trade.[587] An extension to Killhope mines and a branch from Eastgate to Rookhope were also expected to be surveyed. However, another year and a half passed before any further active steps were taken to extend the railway up the Wear Valley.

In June 1886, Sir Joseph Pease, the local Member of Parliament arranged, at his own expense, for a survey to be made from the existing railway terminus at Stanhope to Wearhead.[592] In a long report on the Weardale railway scheme, the *Hexham Courant* started by explaining that simultaneously with the formation of the Weardale Lead Company, the vicar of St John's Chapel, the Rev. R. Shepherd, had proposed the extension of the railway up the Wear Valley from Stanhope and had since acted as secretary to the committee formed to carry out the project.[593] The Board of Admiralty wished the line to go through Killhope to Nenthead and Alston, but the Rev. Shepherd did not think the line that had been surveyed to Wearhead was suitable for such an extension.

At a meeting at St John's Chapel, Sir Joseph Pease said that Mr Lyall of Darlington had surveyed the line and reported that a single line, 9 miles (14.5km) long, could easily be built from Stanhope to Wearhead for £48,627.[595] If it was decided to carry the line through to Alston the cost would be greatly increased, as Killhope would have to be tunnelled. It was estimated that the extension would increase the cost of the line to about a quarter of a million pounds, and Sir Joseph said that, if they desired to secure the line to Wearhead, Alston should be left out of the question. He promised to take a deputation to the board of the NER to state their case for the line to Wearhead. The following week, a detailed description of the proposed railway appeared in the *Hexham Courant*.[596] The line was to start close to the existing terminus in Stanhope, with a new station more convenient for the marketplace, and run for 9 miles 3 furlongs 1.56 chains (15.119km) rising all the way, apart from 3 furlongs (600 metres) of level, to a terminus on the south side of the river Wear, close to Wearhead bridge.

There were to be intermediate stations at Eastgate, Westgate and St John's Chapel, while the Wear was to be crossed three times, and the principal roads would be carried over the railway on arches. The steepest gradient was 1 in 71½ for just over 1 mile and the radius of the sharpest curves was 25 chains (500m). The railway was to keep to the valley bottom, would serve a population of about 9,750 and was expected to save 2s per ton on the cost of transporting ironstone. Despite the views of Sir Joseph Pease on extending through Killhope, those involved in mining in the Nenthead area continued to press for the line to be extended to Alston.[597] However, the committee that was set up decided to stick with their original line, the through line being considered too costly.[599]

In March 1887 the ecclesiastical commissioners told the committee that they would convey the land for the construction of the line through their property for a nominal consideration, but were not able to afford any further financial aid,[600] while Mr J.R.W. Hildyard, who was the owner of the largest section of land required, 15 acres, stated that if the NER Company took up the scheme he would give every facility. The mining of ironstone in the North Pennines now entered another of its periods of decline and, by 1889, most of the ironstone mines in Weardale had ceased working and large numbers of the population were leaving the area.[602] One of the major problems for the ironstone workings was the inability of the Weardale, Steel, Coal and Coke Company to make steel satisfactorily from Weardale ironstone. The company built a special furnace at Tudhoe which was lit up with a blend of 40 tons of ironstone from several of the company's mines in Weardale, upon the result of which the resumption of the ironstone industry in Weardale was said to depend.[604] Three months later it was announced that the mines would resume working.[605]

In 1890 an early example of good environmental policy was made by Durham County Council when it prohibited contaminated water from the lead ore workings being put into the river Wear. Unfortunately this resulted in the employees of the Weardale Lead Company being given notice.[606] At the beginning of 1891, a petition was sent to the ecclesiastical commissioners asking them to prevent the closure of the mines of the Weardale, Steel, Coal and Coke Company.[607] Their assistance was expected to take the form of support for the railway up the Wear Valley. In the same report, the *Hexham Courant* again stated that Weardale ironstone was not suitable for making steel, only wrought or malleable iron.

Further reports appeared in the *Hexham Courant* during the first half of 1891, all of which expected the extension of the railway from Stanhope to Wearhead to provide some relief from the crisis in the mining industry. Sir Joseph Pease continued to assist the local committees in the promotion of the line,[608] and the NER was approached for support.[609] Plans and sections were deposited with the various authorities for a bill to be introduced during the 1892 session of Parliament.[610]

Despite the support from Sir Joseph Pease for the WVER92 Bill, which was to build a line from Stanhope to Wearhead, and the initial continuing support from the Rev. R. Shepherd, a section of the population of the North Pennines still wished to have a line continuing under Killhope to Nenthead and Alston and presented a competing bill to Parliament for a line from Stanhope to St John's Chapel.[611] A meeting held in Nenthead in February 1892 strongly supported the construction of a line from Stanhope to St John's Chapel, while the promoters also wished to extend this to Alston.[612] The Rev. Shepherd said the Alston line would be better than one only going to Wearhead, while the chairman of the meeting, Mr J. Cameron Swan, stated that although the Wear Valley Bill was promoted by Sir Joseph Pease, who was a director of the NER, the NER had agreed to allow Parliament to be arbiter in the matter. He also added that it would be commercially impossible to take the line from the proposed Wearhead terminus to Nenthead. At a meeting later the same day in Alston, a Mr Baker stated that in the construction of the line he did not think much tunnelling would be necessary, as the lords of the Admiralty had given them every facility to get land so they could make a winding line if necessary.

An editorial in the *Hexham Courant* the following week announced: 'In our opinion the large majority of the people will be best served by a line from Stanhope to Alston.'[614] Also in the same issue of the *Hexham Courant*, there was a report of a meeting held in St. John's Chapel where the line to Wearhead was supported.[615] The report stated that Sir Joseph Pease, when he first took up the question in 1886, was anxious that the railway should be made through to Alston, but when a survey showed that the cost would be not less than £260,000 it was dropped in favour of the line to Wearhead. It was pointed out that the only local promoter of the SJCR was Rev. R. Shepherd. Four petitions had been lodged against the Wear Valley Extension Scheme, one by the promoters of the SJCR, one by landowners affected by the Wear Valley scheme, one by the inhabitants of Nenthead and one by the inhabitants of Alston. Only one petition, from the promoters of the Wear Valley scheme, had been lodged against the St John's Chapel line. Despite establishing the aid of Mr J.W. Lowther, the MP for the Alston area,[616] Parliament refused to allow the St John's Chapel Bill to be extended to Alston in the current session.[617]

During May 1892, the two bills came before a select committee of the House of Lords, presided over by Lord Hamilton of Dalziel,[618,619] which considered them as competing lines. Various statements were made by the supporters of the WVER92, including one by the engineer, Mr Lyall. He said:

It was not true as represented that it was impossible to carry the Wear Valley Extension line to Alston. In the event of that being required it would be necessary to start some distance back from Wearhead at New House. It was originally intended to terminate the line at New House, but it was decided to carry it on to Wearhead in response to public demands.

It should be noted that New House is little more than a kilometre west of St John's Chapel. Sir Joseph Pease stated that the NER had agreed to work the WVER92, and the shareholders had confirmed this decision. It was also stated that the WVER92, if sanctioned, would 'be constructed by the NER Company under the superintendence of Mr. Barry'. The committee announced that they had rejected the St John's Chapel Bill, and that the Wear Valley Extension Bill was to be continued with. Before the bill passed the House of Commons, Mr J.W. Lowther, MP, extracted the following assurance from Sir Joseph Pease:

> ... the line was originally laid out with the view of going forward to Alston, but they had only been able to take one step at a time. The line, however, had been carried out in a way that would facilitate its further extension to Alston, and he should only be too happy to level any aid he could to so very desirable development – one the promoters of the line had in view from its inception. He assured his Hon. friend that the line was so laid out that it could be continued to Alston at some future date, and so far as he (Sir. J. Pease) was concerned, he would take care that the arrangements should be carried out.[620]

Attempts continued to be made during the year to revive interest in the extension of the line to Alston,[623] but the failure of the SJCR had ended all realistic hopes of Alston being linked by rail to Weardale. Despite the high hopes for the new railway, at the end of December 1892, all the miners, cartmen, etc. at the Weardale, Steel, Coal and Coke Company's iron mines were discharged.[629]

After the bill for the extension of the WVR to Wearhead had passed through Parliament, it was announced that a meeting would be held in Middleton-in-Teesdale on 22 July 1892 to consider the means best calculated to promote the extension of the railway from Middleton-in-Teesdale to Alston.[622] At the adjourned meeting held on 29 July there was comment on the Weardale schemes, and a Mr Thompson stated that if the line went by Nenthead the promoters of the Wearhead to Alston extension would abandon the scheme.[624] Another speaker stated that Alston was pledged to the Weardale scheme, but it was suggested that Sir Joseph Pease should be approached to secure the assistance of the NER.

The report in the *Teesdale Mercury* of the next meeting stated that a suggestion had been made that the Midland Railway should be approached if the directors of the NER would not take up the matter, and the line could then be extended to join the Midland Railway between Appleby and Carlisle.[625] The *Hexham Courant* reported, from the same meeting, that the chairman had stated a line from Alston to Middleton would considerably shorten the distance and cheapen the carriage of coal and coke to Workington.[626] A committee was formed to pursue the suggestion and two further meetings were held in August 1892 at the first of which it was stated that Mr Baker had agreed to go over the route to

Nenthead.[627] One speaker stated that he felt there was no desire for a railway in the area but another said that the local quarrymen were in favour. At the second meeting there was general agreement to go ahead, and it was stated that the local landowners would not oppose it.[628] The meeting then agreed to collect a petition from the valley between Egglestone and Harwood to prove the general desire for the railway. Despite the obvious wishes of a group of people to resurrect the plans for a railway from Middleton-in-Teesdale to Alston, nothing more was heard of this scheme.

We shall now look at the line authorised by the WVER 92 Act of 1892.[621] Capital of £60,000 was authorised in 6,000 shares of £10 each, of which the NER Company was allowed to subscribe up to £40,000. The NER was authorised to raise this by the creation of new shares and for which it could also appoint one director. The WVER was also authorised to borrow up to £20,000. The land was to be purchased within three years and the line completed within five. There were several clauses specifying which roads and paths could be crossed on the level as well as the gradients of the altered roads, while the tolls were to be the same as those on the Frosterley and Stanhope section of the NER. The plans are to the scale of 6 inches = 1 mile, printed on two sheets with plan and section on the same page.[610] The datum line is stated as being '236.33ft (72.03m) below a point marked X on the surface of the westernmost rail of the NER at the south end of the bridge carrying the said railway over the River Wear marked X on the plan'.

According to the description on the plans, the official starting point was the south end of the bridge over the river Wear at Stanhope, which is 12 miles 5 furlongs 3½ chains (20.39km) from Wear Valley Junction, although the actual point of divergence was 2 chains (40m) further on, or 11 chains (220m) before the F&SR terminus. The line was 9 miles 2 furlongs 8½ chains (15.06km) long,

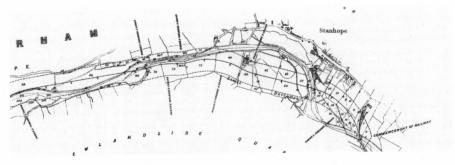

Plans showing the start of the Wear Valley Extension Railway of 1892. Compare this with the image on p. 66 which shows that once the railway had returned to the south bank of the river Wear, immediately west of Stanhope station, the 1892 route followed a similar course to that of the 1845 plans. Reproduced by permission of DRO.

while the radius of all the curves was given as 25 chains (500m). There were few earthworks of significance and while the plans show most of the road crossings on the level, the act required all but two of the public roads to be crossed by bridges, three of which went under the line.[621] The bridges over the roads were to have minimum spans and heights of 12ft (3.66m), although in two cases the width of the roadway under the bridge was specified to be not less than 20ft (6.1m). The line was to rise all the way to Wearhead, with nine changes of gradient, which varied between 1 in 70 and 1 in 198, excluding five level sections for stations at Stanhope, Eastgate, Westgate, St John's Chapel and Wearhead. The point of junction with the F&SR was on a section of level track between the descending gradient before the bridge over the river Wear and the rising gradient after the bridge.

The plans for the F&SR deviation show the line rising at 1 in 377 for 1 furlong (200m) before the south end of the bridge,[434] which makes the height of the bridge 676ft 9in (210m) above sea level. From the junction, the line rose at 1 in 198 for almost ¼ mile (340m) to the level section of 1 furlong (200m) for the new Stanhope station (fig. 9 & 14 col. section). In the space of a single chain (20m) at the end of the level section, the line became straight, started to climb at 1 in 114 and then crossed to the south bank of the river Wear on a viaduct with a single span 7ft (2.1m) high and 45 yards (41m) wide. In general, the railway maintained a relatively sinuous course close to the river, avoiding most areas which would have required major earthworks.

Just under 1¼ miles (1.95km) from the junction the river Wear (see fig. 10 col. section) was crossed again and then the line continued between the river and the former turnpike road (A689). Once the 1892 WVER had crossed the river west of Stanhope station, it followed a very similar course to that of the WVER plans of 1845, as far as St Johns Chapel, although in general the earlier route would have produced a better line but with heavier earthworks. The plans show the road

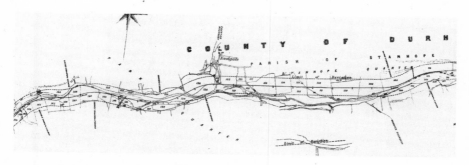

Plan of WVER92 passing Eastgate and crossing the river Wear almost 2 furlongs west of Rookhope Burn. The figure of the 1845 plans on p. 66, shows the WVER45 crossing 4 furlongs west of Rookhope Burn. Reproduced by permission of DRO.

from the south bank of the river to Eastgate crossing the railway on the level, but the act required the road to be carried over the railway.

The river Wear was crossed for the last time just over 3¼ miles (5.35km) from the junction. At Eastgate, a bridge had been required to take a road over the line. (see fig. 11. col. section)

About ¼ mile (35m) beyond Westgate station the river Wear was diverted to the north of the line of the railway.

In this length the plans show a road which crossed the river by a ford to Westgate being raised and crossing the railway on the level.

Plan showing the WVER92 passing Westgate with the river diversion just beyond. Reproduced by permission of DRO.

Plan showing the WVER92 passing Daddry Shield and St John's Chapel, where there was another river diversion. The 1892 route now diverged from the 1845 line, which was to cross the turnpike at the west end of St John's Chapel. Reproduced by permission of DRO.

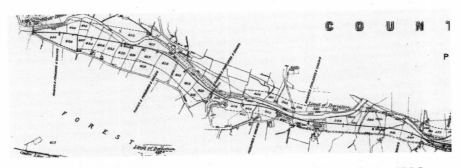

Plan showing the WVER92 terminating at Wearhead. Reproduced by permission of DRO.

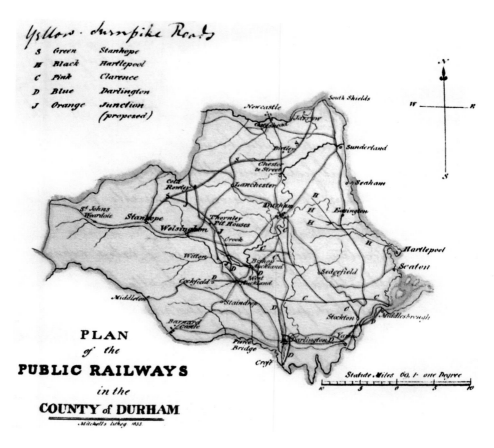

Fig. 1 The plan accompanying the prospectus of the Tees, Weardale and Tyne Junction Railroad. Reproduced by permission of The National Archives (TNA).

Fig. 2 View from the A689 over the unbuilt turnpike, railway embankment and Lintley Farm. This is the point where the route of the WVER would have joined the N&CR branch.

Fig. 5 The site of Scutterhill depot on the west side of the road, before the line reached Slit Pasture ironstone mine. A siding was provided here for loading the lead ore and ironstone brought up from the valley floor on the steep road behind the photographer. On the opposite side of the deep valley is the site of the West Slit lead mine, the terminus of the WICCR.

Opposite top: Fig. 3 View over the road connecting the Turnpike road to Nenthead with the section avoiding Alston via Blagill. The WVER would have crossed the road below the wall on the right above the river Nent, and the N&CR above the next wall on the left, both on the level. Both lines would have been climbing from right to left at 1 in 55 or 54. The earthworks for the WVER would have been extensive on this section.

Opposite bottom: Fig. 4 Site of Bolts Law Junction just north of Parkhead station. The abandoned trackbed of the WI&CCR curves away to the right (west) to cross the Stanhope to Edmondbyers turnpike and then climbs steadily to Bolts Law Summit. Reproduced by permission of NCS.

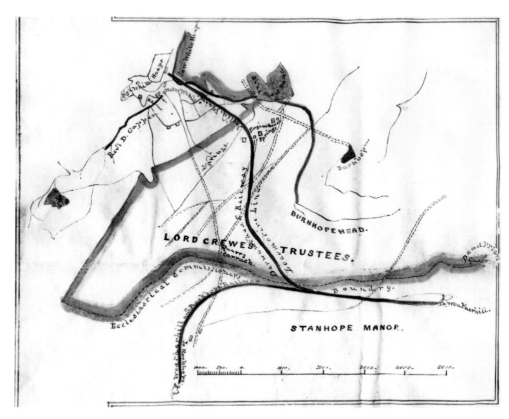

Fig. 6 Map in the copy of the document granting Richard Cordner the lease of a railway from the Weatherhill and Rookhope Railway. Reproduced with permission of Nicholson Portnell solicitors.

Fig. 7 The bridge required by parliament to carry the WVR over the West Auckland to Elishaw turnpike (A68) at Witton-le-Wear in October 2007, by which time the A68 had been diverted.

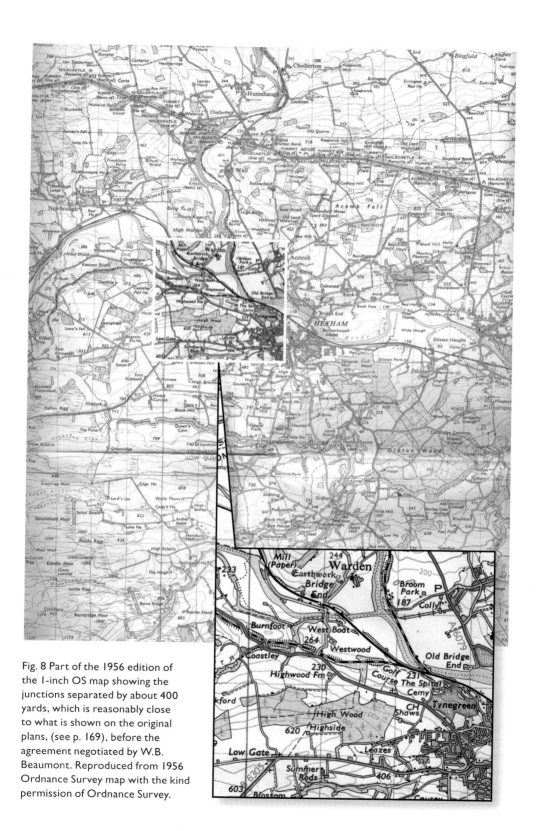

Fig. 8 Part of the 1956 edition of the 1-inch OS map showing the junctions separated by about 400 yards, which is reasonably close to what is shown on the original plans, (see p. 169), before the agreement negotiated by W.B. Beaumont. Reproduced from 1956 Ordnance Survey map with the kind permission of Ordnance Survey.

Fig. 9 Stanhope stations. On the left is the passenger station opened on 21 October 1895. The WVER92 diverged from the original F&SR just behind the point from which the picture was taken. On the right is the original station of 22 October 1862, used for goods traffic since 1895. Reproduced by permission of NCS.

Fig. 10 Bridge carrying the Wear Valley Extension Railway of 1892 to the north bank of the river Wear for the last time. Photographed from the bridge carrying the minor road along the south bank of the river, West of Stanhope, in April 2008. The rails remained in place to Eastgate, but scheduled trains had not run since 1993.

Fig. 11 The remains of Eastgate station photographed, in April 2008, from the bridge required by the act to carry the road from the south bank of the river Wear over the railway.

Fig. 12 *Helen-Kathryn* waiting to leave Lintley Halt with the first return train to Alston on Sunday 1 April 2012.

Fig. 13 Santa Special crossing the river Wear at Broadwood near Frosterley on 17 December 2006 hauled by locomotive No. 40, the Robert Stephenson & Hawthorn 0-6-0T owned by the Weardale Railway Trust. Reproduced by permission of John Askwith of the Weardale Railway Trust.

Fig. 14 The 13.00 Wear Valley Railway train from Wolsingham at Stanhope Station on Wednesday 20 June 2007. At this time the service was being operated under the auspices of the ECT Group, using a pacer unit.

Fig. 15 The coal depot at Wolsingham photographed from the 14.25 train from Bishop Auckland on Sunday 14 August 2011. The building is the former Wolsingham steel works. The blue-painted Weardale Railway 08 shunter HO 50 sits at the head of half the twenty-one coal wagons. The other half of the wagons were stabled on a siding alongside the main line.

There was a further diversion of the river Wear 3 furlongs (300m) past St John's Chapel station.

The terminus was at Wearhead, which lay between the former turnpike (A689) and the south bank of the river, close to the bridge over the river Wear.

A brief look at the unsuccessful SJCR shows that this line would also have risen, at between 1 in 330 and 1 in 80, all the way to the terminus 7 miles 3 furlongs 7 chains (12.01km) from its junction with the F&SR, which was also at the north end of the bridge over the Wear before Stanhope station.[611]

Wearhead station in LNER days with Wearhead bridge in the backbround. Ken Hoole collection, reproduced by permission of HoS-DRM.

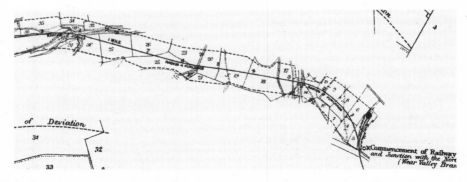

Plan showing the start of the St John's Chapel Railway at Stanhope. Note the similarity of the first 1¼ miles to the WVER92. Reproduced by permission of DRO.

There were to be three level sections, presumably for stations, at Stanhope, Westgate and St John's Chapel, while the section of 1 in 330 was also suitable for a station at Eastgate.

All roads were to be crossed by bridges, with the railway going over four and under two, while the earthworks would have been more severe than on the WVER92.

The route of the SJCR is shown below.

Unlike the WVER of 1845, the SJCR remained on the south side of the A689 after Daddry Shield.

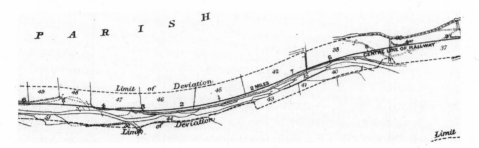

Plan showing the St John's Chapel Railway running closer to the north bank of the river Wear than either WVER line west of Stanhope. Reproduced by permission of DRO.

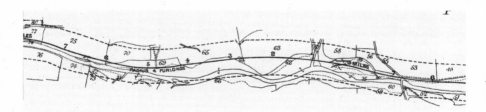

Plan showing the St John's Chapel Railway crossing the Killhope Burn and then continuing along the north bank of the river Wear. Reproduced by permission of DRO.

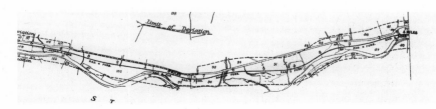

Plan showing the St John's Chapel Railway remaining on the north bank of the Wear between Eastgate and Westgate. Reproduced by permission of DRO.

Plan showing the St John's Chapel Railway crossing the river Wear for the last time near Westgate, 2¾ miles west of Killhope Burn, and terminating to the south of the turnpike (A689) at St John's Chapel. Reproduced by permission of DRO.

Staking out of the WVER92 was completed in time for the ceremony of cutting the first sod to be carried out by Sir Joseph Pease at St John's Chapel on 21 October 1893.[631] In the account of the ceremony, published by the *Hexham Courant*, it was stated that in addition to the £40,000 the NER was allowed to invest, the ecclesiastical commissioners had agreed to subscribe £20,000 to the project, meaning that the WVER92 company did not have to raise any capital of their own. In the middle of December 1893,[632] advertisements appeared for tenders for the contract work of the WVER92 and by the middle of February 1894 the contracts had been let.[633] The work of building the railway commenced in March 1894[634,635] but was soon interrupted by a strike of the workers which was not settled until June,[636] when a compromise was reached with wages raised to between 3*s* (15p) and 3*s* 4*d* (17p) per day. Despite the strike, the *Hexham Courant* was able to report, in March 1894, that considerable progress was being made between Stanhope station and Eastgate,[637] while the low state of the river had allowed the foundations of the bridge near Stanhope to be rapidly constructed.[638] At the beginning of August 1894[640] the *Hexham Courant* reported that preparations were being made for the building of the stations, but later in the same month a mass meeting of the workmen was held at St John's Chapel when it was resolved to ask the contractor to raise their wages from 3*s* 4*d* (17p) to 3*s* 8*d* (18p) per day, and also allow them a half holiday on Saturdays.[641]

By an Act passed on 31 July 1894, the NER absorbed the WVER92.[639] In the preamble the point was made that the WVER92 had not raised any of its authorised capital. At the end of October 1894 a report in the *Hexham Courant* announced that negotiations were under way to commence quarrying whinstone at Cowshill, which was within 1 mile (1.6km) of the 'new extension railway terminus'.[642] By the middle of 1895 the track on the railway was completed, but the Weardale Highway Board refused to take over certain bridge approaches as they felt they were dangerous, with that at Briggin Winch, Stanhope, being the worst, where only a rail fence divided the road from the railway.[644] Nevertheless, by the end of July it was announced that the railway was fast approaching completion, with the permanent line being laid from Stanhope to Wearhead.[645]

The railway was finally opened on 21 October 1895 and, although there was no official ceremony, the local press carried detailed accounts of the day.[646] Sir Joseph Pease, the chairman of the NER, travelled up the line in a special train with a party of directors, and was cheered by crowds assembled at the different stations. In addition to Sir Joseph Pease the company travelling by the special included Sir David and Lady Dale, Sir William Gray, and Messrs. J. Lloyd Wharton, MP, Henry Tennant, C.N. Wilkinson (secretary), C.S. Denniss, E.W. Lyall, Wilson Worsdell, Vincent Raven and J. Cudworth Kendall, whilst Mr J.A. Hildyard and Mr J.W. Roddam joined the train at Stanhope. Unfortunately it rained heavily throughout the day, but the local people made a holiday of the Monday. The opening of the railway saw the end of the coach service to Cowshill, with the coach horses, traps, harness, etc. of Mr R. Mews being sold by auction at the end of November.[647] The first positive result of the new line was the announcement at the end of December 1895 that the whin quarry was about to be opened at Cowshill.[648]

In November 1897, a little more than two years after the line had been opened to Wearhead, a project was announced to connect Weardale to Alston by a railway over Killhope from Wearhead to Alston.[654] Also in the same month both Weardale District Council and Stanhope Urban Council asked the NER to double the Wear Valley line on account of the heavy mineral traffic and the inconvenience to passengers arising out of it by delayed trains.[655]

Early the following year a proposal was made for a light railway to be constructed between Alston and St John's Chapel which would include Nenthead in its route.[656] Mr Baker, of London, who had championed the scheme for a through line some years earlier, was taking an active part and was supported by Mr Fernan, the manager of the Vieille Montagne Mining Company at Nenthead. The proposal was to apply for permission to construct a light railway, with the case for the scheme being argued before three railway commissioners. It was believed the railway would be a great boon to both dales, and would assist the mining industry at Nenthead, but when the Rev. R. Shepherd of St John's Chapel wrote to the NER suggesting the extension of the WVR from Wearhead to Alston, the directors stated they were not prepared to recommend the construction of such a railway.[659]

A report in the *Hexham Courant* in November 1898 stated that ever since the line to Wearhead had been completed, proposals had been made for connecting the lines at Wearhead and Alston, although nothing had come of them, but a survey had recently been made, by Mr Cudworth of the NER and a staff of assistants, of the ground from Eastgate to Alston via Rookhope and Allenheads.[661] The proposed line would tap the two lead mines and smelt mill of the Weardale Lead Company, as well as the Allendale mines, 'now unworked for lack of transit', and the Nenthead Company's works. It was stated that the line could be made without tunnelling, but would be by a rather mountainous route. I have found no evidence for this survey in the relevant NER Minute Books, but on

16 September 1898 it was recorded that a letter had been received from the Rev. W.R. Hartley of Rookhope Vicarage, Eastgate, asking if the directors would be willing to receive a deputation with reference to a branch railway from Eastgate to Rookhope.[659] The deputation was received by the traffic committee at York on Thursday 6 October 1898,[660] but on 3 November 1898 the company declined the application to construct a line from Eastgate to Rookhope.[662]

Nothing more was heard of the Rookhope line, but in December 1898 the NER was asked to make a line over the 4½ miles (7.24km) from Alston to Nenthead or possibly to Wearhead.[663] The proposal had the active support of the Vieille Montagne Mining Company and it was considered probable that the NER directors would give it favourable consideration. A letter dated 7 July 1899 from George Gibb,[664] the general manager of the NER, to Sir Lindsay Wood, an NER director living in Chester-le-Street, sent with a set of plans produced by Harrison, the chief engineer,[665] asked if Sir Lindsay would encourage the company to proceed. In the letter Gibb states that the plans show how the extension of the Alston Branch could be made to Nenthead with a ruling gradient of 1 in 50, and curves no worse than 10 chains (200m) radius, at a cost of about £50,000. Mr St Paul de Sincay, the managing director of the Société des Mines & Fonderies de Zinc de la Vieille Montagne, which had acquired the lead mines on Alston Moor from the Greenwich Hospital Estates, indicated they expected a traffic of about 50,000 tons of ore per annum. Gibb also stated that he thought 'the Society were anxious to get the line and were prepared to make fair financial arrangements to secure it.' At the board meeting held on 17 July 1899, the general manager reported negotiations which had taken place with reference to a proposed light railway from Alston to Nenthead and was authorised to continue negotiations, and to obtain revised estimates of the cost of construction of the proposed railway.[666]

The route was inspected on Tuesday 26 September by a delegation from the NER, composed of three directors, Sir Joseph Pease, Sir Lothian Bell and Sir Lindsay Wood, together with the general manager, Sir G.S. Gibb, and the engineer, Mr C.A. Harrison.[668] On 20 October the general manager reported further correspondence and proposed terms,[669] but on 17 November he reported that the Vieille Montaigne Company of Belgium were not willing to agree to the terms suggested as to rate and guarantee on the proposed railway from Alston to Nenthead and the matter was now left with the Montaigne Company to see Mr C.A. Harrison and to consider whether some cheaper scheme for obtaining railway communication with Nenthead mines could be devised.[670] However, less than two months after the inspection by the NER delegation the *Hexham Courant* reported that the Vieille Montagne Zinc Company was discontinuing night working and laying off forty to fifty workers at Nenthead.[671] The 1899 plans of the NER appear to have been the last serious attempt to extend the Alston branch, or any of the existing lines in the North Pennines, although expansion of facilities continued to occur.

There is an original, but undated, tracing of sections[672] that appear to refer to the plans[665] accompanying George Gibb's letter. This line is shown leaving the Alston branch south of Gilderdale Burn, and following a route to Nenthead significantly different from that of both the earlier N&CR and WVER proposals. The start of the extension was by a junction with the existing Alston branch 4 furlongs 3½ chains (875m) north of the proposed new viaduct over the South Tyne. The datum line is given as 59ft (18m) below the rails at the start of the extension which is, according to the OS map, 260m (853ft) above sea level. This is at the north end of the original Gilderdale Halt of the narrow-gauge STR,[820] or 2 furlongs (402m) south of the point where the route authorised in 1846 was abandoned, or 3 furlongs 3 chains (660m) south of Gilderdale Burn.

The South Tyne was crossed on a viaduct 75ft (22.9m) above the river and 260 yards (238m) long, at the same point as, but at a different angle to, and much

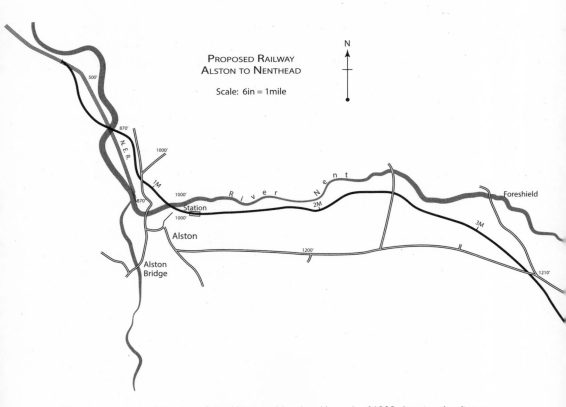

The western part of the plan of the Alston to Nenthead branch of 1899 showing the divergence of the new line from the existing branch just over half a mile north of Alston station and following a route past the town a little to the south of the route proposed by the WVER and the N&CR route authorised in 1846. Traced from the original plans by Mr J. Crompton, Blagill, and reproduced by his permission.

Sites of crossing of the A686 by the WVER, 1845 N&CR and 1899 NER lines. All three lines
would have crossed this road between the North Loaning on the left and Low Byer Inn beyond
the car in the centre. The 1845 N&CR was to cross on the level at the junction of the Loaning,
the WVER was to be on an embankment 31ft high and the 1899 line on one of 18ft, both a
little over a chain (25m) beyond the Loaning, closer to Low Byer Inn.

higher than, the existing viaduct. The proposed viaduct was also 9ft (2.7m) higher
than the viaduct shown in the 1845 plans.

The site for a new Alston station was identified in the valley of the river Nent,
over the ridge to the north-east of Alston's Front Street. There were similarities
with the original N&CR route of 1845, but the steepest gradient in 1899 was 1
in 50.

The terminus was just beyond the level crossing of the road at Holmsfoot in
Nenthead, 5 miles 5 furlongs 5 chains (9.15km) from the junction. The line was
to rise 528.4ft (161m) from just south of Gilderdale viaduct.

Returning to the Wear Valley, the opening of the line to Wearhead proved
successful from the start, with large quantities of minerals being carried soon after
opening. Unfortunately, this also resulted in the closure of the Westgate depot of
the WI&CCR and the lifting of the Westgate incline in 1897, as the traffic was
transferred to the new line.[789]

In the 1880s, the Weardale Steel, Coal and Coke Company opened a large
limestone quarry at Heights alongside but above their line to Middlehope,

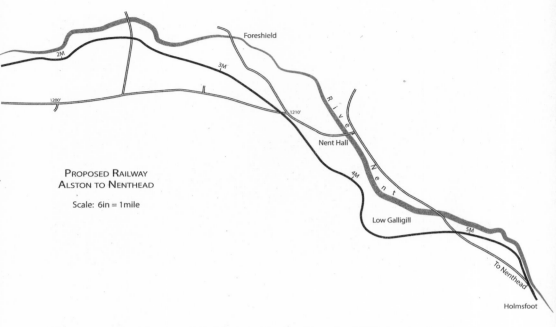

PROPOSED RAILWAY
ALSTON TO NENTHEAD

Scale: 6in = 1mile

The eastern part of the plan of the Alston to Nenthead branch of 1899 showing the alignment between the crossing of the turnpike road before Nenthall to Nenthead, which is much more sinuous than either of the lines on the plans produced in 1845 by the WVER or that of the N&CR authorised by the act of 1846. Traced from the original plans by Mr J. Crompton, Blagill and reproduced by his permission.

about ½ mile (800m) to the east of Scutterhill depot.[728] Initially the output from this quarry was carried down Bishop's Seat and up Bolts Law inclines, but the increased demand for limestone during the First World War was beyond the capacity of these inclines and a new incline was constructed in 1915 by German prisoners of war. This Cambo Keels incline ran from Heights quarry down the hillside to a triangular junction with a siding alongside the Wearhead line between Eastgate and Westgate stations.

Right up to the start of the Second World War there were further suggestions for extensions to the existing railways, from Alston to Wearhead by Weardale District Council in 1906[679] and the vicar of Nenthead in 1911,[687] or to Middleton-in-Teesdale by the people of Alston,[700] but the Cambo Keels incline was the final section of the standard-gauge rail network in the North Pennines to be built. One of the documents in the Stanton, Croft and Company papers is a lease, from the 1940s, of heights quarry which includes a map showing most of the Weardale Iron and Coal Company railway and the incline from Heights quarry down to the triangular junction with the NER near Eastgate, although this is stated as requiring repairs.[694]

The foot of Cambo Keels incline in early 1950 showing the partially dismantled triangular junction where the wagons of stone from Heights quarry had joined the siding between Eastgate and Westgate.

From the beginning of the twentieth century the overall mineral output from the North Pennines started to decrease and as a result the rail system too began to contract. This occurred slowly at first, but became more rapid as the readily accessible mineral resources became exhausted after the Second World War. The next chapter will look at this continuous decline and the final chapter will consider what remains today of the once extensive railway network of the North Pennines.

14

THE LONG DECLINE

We saw in the previous chapter that one of the reasons for extending the railway to Wearhead was an attempt to counteract the depression in the mining industries of the North Pennines. This depression was first felt in lead mining, when the importation of cheap foreign ore made it more and more difficult for the British industry to survive, initially in those areas where transport was difficult and expensive but later extending to most of the ore-fields. The first line to be affected in a serious way was the H&AR, which had been completed for little more than a decade when the major depression in the lead industry occurred.[567] The price of lead ore fell from £17 a ton in 1873–74 to £7 or £8 in 1879, while by November of the following year the price of English pig lead had fallen to £15 5s (£15.25) per ton, a fall of £3 per ton since the beginning of the year.[568] For several years the mines and lead smelters in Allendale were operated on little more than a care and maintenance basis[588] and, although there was a short flurry of activity in Allendale in 1885,[589] the huge Langley smelt mill closed at the end of 1887.[601]

Although the extraction and smelting of lead, and the related ores of zinc and silver, had been the first major industry in the North Pennines, the mining and quarrying of coal, iron ore, limestone and road stone eventually employed even larger numbers of men. Partly because of the investment in a railway by the Weardale Iron and Coal Company, the ironstone workings in the 1880s were mainly in the Wear Valley,[578] although deposits were known to exist over much of the North Pennines. We saw in Chapter 12 that it was the possibility of developing some of these other ore-fields that helped to encourage the promoters of the C&CJR. Unfortunately, in 1890 it was found that although the ironstone from the Wear Valley made excellent wrought iron, it did not prove suitable for making steel.[604,607] Thus, after a short but lucrative boom period, there was a depression in the ironstone quarries to add to that in the lead mines, although the mining of coal and zinc ore and the quarrying of both limestone and road stone continued with vigour.[642,652]

The coal industry in northern England remained healthy until the last quarter of the twentieth century, and small quantities of coal continue to be mined in the South Tyne Valley in the twenty-first century, but the length of time individual mines were in operation was very variable. Prior to the formation of the National Coal Board, individual mines or even entire coalfields could change hands, resulting in different methods being used to take the coal away. Extraction of moderately large amounts of road stone, as well as smaller amounts of other types of stone and metal ores continues in the North Pennines in the twenty-first century, but changing production sites, location of customers and economic considerations have altered the way in which the outputs are moved, while even the modern cement industry in Weardale ended in 2003. The only lines in the North Pennines which did not provide regular passenger services into the twentieth century were the Weardale Iron and Coal Company network, the Lambley Colliery branch from the Alston branch of the N&CR, the section of the W&DJR from Burnhill Junction through Waskerley to Stanhope, and LCR. A passenger service had been operated over LCR from Milton to Brampton town, using horse-drawn 'Dandies' since the 1830s, with horses being replaced by a locomotive and coaches on 1 July 1881.[689] The service ended on 30 April 1890 following an inspection by Major General Hutchinson, when the line did not meet the required standards.[603,689] Following twenty years of local agitation the line was taken over by the North Eastern Railway in 1911[686] and reopened for passenger traffic as a light railway on 1 August 1913.[690]

Like most railways in the United Kingdom, the majority of the lines in the North Pennines survived the First World War, even if passenger services were curtailed, but the arrival of motor buses and road lorries began to eat into their passenger and general goods traffic, while the decline of the staple extractive industries continued. During the nineteenth century the extremities of the WI&CCR near the head of the Rookhope Burn, beyond Grove Rake mine, were closed when the ironstone quarries they served ceased production, while the line to Low White Heaps apparently closed at or before the expiry of the twenty-one-year lease under which it had been built. The remaining lines that were abandoned completely were those replaced by routes that were easier to operate, such as the route from the top of Nanny Mayor's incline to Whitehall on the original part of the S&TR from Waskerley to Rowley, which closed in 1859, and the Sunnyside incline of the former WER closing in 1868. The Westgate depot and incline of the WI&CCR became disused following its replacement by the (second) WVER, which opened in 1895.

The first important sections of railway, both of which were private, to be abandoned without any replacement were the western section of the WI&CCR beyond Slit Pasture from 1905[789] and the short length of LCR from Halton Lea Gate to Lambley Colliery, which was lifted in 1909–10 following the cessation of all operations by Thompson's of Kirkhouse and the transfer of their colliery leases to the new Naworth Coal Company on 1 July 1908.[753] As we saw

Brampton Junction with a train in the platform for the Brampton Town branch on opening day, 31 July 1913. Ken Hoole collection, reproduced by permission of HoS-DRM.

in Chapter 6, this section of line was the western half of the Halton Lea Gate branch authorised by the N&CR Act of 1849, although it was actually built as part of Lord Carlisle's Railway. The closure of this section severed the historic link between LCR and the Alston branch, but the remainder of LCR, as well as the Lambley Colliery branch, continued to be used until well after the Second World War. The Naworth Colliery Company even extended Lord Carlisle's Railway to Gairs colliery in 1909,[685] although this length closed in 1936.[754]

Although the ironstone extracted in the Wear Valley proved unsuitable for the manufacture of steel, that same industry used large quantities of limestone, some of which came from high above the Wear Valley, being taken away over the inclines of the WI&CCR. Some ironstone mining did continue, with Grove Head mine operating into the twentieth century,[675] while the Weardale Lead Company continued to operate mines in the Rookhope valley.[583] Although the Rookhope smelt mill closed in May 1919, mining continued in the valley with the WI&CCR carrying ore from the Rispey preparation mill, about 1¾ miles (2.8km) north-west of Rookhope Village, as well as Boltsburn mine itself. On 20 February 1923 traffic on the last section of the Rookhope Head branch of the WI&CCR ceased when the line from Rispey to Rookhope closed.[808]

We saw in Chapter 13 that during the First World War the requirement for iron and steel increased the demand for limestone, and Cambo Keels incline was built to take the output from the quarry at Heights to the NER line along the valley floor. The WI&CCR line was closed beyond Scutterhill depot around 1915,[789] with the depot officially closing in 1917.[808] The demand for limestone was reduced once the war had ended and with Heights, the only remaining mine or quarry, closing in 1923 the entire line from Rookhope into the Wear Valley became redundant. With the continuing depression in the British lead industry, coupled with the advent of road motor vehicles, the end of the WI&CCR was now in sight.

The construction by the Weardale Lead Company of an aerial flight between Rookhope and Eastgate meant that the remaining parts of the WI&CCR could be closed on 15 May 1923.[808] Although the entire WI&CCR system had officially closed, much of it, including the locomotives, continued to be maintained while, from 1 June 1923, a twice weekly horse-drawn wagon continued to take supplies to the cottages at Bolts Law for some time, and the track was not lifted until the Second World War.[786] Between the wars, shooting parties were carried by A.E. Bainbridge, of Stanhope Castle, using a four-wheeled, battery-operated truck over the section across the Stanhope moors which he called the Stanhope, Rookhope and District Railway.[799] The carriage of shooting parties had ceased by 1939 and final demolition took place in 1943 when the last locomotive was removed from Heights quarry,[810] and the track was finally lifted in June.[809]

The same combination of depression of the lead industry and the use of motor vehicles for the movement of both goods and passengers by road saw the economics of all the railways in the North Pennines beginning to be undermined. However, the Alston branch continued to carry large quantities of coal, especially from its northern end, while the limestone workings which had been established and expanded at Alston[613,681] kept the branch busy and required improvements to loading facilities in the early 1900s.[684,692] Similarly the Wearhead and Middleton-in-Teesdale branches continued to carry large quantities of stone, although all the quarries served by the Bishopley branch had closed by 1925[807], while the W&DJR continued to carry supplies to Consett iron works, along with other traffic, mainly sand and stone. The SD&LUR also remained busy, but even there the last of the Woodland collieries closed in March 1921 with the branch railway being dismantled in 1923[802].

The situation was rather different on the Hexham and Allendale line, where there was virtually no traffic apart from the single daily freight and three passenger trains required to support the local population. Following petitions from the local parish council various alterations and increases to the passenger service, especially during the summer, were implemented in the early 1900s[678] and there were sufficient improvements in the traffic figures to allow Allendale station also to be improved.[680] The extension of the line from Catton station to Allendale town had again been requested when the improvements were being planned,[677] but this was not carried out, and the inconvenience of the station at Catton Road was undoubtedly one of the factors in the fatal decline in passenger numbers after the First World War. In the years immediately prior to the war there were signs of an improvement in the prosperity of the Allen Valley with the establishment of a creamery beside Allendale station, opened on 8 November 1913,[691] and the promises of an improvement in the lead-mining industry closer to Allenheads, starting with the sinking of a new shaft at Ellershope to tap the Swinhope vein.[688] The following year it was reported that the Rookhope lead mines and mills were 'going full swing'.[693] After the war the discovery of a major lead vein was reported in the Sipton District,[695] while the Weardale Lead Company had obtained a long lease of the mineral rights in Allendale, generating considerable activity in the mines in Allendale including a new shaft being dug at Sipton.[702]

Also in the years following the First World War, there was a national move to construct light railways to improve the economies of the more rural areas and there were two proposals which would have affected Allendale. In 1920 Northumberland County Council's reconstruction committee asked the county surveyor and land agent to report on a line from Corbridge or Riding Mill, through Hexhamshire, where a creamery was proposed, to Allendale with branches to Slaley, Lillswood and Whitehall.[696] However, the discovery of lead in Blanchland suggested that a horseshoe route through Blanchland to Shotley Bridge would be better than going across the moors to Allendale.[698] The reconstruction committee stated that while a light railway could be built from Hexham to Dyehouse, unless it could be shown that there would be more traffic than appeared probable, they would not be justified in carrying it out.[699]

A second light railway, this time from Allendale to Eastgate via Rookhope and Allenheads, was also under consideration at this time.[697] That none of these proposed lines had a future was made clear when the government was asked why steps were not being taken to construct railways between Eastgate and Allendale and Middleton-in-Teesdale and Alston. Sir Eric Geddes said that the proposal for a railway between Eastgate and Allendale had not been investigated in detail owing to the decision of the government that schemes involving expenditure not yet in operation were to remain in abeyance. The same observation applied to the railway from Middleton to Alston.[700] Despite the lack of local or central government support further efforts were made to have the line from Allendale to Eastgate built.[702]

The Brampton Town Branch was one of several lightly used lines to be temporarily closed during the First World War, the service being withdrawn on 1 March 1917 and not reinstated until 1 March 1920.[756] The reopening was accompanied by an increase in the fare from 4d (1.7p) to 7d (2.9p), which caused a great decline in passenger traffic,[701] resulting in the line losing about £3,000 per annum. On 26 October 1922 the NER gave notice that they intended to terminate their lease on the branch on 29 October 1923, and the LNER, as the new owner, withdrew the passenger service from that date, although they continued goods services until the end of December.[757]

The decrease in the population which followed the almost total collapse of lead mining in the Allen Valley, and the failure of those who remained to make full use of the branch, resulted in the LNER withdrawing the passenger service over the Allendale branch from 22 September 1930.[712] In fact the last 'milk train' ran on the night of Sunday 21st, although freight trains continued to run,[703] and there was little surprise that this was the first passenger service to be withdrawn from the valleys of the North Pennines. It is interesting to note that passenger services on both the Alston and Allendale branches had been improved in the 1890s following local petitions,[630] but nothing was done for the Wearhead line following similar petitions,[673] while the Middleton-in-Teesdale line had been given an improved service as far back as 1882.[578]

One further closure occurred immediately before the Second World War when the passenger service was withdrawn from the W&DJR between Blackhill and Tow Law on 1 May 1939.[713] Although there was still a considerable amount of limestone and sand being carried from the Stanhope area to Consett, there was virtually nothing which required the section from Burnhill Junction to Tow Law to be kept open, and this was closed to all traffic, although the track was not lifted for almost twenty years.[806] According to Rounthwaite[725] the closure occurred on the same day as the withdrawal of the passenger service, but according to Whittle[733] it was 18 May 1939. Passenger services continued to run from Darlington to Tow Law, and there were no further closures until 1950, after the railways had been nationalised.

The first line to succumb to the less happy economic conditions after the Second World War was the Allendale branch, which was finally closed to goods traffic on 17 November 1950.[711] Again, this came as no surprise, as the steady fall in the local population and the failure of the people of Allendale to support the railway with their goods traffic meant that the quantities of general merchandise no longer warranted a rail service.[710] The discovery of rich deposits of fluorspar at Carrshield had prompted hopes that there would be an industrial revival in the Allen valleys,[707] and the newly formed Allendale Metalliferous Mining Company reported that they had originally intended loading at Allendale,[708] but British Railways had told them that the line was going to close, while Alston and Wearhead stations were closer to the mines.[709]

Like many other lines in the North Pennines, although the railways were affected by bad weather, they still provided a more reliable service than the roads,[581] and the loss of the Hexham and Allendale branch was mourned by the inhabitants of the Allen Valley. The lines of the North Pennines were all suffering from declining traffic, both goods and passengers, and closures of sections of the lines, initially for passengers only, but later more often for all traffic, now became common. At the foot of the Crawleyside incline, Ashes quarry, which had supplied Consett iron works with limestone, ceased production in 1944[803] or 1949[734], and on 28 April 1951, less than six months after the H&AR finally closed, decaying sleepers and declining traffic were the reasons given for the closure of both the Crawleyside and Weatherhill inclines, with the S&TR now terminating at the Parkhead sand quarry.[734] The following year stone traffic ceased from Middleton-in-Teesdale when the output from Ord & Maddison's Crossthwaite quarry was transferred to road.[806]

Although not covered in detail in this survey, it should be noted that passenger services ceased to run between Kirkby Stephen and Tebay on 1 December 1952,[745] the first part of the former SD&LUR to be closed. The following year saw the closure of two more sections of line in the North Pennines. The first was the complete closure of the remaining part of Lord Carlisle's Railway, from Midgeholme to Brampton Junction, by the National Coal Board on 31 March 1953,[755] with demolition starting in October. This was followed, three months later, by the withdrawal of passenger trains between Wear Valley Junction and Wearhead on 29 June 1953,[723] but as was usual at the time, freight traffic continued. The final closure of the 1950s occurred on 11 June 1956 when passenger trains were withdrawn from the steeply graded line between Crook and Tow Law.[734] Goods and passenger facilities were withdrawn from several individual stations, but it was not until the next decade that further line closures occurred in the North Pennines. It was hoped that the introduction of modern motive power would improve the situation, and the December 1959 issue of *The Railway Magazine* carried the following report: 'In an attempt to avoid the necessity of closing the Haltwhistle-Alston branch to passengers, an improved service, with multiple-unit diesel railcars replacing the steam trains, was introduced by the North Eastern Region on November 2.'[715] It was also stated that cheap day fares had been withdrawn and it was hoped that the passenger facilities would become solvent(!).

The Sunniside incline had been closed when the locomotive line from Tow Law to Crook opened for passenger trains on 2 March 1868, but the upper part of the line from Tow Law, which was level, remained open to serve various collieries at Sunnyside Bank Top. The closure of these collieries resulted in the closure of this freight-only section in 1960.[734] Another length of line to be completely closed at this time was from St John's Chapel to Wearhead, from which the remaining goods service was withdrawn on 2 January 1961.[722] However, it was on 20 January 1962 that the first major closure of the decade took place when all services were withdrawn between Barnard Castle and Kirkby Stephen (Merrygill signal box), from Kirkby Stephen Junction to Tebay, and from Appleby East to Clifton on the West Coast main line.[717] Five months later, on 18 June 1962, most of the remaining SD&LUR was closed when passenger services were withdrawn

Diesel train at Alston after the overall roof had been removed, the sidings lifted, the engine shed and other buildings demolished, with the branch in use for passengers only as a basic railway. Reproducd by permission of R. N. Graham.

between Barnard Castle and Bishop Auckland, with Barnard Castle to West Auckland closing to freight traffic as well.[718] The days of eastbound trains of iron ore and westbound trains of coke battling over Stainmore Summit had ended.

For another two and a half years about 1½ miles of the SD&LUR line from Barnard Castle to Tees Valley Junction remained open for all traffic, as this provided the connection between the D&BCR and the TVR which did not close to passengers until 30 November 1964.[719] Following these closures only the section from the connection with the former Midland line at Appleby to Kirkby Stephen remained open for goods and military traffic. The closure to passengers of the last line in the Durham part of the North Pennines area occurred on 22 March 1965 when services were withdrawn between Bishop Auckland and Crook.[720] Two weeks later, on 5 April 1965,[746] goods services were withdrawn from Darlington to Middleton-in-Teesdale, while those between Wear Valley Junction and Tow Law ended on 5 July 1965.[736]

By the middle of 1965 only four sections of the once extensive railway system that had served the North Pennine ore-field remained open. In the south of the area, goods trains continued to run on the Wear Valley line westwards from Bishop Auckland to St John's Chapel. In the west, goods services continued over the remnants of the SD&LUR and the EVR, initially including stone trains from near Kirkby Stephen but later only those serving the military depot at Warcop on

Double-headed train of empties storming past Merrygill signal box, beyond which the line was closed in 1962. Ken Hoole collection, reproduced by permission of HoS-DRM.

the EVR. In the north-east, trains continued to carry sand from Parkhead Quarry and serve the military depot at Burnhill, although Blanchland goods station closed on 2 August 1965,[804] while in the north the Alston branch continued to be served by both passenger and goods trains.

The next casualty was the goods service to Alston, which was withdrawn in September 1965, although the intermediate stations had lost their goods facilities over the preceding years, starting with Featherstone Park in August 1954. Indeed it was something of a miracle that goods trains to Alston lasted until 1965 as most of the mineral traffic had ended several years earlier.[716] The last major colliery, at Lambley, closed at the end of 1958, with the Lambley Fell branch, which had served it, following in 1960. By then the limestone industry at Alston was also virtually dead so that the only mineral carried in any quantity was fluorspar from Anglo-Austral Mines Limited at Nenthead. This company ceased operations in January 1961 and the last consignment of fluorspar left Alston on 24 January, leaving only inward domestic coal as a reliable source of freight revenue. Therefore from 1965 the Alston branch became a basic railway, carrying passenger trains only.[787] On the Wear Valley line goods trains were withdrawn from 1 November 1965 from Westgate to St John's Chapel.[788] By the end of the decade the number of lines still open had been reduced to three when trains were withdrawn from the last part of the former W&DJR, between Burnhill Junction and Weatherhill on 29 April 1968, and Consett to Burnhill Junction on 1 May 1969.[736]

Earlier, on 1 July 1968, ordinary freight services were withdrawn from the Wear Valley line leaving only the trains serving the cement works at Eastgate, with the line beyond completely closed.[788] The passenger service ceased on the Haltwhistle to Alston branch on 1 May 1976, when a new bridge over the river South Tyne, near Lambley, and its connecting roads were completed, allowing a bus service to replace the trains.[821] Military traffic on the remaining section of the Eden Valley Railway, from Appleby to Warcop, ended on 16 March 1989.[794,817] The line from Bishop Auckland to Eastgate continued to carry cement traffic for several more years, but eventually Blue Circle decided that road transport was less expensive and the last train ran on 19 March 1993.[805] On that day normal rail services apparently ended in the North Pennines, although almost ten years earlier tourist trains had started running when the first mile of the narrow-gauge South Tynedale Railway opened on 30 July 1983.[820]

At the start of the twenty-first century, preservation societies were involved with all three sections of railway which remained open for traffic in or adjacent to the North Pennines at the beginning of 1970 and these will be reviewed in the final chapter.

15

THE TOURIST RAILWAYS

In 2014, preservation societies continue to operate tourist rail services on parts of the former Alston branch, the EVR and in Weardale, although an attempt to reintroduce a regular public passenger service on the line from Bishop Auckland to Stanhope failed. We shall now look at these three different organisations in detail, starting with the standard-gauge Eden Valley Railway, followed by the narrow-gauge South Tynedale Railway and ending with the Weardale Railway, now mostly owned by Iowa Pacific Holdings, who have been attempting to restore the line to a full public railway.

Although the military traffic which kept the Appleby to Warcop section of the EVR line open for many years ceased in 1989,[794] the rails remained and in 1995 the Eden Valley Railway Society was formed to reopen it and the lifted section to Kirkby Stephen. The society was later converted into the Eden Valley Railway Trust, a registered charity which, on 1 April 2000, incorporated Stainmore Properties Limited, an organisation originally formed to purchase the Kirkby Stephen East station site (ex-SD&LUR). Next the Eden Valley Railway Company was formed and ownership of the 6 miles of line from Appleby to Warcop was transferred to it, with a tourist passenger service starting in 2006 over a short length of line from Warcop.[812]

The first activity at Warcop occurred in 1996 when, with permission from the BRB property board and a local landowner, a section of track was laid from the BR boundary towards Flithome. Talks were entered into with the BRB property board, then Sustrans, to whom BRB transferred the line upon the privatisation of BR, with the aim of buying the line to Appleby including the track, most of which was still intact. Access was gained to the route and maintenance work was able to start with the removal of ten years of trees and vegetation from the line between Warcop and Appleby. Further track was laid at Warcop and a milestone in the trust's objective to run trains was achieved in 2004 when the railway was granted an order under the Transport and Works Act allowing the operation of passenger-carrying trains. Rolling stock was acquired for both works and passenger trains, culminating in the arrival of a three-coach diesel multiple unit and two four-coach electric units in 2005.[825]

Eden Valley Railway DMU entering Warcop station from Appleby direction in 2006. Reproduced by permission of Mike Butler.

The first narrow-gauge train on the South Tynedale Railway after arrival at the original, temporary, Gilderdale Halt on Saturday 30 July 1983. Looking north, the locomotive, No. 1 *Phoenix*, is running round the train.

Passenger services were started on 14 April 2006, initially only over ¼ mile of track, but by August 2006 2 miles (3.2km) of line were open. After a winter break, the service was restarted at Easter 2007, but on 10 May a lorry hit the bridge just outside Warcop station,[816] causing serious damage and closing the line. The Ministry of Defence accepted liability and the repairs were eventually started on 21 July 2008, with the line reopening in time for the August bank holiday weekend. Work continues to upgrade the track after years of minimal maintenance and to develop the site at Warcop, plans for which include a new station building and a shed for locomotive and coach maintenance.[825] The line was further extended during 2009.[827] Regular but relatively infrequent passenger trains started running over a short section of line at Kirkby Stephen in 2012.[837]

In the north of the Pennines, tourist passenger trains have been running northwards from Alston station along the valley of the river South Tyne since 1983. The South Tynedale Railway Preservation Society was formed in 1973, when the closure of the Alston branch was first announced, and the South Tynedale Railway Company was formed to take over and run the entire standard-gauge branch. These plans collapsed due to lack of finance, the South Tynedale Railway Company was dissolved and all the rails were lifted. However, the members of the South Tynedale Railway Preservation Society decided on 2 July 1977 to build a new narrow-gauge line on the trackbed of the former branch, while Cumbria and Northumberland county councils purchased the trackbed within their boundaries northwards from Alston.

The society, which is a registered charity, obtained a lease of the trackbed in Cumbria from Cumbria County Council, received a Tourist Board grant of £20,000 towards the capital costs and, with the assistance of personnel from the Manpower Services Commission, but using mainly volunteer labour, opened just over a mile of railway on 30 July 1983.[823] A light railway order was obtained for the section in Cumbria and the society became a company limited by guarantee in 1984. The line was extended to the south side of Gilderdale viaduct, the Cumbria county boundary, on 13 December 1986. An agreement to lease the trackbed as far as Slaggyford was obtained from Northumberland County Council, and a second light railway order was obtained on 9 July 1996 to enable the society to extend the railway to Slaggyford, with the first part being opened to a new station at Kirkhaugh, just over 2¼ miles from Alston on 4 September 1999.[793,821] On 21 May 2002, 150 years from the day on which passenger trains first ran from Alston to Lambley in 1852, the society celebrated the 150th anniversary of the branch and, on the same day, launched an appeal to help extend the line another 2¼ miles to Slaggyford.

Following the successful completion of negotiations to lease the 3¼ miles of trackbed and structures as far as Slaggyford, work commenced in July 2007 to clear the trackbed and repair the drains northwards from Kirkhaugh. Grants and support in kind have been received from the Rural Development Commission, the European Community, the Heritage Lottery Fund, the local authorities of Eden and Tynedale District and Cumbria and Northumberland county councils.[823] These have enabled the society to obtain more rolling stock and buildings in which to house and maintain the vehicles used for the passenger service, restore to original condition a historic German First World War locomotive, as well as attend to the maintenance and extension of the tracks. Permission to build the section to Lintley was received and work officially commenced in July 2008.[821] Grants were received in 2009 to fund the expensive repairs required to two occupation overbridges and Lintley viaduct and the section of about 1 mile (1.6km) of line from Kirkhaugh to a new halt at Lintley was opened on 1 April 2012, giving the railway a second point of access from the main road system. (see fig. 12 col. section)

In 2007 grants were obtained to fund the upgrade of the lineside path, which is part of the South Tyne Trail, to make it suitable for walkers of all abilities, wheelchair users and cyclists.[823] The tourist passenger service provided by the volunteers of the South Tynedale Railway Preservation Society attracts about 20,000 visitors a year to the town of Alston, providing a significant contribution to the economy of the area. In 2012 the freehold of the railway land in Cumbria was transferred to the Society while Northumberland granted a 999-year lease on the railway land to a short distance north of Slaggyford. The South Tynedale Railway has become securely established as the main tourist attraction in the upper South Tyne valley with the society celebrating thirty years of running narrow-gauge tourist trains in July 2013.

The success of these Societies in restoring an existing standard-gauge railway and building what is a completely new narrow-gauge railway on a former standard gauge trackbed has been entirely due to the dedication of the members who voluntarily supplied the labour to initially build the new railway and continue to provide the labour, and management, to extend and maintain the railways as well as providing the personnel to operate the tourist passenger services.[824]

In the Wear Valley things have been different. A group called the Friends of the Heritage Line was formed and, for a few years, organised a summer-only passenger service from Saltburn to Stanhope while the cement trains were running. In April 1993, at the invitation of Wear Valley District Council, the Weardale Branch of the Friends helped form the Weardale Railway Society, which evolved into the Weardale Railway Trust. The same year Weardale Railways Limited was established to purchase and maintain the Wear Valley Branch from Bishop Auckland to Eastgate. The company reached an agreement with Railtrack to purchase the line and in the summer of 2002 received the necessary order under the Transport and Works Act to operate passenger trains.

When the order was granted the Weardale Railway stated that it was initially planning to run a seven-day-a-week service between Bishop Auckland and Stanhope, supplemented by steam trains at weekends.[795] In practice a tourist passenger service commenced operating between Stanhope and Wolsingham on 17 July 2004.[796] Weardale Railways Limited carried about 14,000 passengers during the period to the end of December 2004, when it made most of its thirty-plus employees redundant, before going into administration in January 2005 owing over £900,000,[800] despite having received around £5,000,000 in grants. The failure of Weardale Railways Limited is unfortunately reminiscent of the collapse of the Stanhope and Tyne Railway over 160 years earlier, which also operated from Stanhope, and could produce the same end result. At the end of 2005 a £500,000 rescue package was agreed by the local councils and the development agency, One NorthEast, with the creditors agreeing to accept 25p in the pound, although only actually receiving 23.33p.[818]

The ECT Group (Ealing Community Transport) purchased 75 per cent of the shares in a reconstituted Weardale Railway Company with the Weardale Railway Trust holding 12.5 per cent, and Durham County Council and Wear Valley

District Council each holding 6.25 per cent. Services were restarted in August 2006, with the ECT Group promising to underwrite the railway for five years, by which time it was hoped to have reopened the line all the way from the Network Rail interchange at Bishop Auckland to Eastgate.[814]

ECT also started discussions with Network Rail for the purchase of the line as, despite the agreement with Railtrack, the attempt by the original company had failed. In the autumn of 2006 the Weardale Railway Trust purchased an 0-6-0T, operating on the Colne Valley Railway, while RMS Locotec, a subsidiary of the ECT Group, purchased an 0-6-0ST from the North Norfolk Railway.[813] Nevertheless the 2007 operating season commenced using a Pacer DMU, as it was discovered that major boiler repairs were required on the 0-6-0T from the Colne Valley Railway. On 12 April 2007 ownership of the 18.7 miles (30.1km) of line from a point approximately 100 yards west of Bishop Auckland platform to Eastgate was acquired by the Weardale Railway Community Interest Company, the name of the company which ran the line at that time. (see. figs 13 & 14 col. section) [815,818]

In a talk given at 'Transport in the North Pennines, Module 8 of Know Your North Pennines',[818] it was stated that in the twelve months from reopening in 2006 to August 2007 the Weardale Railway carried 10,000 passengers, which is virtually the same as the South Tynedale Railway carried in 1984, its first full year of operation. It was expected that the passenger service would continue to operate only between Wolsingham and Stanhope for two more years while work was undertaken on the line to Bishop Auckland. It was stated that it was expected to appoint a paid General Manager by the end of 2007 while in order for the railway to be viable approximately 70,000 passengers would be required every year. Despite the promise of stability given in 2007, ECT decided to withdraw from all its railway commitments in early 2008[819] and put its 75 per cent share in the Weardale Railway up for sale. Volunteers continued to operate services on the railway during the 2008 season, but without any paid staff.

On 9 September 2008 the sale of the ECT share to Iowa Pacific Holdings was announced.[826] Ed Ellis, president of Iowa Pacific, stated, 'We believe in the community rail model and look forward to developing freight, tourist and passenger services on Weardale Railway.' British American Railway Services (BARS), owned by Iowa Pacific Holdings, purchased most of the railway interests of ECT and it soon became clear that their plans included the expansion of both the Dartmoor and Weardale Railways. A report in *The Railway Magazine* for March 2010 announced that the link from the Weardale Railway to the national network at Bishop Auckland had been completed and they were negotiating with UK Coal to develop a coal depot at Wolsingham to ship large tonnages of coal from a new opencast site by rail.[828] The following month another report stated that the Wolsingham to Bishop Auckland line had been inspected by HMRI on

25 January and that a UK Railtours charter was to be the first train to use it on 19 February.[829] It was also announced that Weardale Railways intended, in addition to the heritage services, to start running commuter trains from Stanhope to Bishop Auckland, using a new temporary platform immediately west of the Network Rail platform. It was hoped that, following the adaptation of the Bishop Auckland platform for through trains, the Weardale service would run through to Shildon.

At the other end of the country, it was announced in June that Devon and Cornwall Railways was applying to run through trains from the Dartmoor Railway to Exeter.[830] The same issue of *The Railway Magazine* reported the building of a loop at Wolsingham to enable the Weardale Railway to run seven daily return trips from Stanhope to Bishop Auckland using a Class 141 DMU.[831] Finally, the July issue of *The Railway Magazine* reported that, following an inspection by HMRI on 27 May, the Wolsingham to Bishop Auckland section of the Weardale railway was officially reopened on 22 May, with the community service timetable commencing the following day.[832]

The plans to run coal trains from Wolsingham came closer to fruition when Durham County Council backed plans to develop a coal-loading facility at Wolsingham on 27 July 2010,[833] and BARS gained European passenger and freight operating licenses.[834] *The Railway Magazine* reported that coal train trials started running to Tata Steel at Scunthorpe on 16 June 2011, using a Colas Rail locomotive and twenty-one wagons of 100 tons.[835] The coal-loading depot at Wolsingham was the former steel works, with the coal brought by road from the opencast site at Tow Law. (see fig. 15 col. section)

Although the first coal train ran on 16 June 2011,[835] and the traffic was successfully established by the end of the year, passenger traffic did not reach the expected levels. An announcement by the president of the Weardale Railway, who also represents BARS, stated that because most of the passenger interest was overwhelmingly in a heritage-type service, the commuter-type service was to be abandoned, at least for the time being, with the daily service ceasing on Saturday 31 December 2011.[836] In 2012 it seemed that with the successful return of freight traffic to the Weardale Railway, the precedent set by the S&TR of initially going bankrupt before becoming an important and successful part of the railway network under new management could be in the process of being repeated. Unfortunately things started to go wrong again in 2013 when Ed Ellis[838] reported that regular passenger services would cease and the Weardale Railway would concentrate on 'up-market dining trains, Polar Express trains at Christmas and coal trains, although even the coal trains ceased in the autumn. Nevertheless, a new company, Weardale Railway Heritage Services Ltd, was formed as a subsidiary of the Weardale Railway Trust and regular heritage services were started again on 14 June 2014.[839]

APPENDIX A

Relationship of Metric to Imperial Units

Imperial unit with abbreviation (x)	Metric equivalent with abbreviation (x)
1 inch (in)	25.4 millimetres (mm)
1 foot (ft) = 12in	304.8mm
1 yard = 3ft	914.4mm
1 chain = 22 yards	20.12 metres (m)
1 link = 1/100 chain = 7.92in	201.2mm
1 furlong = 220 yards = 10 chains	201.2m
1 mile = 8 furlongs = 80 chains = 1,760 yards	1.609 kilometres (km)
£1 = 20 shillings (s)	100 new pence (p)
1 shilling = 12 old pennies (d)	5p
1 old penny (d)	0.42p

Note: When a distance is less than 100 yards or metres, these two units are considered interchangeable over the short and approximate distances described.

APPENDIX B

Railway Companies

Abbreviation	Full title	
BA&WR	Bishop Auckland and Weardale Railway	
BC&BAJR	Barnard Castle and Bishop Auckland Junction Railway	¶
BCR	Border Counties Railway	
BG&HR	Blaydon, Gateshead and Hebburn Railway	
BJR	Brandling Junction Railway	
C&CJR	Cumberland and Cleveland Junction Railway	¶
D&BCR	Darlington and Barnard Castle Railway	
DJR	Derwent Junction Railway	‡
EVR	Eden Valley Railway	
F&SR	Frosterley and Stanhope Railway	
GNER	Great North of England Railway	
H&AR	Hexham & Allendale Railway	
L&CR	Lancaster and Carlisle Railway	
L&NWR	London and North Western Railway	
L&NYR	Lancashire and North Yorkshire Railway	¶
L&TR	Leeds and Thirsk Railway	
LCR	Lord Carlisle's Railway(s)	‡
LM&NJR	Liverpool, Manchester and Newcastle(-upon-Tyne) Junction Railway	†
M&GR	Middlesborough and Guisborough Railway	
M&RR	Middlesborough and Redcar Railway	
N&CR	Newcastle and Carlisle Railway	
N&DVR	Newcastle-upon-Tyne and Derwent Valley Railway	¶
N&LJR	Northumberland and Lancashire Junction Railway	¶
NBR	North British Railway	
NCUR	Northern Counties Union Railway	†
ND&WR	Newcastle, Derwent and Weardale Railway	¶

NE&DGJR	Newcastle-upon-Tyne, Edinburgh and (Direct) Glasgow Junction Railway	¶
NER	North Eastern Railway	
NTR	Leeds and Carlisle or Northern Trunk Railway of England	¶
P&SSR	Pontop and South Shields Railway	
S&DR	Stockton and Darlington Railway	
S&D&N&CUR	Stockton and Darlington and Newcastle and Carlisle Union Railway	†
S&TR	Stanhope and Tyne Railway (or Railroad)	‡
SD&LUR	South Durham and Lancashire Union Railway	
SJCR	St John's Chapel Railway	¶
STR	Shildon Tunnel Railway	°°
TVR	Tees Valley Railway	
W&DJR	Wear and Derwent Junction Railway	
W&DR	Wear and Derwent Railway	‡
WDR	West Durham Railway	
WER	Weardale Extension Railway	‡
WI&CCR	Weardale Iron and Coal Company Railway	‡
WVER	Wear Valley Extension Railway (of 1845)	¶
WVER92	Wear Valley Extension Railway of 1892	
WVR	Wear Valley Railway	
Y&CR	York and Carlisle Railway	¶
Y&GUR	Yorkshire and Glasgow Union Railway	¶
Y&NR	York and Newcastle Railway	
YN&BR	York, Newcastle, and Berwick Railway	

Notes: ¶ = railway not authorised

        † = railway authorised but not built

        ‡ = railway built without initial parliamentary approval

        °° = railway authorised but built by a different, unregistered, group

        All other railways were authorised and built, at least in part.

REFERENCES

(i)   Herepath's Journal is the generic name given to the journals edited by Herepath: *The Railway Magazine* 1835–36; *Railway Magazine and Annals of Science*, New Series 1836–39, *The Railway Magazine and Commercial Journal*, Quarto Series, 1839 onwards.

(ii)   The Libraries, Record Offices, etc. where the reference was found are denoted as follows:

CAS = Cumbria Archive Service (Carlisle Office)
CCL = Carlisle Central Library
CRO (Kendal) = Cumbria Archive Service (Kendal Office)
DPL = Darlington Public Library
DRO = Durham Record Office
DUL = Durham University Library
L&P = Literary and Philosophical Society of Newcastle
NCS = Northumberland Collections Services
NLIS = Local Studies and Family History Centre, Newcastle Libraries and Information Service
NYCRO = North Yorkshire County Record Office
TNA: PRO = The National Archives: Public Record Office
TWAS = Tyne & Wear Archives Service

(iii)   Newspapers, etc. were found as follows:

Auckland Chronicle in DPL or DRO
Auckland Times and Herald in DPL or DRO
Carlisle Journal in CAS
Carlisle Patriot in CCL
Cumberland Pacquet in CAS
Durham County Advertizer in DRO
Hansard in NLIS
Herepath in L&P
Hexham Courant in Courant Offices, Hexham
Newcastle Chronicle in NLIS
Newcastle Courant in NLIS
Newcastle Journal in NLIS
Teesdale Mercury in DPL or Wytham Hall, Barnard Castle
Tyne Mercury in L&P

1.   1767: Report in *Newcastle Journal*, 14 November 1767.
2.   1767: Report in *Newcastle Courant*, 14 November 1767.
3.   1769: Report of Messrs. Brindley and Whitworth, Engineers, Concerning the Practicability and Expence of making a Navigable Canal, from Stockton by Darlington, to Winston, in the County of Durham, with a Plan of the Country, River

Tees, and of the intended Canal. Surveyed and made, By order of the Committee of Subscribers, July 19; 1769. Newcastle: Printed by T. Slack, 1770. DPL.

4.   1793: An Act for repairing, widening, and altering the road from the Turnpike Road between Gateshead and Hexham, near Lobley Hill, in the Parish of Whickham, in the County of Durham, to Burtry Ford, in the Parish of Stanhope, in the same county, and a Branch from the said road, near Bryan's Leap, in the County of Durham, to the Corbridge Turnpike Road, near Black Hedley, in the County of Northumberland, and another Branch from the said road at Wolsingham, in the County of Durham, to Crossgate, near the City of Durham. 33 Geo 3, cap 148; 12 May 1793. L&P: Local Acts, Vol. 16, No. 8.

5.   1794: Editorial, *Cumberland Pacquet*, Volume 21, 14 October 1794.

6.   1794: Ralph Dodd, Letter to Humphrey Senhouse, Esq., M.P., Nether Hall, Cumberland; 21 October 1794. Senhouse Papers, CAS.

7.   1794: Ralph Dodd, Proposed canal from Newcastle to Carlisle. In: report of a meeting held in Newcastle on 1 November 1794. Senhouse Papers, CAS.

8.   1794: Report of a meeting held in Newcastle on 15 November 1794. Senhouse Papers, CAS.

9.   1794: Editorial, *Cumberland Pacquet*, Volume 21, 9 December 1794.

10. 1794: Report of the second meeting of the Northumberland Committee on 27 December 1794. MOUNSEY-HEYSHAM MSS, Volume II, pp.255–256, CAS.

11. 1795: Report of the second meeting of the Cumberland Committee on 3 January 1795. MOUNSEY-HEYSHAM MSS Volume II, pp.256–257, CAS.

12. 1795: Report of the meeting of the delegates from the two Committees held at Hexham on 12 January 1795. MOUNSEY-HEYSHAM MSS Volume II, pp.258–259, CAS.

13. 1795: William Chapman, 5 January 1795. Report on the measures to be attended to in the Survey of a line of Navigation, from Newcastle upon Tyne to the Irish channel; with an estimate of the Probable Annual Revenue that may be derived from it. L&P Tract 8vo Series, Vol. 200, section 1.

14. 1795: R. Dodd, 5 June 1795. Report on the first part of the line of Inland Navigation from the east to the west sea by way of Newcastle and Carlisle, as originally projected and lately surveyed, by R. Dodd, Civil Engineer. L&P Tract 8vo Series, Vol. 38, section 1; NLIS 656.69 vol. 1.

15. 1795: William Chapman, 24 June 1795. Report on the proposed navigation between the East and West seas so far as extends from Newcastle to Haydon Bridge, with observations on the separate advantages on the North and South sides of the River Tyne. L&P Tract 8vo Series, Vol. 38, section 3, part 1.

16. 1795: William Chapman, 10 June 1795. Second Part of a Report on the Proposed Navigation between the East and West Seas, viz from Haydon Bridge to Maryport. With observations on lines to Penrith, Sandsfield, Ravensbank, Bowness, Wigton, etc. L&P Tract 8vo Series, Vol. 38, section 3, part 2.

17. 1795: W. Jessop, 26 October 1795. Report on the proposed line of navigation between Newcastle and Maryport. L&P Tract 8vo Series, Vol. 38, section 4; CAS D/SEN, Newcastle to Maryport Canal 1794–1796; 1807, 1808. Items 3 & 4.

18. 1795(?): Newcastle, Hexham, Carlisle and Maryport Canal. CAS D/Sen Box 158.

19. 1796: Plan of the proposed Canal from Newcastle upon Tyne to Haydon Bridge, by William Chapman, Engineer. July 1796 (deposited 26 September 1796). NCS QRUp 2.

20. 1796: Plan of the Proposed Canal on the South Side of the River Tyne from Hexham to Stella, by John Bell. Deposited 29 September 1796: NCS QRUp 3, deposited 30 September 1796: DRO Q/D/P 1.

21. 1796: John Sutcliffe. Report on the proposed line of navigation from Stella to Hexham, on the south side of the River Tyne; with an estimate of the expense of executing the line. Printed for John Bell, Bookseller & land-surveyor, Union Street; and sold by him and the other booksellers in Newcastle, Hexham, Carlisle, Durham, etc. 5 October 1796. L&P Tracts 8vo Series, Vol. 38, No. 8.

22. 1797: Mr. Whitworth's Report on the proposed canal on the North side of the River Tyne, with observations together with various publications and petitions for and against that line of canal. Printed by Joseph Whitfield, Bookseller, Tyne-Bridge-End, Newcastle-upon-Tyne, 1797. L&P Tract 8vo Series, Vol. 38, section 10, pp. 47–50.

23. 1797: Proposed Bill for Making a Navigable Canal from Newcastle to Haydon Bridge. 37 Geo III, 1797. NCS 404/270.

24. 1808: An Act for making a Navigable Cut from the East Side of the River Tees near Stockton through the Neck of Land into the said River near Portrack in the County of Durham and for making various other improvements in the Navigation of the said River between the Town of Stockton and the Sea. 48 Geo 3, cap 48; 27 May 1808. L&P: Local Acts, Vol. 28.

25. 1810: Report in *Newcastle Chronicle*, 22 September 1810.

26. 1810: Notice in *Newcastle Chronicle*, 22 September 1810.

27. 1818: Plan of a canal from Stockton to Fighting Cocks. DRO Q/D/P 3.

28. 1818: William Chapman. Map of that Part of the County of Cumberland, through which the proposed line of Navigation, from Fisher's Cross or Binnacle to Carlisle would pass. 29 September 1818. CAS Q/RZ/2/1.

29. 1818: Report in *Newcastle Chronicle*, 21 November 1818.

30. 1819: An Act for making and maintaining a Navigable Canal, from or from near the City of Carlisle, to the Solway Frith, at or near Fisher's Cross, in the Parish of Bowness, in the County of Cumberland. 59 Geo 3. cap 13; 6 April 1819. L&P: Local Acts, Vol. 28, No. 2.

31. 1821: An Act for Making and Maintaining a Railway or Tramroad from the River Tees at Stockton to Witton Park Colliery, with several Branches therefrom, all in the County of Durham. 1 & 2 Geo 4, cap 44; 19 April 1821. L&P: Local Acts, Vol. 29, No. 11; DRO: Local & Personal Statutes.

32. 1823: John Loudon McAdam. Plans of the Alston Turnpike Roads, as projected by John Loudon McAdam. CAS: QRZ/2/10; NCS: 317/15.

33. 1823: Report in *Carlisle Journal*, 15 March 1823.

34. 1823: An Act to enable the Stockton and Darlington Railway Company to vary and alter the line of their railway, and also the line or lines of some of the branches therefore, and for altering and enlarging the powers of the Act passed for making and maintaining the said railway. 4 Geo 4, cap 33; 23 May 1823. In: Local Railway Acts 1821–1892; NLIS, L656.2.

35. 1823: Plans of the Railway or Tramroad from the River Tees at Witton Park Colliery, and of the several branches therefrom. Robert Stephenson, Engineer. DRO.

36. 1824: William Chapman. A report on the cost and separate advantages of a Ship Canal and of a Railway from Newcastle to Carlisle. 12 October 1824. L&P Tract 8vo Series, Vol. 198, section 3.

37. 1824: An Act for repairing the road from Burtry Ford in the County of Durham, through Alston in the County of Cumberland, to Burnstones in the County of Northumberland, and from Summerrod's Bar, near Hexham, to Alston aforesaid, and

several other roads in the said counties, and in the North Riding of the County of York, and for erecting bridges over the River Tyne. 5 Geo 4 cap 34; 12 April 1824. L&P: Local Acts, Vol. 18, No. 12.

38.   1824: An Act to authorize the Company of proprietors of the Stockton and Darlington Railway to relinquish one of their branch railways and to enable the said company to make another branch railway in lieu thereof; and to enable the said company to raise a further sum of money, and to enlarge the powers and provisions of the several Acts relating to the said railway. 5 Geo 4 cap 48; 17 May 1824. In: Local Railway Acts 1821–1892; NLIS, L656.2.

39.   1825: Thomas Bell. Plan of a proposed Turnpike Road from Cowes Hill in the County of Durham to the Hexham and Alston Turnpike Road, at the Branch End in the County of Northumberland, and also of the Proposed Branch Roads leading from the said Proposed Turnpike Road from near Beacon Rigg towards Langley Mill, and from Allendale Town past the Riding to Thornley Gate in the County of Northumberland, and from Catton to the Turnpike Road near Nenthead in the County of Cumberland. DRO Q/D/P 20.

40.   1826: An Act for making and maintaining a Turnpike Road leading out of the Alston Turnpike Road, at Branch end, in the County of Northumberland, through Catton, Allendale Town, and Allenheads, to Cows Hill, in the County of Durham, with several branches therefrom. 7 Geo 4, cap 74; 5 May 1826. L&P: Local Acts, Vol. 18, No. 6.

41.   1829: An Act for making and maintaining a railway or tram-road from the town of Newcastle-upon-Tyne in the county of the town of Newcastle upon Tyne, to the city of Carlisle in the county of Cumberland, with a branch thereout. 10 Geo 4, cap 72; 22 May 1829. L&P: Local Acts, Vol. 29, No. 13; NLIS, L656.2.

42.   1832: An Act to accelerate the raising by the Newcastle upon Tyne and Carlisle Railway Company of a certain sum for the more speedy Prosecution of the Undertaking. 2 Wil 4 cap 92; 23 June 1832; NLIS, L656.2.

43.   1833: Prospectus for a proposed railroad, to be called the Tees, Weardale and Tyne Junction Railroad. G. Wilkinson, 27 February 1833. TNA: PRO RAIL 1016/5.

44.   1833: Plans and Sections of an intended Railway or Tramroad from Blaydon in the County of Durham to Gateshead and Hebburn in the said County of Durham. John Blackmore, Civil Engineer, surveyed by T. Sopwith, November 1833. Deposited 30 November 1833. DRO Q/D/P/53.

45.   1834: An Act for making and maintaining a Railway from Blaydon to Hebburn, with six branches thereout, all within the County Palatine of Durham. 4 & 5 Wil 4, cap 26; 22 May 1834. L & P Local Acts, Vol. 28, No. 7.

46.   1834: Report in *Newcastle Courant*, 23 May 1834.

47.   1834: Report in *Newcastle Courant*, 28 November 1834.

48.   1835: Advert in *Tyne Mercury*, 3 March 1835.

49.   1835: Advert in *Tyne Mercury*, 31 March 1835.

50.   1835: Report in *Tyne Mercury*, 5 May 1835.

51.   1835: Plans and Sections of the intended line of Railway or Railways Tramroad or Tramroads commencing at the intended line of the Blaydon, Gateshead and Hebburn Railway in the Parish of Gateshead and Township of Gateshead in the County of Durham and terminating in Monkwearmouth in the township of Monkwearmouth Shore in the Parish of Monkwearmouth in the County of Durham. Thomas Elliott Harrison, Engineer. Deposited 30 November 1835. DRO Q/D/P/62.

52.   1835: Plan and Section of a Proposed Railway to be called the South Durham Railway. From Frosterley in the Parish of Stanhope to the Durham Branch of the

Clarence Railway with four several branches therefrom, all in the County palatine of Durham. Deposited 30 November 1835. DRO Q/D/P 65.

53. 1835: An Act to authorize the Newcastle upon Tyne and Carlisle Railway Company to make an additional branch railway or tramroad, and for other purposes connected with their undertaking. 5 Wil 4, cap 31; 17 June 1835. L&P: Local Acts, Vol. 26, No. 15.

54. 1835: Report in Herepath, Vol. 1, December, p. 272.

55. 1836: Plan and Section of a Proposed Railway to be called the New South Durham Railway, from Frosterley in the Parish of Stanhope to the Byers Green Branch of the Clarence Railway with three several branches therefrom, all in the County palatine of Durham. Deposited 30 November 1836. DRO Q/D/P 74.

56. 1836: An Act for incorporating certain persons for carrying into effect the purposes of an Act passed in the fifth and sixth year of the reign of his present majesty intituled 'An Act enabling John Brandling and Robert William Brandling, Esquires, to purchase and take leases of lands and hereditaments for the formation of a railway from Gateshead to South Shields and Monkwearmouth, all in the County Palatine of Durham, with branches therefrom', and for other purposes. 6 & 7 Wil 4, cap 57; 7 June 1836. L&P: Local Acts, Vol. 28, No. 8.

57. 1836: Share price lists in Herepath, Vol. 1, pp. 48, 160, 200, 248, 296, 344, 400, 480.

58. 1836: Report in Herepath, Vol. 1, July, p. 193.

59. 1836: Plan of a Railway or Tramroad commencing at or in the Stockton and Darlington Railway, near the junction of the said railway with the Black Boy Branch thereof in the Township of East Thickley and terminating in a Field in the occupation of John Bainbridge situate in the Township of Frosterley and on the south side of the Turnpike Road leading from the City of Durham to the Town of Stanhope, with two branches therefrom, all in the County of Durham. 30 November 1836. DRO Q/D/P 76.

60. 1837: Report in Herepath, Vol. 2, January, p. 8.

61. 1837: Report in *Carlisle Journal*, 11 March 1837.

62. 1837: An Act for incorporating certain persons for the making and maintaining a railway from near the Black Boy Branch of the Stockton and Darlington Railway in the township of Saint Andrew Auckland to or near to Witton Park Colliery, with a branch therefrom, all in the County of Durham to be called 'The Bishop Auckland and Weardale Railway'. 7 Wil 4 & 1 Vict, cap 122; 15 July 1837. DRO: Local & Personal Statutes.

63. 1837: Report in Herepath, Vol. 2, July, p. 274.

64. 1837: Report in Herepath, Vol. 3, October, p. 259.

65. 1838: Report in Herepath, Vol. 5, July, p. 63.

66. 1838: Minutes of a Shareholders Meeting of Bishop Auckland and Weardale Railway. 14 December 1838. PRO Rail 46/2.

67. 1839: Report in Herepath, Vol. 5, February 1839, p. 610.

68. 1839: Report in Herepath, Vol. 6, April 1839, p. 172.

69. 1839: Report in Herepath, Vol. 6, April 1839, pp. 204–207.

70. 1839: Minutes of a Special General Meeting of Bishop Auckland and Weardale Railway. 12 April 1839. TNA: PRO Rail 46/1.

71. 1839: Report in Herepath, Vol. 6, June 1839, p. 352.

72. 1839: Report in Herepath, Vol. 1, 28 July 1839, p. 47.

73. 1839: Report in Herepath, Vol. 1, 9 November 1839, p. 305.

74. 1839: Report in Herepath, Vol. 1, 23 November 1839, p. 353.

75.   1839: Report in Herepath, Vol. 1, 14 December 1839, p. 409.

76.   1840: Share price lists in Herepath, Vol. 2.

77.   1840: Report in Herepath, Vol. 2, 1 February 1840, p. 66.

78.   1840: Report in Herepath, Vol. 2, 5 April 1840, p. 242.

79.   1840: Report in Herepath, Vol. 2, 5 December 1840, p. 950.

80.   1840: Report in Herepath, Vol. 2, 26 December 1840, p. 1009.

81.   1841: Share price lists in Herepath, Vol. 3.

82.   1841: Minutes of Meeting of the Subcommittee for the construction of the Shildon Tunnel. 10 March 1841, S&DR Minute Book. TNA: PRO RAIL 667/213.

83.   1841: Report in Herepath, Vol. 3, 29 March 1841, p. 249.

84.   1841: Report in Herepath, Vol. 3, 3 April 1841, pp. 300–301.

85.   1841: An Act to alter, amend, and enlarge the powers granted to the Newcastle upon Tyne and Carlisle Railway company; and to authorize alterations to the line of the railway. 4 & 5 Vict, cap 44; 21 June 1841. L&P: Local Acts, Vol. 26, No. 20.

86.   1841: Report in Herepath, Vol. 3, 6 November 1841, p. 947.

87.   1841: Report in Herepath, Vol. 3, 11 December 1841, p. 1042.

88.   1842: Plan of a tramroad to be called the Weardale Extension Railway, commencing at, or near, the terminus of the Crook branch of the Bishop Auckland and Weardale near Crook in the township of Crook and Billy Row in the Parish of Brancepath and terminating at the south end of Frosterley bridge in the township of Frosterley in the Parish of Stanhope, with a branch therefrom to Bishopley Crags all in the County of Durham. February 1842, Thomas Storey. DRO Q/D/P 114.

89.   1842: Minutes of Meeting of the Subcommittee for the construction of the Shildon Tunnel. 24 February 1842, S&DR Minute Book. TNA: PRO RAIL 667/213.

90.   1842: Minutes of Meeting of the Shildon Subcommittee held on 5 March 1842. S&DR Minute Book. TNA: PRO RAIL 667/169.

91.   1842: An Act to facilitate arrangements consequent upon the dissolution of the Stanhope and Tyne Railroad Company, and to incorporate some of the Proprietors for the purpose of continuing the working of a part of the Railway belonging to the said Company. 5 Vict, cap 27; 13 May 1842. L&P: Local Acts, Vol. 29, No. 9.

92.   1842: Minutes of Board Meeting. 5 July 1842, Bishop Auckland and Weardale Railway: Minutes of Meetings. TNA: PRO RAIL 46/3.

93.   1842: Plan of a tramroad to be called the Weardale Extension Railway, commencing at, or near, the terminus of the Crook Branch of the Bishop Auckland and Weardale Railway near Crook in the township of Crook and Billy Row in the Parish of Brancepath and terminating at the south end of Frosterley bridge in the township of Frosterley in the Parish of Stanhope, with a branch therefrom to Bishopley Crags all in the county of Durham. November 1842, Thomas Storey. DRO: Q/D/P 120.

94.   1843: Minutes of Board Meeting. 17 February 1843, Bishop Auckland and Weardale Railway: Minutes of Meetings. TNA: PRO Rail 46/4.

95.   1843: Report on the proposed extension of the Weardale Railway to join the Stanhope and Tyne Railway as projected by the Derwent Iron Company. Also on a proposed junction between the Auckland and Weardale and Newcastle and Carlisle Railways. John Harris. DRO: D/WHES 15 July 1843.

96.   1843: Minutes of Board Meeting. 17 November 1843, Bishop Auckland and Weardale Railway: Minutes of Meetings. TNA: PRO Rail 46/4.

97.   1844: Report in Herepath, Vol. 6, 24 February 1844, p. 212.

98.   1844: Jenkinson's Report of 30 May 1844 concerning the railway and lime kilns at Stanhope. TNA: PRO RAIL 667/221.

99. 1844: Minutes of a Meeting of Directors held at Low Byer Inn, Alston. 7 September 1844, Minute Books. TNA: PRO RAIL 509/7.

100. 1844: Minutes of a Meeting of Directors held at Allenheads. 5 October 1844, Minute Books. TNA: PRO RAIL 509/7.

101. 1844: Report from William Bouch regarding the engineering features and mode of working from Crawley Incline to Hownes Gil. 24 October 1844. TNA: PRO RAIL 663/1.

102. 1844: Report in Herepath, Vol. 6, 23 November 1844, p. 1411.

103. 1844: Plan and section of an intended railway to be called the Wear Valley Railway with an intended branch therefrom to be called the Bishopley Branch of the said Railway, all in the County of Durham. Deposited on 30 November 1844. John Dixon. DRO: Q/D/P 145.

104. 1844: Report in Herepath, Vol. 6, 7 December 1844, p. 1463.

105. 1845: Report in *Carlisle Journal*, 4 January 1845.

106. 1845: Railway Intelligence in *Tyne Mercury*, 29 January 1845.

107. 1845: Railways in *Carlisle Journal*, 8 February 1845.

108. 1845: Report in *Carlisle Journal*, 15 February 1845.

109. 1845: Report in Herepath, Vol. 7, 15 March 1845, p. 382.

110. 1845: Report in *Tyne Mercury*, 2 April 1845.

111. 1845: Report in Herepath, Vol. 7, 12 April 1845, p. 533.

112. 1845: Railway Intelligence in *Tyne Mercury*, 16 April 1845.

113. 1845: Report in Herepath, Vol. 7, 19 April 1845, p. 563.

114. 1845: Report in *Carlisle Journal*, 19 April 1845.

115. 1845: Advert in *Carlisle Journal*, 26 April 1845.

116. 1845: Railway Intelligence in *Tyne Mercury*, 30 April 1845.

117. 1845: Advert in *Carlisle Journal*, 3 May 1845.

118. 1845: Report in Herepath, Vol. 7, 10 May 1845, p. 700.

119. 1845: Advert in *Tyne Mercury*, 14 May 1845.

120. 1845: Railway Intelligence in *Tyne Mercury*, 14 May 1845.

121. 1845: Report in *Carlisle Journal*, 24 May 1845.

122. 1845: Report in Herepath, Vol. 7, 24 May 1845, p. 781.

123. 1845: Railway Intelligence in *Tyne Mercury*, 28 May 1845.

124. 1845: Railway Intelligence in *Tyne Mercury*, 4 June 1845.

125. 1845: Report in Herepath, Vol. 7, 7 June 1845, p. 861.

126. 1845: Report in Herepath, Vol. 7, 7 June 1845, p. 864.

127. 1845: Railway Intelligence in *Tyne Mercury*, 11 June 1845.

128. 1845: Report in Herepath, Vol. 7, 14 June 1845, p. 945.

129. 1845: Advert in *Newcastle Chronicle*, 14 June 1845.

130. 1845: Records of Stanton, Croft and Company, Solicitors, Newcastle-upon-Tyne. DRO: D/SC 1/134: Lease of crushing mill and land to Charles Attwood, dated 16 June 1845.

131. 1845: Advert in *Tyne Mercury*, 18 June 1845.

132. 1845: Advert in *Carlisle Journal*, 21 June 1845.

133. 1845: Report in Herepath, Vol. 7, 21 June 1845, p. 979.

134. 1845: Minutes of Wear Valley Railway Directors Meeting. 24 June 1845, Wear Valley Railway Directors Meetings Minute Book. TNA: PRO RAIL 718/2.

135. 1845: Advert in *Tyne Mercury*, 2 July 1845.

136. 1845: Railway Intelligence in *Tyne Mercury*, 9 July 1845.

137. 1845: Advert in *Tyne Mercury*, 9 July 1845.

138. 1845: Advert in *Tyne Mercury*, 9 July 1845.
139. 1845: Advert in *Tyne Mercury*, 9 July 1845.
140. 1845: Report in Herepath, Vol. 7, 12 July 1845, p. 1147.
141. 1845: Advert in *Tyne Mercury*, 16 July 1845.
142. 1845: Railway Intelligence in *Tyne Mercury*, 16 July 1845.
143. 1845: Advert in *Tyne Mercury*, 23 July 1845.
144. 1845: Report in Herepath, Vol. 7, 26 July 1845, p. 1207.
145. 1845: An Act for making a Railway, to be called 'The Wear Valley Railway', from and out of the Bishop Auckland and Weardale Railway to Frosterley with a branch terminating at or near Bishopley Crag in Stanhope-in-Weardale, all in the County of Durham. 8 & 9 Vict, cap 152; 31 July 1845. DRO: Local & Personal Statutes.
146. 1845: Report in Herepath, Vol. 7, 9 August 1845, p. 1320.
147. 1845: Railway Intelligence in *Tyne Mercury*, 13 August 1845.
148. 1845: Railway Intelligence in *Tyne Mercury*, 20 August 1845.
149. 1845: Report in Herepath, Vol. 7, 23 August 1845, p. 1417.
150. 1845: Report in Herepath, Vol. 7, 30 August 1845, p. 1509.
151. 1845: Report in *Newcastle Chronicle*, 30 August 1845.
152. 1845: Railway Intelligence in *Tyne Mercury*, 3 September 1845.
153. 1845: Minutes of Meeting of Directors. 17 September 1845, Wear Valley Railway Directors Meetings Minute Book. TNA: PRO RAIL 718/2.
154. 1845: Advert in *Tyne Mercury*, 17 September 1845.
155. 1845: Advert in *Carlisle Journal*, 20 September 1845.
156. 1845: Letter from John Dixon to Joseph Pease. 20 September 1845, Letters regarding the Wear Valley Railway and extension proposals. TNA: PRO RAIL 718/25.
157. 1845: Adverts in *Tyne Mercury*, 24 September 1845.
158. 1845: Article in *Tyne Mercury*, 24 September 1845.
159. 1845: Report in *Carlisle Journal*, 27 September 1845.
160. 1845: Report in Herepath, Vol. 7, 27 September 1845, p. 1783.
161. 1845: Advert in *Tyne Mercury*, 1 October 1845.
162. 1845: Advert in *Tyne Mercury*, 1 October 1845.
163. 1845: Railway Intelligence in *Tyne Mercury*, 1 October 1845.
164. 1845: Advert in *Tyne Mercury*, 1 October 1845.
165. 1845: Advert in *Carlisle Journal*, 4 October 1845.
166. 1845: Report in Herepath, Vol. 7, 4 October 1845, p. 1932.
167. 1845: Minutes of Meeting of Directors. 8 October 1845, Wear Valley Railway Directors Meetings Minute Book. TNA: PRO RAIL 718/2.
168. 1845: Letter of 8 October 1845 from G. H. Wilkinson, Chairman of the Wear Valley Railway to Lord Carlisle. DUL: Howard of Naworth papers: C565/V/1 + 2.
169. 1845: Advert in *Tyne Mercury*, 15 October 1845.
170. 1845: Railway Intelligence in *Tyne Mercury*, 15 October 1845.
171. 1845: Report in Herepath, Vol. 7, 15 October 1845, p. 2136.
172. 1845: Report in Herepath, Vol. 7, 18 October 1845, p. 2166.
173. 1845: Railways in *Carlisle Journal*, 18 October 1845.
174. 1845: Advert in *Newcastle Weekly Chronicle*, 18 October 1845.
175. 1845: Advert in *Tyne Mercury*, 22 October 1845.
176. 1845: Advert in *Tyne Mercury*, 22 October 1845.
177. 1845: Railway Intelligence in *Tyne Mercury*, 22 October 1845.
178. 1845: Railway Intelligence in *Tyne Mercury*, 22 October 1845.
179. 1845: Advert in *Tyne Mercury*, 22 October 1845.
180. 1845: Report in Herepath, Vol. 7, 25 October 1845, p. 2316.

181. 1845: Report in Herepath, Vol. 7, 25 October 1845, p. 2343.
182. 1845: Advert in *Newcastle Weekly Chronicle*, 25 October 1845.
183. 1845: Advert in *Newcastle Weekly Chronicle*, 25 October 1845.
184. 1845: Minutes of Meeting of Directors. 28 October 1845, Wear Valley Railway Directors Meetings Minute Book. TNA: PRO RAIL 718/2.
185. 1845: Railway Intelligence in *Tyne Mercury*, 29 October 1845.
186. 1845: Advert in *Tyne Mercury*, 29 October 1845.
187. 1845: Copy from the Minutes of the Directors Meeting of the Wear Valley Railway of 4 November 1845. DUL: Howard of Naworth papers: C565/V/3.
188. 1845: Advert in *Newcastle Weekly Chronicle*, 1 November 1845.
189. 1845: Minutes of Meeting of Directors. 4 November 1845, Wear Valley Railway Directors Meetings Minute Book. TNA: PRO RAIL 718/2.
190. 1845: Railway Intelligence in *Tyne Mercury*, 5 November 1845.
191. 1845: Advert in *Tyne Mercury*, 5 November 1845.
192. 1845: Advert in *Tyne Mercury*, 12 November 1845.
193. 1845: Advert in *Tyne Mercury*, 12 November 1845.
194. 1845: Report in Herepath, Vol. 7, 15 November 1845, p. 2534.
195. 1845: Railway Intelligence in *Tyne Mercury*, 19 November 1845.
196. 1845: Report in Herepath, Vol. 7, 22 November 1845, p. 2583.
197. 1845: Plans and sections of the Newcastle and Leeds Direct Railway. Deposited 28 November 1845. Thomas Story, Engineer. DRO: Q/D/P/147.
198. 1845: Plans, sections and books of reference for the Wear Valley Extension Railway. Deposited 28 November 1845. John Dixon, Engineer. CAS: Q/RZ/1/132; DRO: Q/D/P/148; NCS: QRUp65.
199. 1845: Plans of the Northumberland and Lancashire Junction Railway. Deposited 29 November 1845. Thomas Story, Engineer. TWAS: D/NCP/4/66.
200. 1845: Plans, sections and books of reference for the York, Carlisle and Durham, Westmoreland and Lancashire Railway. Deposited 30 November 1845. J. M. Rendell, Engineer. DRO: Q/D/P/154; NYCRO: QDP(M)62.
201. 1845: Minutes of Meeting of Directors. 2 December 1845, Wear Valley Railway Directors Meetings Minute Book. TNA: PRO RAIL 718/2.
202. 1845: Report in Herepath, Vol. 7, 6 December 1845, pp. 2648–2652.
203. 1845: Report in Herepath, Vol. 7, 6 December 1845, pp. 2673–2675.
204. 1845: Railway Intelligence in *Tyne Mercury*, 10 December 1845.
205. 1845: Railway Intelligence in *Tyne Mercury*, 10 December 1845.
206. 1845: Advert in *Tyne Mercury*, 10 December 1845.
207. 1845: Report in Herepath, Vol. 7, 13 December 1845, p. 2690.
208. 1845: Minutes of Meeting of Directors. 16 December 1845, Wear Valley Railway Directors Meetings Minute Book. TNA: PRO RAIL 718/2.
209. 1845: Railway Intelligence in *Tyne Mercury*, 17 December 1845.
210. 1845: Report in Herepath, Vol. 7, 20 December 1845, p. 2750.
211. 1845: Advert in *Newcastle Chronicle*, 20 December 1845.
212. 1845: Report in Herepath, Vol. 7, 27 December 1845, p. 2757.
213. 1845: Plans, sections and books of reference for the Leeds and Carlisle, or Northern Trunk Railway of England, 1845. G. and J. Rennie, Engineers. NYCRO: QDP(M) 64.
214. 1845: Plans, sections and books of reference for the Yorkshire and Glasgow Union Railway, 1845. W. Cubitt and H.H. Fulton, Engineers. NYCRO: QDP(M) 65.
215. 1845: Plans and sections of an extension of the Newcastle upon Tyne and Carlisle Railway and branches from the same railway, 1845. John Bourne, Acting Engineer. CAS: Q/RZ/1/5; NCS: QRUp 67a; TWAS: D/NCP/4/69.

216. 1846: Report in Herepath, Vol. 8, 11 January 1846, pp. 35–38.
217. 1846: Report in Herepath, Vol. 8, 11 January 1846, p. 44.
218. 1846: Report in Herepath, Vol. 8, 7 February 1846, p. 194.
219. 1846: Report in Herepath, Vol. 8, 14 February 1846, p. 208.
220. 1846: Report in Herepath, Vol. 8, 21 February 1846, p. 273.
221. 1846: Report in Herepath, Vol. 8, 28 February 1846, p. 317.
222. 1846: Report in Herepath, Vol. 8, 4 April 1846, pp. 455–456.
223. 1846: Report in Herepath, Vol. 8, 4 April 1846, p. 459.
224. 1846: Report in Herepath, Vol. 8, 25 April 1846, p. 533.
225. 1846: Report in Herepath, Vol. 8, 2 May 1846, p. 570.
226. 1846: Report in Herepath, Vol. 8, 9 May 1846, pp. 599–600.
227. 1846: Report in Herepath, Vol. 8, 16 May 1846, p. 627.
228. 1846: Report in Herepath, Vol. 8, 16 May 1846, p. 655.
229. 1846: Report in Herepath, Vol. 8, 23 May 1846, p. 683.
230. 1846: Report in Herepath, Vol. 8, 30 May 1846, pp. 713–714.
231. 1846: Report in Herepath, Vol. 8, 13 June 1846, pp. 760–762.
232. 1846: Report in Herepath, Vol. 8, 20 June 1846, p. 792.
233. 1846: Act Incorporating the Liverpool, Manchester & Newcastle-upon-Tyne Railway. 9 & 10 Vict, cap 90; 26 June 1846. DRO: Local & Personal Statutes.
234. 1846: Report in Herepath, Vol. 8, 27 June 1846, p. 815.
235. 1846: Report in Herepath, Vol. 8, 27 June 1846, p. 816.
236. 1846: Report in Herepath, Vol. 8, 27 June 1846, p. 831.
237. 1846: An Act for making a Railway from the Great North of England Railway at Thirsk in the North Riding of Yorkshire to the Lancaster and Carlisle Railway at Clifton in Westmoreland, and a Railway from Bishop Auckland in the County of Durham to the Lancaster and Carlisle Railway at Tebay in Westmoreland, to be called the Northern Counties Union Railway. 9 & 10 Vict, cap 260; 27 July 1846. DRO: Local & Personal Statutes.
238. 1846: Report in Herepath, Vol. 8, 11 July 1846, p. 870.
239. 1846: Report in Herepath, Vol. 8, 1 August 1846, p. 938.
240. 1846: Report of the Directors of the Wear Valley Railway to the Half-yearly meeting. 26 August 1846, Wear Valley Railway General Meetings Minute Book. TNA: PRO RAIL 718/1.
241. 1846: Report in Herepath, Vol. 8, 29 August 1846, p. 1084.
242. 1846: Report in Herepath, Vol. 8, 12 September 1846, p. 1165.
243. 1846: Report in Herepath, Vol. 8, 12 September 1846, p. 1169.
244. 1846: Report in Herepath, Vol. 8, 19 September 1846, p. 1210.
245. 1846: Report in Herepath, Vol. 8, 3 October 1846, pp. 1273–1274.
246. 1846: Report in Herepath, Vol. 8, 14 November 1846, p. 1435.
247. 1846: Report in Herepath, Vol. 8, 28 November 1846, p. 1501.
248. 1846: Report in Herepath, Vol. 8, 5 December 1846, pp. 1529–1530.
249. 1846: An Act to authorise the Newcastle-upon-Tyne and Carlisle Company to extend their railway in Newcastle-upon-Tyne, to make a branch railway and for other purposes connected with their undertaking. 9 & 10 Vict, cap 394; 28 August 1846. LSD: NLIS, L656.2.
250. 1846: Plans of the Aysgarth Alteration of the Liverpool, Manchester and Newcastle-upon-Tyne Junction Railway. 27 November 1846. NYCRO: QDP(M) 80.
251. 1846: Plans of the Deviation of the Main Line of the Northern Counties Union Railway. NYCRO: QDP(M) 86.
252. 1847: Report in Herepath, Vol. 9, 23 January 1847, p. 82.

253. 1847: Report in Herepath, Vol. 9, 6 February 1847, p. 147.
254. 1847: Report in Herepath, Vol. 9, 27 February 1847, p. 275.
255. 1847: Report in Herepath, Vol. 9, 27 February 1847, p. 276.
256. 1847: Report in Herepath, Vol. 9, 27 February 1847, p. 286.
257. 1847: Advert in *Newcastle Courant*, 26 March 1847.
258. 1847: Advert in Herepath, Vol. 9, 27 March 1847, p. 446.
259. 1847: Report in Herepath, Vol. 9, 3 April 1847, p. 453.
260. 1847: Report in Herepath, Vol. 9, 3 April 1847, p. 458.
261. 1847: Advert in *Newcastle Courant*, 9 April 1847.
262. 1847: Advert in Herepath, Vol. 9, 17 April 1847, p. 519.
263. 1847: Report in Herepath, Vol. 9, 1 May 1847, p. 561.
264. 1847: Minutes of a Meeting of Directors. 3 May 1847, Newcastle and Carlisle Railway Minute Books. TNA: PRO RAIL 509/8.
265. 1847: Minutes of a Meeting of Directors. 10 May 1847, Newcastle and Carlisle Railway Minute Books. TNA: PRO RAIL 509/8.
266. 1847: The Alston Branch, *Newcastle Chronicle*, 25 June 1847.
267. 1847: Report in Herepath, Vol. 9, 3 July 1847, p. 768.
268. 1847: Evidence for the Amalgamation of WVR, BA&WR, WER, W&DR, Shildon Tunnel. TNA: PRO RAIL 718/20.
269. 1847: An Act for enabling the Wear Valley Railway Company to purchase or lease the Bishop Auckland and Weardale Railway, the Wear and Derwent Railway, the Weardale Extension Railway, and the Shildon Tunnel, and to raise an additional sum of money; and for other purposes. 10 & 11 Vict, cap 292; 22 July 1847. DRO: Local & Personal Statutes.
270. 1847: An Act to authorise certain alterations in the line of the Liverpool, Manchester & Newcastle-upon-Tyne Junction Railway; and for other purposes. 10 & 11 Vict, cap 227; 22 July 1847. NYCRO: Local & Personal Acts – 10 & 11 Vict, session 7.
271. 1847: An Act to enable the Liverpool, Manchester & Newcastle-upon-Tyne Junction Railway Company to make a railway from the Burnley branch of the Manchester and Leeds Railway in the township of Habergham Eaves in the Parish of Whalley in the county of Lancaster to the East Lancashire Railway in the same township; and for other purposes. 10 & 11 Vict, cap 240; 22 July 1847. NYCRO: Local & Personal Acts – 10 & 11 Vict, session 7.
272. 1847: An Act to enable the Northern Counties Union Railway Company to make certain alterations to their Railway in the Parishes of Aysgarth and Wensley in the North Riding of the County of York. 10 & 11 Vict, cap 290; 22 July 1847. NYCRO: Local & Personal Acts – 10 & 11 Vict, session 7.
273. 1847: Report in Herepath, Vol. 9, 24 July 1847, pp. 839–841.
274. 1847: Report in Herepath, Vol. 9, 31 July 1847, p. 886.
275. 1847: Report in Herepath, Vol. 9, 7 August 1847, p. 902.
276. 1845: Minutes of Meeting of Directors. 11 August 1847, Wear Valley Railway Directors Meetings Minute Book. TNA: PRO RAIL 718/2.
277. 1847: Report in Herepath, Vol. 9, 28 August 1847, p. 988.
278. 1847: Report in Herepath, Vol. 9, 4 September 1847, p. 1043.
279. 1847: Report in Herepath, Vol. 9, 11 September 1847, p. 1062.
280. 1847: Report in Herepath, Vol. 9, 11 November 1947, p. 1076.
281. 1847: Report in Herepath, Vol. 9, 9 October 1847, p. 1157.
282. 1847: Report in Herepath, Vol. 9, 9 October 1847, p. 1162.
283. 1847: Report in Herepath, Vol. 9, 27 November 1847, p. 1323.
284. 1847(?): Undated Map of Part of the Alston Branch. NCS ZLC/C/162.

285. 1847–48: Northern Counties Union Railway plans and sections of deviations of Auckland and Tebay line and of Thirsk and Clifton line at Birkett, 1847–1848. H.H. Fulton, Engineer. DRO: Q/D/P/174.
286. 1848: Report in Herepath, Vol. 10, 5 February 1848, p. 129.
287. 1848: Report in Herepath, Vol. 10, 19 February 1848, p. 190.
288. 1848: Report in Herepath, Vol. 10, 4 March 1848, p. 277.
289. 1848: Report in Herepath, Vol. 10, 1 April 1848, p. 363.
290. 1848: Report in Herepath, Vol. 10, 1 April 1848, p. 365.
291. 1848: Report in Herepath, Vol. 10, 15 April 1848, p. 418.
292. 1848: Report in Herepath, Vol. 10, 20 May 1848, p. 546.
293. 1848: Report in Herepath, Vol. 10, 10 June 1848, p. 605.
294. 1848: Report in Herepath, Vol. 10, 29 July 1848, pp. 787–788.
295. 1848: Report in Herepath, Vol. 10, 26 August 1848, p. 910.
296. 1848: Report in Herepath, Vol. 10, 9 September 1848, p. 967.
297. 1848: Report in Herepath, Vol. 10, 7 October 1848, p. 1050.
298. 1848: Report in Herepath, Vol. 10, 7 October 1848, p. 1065.
299. 1848: Report in Herepath, Vol. 10, 4 November 1848, p. 1163.
300. 1848: Report in Herepath, Vol. 10, 18 November 1848, p. 1208.
301. 1848: Report in Herepath, Vol. 10, 18 November 1848, p. 1210.
302. 1848: Report in Herepath, Vol. 10, 25 November 1848, p. 1236.
303. 1848: Newcastle & Carlisle Railway plans for deviations of, and a branch from the Alston branch authorised in 1846. November 1848. CAS QRZ/1/8; NCS QRUp/75.
304. 1848: Report in Herepath, Vol. 10, 9 December 1848, p. 1283.
305. 1848: Share price lists in Herepath, Vol. 10, pp. 372, 612, 636, 832, 988, 1300, 1344.
306. 1849: Report in Herepath, Vol. 11, 3 February 1849, p. 110.
307. 1849: Report in Herepath, Vol. 11, 10 February 1849, p. 121.
308. 1849: Report in Herepath, Vol. 11, 17 February 1849, p. 157.
309. 1849: Report in Herepath, Vol. 11, 3 March 1849, p. 229.
310. 1849: Report in Herepath, Vol. 11, 10 March 1849, p. 251.
311. 1849: Report in Herepath, Vol. 11, 17 March 1849, p. 277.
312. 1849: Report in Herepath, Vol. 11, 31 March 1849, p. 325.
313. 1849: Report in Herepath, Vol. 11, 5 May 1849, p. 461.
314. 1849: Report in Herepath, Vol. 11, 23 June 1849, p. 638.
315. 1849: Report in Herepath, Vol. 11, 30 June 1849, p. 648.
316. 1849: Report in Herepath, Vol. 11, 7 July 1849, p. 684.
317. 1849: An Act to authorize the Newcastle-upon-Tyne and Carlisle Railway Company to alter the Alston branch of their railway, to make a branch railway therefrom, and for other purposes. 12 & 13 Vict, cap 43; 13 July 1849. L&P: Local Acts Vol. 26, No. 27.
318. 1849: An Act to consolidate the several Acts relating to the Stockton and Darlington Railway Company, to enable the Company to alter their line of railway in the Parishes of Egglescliffe and Stockton-on-Tees, and to increase their capital, and to vest in them the Middlesborough Dock. 12 & 13 Vict, cap 54; 13 July 1849. DRO: Local & Personal Statutes.
319. 1849: Report in Herepath, Vol. 11, 21 July 1849, p. 731.
320. 1849: Report in Herepath, Vol. 11, 4 August 1849, p. 777.
321. 1849: Report in Herepath, Vol. 11, 1 September 1849, p. 901.
322. 1849: Report in Herepath, Vol. 11, 1 September 1849, p. 902.
323. 1849: Report in Herepath, Vol. 11, 27 October 1849, p. 1088.
324. 1849: Report in Herepath, Vol. 11, 10 November 1849, p. 1149.

325. 1849: Minutes of a Meeting of Directors. 5 December 1849, Newcastle and Carlisle Railway Minute Books. TNA: PRO RAIL 509/8.

326. 1849: Minutes of a Committee Meeting. 20 December 1849, Newcastle and Carlisle Railway Minute Books. TNA: PRO RAIL 509/8.

327. 1849: Share price lists in Herepath, Vol. 11, pp. 184, 248, 1256, 1276.

328. 1850: Report in Herepath, Vol. 12, 9 February 1850, p. 134.

329. 1850: Report in Herepath, Vol. 12, 6 April 1850, p. 333.

330. 1850: Report in Herepath, Vol. 12, 13 April 1850, p. 360.

331. 1850: Report in Herepath, Vol. 12, 9 April 1850, p. 399.

332. 1850: Report in Herepath, Vol. 12, 4 May 1850, p. 443.

333. 1850: An Act to extend the Powers of the Newcastle-upon-Tyne and Carlisle Railway Company, and to amend Acts relating to their Railway. 13 & 14 Vict, cap 72; 29 July 1850. L&P: Local Acts Vol. 26, No. 28.

334. 1850: Report in Herepath, Vol. 12, 31 August 1850, p. 864.

335. 1850: Report in Herepath, Vol. 12, 5 October 1850, p. 967.

336. 1850: Report in Herepath, Vol. 12, 23 November 1850, p. 1138.

337. 1850: Minutes of a Committee Meeting. 28 November 1850, Newcastle and Carlisle Railway Minute Books. TNA: PRO RAIL 509/8.

338. 1850: Report in Herepath, Vol. 12, 30 November 1850, p. 1170.

339. 1850: Letter in Herepath, Vol. 12, 21 December 1850, p. 1245.

340. 1850: Contract Payments. TNA: PRO RAIL 509/49.

341. 1850: Share price lists in Herepath, Vol. 12, pp. 997, 1069, 1189, 1257.

342. 1851: Letter in Herepath, Vol. 13, 25 January 1851, p. 90.

343. 1851: Report in Herepath, Vol. 13, 25 January 1851, p. 93.

344. 1851: Report in Herepath, Vol. 13, 8 February 1851, p. 130.

345. 1851: Report in Herepath, Vol. 13, 15 February 1851, p. 177.

346. 1851: Share price lists in Herepath, Vol. 13, 22 February 1851, p. 198.

347. 1851: Notice in *Newcastle Journal*, 8 February 1851.

348. 1851: Report in *Newcastle Weekly Chronicle*, 4 April 1851.

349. 1851: Report in *Newcastle Weekly Chronicle*, 9 May 1851.

350. 1851: An Act for empowering the Stockton and Darlington Railway Company, and their lessors, the Wear Valley Railway Company and the Middlesborough and Redcar Railway Company, to raise more money and for other purposes, 14 Vict, cap 23; 19 May 1851. DRO: Local & Personal Statutes.

351. 1851: Local & General Intelligence in *Newcastle Journal*, 7 June 1851.

352. 1851: Local & General Intelligence in *Newcastle Journal*, 21 June 1851.

353. 1851: Minutes of a Committee Meeting. 9 July 1851, Newcastle and Carlisle Railway Minute Books. TNA: PRO RAIL 509/9.

354. 1851: Minutes of a Committee Meeting. 14 July 1851, Newcastle and Carlisle Railway Minute Books: TNA: PRO RAIL 509/9.

355. 1851: Advert in *Newcastle Weekly Chronicle*, 1 August 1851.

356. 1851: Newcastle and Carlisle Railway, Alston Branch in *Newcastle Journal*, 13 September 1851.

357. 1851: Railway Intelligence in *Carlisle Journal*, 3 October 1851.

358. 1851: Advert in *Newcastle Weekly Chronicle*, 3 October 1851.

359. 1851: Advert in *Newcastle Weekly Chronicle*, 31 October 1851.

360. 1851: Minutes of a Committee Meeting. 17 November 1851. Newcastle and Carlisle Railway Minute Books. TNA: PRO RAIL 509/9.

361. 1852: Religious and Charity Notes in *Newcastle Journal*, 10 January 1852.

362. 1852: Report in *The Carlisle Patriot*, 10 January 1852.
363. 1852: Advert in *Newcastle Weekly Chronicle*, 30 January 1852.
364. 1852: Report in *Newcastle Weekly Chronicle*, 2 April 1852.
365. 1852: Advert in *Newcastle Weekly Chronicle*, 23 April 1852.
366. 1852: Railway Timetables in *Newcastle Weekly Chronicle*, 7 May 1852.
367. 1852: Report in *Newcastle Weekly Chronicle*, 14 May 1852.
368. 1852: An Act for increasing the Capital of the Stockton and Darlington Railway Company, and for other purposes. 15 Vict, cap 19; 28 May 1852. DRO: Local & Personal Statutes.
369. 1852: Advert in *Newcastle Weekly Chronicle*, 18 June 1852.
370. 1852: Advert in *Newcastle Weekly Chronicle*, 23 July 1852.
371. 1852: Railway Timetables in *Newcastle Weekly Chronicle*, 23 July 1852.
372. 1852: Advert in *Newcastle Weekly Chronicle*, 20 August 1852.
373. 1852: Railway Timetables in *Newcastle Weekly Chronicle*, 20 August 1852.
374. 1852: Plans, sections and notice of Application to Parliament for the Darlington and Barnard Castle Railway. Thomas Bouch, Engineer. November 1852. DRO: Q/D/P/193.
375. 1853: Railway Timetables in *Newcastle Weekly Chronicle*, 14 January 1853.
376. 1853: Report of the Directors of the Newcastle and Carlisle Railway. 17 March 1853. NLIS: L656.2.
377. 1853: Report in *Newcastle Weekly Chronicle*, 18 March 1853.
378. 1853: An Act to repeal the Act for repairing the Alston Turnpike Roads, and to make other provisions in lieu thereof. 16 & 17 Vict, cap 112; 4 August 1853. DRO: Local & Personal Acts.
379. 1853: Plans, sections, book of reference and Parliamentary notice of the Darlington and Barnard Castle Railway. Thomas Bouch, Engineer. November 1853. DRO: Q/D/P/196.
380. 1853: Plans and Section of a proposed branch railway from and out of the Stockton and Darlingont Railway commencing at the junction therewith of the Haggerleases Branch thereof and terminating near the north end of the Shildon Tunnel; and plan of additional land proposed to be taken for the general purposes of the railway in the Township of Thickley. 29 November 1853. DRO: Q/D/P 198.
381. 1853: Plans, sections, Parliamentary notice for the Barnard Castle & Bishop Auckland Junction Railway. Deposited 30 November 1853. DRO: Q/D/P/ 205.
382. 1854: An Act for making a railway from the Stockton and Darlington Railway near Darlington to or near Barnard Castle, both in the County of Durham, and for making arrangements with the Stockton and Darlington Railway Company; and for other purposes. 17 & 18 Vict, cap 115; 2 July 1854. DRO: Local & Personal Acts.
383. 1854: An Act for authorizing the Stockton and Darlington Railway Company to make new works; and for other purposes, and of which the short title is 'The Stockton and Darlington Railway Act, 1854'. 17 & 18 Vict, cap 128; 3 July 1854. DRO: Local and Personal Statutes.
384. 1854: Border Counties Railway Act; 17 & 18 Vict, cap 212; 31 July 1854. L&P: Local Acts Vol. 26, No. 17.
385. 1854: Plans, book of reference notice of application for an Act to enable the Stockton and Darlington Railway Company to make and maintain railways or branch railways. 9 November 1854. DRO: Q/D/P 207.
386. 1855: An Act for enabling the Stockton and Darlington Railway Company to make new branches and other works; to acquire additional lands; and for other purposes. 18 & 19 Vict, cap 149; 16 July 1855. DRO: Local & Personal Statutes.

387. 1855: Plans and Sections of the Stockton and Darlington and Newcastle and Carlisle Union Railway. November 1855. DRO: Q/D/P 219.

388. 1856: Local and General News in *Teesdale Mercury*, 25 June 1856.

389. 1856: Advert in *Teesdale Mercury*, 2 July 1856.

390. 1856: Local and General News in *Teesdale Mercury*, 9 July 1856.

391. 1856: An Act for making a railway from the Stocksfield station of the Newcastle-upon-Tyne and Carlisle to the Stockton and Darlington Railway near Conside iron works, with a branch to the Derwent Iron Company Railway, and for other purposes. 19 & 20 Vict, cap 94; 10 July 1856. DRO: Local & Personal Acts.

392. 1856: Local and General News in *Teesdale Mercury*, 16 July 1856.

393. 1856: Report in *Teesdale Mercury*, 13 August 1856.

394. 1856: Report in *Teesdale Mercury*, 20 August 1856.

395. 1856: Report by William Bouch on the S&D&N&CUR. 31 October 1856. TNA: PRO RAIL 667/207

396. 1856: Letter from David Dale to Henry Pease. TNA: PRO RAIL 667/207.

397. 1856: Report in *Teesdale Mercury*, 26 November 1856.

398. 1856: Plans and sections for the South Durham and Lancashire Union Railway. Thomas Bouch, C.E., Engineer. DRO: Q/D/P/225.

399. 1857: An Act for making a railway commencing by a junction with the Haggerleases Branch of the Stockton and Darlington Railway near the Lands Colliery in the County of Durham, and terminating by a junction with the Lancaster and Carlisle Railway at or near Tebay in the County of Westmorland; and for making arrangements with the Stockton and Darlington Railway Company; and for other purposes. 20 & 21 Vict, cap 40; 13 July 1857. DRO: Local & Personal Statutes.

400. 1857: Local and General News in *Teesdale Mercury*, 26 August 1857.

401. 1857: Plans and sections for the Eden Valley Railway. 1857. CRO(Kendal): WD/Hoth.

402. 1857: Plans and sections of proposed new railways and works in the County of Durham; and plans of additional lands in that County, Session 1857–8. John Dixon, William Cudworth, Engineers. 30 November 1857. DRO: Q/D/P/237.

403. 1857–58: Ordnance Survey maps, 6 inches to the mile, 1857–58 survey. DRO.

404. 1858: Report in *Durham County Advertizer*, 29 January 1858.

405. 1858: An Act to authorise the making of a railway from the Lancaster and Carlisle Railway at or near Clifton to the South Durham and Lancashire Union Railway at or near Kirkby Stephen, all in the County of Westmorland; and for other purposes. 21 & 22 Vict, cap 14; 2 May 1858. DRO: Local & Personal Statutes.

406. 1858: Report in *Newcastle Courant*, 2 July 1858.

407. 1858: An Act for enabling the Stockton and Darlington Railway Company to make a new Railway in the County of Durham in connection with the Wear Valley and Stockton and Darlington Railways; to acquire additional land; and for other purposes. 21 & 22 Vict, cap 115; 23 July 1858. DUL: Statutes at Large, Vol. 98.

408. 1858: An Act for the amalgamation of the Stockton and Darlington, the Wear Valley, the Middlesborough and Guisbrough, and the Darlington and Barnard Castle Railway Companies, and for regulating the capital and borrowing powers of the Stockton and Darlington Railway Company formed by the amalgamation, and for other purposes. 21 & 22 Vict, cap 116; 23 July 1858. DRO: D/X 339/16.

409. 1858: Report in *Teesdale Mercury*, 11 August 1858.

410. 1858: Plans, sections, book of reference and notice of application to Parliament of the Deviation of the South Durham and Lancashire Railway. 29 November 1858. DRO: Q/D/P/241.

411. 1859: Joseph Pearson, unpublished diary. Property of the Kearton Family, Alston.

412. 1859: Report in *Durham County Advertizer*, 8 July 1859.

413. 1859: An Act to enable the South Durham and Lancashire Union Railway Company to deviate their authorized line of railway; to carry their line over a certain road by a level crossing; and to construct a road for providing better access to the railway at or near to Barnard Castle; and for other purposes. 22 & 23 Vict, cap 73; 1 August 1859. DRO: Local & Personal Acts.

414. 1859: Plans, Section, Book of Reference and notice of application to Parliament by the North Eastern Railway for power to construct a branch from Blaydon to Conside. November 1859. DRO: Q/D/P/249.

415. 1859: Plans, Sections, Book of reference, and Notice of Application to Parliament for the Newcastle Upon Tyne and Derwent Valley Railway. 30 November 1859. Thomas Bouch, Engineer. TWAS: D/NCP 118; DRO: Q/D/P/247

416. 1859: Report in *Durham County Advertiser*, 6 December 1859.

417. 1859: Report in *Newcastle Courant*, 16 December 1859.

418. 1860: An Act for authorizing the Stockton and Darlington Railway Company to raise additional capital; and for other purposes. 22 & 23 Vict, cap 44; 15 May 1860. DRO: Local & Personal Statutes.

419. 1860: Report in *Newcastle Courant*, 24 November 1860.

420. 1860: Plans, Sections, Book of Reference and Application to Parliament of the Frosterley and Stanhope Railway and approach road to station. Wm. Bryson, Engineer. 27 November 1860. DRO: Q/D/P/252.

421. 1860: Report in *Durham County Advertiser*, 30 November 1860.

422. 1860: Plans and Sections of the Newcastle, Derwent and Weardale Railway. Thomas Bouch, Engineer. 30 November 1860. TWAS: D/NCP 124; DRO: Q/D/P/254.

423. 1860: Advert in *Newcastle Courant*, 28 December 1860.

424. 1861: Advert in *Newcastle Courant*, 11 January 1861.

425. 1861: An Act to authorize the making of a railway from the Stockton and Darlington Railway at or near the Frosterley station to Newlandside near Stanhope, with a road approach from Stanhope, all in the County of Durham; and for authorizing working arrangements with the Stockton and Darlington Railway Company; and for other purposes. 24 & 25 Vict, cap 72; 28 June 1861. DRO: Local & Personal Statutes.

426. 1861: Report in *Teesdale Mercury*, 10 July 1861.

427. 1861: Local and General News in *Teesdale Mercury*, 10 July 1861.

428. 1861: Advert in *Teesdale Mercury*, 10 July 1861.

429. 1861: An Act for enabling the Stockton and Darlington Railway Company to raise additional capital; and for other purposes. 24 & 25 Vict, cap 157; 22 July 1861. DRO: Local & Personal Statutes.

430. 1861: Local and General News in *Teesdale Mercury*, 31 July 1861.

431. 1861: Report in *Teesdale Mercury*, 7 August 1861.

432. 1861: Timetable in *Teesdale Mercury*, 7 August 1861.

433. 1861: Local and General News in *Teesdale Mercury*, 21 August 1861.

434. 1861: Plans and sections of Frosterley and Stanhope Railway, Deviation of a line, branch line, road approach and abandonment of portion of a railway and approach road. Wm. Bryson, Engineer. 27 November 1861. DRO Q/D/P 259.

435. 1861: Stockton and Darlington Railway: Plan of a Proposed line of railway from Tow Law to Crook in the County of Durham. John Dixon and W. Cudworth, Engineers. 29 November 1861. DRO: Q/D/P/260.

436. 1862: Advert in *Teesdale Mercury*, 2 April 1862.

437. 1862: Directors' Meeting. 25 April 1862, Frosterley and Stanhope Railway Minute Book. PRO RAIL 212/1.

438. 1862: Lease. 26 April 1862. NCS ZNI 14.
439. 1862: The Stockton and Darlington Railway (Towlaw and Crook) Act, 1862. 25 & 26 Vict, cap 54; 3 June 1862. DRO: Local & Personal Statutes.
440. 1862: Local and General News in *Teesdale Mercury*, 11 June 1862.
441. 1862: An Act to Authorise a Deviation of part of the Authorised line of the Frosterley and Stanhope Railway, to construct a new branch and other works, to abandon portions of the authorised line and approach to Stanhope, to raise additional capital, amend and repeal Acts; and for other purposes. 25 & 26 Vict, cap 40; 3 June 1862. DRO: Local & Personal Statutes.
442. 1862: An Act for the amalgamation of the South Durham and Lancashire Union and Eden Valley Railway Companies with the Stockton and Darlington Railway Company; for the transfer to the last-named Company of the Frosterley and Stanhope Railway; and for other purposes. 25 & 26 Vict, cap 106; 30 June 1862. DRO: D/X 339/17.
443. 1862: An Act to enable the Eden Valley Railway Company to construct certain extension and branch railways; to use portions of other railways; to raise additional capital; and for other purposes. 25 & 26 Vict, cap 118; 7 July 1862. DRO: Local & Personal Acts.
444. 1862: An Act to enable the North-eastern Railway Company to construct a branch railway between Blaydon and Conside, with branches thereform; to acquire additional lands; and for other purposes. 25 & 26 Vict, cap 146; 17 July 1862. NLIS 656.2, North Eastern Railway Acts, 1842–1883, Vol. 1.
445. 1862: Report in *Auckland Times and Herald*, 25 October 1862.
446. 1863: An Act for the amalgamation of the Stockton and Darlington Railway Company with the North-eastern Railway Company; and for other purposes. 26 & 27 Vict, cap 122; 13 July 1863. DRO: Local & Personal Acts.
447. 1863: Local and General News in *Teesdale Mercury*, 29 July 1863.
448. 1864: Railway Timetables in *Teesdale Mercury*, 5 August 1864.
449. 1864: Report in *Hexham Courant*, 24 August 1864.
450. 1864: Report in *Hexham Courant*, 7 September 1864.
451. 1864: Supplement to *Hexham Courant*, 28 September 1864.
452. 1864: Minutes of meeting. 8 October 1864, Minute Book of the Proceedings of General Meetings of the Tees Valley Railway. TNA: PRO 687/1.
453. 1864: Report in *Hexham Courant*, 12 October 1864.
454. 1864: Notice in *Hexham Courant*, 16 November 1864.
455. 1864: Plans and Sections of the Hexham and Allendale Railway. November 1864. NCS: QRUp 114.
456. 1864: Plans and Sections of the Tees Valley Railway. Nimmo & MacNay, Engineers. 29 November 1864. NYCRO: QDP(M) 149.
457. 1864: Report in *Hexham Courant*, 7 December 1864.
458. 1864: Report in *Teesdale Mercury*, 14 December 1864.
459. 1864: Local News in *Hexham Courant*, 21 December 1864.
460. 1865: Local and Miscellaneous in *Hexham Courant*, 18 January 1865.
461. 1865: Local and Miscellaneous in *Hexham Courant*, 25 January 1865.
462. 1865: Local and Miscellaneous in *Hexham Courant*, 15 March 1865.
463. 1865: Papers from the estate of Henry Bacon Grey. 27 March 1865. NCS, ZLO XVIII/22a & b.
464. 1865: Report in *Hexham Courant*, 5 April 1865.
465. 1865: Local and Miscellaneous in *Hexham Courant*, 17 May 1865.

466. 1865: An Act for authorising the construction of railways in the county of Northumberland to be called the 'Hexham and Allendale Railway', and for other purposes. 28 Vict, cap 87; 19 June 1865. NLIS: L656.2.

467. 1865: An Act to incorporate a Company for making a Railway from the South Durham and Lancashire Union branch of the North-eastern Railway at Lartington to Middleton-in-Teesdale; Working arrangements with the North- eastern Railway Company; Powers to that Company to subscribe; and other powers. 28 Vict, cap 91; 19 June 1865. DRO: Local & Personal Statutes.

468. 1865: Minute from the North Eastern Railway, S&DR Section, Board Meeting. 27 June 1865, Tees Valley Railway Book of Reports, Letters, etc. TNA: PRO RAIL 687/9

469. 1865: Report in *Hexham Courant*, 13 September 1865.

470. 1865: Report in *Newcastle Daily Chronicle*, 16 September 1865.

471. 1865: *Newcastle Daily Chronicle*, 4 October 1865.

472. 1865: Local and Miscellaneous in *Hexham Courant*, 4 October 1865.

473. 1865: Report in *Hexham Courant*, 25 October 1865.

474. 1865: Advert in *Hexham Courant*, 15 November 1865.

475. 1865: Advert (North Eastern Railway) in *Hexham Courant*, 15 November 1865.

476. 1866: Notice in *Teesdale Mercury*, 3 January 1866.

477. 1866: Local and District News in *Hexham Courant*, 17 January 1866.

478. 1866: Local and General News in *Teesdale Mercury*, 7 February 1866.

479. 1866: Local and District News in *Hexham Courant*, 21 February 1866.

480. 1866: Report in *Hexham Courant*, 11 April 1866.

481. 1866: Local Bills in *Hexham Courant*, 2 May 1866.

482. 1866: An Act to enable the Greenwich Hospital Estates and the North-Eastern Railway Company to aid in the completion of the Hexham and Allendale Railway; and for other purposes. 29 Vict, cap 128; 11 June 1866. LSD: NLIS: L656.2.

483. 1866: Report in *Teesdale Mercury*, 8 August 1866.

484. 1866: Report in *Hexham Courant*, 5 September 1866.

485. 1866: Local and General News in *Teesdale Mercury*, 7 October 1866.

486. 1866: Editorial in *Teesdale Mercury*, 29 December 1866.

487. 1867: Report in *Hexham Courant*, 6 February 1867.

488. 1867: Local and General News in *Teesdale Mercury*, 13 February 1867.

489. 1867: Report in *Teesdale Mercury*, 27 February 1867.

490. 1867: Report in *Teesdale Mercury*, 24 April 1867.

491. 1867: Letter from Thomas MacNay Secretary to the Board of Trade. 12 June 1867, Deviation of the line from Crook to Tow Law: Correspondence with the Board of Trade, 1867. TNA: PRO 667/1182.

492. 1867: Letter from Thomas MacNay Secretary to the Board of Trade. 12 July 1867, Deviation of the line from Crook to Tow Law: Correspondence with the Board of Trade, 1867. TNA: PRO 667/1182.

493. 1867: Letter from Col. Hutchinson. 12 July 1867, Deviation of the line from Crook to Tow Law: Correspondence with the Board of Trade, 1867. TNA: PRO 667/1182.

494. 1867: Letter from Col. Hutchinson. 17 July 1867, Deviation of the line from Crook to Tow Law: Correspondence with the Board of Trade, 1867. TNA: PRO 667/1182.

495. 1867: Statement by Thomas MacNay. 19 July 1867, Deviation of the line from Crook to Tow Law: Correspondence with the Board of Trade, 1867. TNA: PRO 667/1182.

496. 1867: Letter from Col. Hutchinson. 19 July 1867, Deviation of the line from Crook to Tow Law: Correspondence with the Board of Trade, 1867. TNA: PRO 667/1182.

497. 1867: Extract from Minutes of the Traffic Committee Meeting. 24 July 1867, Deviation of the line from Crook to Tow Law: Correspondence with the Board of Trade, 1867. TNA: PRO 667/1182.

498. 1867: Local and District News in *Hexham Courant*, 21 August 1867.

499. 1867: Report in *Hexham Courant*, 28 August 1867.

500. 1867: Extract from the minutes of the General Committee Meeting, N.E.R. S&DR section. 9 October 1867, Deviation of the line from Crook to Tow Law: Correspondence with the Board of Trade, 1867. TNA: PRO 667/1182.

501. 1867: Letter from Thomas MacNay to Col. Hutchinson. 29 November 1867, Deviation of the line from Crook to Tow Law: Correspondence with the Board of Trade, 1867. TNA: PRO 667/1182.

502. 1868: Report in *Hexham Courant*, 14 January 1868.

503. 1868: Railway Timetables in *Auckland Chronicle*, 17 January 1868.

504. 1868: Advert in *Hexham Courant*, 18 January 1868.

505. 1868: Letter from Thomas MacNay to Col. Hutchinson. 31 January 1868, Deviation of the line from Crook to Tow Law: Correspondence with the Board of Trade, 1867. TNA: PRO 667/1182.

506. 1868: Report in *Hexham Courant*, 4 February 1868.

507. 1868: Report in *Newcastle Courant*, 28 February 1868.

508. 1868: Notice. 2 March 1868, Deviation of the line from Crook to Tow Law: Correspondence with the Board of Trade, 1867. TNA: PRO 667/1182.

509. 1868: Local Gossip in *Hexham Courant*, 28 March 1868.

510. 1868: Report of inspection by Col. C.L. Hutchison. 1 May 1868, Tees Valley Railway Book of Reports, Letters, etc. TNA: PRO RAIL 687/10

511. 1868: District News in *Auckland Chronicle*, 8 May 1868.

512. 1868: Report in *Auckland Chronicle*, 15 May 1868.

513. 1868: Letter from Col. Hutchison. 16 May 1868, Tees Valley Railway Book of Reports, Letters, etc. TNA: PRO RAIL 687/10

514. 1868: Letter from Board of Trade. 18 May 1868, Tees Valley Railway Book of Reports, Letters, etc. TNA: PRO RAIL 687/10

515. 1868: Local and District News in *Hexham Courant*, 23 May 1868.

516. 1868: Advert in *Hexham Courant*, 18 July 1868.

517. 1868: Report in *Hexham Courant*, 1 September 1868.

518. 1868: Advert in *Newcastle Journal*, 30 November 1868.

519. 1869: Report in *Hexham Courant*, 6 February 1869.

520. 1869: Report in *Hexham Courant*, 27 February 1869.

521. 1869: Advert in *Hexham Courant*, 27 February 1869.

522. 1869: Reports in *Hexham Courant*, 2 March 1869.

523. 1869: Railway Timetable in *Teesdale Mercury*, 14 July 1869.

523a. 1869: Meeting of the Land Committee. 12 June 1869, Tees Valley Railway Minute Books. TNA: PRO RAIL 687.

524. 1870: Report in *Hexham Courant*, 12 April 1870.

525. 1870: Report in *Hexham Courant*, 30 April 1870.

526. 1871: Report in *Teesdale Mercury*, 8 July 1871.

527. 1871: Editorial in *Teesdale Mercury*, 8 November 1871.

528. 1871: Report in *Carlisle Patriot*, 10 November 1871.

529. 1871: Local News in *Hexham Courant*, 11 November 1871.

530. 1871: Report in *Carlisle Journal*, 17 November 1871.

531. 1871: Editorial in *Teesdale Mercury*, 22 November 1871.

532. 1871: Editorial and Report in *Auckland Times and Herald*, 24 November 1871.
533. 1871: District News in *Hexham Courant*, 25 November 1871.
534. 1871: Plans, sections, and books of reference for the Cumberland and Cleveland Junction Railway. Deposited 30 November 1871. CAS: Q/RZ January 139; DRO: Q/D/P/311; NYCRO/QDP(M)/182.
535. 1871: Local and District News in *Carlisle Patriot*, 1 December 1871.
536. 1871: Miscellaneous News in *Hexham Courant*, 2 December 1871.
537. 1871: Report in *Auckland Times and Herald*, 22 December 1871.
538. 1871: Report in *Carlisle Journal*, 26 December 1871.
539. 1871: Report in *Teesdale Mercury*, 27 December 1871.
540. 1871: Schedule of Land required by the Cumberland and Cleveland Junction Railway from John Bowes Esq., Streatland Castle, near Darlington. All in the Parish of Romaldkirk. DRO, D/St/D3 November 16.
541. 1871: Hanby Holmes Archive. DRO, D/HH October 18/307-308.
542. 1872: Letter from Richardson Gutch & Co.; to C.R. Wilkinson, Esq., Secretary, NER; York. 17 January 1872. TNA: PRO RAIL 527-1772.
543. 1872: Report in *Carlisle Journal*, 6 February 1872.
544. 1872: Report in *Teesdale Mercury*, 7 February 1872.
545. 1872: Letter from Tilleard & Co. to J. D. Holmes. 9 March 1872. DRO, D/HH January 4/71/13.
546. 1872: Post Office Telegraph of 11 March 1872 from Tilleard & Co. to J.D. Holmes. DRO, D/HH 4/71/16
547. 1872: District News in *Hexham Courant*, 16 March 1872.
548. 1872: Report in *Carlisle Journal*, 16 April 1872.
549. 1872: Report in *Carlisle Patriot*, 17 May 1872.
550. 1872: Report in *Newcastle Weekly Chronicle*, 18 May 1872.
551. 1872: Editorial in *Teesdale Mercury*, 19 June 1872.
552. 1872: Report in *Carlisle Journal*, 25 June 1872.
553. 1872: Reports in *Carlisle Patriot*, 28 June 1872.
554. 1872: Report in *Hexham Courant*, 9 November 1872.
555. 1872: Hansard, Third Series, Vol. 213, Local Acts, 1872.
556. 1873: District News in *Hexham Courant*, 19 July 1873.
557. 1875: District News in *Hexham Courant*, 23 January 1875
558. 1875: District News in *Hexham Courant*, 1 May 1875.
559. 1876: District News in *Hexham Courant*, 11 December 1875.
560. 1876: Report in *Hexham Courant*, 30 September 1876.
561. 1877: District News in *Hexham Courant*, 27 January 1877.
562. 1878: District News in *Hexham Courant*, 9 March 1878.
563. 1878: District News in *Hexham Courant*, 19 October 1878.
564. 1878: Local News in *Hexham Courant*, 19 October 1878.
565. 1878: Report in *Hexham Courant*, 16 November 1878.
566. 1879: Report in *Hexham Courant*, 29 March 1879.
567. 1879: Report – North of England Lead Mining, *Hexham Courant*, 7 June 1879.
568. 1880: Report – Northern Lead Mining, *Hexham Courant*, 6 November 1880.
569. 1880: Plan of Middleton-in-Teesdale station. DRO, D/St/p14.
570. 1881: District News in *Hexham Courant*, 26 February 1881.
571. 1881: Local Census Returns in *Hexham Courant*, 23 April 1881.
572. 1881: Alstonia, by Gario in *Hexham Courant*, 9 July 1881.
573. 1881: Report – Durham Lead Mines, *Hexham Courant*, 13 August 1881.
574. 1881: District News in *Hexham Courant*, 20 August 1881.

575. 1881: District News in *Hexham Courant*, 31 December 1881.

576. 1882: Letter in *Hexham Courant*, 10 June 1882.

577. 1882: An Act for enabling the North Eastern Railway Company to make new railways and for conferring additional powers on the Company in relation to their undertaking and for vesting in them the undertaking of the Tees Valley Railway Company; and for other purposes. 45 Vict, cap 1; 19 June 1882. L&P: Local Acts, Vol. 31.

578. 1882: Railway Timetable in *Teesdale Mercury*, 8 July 1882.

579. 1882: District Notes in *Hexham Courant*, 2 September 1882.

580. 1882: Indenture made on 23 September 1882. Records of Stanton, Croft and Company, Solicitors, Newcastle-upon-Tyne. DRO: D/SC 1/2.

581. 1882: Report in *Hexham Courant*, 9 December 1882.

582. 1883: District News in *Hexham Courant*, 2 June 1883.

583. 1883: District News in *Hexham Courant*, 14 July 1883.

584. 1884: Heads of proposed agreement between Lindsey Wood, et al. and Weardale Ironstone etc. 2 August 1884, Records of Stanton, Croft and Company, Solicitors, Newcastle-upon-Tyne. DRO: D/SC 1/122.

585. 1884: District News in *Hexham Courant*, 13 September 1884.

586. 1884: District News in *Hexham Courant*, 1 November 1884.

587. 1885: District News in *Hexham Courant*, 28 February 1885.

588. 1885: District News in *Hexham Courant*, 17 October 1885.

589. 1885: District News in *Hexham Courant*, 19 December 1885.

590. 1886: Report – Heavy Snowstorms in Weardale, *Hexham Courant*, 30 January 1886.

591. 1886: Report – Great Snowstorm, *Hexham Courant*, 6 March 1886.

592. 1886: District News in *Hexham Courant*, 12 June 1886.

593. 1886: Report in *Hexham Courant*, 9 October 1886.

594. 1886: District News in *Hexham Courant*, 6 November 1886.

595. 1886: District News in *Hexham Courant*, 6 November 1886.

596. 1886: Report in *Hexham Courant*, 13 November 1886.

597. 1886: District News in *Hexham Courant*, 27 November 1886.

598. 1887: Weardale Intelligence in *Hexham Courant*, 8 January 1887.

599. 1887: Report in *Hexham Courant*, 15 January 1887.

600. 1887: Report – The Proposed Weardale Railway, *Hexham Courant*, 26 March 1887.

601. 1887: Local Gossip, *Hexham Courant*, 31 December 1887.

602. 1889: Weardale Intelligence in *Hexham Courant*, 26 October 1889.hhh

603. 1890: District News, Brampton in *Hexham Courant*, 29 March 1890.

604. 1890: District News in *Hexham Courant*, 29 March 1890.

605. 1890: Weardale Intelligence in *Hexham Courant*, 21 June 1890.

606. 1890: Weardale Intelligence in *Hexham Courant*, 20 September 1890.

607. 1891: Report – The Iron Mines Crisis in Weardale, *Hexham Courant*, 24 January 1891.

608. 1891: Report – Proposed Upper Weardale Railway, *Hexham Courant*, 4 July 1891.

609. 1891: Weardale Intelligence in *Hexham Courant*, 25 July 1891.

610. 1891: Wear Valley Railway Extension, plans and sections. Deposited 27 November 1891. Edward Whyte Lyall, C.E., Engineer. DRO: Q/D/P 402.

611. 1891: Plans, section, book of reference and notice of application to Parliament, for the St. John's Chapel Railway. Deposited 30 November 1891. R. Elliott Cooper, Engineer. DRO: Q/D/P 405.

612. 1892: Report – Weardale and Alston Railway, *Hexham Courant*, 27 February 1892.

613. 1892: Alston Intelligence in *Hexham Courant*, 5 March 1892.

614. 1892: Editorial in *Hexham Courant*, 5 March 1892.

615. 1892: Report – Rival Railway Schemes in Weardale, *Hexham Courant*, 5 March 1892.

616. 1892: Alston Intelligence in *Hexham Courant*, 12 March 1892.

617. 1892: Alston Intelligence in *Hexham Courant*, 26 March 1892.

618. 1892: Report – St. John's Chapel and Wear Valley Extension Railway Bills, *Hexham Courant*, 14 May 1892.

619. 1892: Report – Railway Extension in Weardale, *Hexham Courant*, 21 May 1892.

620. 1892: Alston Intelligence in *Hexham Courant*, 18 June 1892.

621. 1892: An Act for making a railway from Stanhope to Wearhead in the County of Durham to be called the Wear Valley Extension Railway and for other purposes. 55 & 56 Vict, cap 128; 20 June 1892. L&P: Local Acts, Vol. 33, No. 21.

622. 1892: Editorial in *Teesdale Mercury*, 20 July 1892.

623. 1892: Alston Intelligence in *Hexham Courant*, 30 July 1892.

624. 1892: Report in *Teesdale Mercury*, 3 August 1892.

625. 1892: Middleton-in-Teesdale in *Teesdale Mercury*, 10 August 1892.

626. 1892: Alston Intelligence in *Hexham Courant*, 6 August 1892.

627. 1892: Editorial in *Teesdale Mercury*, 17 August 1892.

628. 1892: Middleton-in-Teesdale in *Teesdale Mercury*, 24 August 1892.

629. 1892: District News: Weardale in *Hexham Courant*, 24 December 1892.

630. 1893: District News: Alston in *Hexham Courant*, 8 April 1893.

631. 1893: Weardale Valley Extension Railway, *Hexham Courant*, 28 October 1893.

632. 1893: District News in *Hexham Courant*, 16 December 1893.

633. 1894: The New Railway, *Hexham Courant*, 17 February 1894.

634. 1894: The New Railway, *Hexham Courant*, 10 March 1894.

635. 1894: District News in *Hexham Courant*, 17 March 1894.

636. 1894: District News in *Hexham Courant*, 23 June 1894.

637. 1894: District News in *Hexham Courant*, 14 April 1894.

638. 1894: District News in *Hexham Courant*, 5 May 1894.

639. 1894: An Act to confer additional powers upon the North Eastern Railway Company and upon that Company and the London and North Western Railway Company for the construction of new railways and other works and the acquisition of additional lands, for transferring to the North Eastern Railway Company the powers of the Wear Valley Extension Railway Company and for other purposes. 57 & 58 Vict, cap 153; 31 July 1894. L&P: Local Acts, Vol. 31, No. 18.

640. 1894: District News in *Hexham Courant*, 4 August 1894.

641. 1894: District News in *Hexham Courant*, 25 August 1894.

642. 1894: District News in *Hexham Courant*, 27 October 1894.

643. 1895: District News in *Hexham Courant*, 19 January 1895.

644. 1895: District News in *Hexham Courant*, 13 July 1895.

645. 1895: District News in *Hexham Courant*, 27 July 1895.

646. 1895: Report in *Hexham Courant*, 26 October 1895.

647. 1895: District News in *Hexham Courant*, 7 December 1895.

648. 1895: District News in *Hexham Courant*, 21 December 1895.

649. 1895: Ordnance Survey maps, 6 inches to the mile, 1895 survey. DRO.

652. 1897: District News in *Hexham Courant*, 6 March 1897.

653. 1897: Minute 10712 – Meeting of Board. 5 November 1897, North Eastern Railway Board Minute Book, Vol. 13. TNA: PRO RAIL 527/19.

654. 1897: District News in *Hexham Courant*, 20 November 1897.

655. 1897: District News in *Hexham Courant*, 27 November 1897.

656. 1898: District News in *Hexham Courant*, 5 March 1898.

657. 1898: Minute 19845 of 31 March 1898. NER Traffic Committee Minute Book. TNA: PRO RAIL 527/74.

658. 1898: Allendale Notes in *Hexham Courant*, 9 July 1898.
659. 1898: Minute 10 of 16 September 1898. NER Chairman's Business Book 17 July 1897 to 18 July 1902. TNA: PRO RAIL 527/148.
660. 1898: Traffic Committee – 6 October 1898. NER Co. – Engineers Minute Book 5 May 1898 to 2 March 1899. TNA: PRO RAIL 527/377.
661. 1898: District News in *Hexham Courant*, 22 October 1898.
662. 1898: Minute 20043, 3 November 1898. NER Traffic Committee Minute Book. TNA: PRO RAIL 527/74.
663. 1898: Proposed Railway from Alston, *Hexham Courant*, 17 December 1898.
664. 1899: Letter from the General Manager of the North Eastern Railway, George S. Gibb to Sir Lindsay Wood. 7 July 1899. The property of Mr J. Crompton, Blagill.
665. 1899: Plans of Proposed Railway: Alston to Nenthead, undated but accompanying the letter from George S. Gibb, dated 7 July 1899. The property of Mr J. Crompton, Blagill.
666. 1899: Minute 10885 – Special meeting of Board. 21 July 1899, North Eastern Railway Board Minute Book, Vol. 13. TNA: PRO RAIL 527/19.
667. 1899: Allendale Notes in 'Hexham Courant*, 5 August 1899.
668. 1899: The Alston and Nenthead Light railway scheme, *Hexham Courant*, 30 September 1899.
669. 1899: Minute 14 of 20 October 1899. NER Chairman's Business Book 17 July 1897 to 18 July 1902. TNA: PRO RAIL 527/148.
670. 1899: Minute 10907 – Board Meeting. 17 November 1899, North Eastern Railway Board Minute Book, Vol. 13. TNA: PRO RAIL 527/19.
671. 1899: District News: Nenthead in *Hexham Courant*, 18 November 1899.
672. 1899: Sections of the Alston to Nenthead Railway; undated but probably July 1899, and with the following written on the right-hand end of each sheet: 2B 9 5. STRPS archives.
673. 1900: District News: Weardale in *Hexham Courant*, 31 March 1900.
675. 1902: District News: Weardale in *Hexham Courant*, 14 June 1902.
676. 1903: J. Robinson, *The Attwood Family*, 1903. Printed by Hills and Company, Sunderland. Privately published, pp. 74–75. NLIS L 929.2
677. 1905: District News: Allendale in *Hexham Courant*, 16 September 1905.
678. 1906: Correspondence in *Hexham Courant*, 9 June 1906.
679. 1906: District News: Weardale in *Hexham Courant*, 28 July 1906.
680. 1906: District Notes: Allendale Town in *Hexham Courant*, 3 November 1906.
681. 1908: District News: Alston in *Hexham Courant*, 7 November 1908.
682. 1908: Records of Stanton, Croft and Company, Solicitors, Newcastle-upon-Tyne. DRO: D/SC 1/203.
683. 1908?: Records of Stanton, Croft and Company, Solicitors, Newcastle-upon-Tyne. DRO: D/SC 1/201.
684. 1909: District News: Alston in *Hexham Courant*, 3 April 1909.
685. 1909: Report in *Hexham Courant*, 1 May 1909.
686. 1911: Report – Brampton Light Railway Scheme, *Hexham Courant*, 1 July 1911.
687. 1911: Report – Alston and Nenthead Railway, *Hexham Courant*, 8 July 1911.
688. 1913: Report in *Hexham Courant*, 22 February 1913.
689. 1913: Cutting from *Newcastle Daily Journal*, 1 August 1913. Collection of Papers on Brampton Branch. TNA: PRO RAIL 527/986/3.
690. 1913: Local Notelets in *Hexham Courant*, 2 August 1913.
691. 1913: Report in *Hexham Courant*, 15 November 1913.

692. 1913: North Eastern Railway Plans and Sections, 1913 Session. CAS Q/RZ 1 174.

693. 1914: Allendale Notes in *Hexham Courant*, 4 July 1914.

694. 1919: Lease of Heights Quarry. 6 March 1919. DRO D/SC 1/140.

695. 1919: Notelets in *Hexham Courant*, 17 May 1919.

696. 1920: Gossip and Comment in *Hexham Courant*, 7 February 1920.

697. 1920: Report in *Hexham Courant*, 2 October 1920.

698. 1920: Gossip and Comment in *Hexham Courant*, 16 October 1920.

699. 1920: Notelets in *Hexham Courant*, 13 November 1920.

700. 1921: Gossip and Comment in *Hexham Courant*, 26 February 1921.

701. 1922: Local and District News in *Hexham Courant*, 2 September 1922.

702. 1924: Allendale Notes in *Hexham Courant*, 19 January 1924.

703. 1930: Occasional Notes in *Hexham Courant*, 17 September 1930.

704. 1948: John S. MacLean, *The Newcastle & Carlisle Railway, 1825–1862*, John S. MacLean, Newcastle, pp. 11–12.

705. Ibid. p. 112.

706. 1948: Table of Locomotives, in John S. MacLean, *The Newcastle & Carlisle Railway, 1825–1862*, John S. MacLean, Newcastle, pp. 74–75.

707. 1950: Report in *Hexham Courant*, 5 May 1950.

708. 1950: Report in *Hexham Courant*, 23 June 1950.

709. 1950: Report in *Hexham Courant*, 14 July 1950.

710. 1950: Editorial in *Hexham Courant*, 22 September 1950.

711. 1950: Article in *Hexham Courant*, 24 November 1950.

712. 1951: H.C. Casserley, *Service Suspended*, Ian Allen Ltd, London, p. 33.

713. Ibid. p. 34.

714. 1958: *Railway Magazine*, Vol. 104, p. 58.

715. 1959: *Railway Magazine*, Vol. 105, p. 877.

716. 1961: Memorandum for Consultation with Staff Representatives of Sectional Councils 1, 2, 3, 4 & 5: Haltwhistle – Alston Branch: Proposed Closure. British Railways.

717. 1962: *Railway Magazine*, Vol. 108, p. 138.

718. 1962: *Railway Magazine*, Vol. 108, p. 576.

719. 1964: *Railway Magazine*, Vol. 110, p. 920.

720. 1965: *Railway Magazine*, Vol. 111, p. 235.

721. 1965: T.E. Rounthwaite, *The Railways of Weardale*, The Railway Correspondence and Travel Society, pp. 4–5.

722. Ibid. p. 16.

723. Ibid. p. 17.

724. Ibid. p. 19.

725. Ibid. p. 22.

726. Ibid. p. 23.

727. Ibid. p. 26–32.

728. Ibid. p. 30.

729. 1969: *Bradshaw's Railway Manual Shareholder's Guide and Directory*, 1869 New Edition, David & Charles, Newton Abbot, pp. 314–315.

730. Ibid. pp. 438–439.

731. 1971: G. Whittle, *The Railways of Consett and North-West Durham*, David & Charles, Newton Abbot, pp. 55–56.

733. Ibid. p. 160.

734. Ibid. p. 161.

735. Ibid. p. 215.

736. Ibid. p. 216.

737. 1973: K. Hoole, *The Stainmore Railway.*, Dalesman Books.

738. 1974: J.S. Jeans, *History of the Stockton and Darlington Railway, Jubilee Memorial of the Railway System 1875*, Frank Graham, Newcastle, p. 6.

739. Ibid. pp. 21–26.

740. Ibid. pp. 109–110.

741. Ibid. p. 266.

742. 1974: A.W. Skempton, William Chapman (1749–1832), Civil Engineer. The Eleventh Dickinson Memorial Lecture. In *Transactions of the Newcomen Society*, Vol. 46, pp. 45–82.

743. 1975: Hugh McKnight, *The Shell Book of Inland Waterways*, David & Charles, Newton Abbot, p. 261.

744. 1976: J.G. James, Ralph Dodd, The Very Ingenious Schemer. In *Transactions of the Newcomen Society*, Vol. 47, pp.61–178, 1974–76. L&P.

745. 1978: K. Hoole, *A Regional History of the Railways of Great Britain, Vol. 4 – The North East*, David & Charles, Newton Abbot, p. 136.

746. Ibid. p. 137.

747. Ibid. pp. 184–185.

748. 1978: Brian Webb & David A. Gordon, *Lord Carlisle's Railways*, Railway Correspondence & Travel Society, London.

749. Ibid. p. 3.

750. Ibid. p. 21.

751. Ibid. p. 58.

752. Ibid. pp. 58–59.

753. Ibid. p. 64.

754. Ibid. p. 66.

755. Ibid. p. 70.

756. Ibid. p. 96.

757. Ibid. p. 97.

758. 1985: *Bradshaw's July 1922 Railway Guide*, Book Club Associates, p. 747.

759. 1987: *Tomlinson's North Eastern Railway*, New Edition, David & Charles, Newton Abbot.

760. Ibid. pp. 34–35.

761. Ibid. pp. 37–38.

762. Ibid. pp. 40–49.

763. Ibid. p. 174.

764. Ibid. pp. 211–218.

765. Ibid. pp. 240–247.

766. Ibid. pp. 243–245.

767. Ibid. p. 263.

768. Ibid. p. 298.

769. Ibid. p. 437.

770. Ibid. p. 443.

771. Ibid. pp. 441–444.

772. Ibid. p. 474.

773. Ibid. p. 511.

774. Ibid. p. 513.

775. Ibid. p. 521.

776. Ibid. pp. 523–524.

777. Ibid. pp. 529–530.

778. Ibid. p. 559.

779. Ibid. p. 568.

780. Ibid. p. 570.
781. Ibid. p. 584.
783. Ibid. p. 606.
784. Ibid. p. 607.
785. Ibid. p. 646.
786. 1988: A. Earnshaw, *Rails in the Durham Fells*. In *Back Track*, Vol. 2 (Autumn), pp. 125–131. NLIS L656.2.
787. 1991: S.C. Jenkins, *The Alston Branch*, The Oakwood Press, Oxford, pp. 100–102.
788. 1994: A. Earnshaw, *The Weardale Steam Railway Development Plan*.
789. 1996: L.E. Berry, The Remarkable Rookhope Railway. In *Back Track*, Vol. 10, part 8 pp. 397–404 and part 9 pp. 495–499.
790. 1997: Lambley Viaduct, by "Wanderer". In *Tynedalesman* No. 112 (October), reproduced from the North Eastern *Railway Magazine*, November 1912.
791. 1997: Robert Watson, *The Eden Valley Railway*, The Oakwood Press, Oxford.
792. 1998: R. Forsythe & C. Blackett-Ord, *Lambley Viaduct*, North Pennines Heritage Trust.
793. 1999: Editorial, *Tynedalesman*, No. 120 (October 1999), South Tynedale Railway Preservation Society, Alston.
794. 2001: Report in *Steam Railway*, September–October 2001.
795. 2002: Report in *Railway Magazine*, October 2002, p. 82.
796. 2004: Report in *Newcastle Journal*, 18 July 2004.
797. 2004: William Morley Egglestone [June 1887], *The Projected Weardale Railway*, The Weardale Museum.
798. 2004: Colin E. Mountford, *The Private Railways of County Durham*, Industrial Railway Society, pp. 388–403.
799. Ibid. pp. 400–401.
800. 2005: Reports in *Newcastle Journal*, 30 March 2005.
801. 2006: Colin E. Mountford & Dave Holroyde, *The Industrical Railways & Locomotives of County Durham*, Industrial Railway Society, p. 53.
802. Ibid. p. 72.
803. Ibid. p. 111.
804. Ibid. p. 151.
805. Ibid. p. 213.
806. Ibid. p. 269.
807. Ibid. p. 289.
808. Ibid. p. 411.
809. Ibid. p. 412.
810. Ibid. p. 417.
811. Ibid. pp. 439–440.
812. 2006: Eden Valley Railway, Opening Times and Timetable [Leaflet] 2006.
813. 2007: Report in *Railway Magazine*, January 2007, p. 63.
814. 2007: Phil Marsh, Community Railway Champions. In *Railway Magazine*, February 2007, pp. 26–29.
815. 2007: Report in *Railway Magazine*, August 2007, p. 65.
816. 2007: Report in *Railway Magazine*, October 2007, p. 80.
817. 2007: Eden Valley Railway website, www.evr.org.uk
818. 2007: S. Raine, Talk given to *Know Your North Pennines*, Langley, 10 October 2007.
819. 2008: Report in *Railway Magazine*, June 2008, p. 8.
820. 2008: T.M.Bell, *The South Tynedale Railway, Visitor's Guide*, 5th Edition, South Tynedale Railway (Sales) Ltd, Alston, p. 1.
821. Ibid. p. 2.

822. Ibid. p. 5.
823. Ibid. pp. 6–7.
824. Ibid. p. 24.
825. 2008: David Heywood, personal communication, Eden Valley Railway Trust, August 2008.
826. 2008: Report in *Newcastle Journal*, 9 September 2008.
827. 2010: Eden Valley Railway website, www.refprint.plus.com/evr/eden_valley_railway_main.htm
828. 2010: Report in *Railway Magazine*, March 2010, p. 54.
829. 2010: Report in *Railway Magazine*, April 2010, p. 54.
830. 2010: Report in *Railway Magazine*, June 2010, p. 8.
831. 2010: Report in *Railway Magazine*, June 2010, p. 56.
832. 2010: Report in *Railway Magazine*, July 2010, p. 11.
833. 2010: Report in *Railway Magazine*, October 2010, p. 55.
834. 2010: Report in *Railway Magazine*, November 2010, p. 6.
835. 2011: Report in *Railway Magazine*, August 2011, p. 6.
836. 2012: Report in *Northern Echo*, 3 January 2012.
837. 2012: Report in *Railway Magazine*, September 2012, p. 60.
838. 2013: Report in *Railway Magazine*, May 2013, p. 10.
839. 2014: Report in *Railway Magazine*, July 2014, p. 105.

INDEX

Note numbers in **bold** refer to an illustration, although there may be other mentions in the text on the same page. F1CS = Figure 1 in the Colour Section.

Admiralty, Lord of 216–18, 220.
Allen 7, 29–31, 76-84–85, 165–82, 238–39.
Allen Foot 24.
Allendale 7, 8, 12, 20, 29, 34, **68**, 69, 75, 78, **79**, 80, **81**, **82**, 83–84, 165, **166**, 172, **173**, 174–76, **178**, 179–80, 182, 216, 228, 234, 238–39.
Allendale Metalliferous Mining Company 239.
Allendale Town **17**, 76–79, **83**, 165–68, **173**, 176–77, 180, 237.
Allenheads 7, 9, **17**, 20, 31, 47–48, 76–80, **81**, 83–85, 155, 165, 167–68, 174, **175**, 215–16, 228, 238.
Allensford 52.
Allport 110.
Alston 7–9, 12–13, **19**, 20, 22–24, **29**, 30, **31**, **32**, 34, 41–42, 45–48, 55, 57, 62–63, 70, **71**, 76–78, 80, 83, 85–117, **93**, **112–13**, 140, 164–65, **168**, 172, **178**, 182–83, 191–92, **194**, 198–99, 201, **202**, 206, **208**, 210, 212, 214–22, 228–29, **230**, 231, **232**, 235–40, **241**, 242–47, F3CS, F12CS.
Anglo-Austral Mines Limited 242.
Anglo-Mediterranean Telegraph Company 199.
Annfield 36.
Appleby **18**, 43, 49, 51–52, 56, **61**, 186, 221, 240, 241, 243–44.
Appleby, D. P. 195.
Ashes Quarry 240.
Ashgill **17**, **205**, 206, **207**, 216.
Askrigg 53, **59**, **61**.
Attwood, Charles 142, 149, 152–53, 157, 163, 216.
Auckland 12, 35, 37, 46, 50, 54, 60, 126, **189**.
Auckland Chronicle 151.
Auckland Times and Herald 198.
Aysgarth 58.

Bainbridge, A.E. 237.
Baker, Mr. 220, 221, 228.
Balder 192, **193**, 195.
Baring (family) 153.
Barnard Castle **14**, 20, 30, 50, 57, **59**, 60, 85, 182, **183–85**, 186, **187**, 188, **189–90**, 191–93, 195–96, 240–41.
BARS (British American Railway Services) 248–49.

Bartholomew 181.
Barton 54.
Beaumont, Wentworth Blackett 165–67, **178**, 179–81, 215, 217, F8CS.
Beaumont Lead Company 165, 218.
Bedale 51, 54, **59**, 60, **62**.
Bell, John 25.
Bell, Sir Lothian 229.
Bell, Thomas 31.
Bellingham 30, 47–48, 77, 86.
Berwick 117.
Bewick 166–67, 176, 179.
Binnacle 27.
Birtley 51.
Bishop Auckland **14**, 20, 41, 44, 47, 54, **59**, 60, 131, **141**, 146–47, **148**, 151, 157, 160–61, 182–83, 185, **186**, 188–89, 241, 243–44, 247–49, F15CS.
Bishop's Seat 154, 156, 232.
Bishopley 39, 44, 157, 159, **161**, 237.
Bitchburn Beck 37.
Black Boy 40.
Black Bull 120.
Black Burn 74, 201–02, **203**, 212, **213**.
Blackhill **15**, 140, 239.
Blagill **19**, 93, **94**, F3CS.
Blanchland **133**, 153, 156, 238, 242.
blast furnace 142, **143**.
Blaydon **15**, 33–34, 142, **144**, 148–49, 151.
Blenkinsopp 34.
Blue Circle 243.
Board of Trade 45–46, 50, 52–54, 63, 76, 86, 150–51, 180, 196–97.
Bolt's Burn (Bolts Burn) **17**, 153–56, 163, **164**.
Bolton & Co. 192.
Bolts Law **17**, 146, 154, **155**, 163, 232, 237, F4CS.
Border Counties Junction **17**, 165, **169**, 172–73, **181**.
Boroughbridge 21.
Bouch, William 132–33, 140.
Bourne, John 88.
Bowes **14**, **16**, 49, **59**, **61**.
Boews, Mr 217.
Bowlees 199.

Bradford 52.
Brampton 12, **27**, 28, **29**, **30**, 31–32, **34**, 96, **202**, 235.
Brampton Junction 32, **236**, 240.
Brampton Town **19**, 32, **236**, 238.
Brewery Bridge 216.
Briggin Winch 227.
Brindley, James 21.
British Isles 11, 43, 201, 214.
British Rail 181, 197, 239.
Broomhouse 88.
Brough 49, 184, 193, 209.
Brougham, Lord 186.
Bruce, George Barclay 117.
Brusselton **134**.
Bryson, William 157, 159.
Buck, George Watson 53.
Burnhill **15**, **137**, **138**, 233, 239, 242.
Burnstones 30, **72**, 73, **91**, 96, 104, **107**, 113, 117.
Burtreeford 30.
Buses Hill 200.
Byerhope Burn 174, **175**.
Byng, Colonel 217.

Caldron Snout 199, 206.
Cambo Keels 232, **233**, 236.
Canal(s) 11, 12, 13, 16, 21, **22**, 23, 24, **25**, **26**, **27**, **28**, **29**, 34, 76.
Capper, Rev. David 157.
Carlisle, City of 9, 12, 17, **22**, 23, **27**, 28, 34, 43, 55, 88, 100, 113–15, 139, 142, 145, 221.
Carlisle, Earl of (Lord) 28, 31–32, 45, 74, 96–98.
Carlisle (locomotive) 116.
Carlisle Canal 11, 28, 34.
Carlisle Journal 49–52, 54, 198–99, 201.
Carlisle Patriot 198, 201, 214.
Carrhouse 38–39, 41–42, 119, 131.
Carrshield 239.
Carts Bog 172.
cast iron 28.
Catherill, J. 216.
Catterick 54, **59**.
Catton **83**, 84, 166–68, **172**, 176, **177–78**, 237.
Catton Road **17**, 83, **177–78**, 179–80, 237.
Central Station (Newcastle) 47–48, **49**, 77, 87, 111, 147.
Champion, Edward 48.
Chapman, William 23–25, 27–28, 37.
Charlton 117.
Chesterhope-le-Street 229.
Chesterhope 48.
Chipchase Castle 48, 86.
Chollerford 165.
Church Walk 146.
Cleveland 135, 182.
Cleveland, Duke of 50, 185, 191, 217.
Clifton **18**, 49–51, 56, 59, **61**, 186, 240.
Clitheroe 53.
Coal 11, 29, 32, 36, 41, **105**, 112, 114, 122, 154, 156, 163, 184, 189, 221, 234–35, 237, 243, 248, 249.
Coalcleugh 31.
Coalfell Beck **73**.
Coalfield 12, 21–22, 35–37, 186, 235.

Coanwood **19**, **104**, 113, 115–16.
Coastley 166, **169**, **170**, 176–77.
Cockfield Fell 50.
Coddrington, Captain 119.
Coke 186, 189, 221, 241.
Colas Rail 249.
colliery(ies) 11, 24, 28, 32, 35, 37, 75, 101, **102**, **103**, **105**, **109**, 114, **135**, 137, 138, 185, 189, 235, 236, 237, 240, 242.
Colne 51, 248.
Commons, House of 44, 56–58, 85–86, 99, 111, 167, 200–01, 221.
Consett (Conside) **15**, 36, 38, 119, 131–32, 135, 137–41, **144**, 145, 149, 151, 188, 237, 239–40, 242.
Cookson, Charles 149.
Copper 45.
Corbridge **17**, 137, 142, 189, 238.
Cordner, Richard 157, 163, F6CS.
Corsenside 48.
Cotherstone **14**, **191**, 192, **193**, 195.
Coverale 51.
Cowan, Marshall and Ridley 97, 104.
Cowgap 216.
Cowshill **17**, 30, **68**, 94, 215, 227–28.
Cowton 58.
Crawford, John 48.
Crawley(side) **17**, 36, 38, **66**, 75, 132, **133**, 157, 240.
Croft Bridge 21.
Crook **15**, 31, 39, **40**, 41–43, 83, 118–19, 124, 131–32, 137, **138**, 139, 142, **149**, **150**, 151, 240, 241.
Crook Burn **206**.
Cross Gill 204.
Crossthwaite 212, 240.
Cruchley, G.F. **185**.
Cudworth, William 135, 228,
Cumberland 23, 46, 55, 63, 70, 72, 74, 88, 92, 99, **108**, 186, 188, 198, 201, 206.
Cumbria(n) 9, 16–17, **22**, **25–27**, **29**, 135, 138, 139, **141**, 246, 247–48.
Cupola Bridge 30–31.
Cutting 13, 21, **30**, 40, 64, 67, **69**, 70, 74, **82**. 89, 107, 149, 154, 181, 192, 194, 197, 206, **210**, 214, 227.

Daddry Shield 65, **67**, 226.
Dale, David 140.
Dalziel, Lord Hamilton of 220.
Darlington 9, 11, 21–22, 35, **37**, 43, 52, 59, 119, 121, 124, 129, 157, 183, 184, 186, 188–89, 218, 239, 241.
Darnel, William Nicholas 161.
Dartmoor 248–49.
Denniss, C.S. 228.
Dent's School 216.
Derwent 34, 131, 139–40, 142–43, 145–47, 156–57.
Derwent Cote iron works 149.
Derwent Iron Company 41, 119, 131, 139–40.
Derwentwater 76.
Devonshire, Duke of 217.
Dickinson, Barnard, Jun. 53.

Dickinson, Solicitors 198.
Dilston 216.
Dinning 166.
Dirt Pot 80, **81**, 83.
Dixon, John 44, 45, 46, 63, 78, 83, 120, 135.
DMU 248, 249.
Dodd, Ralph 21–25, **28**, **29**.
Doncaster 62.
Dougang Mining Company 94.
Doves Pool 80.
Dowgang 94.
Duke Street 216.
Dunston 147.
Durham 9, 13, **15**, 16–17, 21, 31, 36, **37**, 39–40,
     45–46, 50, 52, 63, 70, 142, 147, 152, 186, 191,
     ·199, 206–07, 218–19, 241, 247, 249.
Durham Advertiser 143, 146.
Dyehouse 238.

Ealing Community Transport (ECT) 247, 248,
     F14CS.
Earl Grey Inn 189.
Eastgate **17**, 154, 218, **223**, 224, **226**, 227–29,
     232, **233**, 237–38, 243, 247–48, F10CS,
     F11CS.
Eden 12, 24, 46, 49, 60, **73**, 212, 246.
Edinburgh 47, 57, 143, 183, 217.
Ecclesiastical Commissioners 219, 227.
Egglestone 30, 191, 209, 222.
Elfoot 181.
Elishaw 161, F7CS.
Ellershope 238.
Ellis, Ed 248, 249.
Elrington **17**, 166, **170, 171**, 179, 180.
Elswick 48.
Embankment 13, **33**, 40, 64, 67, 69, 80, 82, **89**,
     90, 92, 101, 103, **104, 106**, 107, 116, 117, 154,
     168, **170**, 171, 174, 176–77, 180, 189, 192,
     197, **231**.
Etherley **14**, 36, 37.
Evenwood **14**.

Farlam **29, 30, 73**, 74.
Farnley 47.
Featherstone **19**, 89, 101, **102**, 242.
Fernan 228.
Fighting Cocks 22.
Fisher's Cross 27.
Flithome 244.
Foreshield 230, **232**.
Forest Head **19**, 28.
Forrest and Frith 199.
Fourstones **17**, 30, **169**.
Fraser's Hush 155, 156.
Frosterley **15**, 39, **40**, 41, 44–45, 55–56, 63–64,
     65, 70, 73, 75, 78, 80, 96, 119, 124, 129, 157,
     158, 159, 160, 161, 162, 222, F13CS.
Fulton, Hamilton H. 51, 60.
Furness 188.

Gairs **19**, 236.
Galligill 232.

Garrigill **19**, 94, 198, **203**, 206, 212, 214, 216.
Gateshead **15**, 31, 34, 50, 146.
Gaunless 40, **189, 190**.
Geddes, Sir Eric 238.
German(y) 232, 246.
Gibb, George 229–30.
Gilderdale 92, **93**, 100, 113, 116–17, 230–31,
     245–46.
Glasgow 8, 43, 52.
Glendue **72**, 104, **106**, 117, 166.
Glenwhelt 23–24. **26**.
Gloucestershire 157.
Gordon, David 29, 45, 74, 97.
Gordon Beck 189.
Gossipgate 70, 93.
Grassington 51, **59, 61**.
Green, John 48.
Green Hurth **16, 17,** 199, 214, 217.
Greenhead 34, 198.
Greenshaw 166.
Greenwich (Hospital) 76, 165–67, 172, 17–76,
     179, 181, 216, 229.
Greta 49.
Greta Bridge 49, 50.
Grey, Charles 165, 216–17.
Grey, Charles Bacon 33.
Grey, Ralph William 48, 86–87.
Grove Head 236.
Grove Rake 155, 157, 235.

Haematite 138.
Haggerleases (Hagger Leases) 35, 37, 50, 134, **135**,
     140, 141, 146–47, **150**, 185, **186**, 187–89.
Haining Burn **33**, 74.
Hall Bank Toll **73**.
Hallbankgate 7, **19, 29, 30**, 31, 32, **34**, 37.
Halton Lea Gate **19**, 32, 75, 99, 109, **110**, 114,
     235–36.
Haltwhistle 12, **19**, 23, 34–35, 42–43, 47–48, 57,
     74, 78, 85, **88, 89**, 92, 97, 99, **100, 101, 105**,
     107, 109–11, **112–13**, 114–16, 165, 183, 202,
     216, 240, 243.
Hareshaw 48.
Harper Town 114.
Harperley **15**.
Harris, John 41–42, 44, 215.
Harrison, C.A. 229.
Harrison, J.T. 116–17.
Harrison, Thomas Elliot 36, 53.
Harrogate 54.
Hartley, Rev. W.R. 229.
Hartleyburn (Hartley Burn) **19**, 24, 32, 34, 47,
     72, 74, 109, 110.
Harwood 198, **206, 207**, 222.
Hawes 51–53, 56–57, **61**.
Hawick 52, 57, 183.
Hawkshaw, John 51.
Hay, Lord William Montagu 199.
Haydon Bridge **17**, 24–25, **26**, 28, 30, 33–34,
     35, 76, 79, 83, 92, 165.
Heathery Cleugh **79**, 80, 83.
Hebburn 34.

Heights Quarry 231–32, **233**, 236–37.
Hepworth, B. 195.
Herdley 89, 103, **104**, **106**, 118.
Herepath 38, 43, 49–58, 60, 76, 86–87, 97, 99, 118, 121–24, 182.
Hexham 8, **17**, 22–25, **28–29**, 30, **31**, 33, 52, 70, 78, 85–86, **93**, 108, 147, 166–68, **169**, **170**, 171, 174, 177, 179–82, 238.
Hexham Courant 9, 156, 163, 165–66, 174, 179, 197–98, 215–21, 227–29.
Hexhamshire 238.
High Force **16**, 199, 208, **209**, 213–14.
High Level Bridge 146.
High Stoop **15**, 142, **143**.
High Waterhouses 137.
Hildyard, J.A. 228.
Hildyard, J.R.W. 219.
Hillgate 146.
Hilltop 70.
Holmes **174**.
Holmes, J.D 200–01.
Holmsfoot 231, **232**.
Holwick **16**, 199, 208, **209–10**.
Hoole, K. 188–89.
Hopkins 218.
Hopkins, John Castell 41, 118–19.
Horrocks, Mr & Mrs 200–02.
Howgillrigg 107.
Hownes Gill **15**, 38, 131–32, 135, **136**, 138–39, 142, **144**, 145, **147**.
Hudgill **94**.
Hudson, George 50, 53, 57, 99, 110–11.
Hunderthwaite 197.
Hunstanworth 157.
Hunter 177.
Huntley Rectory 157.
Hutchinson, Col. (later Major General) 150–51, 196, 235.

Imperial units 13, 15.
Incline 7, **34**, 36–39, 41, **66**, 74–75, 77, **79**, 80–81, 83, 119, **120**, 132, **134**, 135, **136**, 137, **138**, 139, **142**, **143**, 146, 149, **150**, 151, 154, **155**, 156–57, 162–63, **164**, 212, 231–32, **233**, 235–36, 240.
Ingleton 53, **61**.
Iowa Pacific Holdings 244, 248.
Irish Channel 23.
Iron 12, 19, 28, 36, 37–38, 45–46, 86, 141, 152–53, 197–98, 218–19, 221, 234, 236, 241.
Ironstone 41, 153–57, 163, 186, 197, 214, 216–17, 219, 234–36, F5CS.
Iron works 48, 131–32, 135, 138, 140–41, **143**, 147, **149**, 153, 157, 186, 217, 237, 240,
Ireshope 67.
Irthing 12, 23–24, 74.

Jeans, J.S. 118.
Jee, Alfred S. 51.
Jenkinson 132
Jessop, Josias & William 23, 37.
Johnson, Matthew Foster 153.

Justices of the Peace 12, 16, 45–46, 54, 63, 76, 88, 99, 198, 201.

Kendal 11.
Kettlewell 51, 52, **59**, **61**.
Killhope 12, **17**, 41, 55, 63, 67, **68**, **69**, 70, 74, 80, 215. 216, 217, 218, 219, 220, **226**, 228.
Kirkby Lonsdale 54.
Kirkby Stephen **16**, 49, 51, 52, 54, 60, **61**, 141, 182, 183, 185, 186, 240, 241, 244, 245.
Kirkhaugh **19**, 23, 31, 63, 70, 72, 246.
Kirkhouse 24, 28, **34**, 74, 235.
Knar Burn 90, **91**, 117.
Knaresdale (Knarsdall) 23, 92.
Knitsley 52.

Lambley 12, **19**, **72**, 75, 89, **90**, 96, **98**, 100, **101**, 103, **104**, **105**, 107, **109**, **110**, 111–17, 235–36, 243, 246.
Lancashire 51, 54.
Lancaster 11, 54.
Lanchester **15**, 38, 52, 145, 147.
Lands 185, 189, **190**.
Lanehead **17**, **68**, **79**, 80, 153.
Lanercost 74.
Langdon (Beck) **16**, 199, **207**, **208**.
Langley **17**, 24, 76, 84, 165, 166, **172**, 176, 177, 179, 181, 234.
Langley Beck 189.
Lead 7, 12, 22, 23, 24, 33, **35**, 45, 48, 76, 77, 83, 85, 87, 153, 154, 155, 163, 165, 166, 167, 172, 179, 180, 182, 190, 197, 199, 201, 212, 213, 214, 217, 218, 219, 228, 229, 234, 237, 238, 239, F5CS.
Leadbitter 176, 181.
Leadgate **15**, **19**, 180, 198, **203**.
Leeds 60, 62.
Leeman, George 60.
level crossing 69, 91, 107, 192, 209, **210**, 231.
Leyburn 51, **59**, 60, 62.
light railway 228, 229, 235, 238, 246.
Lime 123, 132.
limekiln 38, 65, 75.
limestone 36, 41, 44, 45, 65, 131, 153, 154, **158**, 163, 197, 231, 232, 234, 236, 237, 239, 240, 242.
Lintley **19**, 63, **71**, 72, 73, 92, 117, 246, F2CS, F12CS.
Lintzgarth 155.
Liverpool 51, 143, 146.
Lobley Hill 31, 40, 65, **67**, 160.
Lock 23, 24, **27**.
Locke, Joseph 51, 54.
London 8, 36, 121, 124, **145**, 197, 217, 228.
London Road 34.
Lords, House of 57, 58, 86, 99, 149, 200, 201, 220.
Lort Burn 117.
Losh, James 112.
Lovelady Shield 94.
Low Ash Holm 98, **105**.
Low Byer 70, **71**, **232**.
Low White Heaps **17**, 157, 163.

Lowgate **170**.
Lowther, J.W 220, 221.
Lune 193, **194**, 195.
Lyall, E.W. 218, 220, 228.

McAdam, John Loudon 30, **31**.
MacNay, Thomas 119, 120, 126, 150, 151, 191, 201.
Mallerstang 51, 56, **61**.
Manfield 54.
Maryport 24.
Masham 54.
Medomsley 36.
Meeting Slacks 38, 41, 42, 119, 131, 132, 133.
Melmerby **59**, **62**, 212, **213**.
Merry Knowe 107.
Merrygill 240, **242**.
Merseyside 13, 52, 151.
Mews, R. 228.
Meynell, Thomas (Junior) 40, 41, 118, 119.
Mickleton **16**, 191, **193**, **194**, 195, 197.
Midderidge 39.
Middleham 51.
Middlehope **17**, 154, 155, 156, 157, 231,
Middlehope Burn 154, 156, 157.
Middlehope Shield 156.
Middlesbrough 122.
Middleton-in-Teesdale 7, 12, **16**, 35, 65, 75, **183**, **187**, 190, 191, **192**, 193, **195**, 197, 198, 201, 206, 208, 209, **210**, **211**, 215, 221, 222, 232, 238, 239, 241.
Middleton Tyas 54.
Midgeholme **19**, 32, 34, 240.
Milton **19**, **30**, 32, 34, 37, 45, 54, 63, 64, **72**, 74, 75, 235.
mine(s) 8, 11, 12, 23, 24, 45, 76, 77, 84, 85, 97, 153, 154, 155, 156, 157, 162, 163, 164, 166, 167, 199, 200, 201, 202, 212, **213**, 214, 216, 217, 218, 219, 221, 228, 229, 234, 235, 236, 237, 238, 239, F5CS.
mineral(s) 28, 85, 111, 153, 161, 163, 177, 178, **196**, 198, 199, 201, 212, 231, 233, 238, 242.
mineral traffic 160, 184, 187, 197, 228, 242.
mining 12, 22, 35, 48, **69**, 70, 76, **81**, 87, 94, 153, 165, 182, 189, 190, 212, 215, 217, 219, 228, 229, 234, 236, 238, 239.
Monck, Charles Atticus 87.
Morralee 76, 77, 78.
Morpeth, Lord 74,
Muggleswick 37, 119.
Muker 53.
Muschamp, Emerson 41.

Nanny Mayor's incline 38, 119, **138**, 235.
Napoleonic War 26.
National Archives 9, 199.
National Coal Board 235, 240.
Naworth Coal Company 235.
Neild, Jonathan 199.
Nent (river) 42, 43, 63, 64, 70, **71**, 80, 93, **108**, 109, 231, F3CS.
Nenthall **17**, **19**, **71**, 94, **95**, 109, **232**.

Nenthead 12, **17**, 32, 47, 63, **69**, 70, 73, 74, 77, 78, 85, 86, **88**, **89**, **90**, **91**, **93**, **94**, **95**, 96, 97, 99, 102, **113**, 117, 215, 216, 218, 220, 221, 222, 228, 229, **230**, 231, **232**, 242, F3CS.
Nentsberry **71**, 94.
Network Rail 248, 249.
Neville Street 47, 48.
New House 220, 221.
Newbiggin 60.
Newcastle-upon-Tyne 9, 12, 13, **15**, 16, 22, 23, 24, 25, 26, 28, 34, 43, 47, 48, **49**, 50, 52, 54, 77, 86, 87, 88, 99, 100, 111, 113, 114, 115, 142, 143, **146**, 148, 151, 152, 192.
Newcastle Chronicle 47, 48, 97, 115.
Newcastle Courant 33, 136, 146, 147, 148.
Newcastle Journal 112.
Newcastle and Maryport Canal 12, **25**, **26**, **27**.
Newlandside 158, 160.
Newshield 31.
Nilstone Rigg (Ridge) 172, 176.
Nook 48.
North Eastern Region 249.
North Grain 156.
North Loaning 92, **231**.
North Pennines 7, 8, 12, 13, **14–19**, 21, 23, 28, 29, 30, 34, 35, 36, 42, 43, 48, 54, 56, 57, 62, 76, 85, **103**, 152, 164, 180, 182, 197, 204, 212, 214, 215, 217, 219, 220, 229, 232, 233, 234, 235, 237, 239, 240, 243, 248.
North Riding (of Yorkshire) 9, 191, 198, 201, 208.
North Tyne 47, 48, 52, 85, 86, 96.
North Yorkshire 16.
Northallerton 43, 48, 49, 50, 57, **59**, **62**, 85, 183.
Northbrook, Earl of 153.
Northumberland 9, 16, 23, 46, 63, 72, 74, 80, 88, 99, 238, 246, 247.
Northumberland and Durham District Bank 140.
Northumbria Water 202.

Ord & Maddison 196, 197, 211, 240.
Ordnance Survey (OS) 64, 88, 92, 137, 153, 154, 155, 156, 163, **181**, 201, 230.
ore 12, 135, 137, 138, 139, 141, 151, 155, 156, 163, 197, 198, 199, 219, 229, 234, 235, 236, 241, F5CS.
ore-field 12, 21, 29, 33, 36, 44, 56, 182, 186, 234, 241.
Orton 50, 51.
Otley 52.
Overton, George 22, 35.

Pacer 248.
Park Burn **89**, **90**.
Park End 197, 211.
Park Head Wheel 132, **133**, 134.
Park Village 89.
Parkhead **15**, **17**, 152, 153, 154, 155, 156, 157, 240, 242, F4CS.
Parliament(ary) 11, 12, **14**, 16, 18, 22, 25, 26, 27, 29, 30, 33, 35, 36, 39, 41, 43, 44, 45, 48, 50, 51, 54, 55, 56, 57, 58, 60, 62, 63, 64, 76,

77, 78, 85, 86, 96, 97, 98, 99, **100**, 101, 103, 104, 107, 108, 109, 111, 117, 118, 122, 123, 124, 127, 128, 131, 134, 145, 148, 149, 152, 153, 160, 165, 166, 167, 175, 176, 183, 185, 188, 198, 201, 212, 215, 217, 218, 219, 220, 221, F7CS.
Parson Byers 159.
Pearson, Joseph 114, 115, 116.
Pease, Henry 40, 41, 50, 118, 125, 126, 127, 140, 158, 191.
Pease, Henry Fell 191.
Pease, John 40.
Pease, Joseph 41, 50, 78, 118, 119, 125, 218, 219, 220, 221, 227, 228, 229.
Pease, Messrs. 197, 199.
Peasmeadows 174, **175.**
Pennine Way **204.**
Penrith **18**, 24, 30, 49, 52, **61**, 141, 182, 184, 186, 187, 188, 198, **202.**
Peterborough 62.
Phoenix Pit 36.
Plenmeller **19**, 101, **102.**
Plummer, Matthew 85, 97, 112.
Polar Express 249.
Pont Burn 144, 147.
Pontop 39.
Portrack 21.
Post Office 197.
Preston 53.
Private Bill Office 48, 56, 99, 198.

quarry(ies)(ing) 8, 44, **65**, 131, 132, 153, 156, **158**, 160, 162, 163, 164, **195**, **196**, 197, 211, 213 214, 222, 227, 228, 231, 232, **233**, 234, 235, 236, 237, 240, 243.

RAILWAYS
Barnard Castle and Bishop Auckland Junction Railway (BC&BAJR) 183.
Bishop Auckland & Weardale Railway (BA&WR) 39, **40**, 41, 44, 45, 46, 63, 118, 119, 120, 121, 126, 131, 132, 134, 141, 147, **148**, **150**, 160, 161, 162.
Blaydon, Gateshead and Hebburn Railway (BG&HR) 34.
.order Counties Railway (BCR) 165, 168, **169**, 172, 173, 180, **181.**
Brandling Junction Railway 34, 135, 146.
Caledonian Railway 43, 44, 49.
Clarence Railway 36, 39.
Clitheroe Junction Railway 53.
Cockermouth, Keswick and Penrith Railway (CK&PR) 141, 187.
Colne Valley Railway 248.
Cumberland and Cleveland Junction Railway (C&CJR) 7, 12, 23, 198–214, 216, 234.
Darlington and Barnard Castle Railway (D&BCR) 125, 126, 127, 183, 184, 185, 186, 187, 192, 241.
Derwent Junction Railway 7, 65, **66**,.
East and West Durham, Northumberland and Scottish Junction Railway 52.

Eden Valley Railway (EVR) 64, 125, 129, 186, 188, 243, 244.
Frosterley and Stanhope Railway (F&SR) 65, 121, 127, 128, 129, 152, 157, **158**, **159**, **160**, 161, 222, 223, 225, F9CS.
Glasgow, Dumfries and Carlisle Railway 43.
Great North of England Railway (GNER) 48, 49, 50, 51, 53, 54.
Great Northern Railway 57, 62.
Hexham and Allendale Railway (H&AR) 8, 12, 20, 31, 78, 79, 83, 165–181, 195, 197, 215, 234, 237, 239, 240.
Lancashire and North Yorkshire Railway 51, 53, 54, 56, 57.
Lancashire & Yorkshire Railway 58.
Lancashire, Weardale and Hartlepool Union Railway 45.
Lancaster and Carlisle Railway (L&CR) 43, 46, 49, 50–52, 60, 126, 141, 185, 186.
Lancaster and Newcastle-upon-Tyne Direct Railway 54.
Leeds and Bradford Extension Railway 51.
Leeds and Carlisle Railway 52, 56, **61.**
Leeds and Thirsk: Auckland Extension 54,
Leeds & Thirsk Railway (L&TR) 52, 54, 56, 60, **62.**
Leeds Northern Railway **62.**
Liverpool and Preston Railway 51.
Liverpool, Manchester & Newcastle Junction Railway (LM&NJR) 53, 57, 58, 60, **61.**
London and Edinburgh Direct Railway 52.
London and North Eastern Railway (LNER) **225**, 238.
London and North Western Railway 13, 146, 151.
London & York Railway 52, 57, 183.
Lord Carlisle's Railway (LCR) (Brampton Railway) 28, **29**, **30**, 31, 32, **33**, 34, 45, 47, 63, **72**, **73**, 74, 75, 97, 99, 103, **104**, **105**, **109**, **110**, 114, 235, 236, 240.
Manchester, Liverpool & Great North of England Union Railway 51, 52, 53.
Maryport & Carlisle Railway 99.
Middlesbrough and Guisbrough Railway (M&GR) 126, 127, 135.
Middlesbrough and Redcar Railway (M&RR) 121, 123, 124, 125, 126, 127.
Midland Railway 221, 241.
Newcastle and Berwick Railway 43, 86.
Newcastle & Carlisle & North Tyne Junction Railway 47.
Newcastle & Carlisle Railway (N&CR) 7, 12, 20, 26, 28, 32–35, 37, 41–43, 45, 46–48, **49**, 56, 62, 63–64, 70, **71–73**, 74–78, 85–117, 139–40, 142, 144–45, **146**, 147, 165–66, 168, **169**, 176, 179, 181–82, 185, 202, 230, **231**, **232**, 235–36, F2CS, F3CS.
Newcastle & Leeds Direct Railway 54.
Newcastle, Derwent and Weardale Railway (ND&WR) **145**, **146**, 147, **148**, 149.
Newcastle, Durham, & Lancashire Junction Railway 50–51.

Newcastle-upon-Tyne, Edinburgh & (Direct) Glasgow Junction Railway (NE&DGJR) 48, 85–86, 96.
Newcastle upon Tyne and Derwent Valley Railway (N&DVR) 142, **144**, 145–46.
Newcastle-upon-Tyne, Hawick & Edinburgh & Glasgow Junction Railway 47.
North British Railway (NBR) 43, 146, 149.
North Eastern Railway (NER) 36, 113, 129, 130–31, **143**, **144**, 145–49, 151, 154, 165–67, 169, 175–77, 179–81, 188–92, 194, 197, 199, 211–12, 216–22, 227–29, **231**, 232, 235–36, 238.
North Norfolk Railway 248.
North Western Railway 52, 53.
Northern Counties Union Railway (NCUR) 56–58, **59**, 60, **61**, **62**, 126, 182, **183**, 185–86, **187**.
Northern Trunk Railway of England 52.
Northumberland and Lancashire Junction Railway (N&LJR) 51, 53–54, 56–57, 86.
Pontop & South Shields Railway (P&SSR) 39, 41, 135.
St. John's Chapel Railway (SJCR) 215, 220, 221, 225, **226**, **227**.
South Durham and Lancashire Union Railway (SD&LUR) 13, 20, 126, 128–29, **140**, 141, 143, 146–47, 184–86, **187**, 188–89, 191–92, 194–96, 237, 240, 241, 244.
South Tynedale Railway (STR) 7–9, **103**, 202, 243, 244, **245**, 246–248.
Stanhope and Tyne Railway (S&TR) 36–39, 41, 65, **66**, 75, 118, 125, 131, 132, **136**, 152–53, 157, 235, 240, 247, 249.
Stanhope, Rookhope and District Railway 237.
Stockton & Darlington & Newcastle & Carlisle Union Railway (S&D&N&CUR) **139**.
Stockton & Darlington Railway (S&DR) 11, 12, 22, 32, 36, **37**, 39–47, 49–50, 55, 63, 75, 77, 78, 80, 83, 96, 118–32, 134–43, 146–49, 152–56, 159–63, 182, 183, **185**, 186–89, **190**, 191–92.
Sunderland, Durham and Auckland Union Railway 50.
Tees Valley Railway (TVR) 8, 12, 191–99, 201, 209, **211**, 212, 217, 241.
Tees, Weardale and Tyne Junction Railroad 37, 39, F1CS.
Wear and Derwent Junction Railway (W&DJR) 7, 8, 42, 75, 80, 83, 120, 124, 131–151, 162–63, 235, 237, 242, 239.
Wear and Derwent Railway (W&DR) 41, 118, 124, 131, 132, 134, 135, 137, 139.
Wear Valley Extension Railway of 1845 (WVER) 7, 8, 20, 32, **33**, 45, **46**, 48, 55–56, 63–75, 76, 78–85, 89–90, 92, 93, 95–97, 104, 118, 152, 157, 165, 174, **175**, 176, 216, 223, 226, **230**, **231**, **232**, 235, F2CS, F3CS, F10CS.
Wear Valley Extension Railway of 1892 (WVER92) 20, 215, 219–21, **222–25**, 226–27, F9CS.
Wear Valley Railway (WVR) 12, 20, 41, 44–46,

48, 55, 56, 63, 65, 74, 75, 78, 85, 90, 96. 118–27, 131–35, 137, 152, 157, 160, **161**, 162, 183, 221, 228, F7CS.
Weardale Extension Railway (WER) 41, 42, 119, **120**, 131–32, 134–35, 137, 138, 142–43, 153, 235,
Weardale Iron and Coal Company Railway (WI&CCR) 7, 140, 152–57, **158**, 162–64, 231–32, 234–37, F4CS, F5CS.
Weardale Railway 7, 218, 244, 247–49, F13CS, F14CS, F15CS,
West Durham Railway (WDR) 41, 42, 138.
York and Carlisle Railway (Y&CR) 49–51, 56–57, **59**, **183**.
York and Newcastle railway (Y&NR) 58.
York, Newcastle, and Berwick Railway (YN&BR) 58, 60, 99, 110, 183.
Yorkshire and Glasgow Union Railway (Y&GUR) 51–52, 56–58, 183.

Railtrack 247, 248.
Railway Abandonment Act 58.
Railway Mania 7, 43–62, 79, 96–97.
Raise 198.
Ramshaw 156–157, 163.
Ramshay, John 97.
Randalholme 70, **71**, 72.
Raven, Vincent 228.
Ravenstonedale 49.
Redcar 123–24, 128, 174, 183.
Redesdale, Lord 201.
Redgate Head 154.
Redmire 51, **59**.
Rednorth 39.
Reed, Edward 97.
Reedsmouth 47.
Reeth 53.
Rendel, J.M 50.
Rennie, Sir John 52, 54.
Ribble 53.
Ribble Link 11.
Rich, Col. 150–51.
Richardson, Gutch & Co. 199.
Richmond 43, 49, 51, 53–54, 58–**59**.
Riding Mill 238.
Ridley, Sir Matthew White 87.
Ridsdale 48.
Ripley 54.
Ripon 53–54, **59**.
Rispey 236.
Ritson, W. 174, 179.
RMS Locotec 248.
Robinson, Examiner 200–01.
Roddam, J.W. 228.
Rodderup Fell 198.
Roddymoor 138.
Rotherhope **19**, 212, **213**, 214.
Romaldkirk **16**, 191, **193**, 208.
Rookhope **17**, 152–54, **155**, 156–57, 163, **164**, 165, 218, **223**, 226, 228–29, 235, 237–38.
Rose and Crown 190.
Rounthwaite 153–54, 239.

Rowfoot 89.
Rowlands Gill 15.
Rowley 15, 83, 131–32, 137, 235.
Royal Assent 39, 45, 56–57, 60, 86, 99, 111, 118, 125–27, 130, 141, 149, 167, 175, 183, 185, 188, 191, 201.
Rush & Lawton 116.

St Andrew Auckland 40, 45.
St Helen Auckland 188.
St. John's Chapel 220.
Saltburn 247.
Scargill 49, 59.
Scarth, Wm. Thos. 199.
Scotch Isle 15.
Scotland 11, 43, 45, 46, 52, 57, 63, 74, 198.
Scotswood 142, 144.
Scunthorpe 249.
Scutterhill 17, 154–56, 232, 237, F5CS.
Sedbergh 54.
Seldom Seen 216.
Settle 53, 61.
Shafthill 97, 98, 112–13, 115–16.
Shaw, William 157.
Shepherd, Rev. R. 218, 220.
Shield Water 19, 200, 212–13.
Shildon 14, 35, 37, 39–41, 59, 83, 118, 119, 120, 124, 131–32, 134, 161, 249.
Shot Tower 34.
Shotley Bridge 15, 140, 238.
Sincay, St Paul de 229.
Sinderhope 17, 82, 174.
Sipton 82, 238.
Skipton 51.
Slaggyford 19, 31, 72, 73, 91, 92, 93, 96, 113, 114, 117, 246–47.
Slaley 238.
Slit Pasture 155, 235, F5CS,
Slit Vein 156.
Smails Burn 154.
smelt mill (smelter) 70, 76–80, 83–84, 155, 163, 165–66, 172, 177, 179–81, 228, 234, 236.
Smith, John Abel 86–87, 96.
Snow 163, 175, 214.
Softly 72, 91, 104, 107.
Solway Firth 27.
South Church 40.
South Loaning 70, 231.
South Shields 36, 39, 135.
South Tyne 7, 12, 23–24, 29, 31, 35, 42–43, 48, 49, 57, 64, 71, 72–74, 76–77, 85, 88, 89, 90, 96, 97, 98, 99–100, 102–03, 104, 108, 109–11, 116, 165, 185, 199, 202, 204–05, 206, 212, 214, 230, 235, 243, 245–47.
Spar 45, 239, 242.
Spartylea 81.
Spency Croft 70.
Staindrop 50–51.
Stainmore 16, 50, 182, 188–89, 198, 241.
Stainmore Properties Limited 244.
Stanhope 7, 12, 17, 36, 38–39, 41–43, 45, 66, 70, 75, 80, 118, 131–32, 139, 152–53,

157–58, 159, 160, 162, 164, 174, 215–16, 218–20, 222, 223, 225, 226–28, 235, 237, 239, 244, 247, 248–49, F4CS, F9CS, F10CS, F14CS.
Stanhope Railroad Company 36.
Stanton, Croft and Company 152, 157, 158, 232.
Staward 17, 78, 166–67, 168, 172, 177, 178, 179.
Steel 214, 219, 234, 236, 249.
Step Ends 193.
Stephenson, George 32, 35, 45, 74.
Stephenson, Robert 36, 37, 39, 44, 53, 188.
Stobart, Henry 40–41, 118–19.
Stockton 21, 22, 35, 39, 62, 118.
Stocksfield 33, 139, 141.
Storey, Thomas 41, 44, 51, 54.
Strathmore, Lord 196.
Styford 33.
Summerrods 31.
Summit 23–24, 26, 31, 38, 64, 69, 70, 80, 140, 154, 168, 172, 185, 193, 194, 202, 206, 210, 214, F4CS.
Sunderland Cleugh 154.
Sunniside 41, 120, 132, 135, 137, 138, 142, 143, 149, 150, 151, 240.
Sutcliffe, John 24.
Swale 53.
Swalwell 15, 147.

Swan, J. Cameron 220.
Swinhope 81, 28.

Talkin 28.
Tate, Peter 104, 116.
Team 34, 50, 147.
Tebay 18, 49, 60, 61, 116, 183, 185–86, 188, 240.
Tees 7, 8, 21, 29, 49, 57, 141, 182, 187, 190, 191, 192, 193, 199, 201–02, 205, 206–07, 208–09, 212, 214, 241.
Teesdale 12, 164, 195, 197, 206, 221.
Teesdale Mercury 184, 187, 195, 197–99, 201,
Telegraph 115, 199.
Tennant, Henry 228.
Thinhope 72, 90, 117.
Thompson, Benjamin 37.
Thompson Brothers 116.
Thompson, James 32–33, 45.
Thompson, Robert 199.
Thompson's of Kirkhouse 109–10, 235.
Thompson's Well 92.
Thirsk 51, 59, 60, 182.
Thornhope 92, 117.
Thornley Gate 31, 83.
Thornley Pit Houses 37.
Tilleard & Co. 200.
Tindale Fell 19, 24, 28, 33.
Tipalt 23–24, 88, 89, 101.
Tomlinson 33, 36, 41–42, 113, 131–32, 136, 142, 146, 152, 199, 200.
Tow Law 15, 37, 120, 135, 136, 137, 138, 142, 143, 147, 149, 150, 151, 153, 157, 217, 239, 240–41, 249.
Tudhoe 153, 219.

Tunnel(led,/lling) **17**, 40–41, 47, 67, **69**, 118, **119**, 120, 131–32.
Tunnel Branch **134–35**, **141**.
Turnpike 29, 30, **31–32**, **67**. 72, 90, 92, 107, 192.
Tyler, Captain 151.
Tyne 12, 23–24, 33–34, 36, 46, 50, 63, 74, 139, 147, 182, 198, 201.
Tyne & Wear 9, 16, 49.
Tyne Mercury 42, 47–54, 131.
Tynedale 216, 246.
Tynehead **17**, **205**.

Ullswater 24.
Ulverston Canal 11.
Ure 21.

van de Weyer, Victor William Bates 153.
Viaduct 13, 40, 56, 64, 71–72, **82**, 84, 89, 97, 98, 100, **101**, **103**, **104–06**, 107, **108**, 111–13, **114**, 115–17, **126**, 138, 140, 142–43, 145, 147, 154, 189, **190–91**, 192, **193–94**, 195, 198, 202, **203–04**, 206, **207**, **208**, 212, **213**, 223, 230–31, 246.
Vieille Montagne Mining Company 228–29.

Warcop **18**, 241, 243–45.
Warden 47–48.
Waskerley 15, 37, 119, 131–32, 137, **138**, 142, 153, 235.
Water Authority Crossing 202.
Watershed 12, 57, 73–74, 139, 201, 205–06.
Wath 54, **59**, 60, 62.
Waughold Holme **98**.
wayleave(s) 36, 39, 131, 124
Wear 7, 12, 22, 29, 36–38, 44, 57, 65, **66**, 75, **79**, **147**, 154, 157–58, **159**, **160**, 161–62, 165, 182, 218, **222**, **223**, 224–27, F10CS, F11CS, F13CS.
Wear Valley 29, 36, 39, 42, 46, 63, 79, 121, 131, 152, 156–57, 160, 163, 215, 218–19, 220, 231, 234, 236–37, 241–43, 247.
Wear Valley Junction 15, **44**, 56, 160–61, 222, 240–41.
Weardale 12, 44, 46, 70, 143, 146–47, 154, 215–19, 221, 227–28, 232, 235, 244, 247, 249.
Weardale Iron & Coal Company 142, 152, 153, 157, **158**, 163, 217, 232, 234–35.
Weardale Lead Company 163, 218, 228, 236–38.
Weardale Steel, Coal and Coke Company 152–53, 219, 221, 231.
Wearhead 7–8, **17**, 41, 63, 65, 67, **68**, **162**, 164, 215, 218–21, 223, **224**, **225**, 227–29, 231–32, 234, 237–40.
Weatherhill 36, 38, 132, **133**, 134, 153, 157, 240, 242.

Webb, Brian 29, 74, 97.
Wensleydale 58, 60.
West Auckland **14**, 49–50, 161, 186, 188, 241, F7CS.
West Boat **170**.
West Ferryfield 158, 162.
West Level 155.
West Slit **17**, 154, 156, F5CS.
Westgate **17**, **66**, 67, 154–57, 163–64, 217–18, 223, **224**, **226–27**, 231–32, **233**, 235, 242.
Westminster 216.
Westwood 166.
Wharfedale 52.
Wharton, J. Lloyd 228.
Whickham 153.
Whinstone 197, 227.
Whitehall **137**, 235, 238.
Whitfield **31**, **32**, 165.
Whitesyke 216.
Whitley 117.
Whittle 153, 239.
Whittonstal 52.
Whitwham 91.
Whitworth, Robert 21, **22**, 23.

Wilkinson and Smith 216.
Wilkinson, C.N. 199, 228.
Wilkinson, George H. 37, 39, 42.
Wilson, C. 199.
Wilson, L. 9.
Winlaton Mill 147.
Winston 21, **22**.
Witham, Thomas 191.
Witton 39, 119, 124, **139**.
Witton-le-Wear **14–15**, 44, 161, F7CS.
Wolsingham **15**, 38, 45, 119–20, 135, 137–38, 153, 247–49, F14CS, F15CS,
Wood, Sir Lindsay 229.
Woodburn 47, 48.
Woodhorn 88.
Woodlands 189, 237.
Woods, N. 87.
Workington 221.
Worsdell, Wilson 228.
wrought iron 28, 234.

Yadmoss **17**, 198, 214.
Yeats 123.
Yolland, Colonel 179.
York 130, 229.
Yorkshire 24, 191.

Zinc 45, 229, 234..

Visit our website and discover thousands of other History Press books.

www.thehistorypress.co.uk